Israel

versus

Israel

The Great Paradox of Scripture

by Clyde F. Whitehead

Published by

Covenant House Books
P.O. Box 4690
Sevierville, TN 37864
615/428-5176

ISBN 0-925591-18-1
Printed in the United States of America.

TABLE OF CONTENTS

To my beloved wife for her patience and support through several months of study and preparation for this book.
Also, to my wonderful mother who prayed for a minister-son before I was born.

INTRODUCTION

Many, many years ago Solomon wrote: "... of making many books there is no end; and much reading is a weariness of the flesh" (Ecclesiastes 12:12). Solomon was a prophet in every sense of the term. He saw far beyond his own day. This wise man could not have described the Twentieth Century with more accuracy if he had been living at this very hour.

Without doubt, our generation can relate to the first part of Solomon's statement — our age has produced millions of books. But few people know anything about "reading being a weariness to the flesh," especially regarding the Book of Books. Today's world abounds with books. And for every practical and helpful book that comes from the press there are scores of books to counteract it. Error and falsehood come to us in very neat, sophisticated packages — they are all bound up in very colorful, picturesque, schematic, thought-provoking books.

Modern day methods of communication have enabled men to spread their beliefs in an unprecedented way. But truth, from a human point of view, rarely keeps abreast with error. I believe it was Charles H. Spurgeon who said that a lie will travel around the world while truth is putting its shoes on. Books and other mass media have drawn men away from the Scriptures to depend upon someone else for their knowledge and understanding of God. But this is not a new problem — just an old problem multiplied manyfold.

If the Jews of Jesus' day had understood the Scriptures they would have recognized Him. But this exchange of the Scriptures for the works of men is to be seen in every age and generation. Second-hand Christianity has been — and still is — the curse of mankind. The majority of people come to the Scriptures out of a pre-conceived, family, or church imposed religious background. This can be very helpful but in many cases it is just the opposite. Even ministers of the Gospel are content to accept the opinions of others without testing them thoroughly by the

Scriptures. Ministers and laymen alike will sometimes be very vocal on issues with which they have only a faint knowledge. The attitude of the Bereans who "searched the Scriptures daily" to confirm the preaching of Paul and Silas is a good guideline for those who wish to know the truth. The Scriptures should be approached with an unbiased mind and with the leadership of the Holy Spirit (I John 2:27).

The churches of America have inherited a Christian legacy that makes few demands upon them. We have not had to "struggle" and "pioneer" in a new theological world as some of our forefathers did. Everything has been handed to us on a "silver platter" and we have become very complacent in our quest for Biblical knowledge. American Christianity is like a spoiled child who has been pampered with an abundance of wealth. We can very well compare ourselves to the Church of Laodicea who had "need of nothing" (Revelation 3:17).

The political world is not the only group that is guilty of "coat-tailing." The ministers of the Gospel in this country have depended almost totally upon the fathers of the Reformation era and other European and British theologians for their understanding of the Scriptures. We have become a nation of theological freeloaders — homiletical hitch-hikers who refuse to fend for ourselves.

The Christianity of America has produced few, if any, notable theologians. Deep-rutted traditional loyalty and an ecclesiastical hierarchy in almost every denomination have kept ministers of the Gospel well-contained. Fear of non-conformity has resulted in many theological robots who are unable to "think" for themselves. All the light of Scripture has not been tapped and there is an urgent need of ministers who will "study to show themselves approved unto God" and not unto men.

Second-hand Christianity tends to lead men away from the Scriptures, leading them to third-hand and fourth-hand theology and oftentimes to cultism. Men begin to "interpret the interpreters" rather than the Word itself. It is a repeat of the Rabbinical system prior to and during New Testament days. The Scriptures should be our first and foremost textbook instead of the traditions of men. Generally speaking, there is a price to pay when we break with tradition and return to the Fountainhead of truth.

It was a return to the Scriptures that brought the wrath of the religious zealots upon Jesus and the Apostles. Jesus and the early church did not introduce any new or novel ideas into the religious climate of their day.

They simply interpreted the Old Testament as it should have been understood. Truth is eternal — it does not change from one generation to the next — therefore, it is always subject to attack by its opponents. The Protestant Reformation is a classic example of this fact.

There are no new or innovative ideas in this work — it is a break with a good deal of tradition and a reclamation of that which has been lost in the shuffle from one Bible interpreter to another. The truths set forth in this work on the Jewish people are not a "breakthrough" in Biblical revelation. They may contradict many current views but they are no different from what Moses, the prophets, and the New Testament apostles taught concerning the seed of Abraham. It would be most unusual if there were no repercussions coming from this work.

The Scriptures do not yield their treasures to every passer-by. Their riches do not always lie on the surface but are deeply embedded in the mind and heart of God. Certain conditions must be met if they are properly understood. It is possible for men to interpret the Scriptures to their own destruction (2 Peter 3:16). There is no area of life that men should approach with more caution and reverence than the interpretation of God's Holy Word.

Many passages of Scripture are quoted in this work. It has been my observation that few people will take the time to look up Scripture references while reading a book — for this reason I have gone to great lengths to print them for the reader. A careful examination of every passage is very important. There is no substitute for the "pure milk of the Word."

All the scriptural quotations in this work are from the King James Version unless otherwise specified. Italics are often used in this work for emphasis, both in Scripture quotations and in the text.

Chapter 1

The State Of The Jew:
Modern Day Opinions vs. The Scriptures

Since the days of John N. Darby (1830) and more especially since the days of the Scofield Bible (1909) there have arisen certain beliefs and attitudes toward the Jewish people that need to be challenged. For many individuals there is a divinity or sacredness about the Jewish people that cannot be said of any other people on the face of the earth. To read and listen to the opinions of some Bible interpreters one would think that the natural descendants of Abraham are earmarked with a hallowed or sanctified flesh, even in their *unbelief.* There is a holy aura about them that is unlike any other human beings. We are led to believe that the Jewish people are a breed apart from all other homo sapians. They are a miracle-people even though many of them have rejected the Word of God in every generation.

The Bible gives us an entirely different picture of the physical seed of Abraham than is conjured up in the minds of many speakers and writers today. If one spells out the true state or condition of fleshly Israel, as found in the Scriptures, he is branded as anti-Semitic or neo-Nazi.

Some students of the Scriptures should read again what many of the Old Testament prophets had to say about unbelieving Israel. They need to be reminded of the curses and judgments pronounced upon these people because of their sin and unbelief. If the prophets of the old dispensation were inspired of God, as the Bible declares they were, then these calamitous pronouncements came from Him.

John the Baptist sets the stage for the thesis of this work by laying the axe at the very root of Israel's false hope, their carnal ties with Abraham. John informed the Jews who came to his baptism that God's reputation does not stand or fall on their religiosity and if needs be "God is able of these stones to raise up children unto Abraham" (Luke 3:8). He referred to them as a "generation of vipers" and insisted upon genuine repentance if they were to enter the Kingdom of God.

Jesus, perhaps more than anyone else, denounced their life style. "Ye hypocrites ... fools and blind ... whited sepulchres ... ye serpents ... ye generation of vipers ... ye blood shedders" (Matthew 23:13-35).

The Apostle Paul refused in no uncertain terms to laud them in their unbelief. When the Thessalonian Christians were being persecuted by their own Gentile brethren, Paul tried to console them by the example of the Jews against their own kin:

> For ye, brethren, became followers of the churches of God which in Judaea are in Christ Jesus: for ye also have suffered like things of your own countrymen, even as they have the Jews.
> *Who killed the Lord Jesus,* and *their own prophets,* and *have persecuted us;* and they *please not God,* and *are contrary to all men* (1 Thessalonians 2:14-15).

If verbal assault can be called anti-Semitism then the prophets in the Old Testament were guilty; so were John the Baptist, Jesus, Paul, and Stephen. If these men were living today their names would go down in infamy. The tribunal court that the premillennialists have so cleverly established to defend Jewry would never acquit them.

One of the key passages in the book of Romans is given in chapter two, verse eleven: "For there is *no respect of persons with God."* This is the theme that Paul wants to develop throughout this epistle. When he comes to prove this truth he shows that all men are sinners (including the Jewish people) and quotes from their own Scriptures, Psalms 14 and 53:

> What then? Are we [Jews] better than they [Gentiles]? *No, in no wise:* for we have before *proved both Jews* and *Gentiles,* that *they are all under sin.*
> As it is written, there is *none righteous, no not one:* There is *none that understandeth,* there is *none that seeketh after God* (Romans 3:9-11).

Will some of the evangelical church crucify me if I put the Jewish people in the same category as does the Bible? Has the Word of God changed since the Scofield Bible was printed or since 1948? Could it be that the Jew has evolved into some kind of holy species since the Scriptures were written? Does the Jew today, in his natural state, have a different heart from the unbelieving Jew of the Old and New Testament days?

The Jewish mentality that has infiltrated the Christian church today knows no bounds. We are told by many futurists that men and nations (past and present) decide their destiny according to their attitude and relationship to Israel. Those who revel in Jewish prophecy see Israel as a barometer by which nations rise or fall. Current events inside and outside the state of Israel have become the criteria for judging men rather than the Word of God.

Some premillennialists would have us believe that men are "blessed" or "cursed" to the degree they "bless" or "curse" Israel. God's initial word to Abraham in Genesis 12:2-3 has become a theological panacea for this doctrine:

> And I will make of thee a great nation, and I will bless thee, and make thy name great: and thou shalt be a blessing:
> And I will bless them that bless thee, and curse him that curseth thee: and in thee shall all families of the earth be blessed.

Those who provide for and protect Israel, so the teaching goes, are assured of God's blessings. Israel is the focal point of God's activity in the world today rather than Christ and His church.

The premillennialists' interpretation of Genesis 12:2-3 is a good eye opener for the uninitiated in millennial tactics. This passage is generally understood as the cornerstone of their "doctrine" but when properly interpreted it becomes their demise. The millenarians are guilty of taking the first half of verse 3 and applying it to all Jews and all Gentiles in every period of history, but when the entire verse is considered (as it should be) it exposes one of the greatest doctrinal errors ever perpetrated on the Christian church. If the Gentiles are to be "blessed" or "cursed" by their treatment of the carnal seed of Abraham in every period of history, then we must conclude that it is through the *same* carnal seed that "all the families of the earth are blessed:"

> And I will bless them [Gentiles] that bless thee [Jew], and curse him [Gentile] that curseth thee [Jew]; and in thee [Jew] *shall all families of the earth be blessed.*

If the first half of verse 3 is speaking of the carnal seed of Abraham, then so is the second half. Is there a remote possibility that the carnal seed of Abraham are capable of blessing "all the families of the earth?"

To fantasize Genesis 12:2-3 and apply it indiscriminately to the unbelieving Jews of today is to pour contempt upon the Gospel of Christ. The "blessing" and "cursing" in this passage of Scripture pertain to Christ and His elect and not the carnal offspring of Abraham (Galatians 3:16, 29). The Jewish people in unbelief are not the source of "blessing" or "cursing" for the rest of the world. How can unregenerate, unenlightened people (Jew or Gentile) be a blessing to others when they have a "curse" upon themselves (Galatians 3:8-14)?

The zealotic slogans, "bless Israel" and "comfort Israel," of the futurists are like wells without water. There are no more advantages in "blessing" and "comforting" Israel than there are in "blessing" and "comforting" other peoples of the world (Romans 3:9ff). These pious slogans, flavored with premillennial incense, are meant to rally political, financial, and "religious" fervor for the state of Israel.

There are some Christian groups in the state of Israel today whose only purpose for being there is to "comfort" the Jews. They are not motivated to *convert* them to Christianity, but to "comfort" them. International Christian Embassy, Jerusalem (ICEJ) is one of those organizations. This Christian group was founded in 1980 for the explicit purpose of "supporting" and "comforting" Israel. Kenneth H. Sidey, one of the associate editors of *Christianity Today,* in an article entitled "For the Love of Zion," quotes the officials of ICEJ as saying "No one can point to a single Jewish person converted to Christianity as a result of our efforts."[1] In the light of ICEJ's current operating budget (about $80,000 per month), we can conclude that millions of dollars have passed through the hands of this organization without a "single convert."

It seems that human emotions have replaced sound theology. Sentiments for the Jewish people in their plight to maintain a political state is far more important than their eternal welfare. There is more interest in making them "comfortable" here and now than there is in making them "comfortable" in a world to come. While the Apostle Paul was willing to face an angry mob in Jerusalem, be bound, and even die for the Gospel's sake (Acts 21:11-13), the millenarians are willing to hold the Gospel at arm's length and "comfort" the Jews. There is reason to believe that some premillennialists have created a "comfort zone" for themselves rather than the Jews. See also Acts 5:28-29.

The first and foremost task of the evangelical church is not to "bless" and "comfort" the state of Israel, but to understand Israel's *state* — i.e., to see her lost condition. The New Testament is not concerned with Israel as a secular nation, but a "holy nation" — comprised of both Jews and Gentiles (1 Peter 2:9). The Jewish people, whether in the state of Israel, or outside the state of Israel, can never be "blessed" until they acknowledge the "blessed" Saviour. They can never be "comforted" in

---

1. *Christianity Today,* Vol. 36, No. 3, March 9, 1992, 48.

the proper sense of the term until they are indwelled by the Great Comforter—the Holy Spirit of God. As long as the Jewish people reject the Word of the Gospel, the wrath of God will be upon them. Instead of being "blessed" and "comforted" they will continue to experience indignation, wrath, tribulation, and anguish (Romans 2:8-11).

We sometimes hear and read that the Jews are a "destined" people. If so, may I ask: to *what* are they destined? And *when* will they arrive at their destination? Is their "destination" like the proverbial carrot and stick? Will they always be a people "in waiting"? Will the Jewish families continue to end the Seder (Passover) by crying *"L'shana Tova b'Yerushalayim!"* (Next year in Jerusalem!)? Are they "destined" for the so-called thousand year reign? What about the other four thousand years of Jewish history? Dare we compare one thousand years of bliss to four thousand years of misery?

What "destiny" can we claim for the millions and millions of Jews who have lived and died since Abraham's day? Will God show favoritism to a few thousand Jews in some millennial age to the exclusion of millions who have come and gone? Is there not a better answer for the stock of Abraham? Is there no balm in Gilead? Will the present generation lead the next generation into the same pitfall?

Also, there is the fabled concept that the Jews are God's "chosen people." This unqualified, blanket statement on the Jewish people has been in vogue for a number of years. We are told that God has "unconditionally" bound Himself to Abraham's descendants. If they are God's "chosen people," I would like to ask: *for what* and *to what* are they chosen? Have they been chosen for Roman persecution, for Moslem tyranny, for the sword of the Crusaders, for the ruthlessness of the Turks, for the Spanish Inquisition, for Russian *pogroms;* have they been chosen for the concentration camps and holocausts of Auschwitz, Poland and other cities such as Dachau, Belsen, and Buchenwald, Germany; are they chosen for the ghetto, for goy fear; have they been chosen for kosherism and legalistic Judaism? Over the years the words "persecution" and "Jew" have become synonymous terms. Did God "choose" the Jewish people for such anti-Semitism? Is God glorified by such deplorable inhumanities?

Is there some kind of hidden, latent factor in the Jewish race that will commend itself to God in the future but is not present today? Would the premillennialists have us stick our heads in the sand and ignore the facts of Scripture and history? Are they asking us to play a game of pretense? Must we abandon our rationality for this make-believe theology? This is not to put the Jewish people down — rather it is an effort to circumvent some of the false ideas concerning them. The Bible declares them to be "sinners" — not *chosen*.

One of the greatest heresies being propagated in some areas of the church today is the equality of Jew and Christian. Some futuristic teachers make no difference between Abraham's carnal descendants and born again Christians. We are told that both are fulfilling a divine role in God's redemptive program — both serve the same God. There are those who have the audacity to say that the Jewish people do not need conversion as the Gentiles. We are made to wonder what is on the heresy agenda of the futurists in the days ahead.

Some of the current views on the Jewish people need to be de-mythologized. If Jewish flesh and blood have redemptive merit in them in some future millennial age, why not *now?* Will the blood of the Jews be purer in the future than now? All history proves that the longer the world stands the less pure races become. An untainted blood line from Abraham to the present hour is a highly debatable matter. I question whether or not a pure blood line is traceable to Abraham. What percentage of Jewish blood must one have in his body to be classified as a Jew? If the so-called millennial reign should occur today, how many present-day Jews would qualify to share in it?

Marriages between Jews and non-Jews go all the way back to the beginning of the Israelite nation. Some of the most prominent characters in Jewish history married outside their race. Joseph married an Egyptian; Judah married a Canaanite; Moses married a Midianite; Boaz married Ruth, the Moabitess; David married Maacah, a Geshurite; Solomon married the daughter of an Egyptian Pharoah; Ahab married Jezebel, a Phoenician princess; and Jehoram married Athaliah, the half Hebrew and half Gentile daughter of Ahab and Jezebel.

Even Jesus had a shade of Moabite blood in Him that came as a result of a Hebrew man (Boaz) marrying a Moabite woman (Ruth). We read that "Boaz begat Obed of Ruth; and Obed begat Jesse; and Jesse begat David the king" (Matthew 1:5b-6a). All Scripture attests that Jesus was the Son of David as well as the Son of God.

Generally speaking, genealogical reading in the Scriptures ends in boredom; but on the other hand an inquiry of this nature can be very revealing. We discover a series of mixed marriages among the Hebrew people that usually go unnoticed by the average Bible student. For

example, the marriage of Joseph to Asenath, the daughter of Poti-
pherah, priest of On (a city in southern Egypt), resulted in the birth of
two sons: Manasseh and Ephraim. Manasseh and Ephraim are half
Egyptian and half Hebrew. Both became heads of tribes after the
conquest of Canaan under Joshua. 1 Chronicles 7:14-19 and 20-29
respectively, trace the occupants of these tribal territories directly to the
sons of Joseph. Therefore the tribe of Ephraim, the largest tribe of the
northern kingdom, and the tribe of Manasseh are a mixed race of people.

No information is given on the wives of Jacob's sons who became
the heads of the other ten tribes except Judah and Simeon. Judah married
a Canaanite woman whose father's name was Shuah (Genesis 38:2).
Judah had three sons by this Canaanite wife: Er, Onan, and Shelah.
When Er became of age, his father, Judah, selected a wife for him by the
name of Tamar (Genesis 38:6). Some scholars believe that Tamar was
also a Canaanite and more especially of Philistine descent.[2]

Er, because of his wickedness, was smitten by the Lord and Onan's
disobedience resulted in a similar fate. According to ancient marital
customs, Tamar was to have married Shelah, the youngest and last of
Judah's sons. For some unknown reason she was denied this relationship, which in turn, provoked her into a sexual intrigue with her father-
in-law. This incontinent involvement with Judah resulted in the birth of
twin sons who were given the names of Pharez and Zarah. Pharez
became the progenitor through which the tribe of Judah would evolve
(1 Chronicles 4:1ff). If Tamar was of Canaanite descent, then the entire
tribe of Judah, the largest of the twelve tribes, was tainted with Gentile
blood — of course, this is only conjecture.

Furthermore, if Judah had no reservations about marrying a Canaanite woman, and if he chose one for his son Er, then it is possible that
the other sons of Jacob would have few qualms about marrying
Canaanite wives (See Genesis 34:16). Some writers on the subject
believe they married women from Mesopotamia. However, the Scriptures are silent on the matter. Simeon's son, Shual, by a Canaanite
woman, could tip the scales in favor of Canaanite wives for all of Jacob's
sons (Genesis 46:10).

The Jewish people have been everything but immune to mixed
marriages. After Solomon's death and the dividing of the nation, the

---

2. *The Pulpit Commentary*, Wm B. Eerdman's Publishing Company, Grand Rapids,
   Michigan, 1950, Vol. I, 441.

stage was set for many interracial marriages. The corrupt leadership and religious decline in both kingdoms, especially the northern kingdom, prepared the way for a mixed race of people. The neglect of God's Word and their interactions with foreign countries made them more vulnerable to Gentile marriages. The centuries during and after the captivity would take their toll in Jewish blood.

A part of the reform under Ezra and Nehemiah, in the reconstruction period, consisted of a ban on the Jews marrying foreign wives. Some of their contemporaries had married wives of the Canaanites, the Hittites, the Perizzites, the Jebusites, the Ammonites, the Moabites, the Egyptians, and the Amorites (Ezra 9:1). The gravity of this sin is attested by Ezra's reaction to it. He rent his garment and mantle; he plucked off the hair of his head and beard; he sat in astonishment (Ezra 9:3). In addition to this, he was ashamed and blushed at the very thought of such an abominable act against God (Ezra 9:6). The "princes," "rulers," and "Levites" were among the offenders:

> For they [Israelites] have taken of their [foreign] daughters for themselves, and for their sons: so that the holy seed have *mingled themselves with the people of those lands:* yea, the hand of the princes and rulers hath been chief in this trespass (Ezra 9:2).

Marriages between Jews and non-Jews caused Ezra more anguish of soul than any other problem he faced. It had reached alarming proportions. Ezra lamented: "we are *many* that have transgressed in this thing" (Ezra 10:13). So serious was the matter that he felt the people could not stand before God unless it was abolished (Ezra 9:15). Ezra established a divorce system to annul existing mixed marriages. Two entire chapters (9 and 10) are devoted toward the correction of this offense.

A few years after Ezra's efforts to curb such marriages, Nehemiah is faced with the same difficult situation. Nehemiah was shocked and very indignant when he discovered that some of the Jews'

> ... children *spake half in the speech of Ashdod,* and *could not speak in the Jews' language,* but according to the language of each people [i.e., Ashdod, Ammon, and Moab] (Nehemiah 13:24).

If there was a pure blood line traceable to Abraham after the captivity, it would have to be through the small remnant that returned to Palestine under Zerubbabel, Ezra, and Nehemiah. Only a few of the

Jews that once comprised the southern kingdom would return to their homeland to begin the restoration era. Nehemiah leaves us with little doubt about these facts:

> Now the city [Jerusalem] was large and great but the *people were few,* and the houses were not built (Nehemiah 7:4).

Ezra gives the exact figure of 42,360 people who returned to their native land (Ezra 2:64). Ezra's figures seem to be the only reliable source for the number of people who returned from the captivity. This is a very small number in comparison to the multitude who came out of Egypt under Moses. The figure is dwarfed even more when we consider the thousands of Israelites who lived in both kingdoms prior to the captivity.

Most of the Jews in the northern kingdom lost their identity in one way or another; the Judean Jews who sought a sanctuary in Egypt, under the leadership of Johanan (Jeremiah 43:4-7), never returned to Palestine, except a few who were able to escape (Jeremiah 44:13-14; 28); and those who were allowed to remain in their homeland (the poor Jews of both Israel and Judah) intermarried with surrounding nations.

In the years following the restoration, many Jews became scattered throughout the Gentile world. They were known as the Jews of the diaspora. Most of these Jews became cosmopolitan in their life style and had little or no interest in Jewish nationalism. Jewish nationalism and Judaism have been the prime factors in preserving the Jewish race. Where these diminish, the door is open for mixed marriages.

In more modern days, the Jewish people have been deported or have migrated to almost every country in the world — Russia, Poland, Spain, France, Germany, America — to name a few. Living *in* and *under* foreign domination for hundreds of years has naturally led to many mixed marriages. Small pockets of Jewish people in certain parts of the world have been swallowed up by intermarrying with non-Jews; or else become extinct for the refusal of it.

Intermarriages on the European scene must have been very high after World War I. Nathan Glazer, in his book, *American Judaism,* states that "intermarriage rates had been very high in Germany, Austria, and Hungary between the wars."3

---

3. Nathan Glazer, *American Judaism,* The University of Chicago Press, Chicago and London, 1972, 161

The same pattern of mixed marriages is found on this side of the Atlantic and perhaps with greater gusto. Over one-third of the world's Jewish population is found in the United States (see statistical quote from the *American Jewish Year Book* below). Following World War II, religious freedom, equal rights, and prosperity in this nation created a seedbed for intermarriages among the Jewish people. In the early 1960s there developed a Jewish survival syndrome in this country that is a concern for the establishment to this hour. The exact date of the following newspaper article is not known, but it is certainly later than 1960. It is a quote from Rabbi Harold I. Saperstein, president of the New York Board of Rabbis:

> NEW YORK (RNS) — The growing number of marriages between Jews and non-Jews "threatens the very survival of the Jewish community," declared Rabbi Harold I. Saperstein, president of the New York Board of Rabbis ...

Statistics are not available to confirm the exact number of marriages between Jews and non-Jews in this nation and opinions on the subject vary. The February (1993) issue of *Moment* magazine, a Jewish publication designed to promote Jewish culture and opinion, has an article by Dennis Prager entitled "Prager's Thirteen Principles of Intermarriage" which opens with this lead line: "With intermarriage rates running at about 50 percent, intermarriage has become the most discussed topic in American Jewish life."[4] This writer has described the problem in a nutshell. According to Mr. Prager, the nearest solution to these runaway marriages is to make Jewish homes and schools. Dennis Prager writes and publishes *Ultimate Issues*, a quarterly publication containing his thoughts about life and Judaism. He is also a nightly talk show host on KABC Radio in Los Angeles.

The above statement by Dennis Prager agrees with most of the information the writer has been able to obtain on Jewish marriages. A good deal of time and money has been spent by the establishment to avert this trend but with little success.

---

4. *Moment* magazine, a division of Jewish Educational Ventures, Inc., 3000 Connecticut Ave. N.W., Suite 300, Washington, D.C., 20008, February, 1993, Volume 18, Number 1, p. 18.

The 1977 edition of the *American Jewish Year Book* reported a drop of 86,000 in the Jewish world population. This figure represents only one year's decline:

> NEW YORK (AP) — The world's Jewish population now is estimated at 14,145,000 says the 1977 edition of the *American Jewish Year Book*. The figure represents a year's drop of 86,000.
>
> The volume, issued jointly by the American Jewish Committee and the Jewish Publication Society of America, puts the number of U. S. Jews at 5,845,000.
>
> After the United States, countries with the largest Jewish populations were listed as Israel, 2,953,000; Soviet Union, 2,680,000; France, 550,000; Great Britain, 410,000; Canada, 305,000; and Argentina, 300,000. [5]

And what is to be said of the Jewish people now living in the state of Israel? Can they claim a pure blood line with Abraham? In the October 6, 1978 issue of *Christianity Today* there appeared a series of articles under the title, "Israel: The Unbroken Line." One of the subtopics in this series was written by George Shama, counselor, Jordan Mission to the United Nations, New York, New York. The title of Mr. Shama's article was, "A False Claim To Palestine." The premise of this writer's work is that the Jewish people have no claim upon Palestine by virtue of their blood ties: they are a mixed race of people. I quote a part of his article:

> Not only are Jews wrongly claiming any exclusive right to the promises made to all Abraham's seed, religious Jews today, and especially contemporary Zionists, are *not physical descendants from Abraham's stock*. There are *black Jews, blond Jews, and blue-eyed Jews*. The current political leaders in Israel and Jewish immigrants from Russia, Central America, and the United States *are mostly of Khazar descent* — Caucasian Russians converted to Judaism in the Eighth Century by Byzantine Jews.
>
> Zionist claims to the land of Palestine, therefore, cannot be based on *physical descent* or ancient promises. They have no basis in the

---

5. *The Maryville-Alcoa Times*, Maryville, Tennessee January 21, 1977.

century-long possession of the land. In fact, their sole claim to the land is the right of invasion and conquest.[6] (Author's emphasis).

A new study by two professors at the Hebrew University in Jerusalem reveals that within 30 years the state of Israel could have more Arabs than Jews if the population trends continue:

> WASHINGTON (AP) — The fast-growing Arab population could constitute nearly half the people in Israel in 30 years, a new study by two Hebrew University professors speculates.
>
> The study estimates that if Israel annexes the disputed West Bank lands, and if current population growth trends continue, Jews could make up as few as 50.04 percent of the Israeli population by the year 2015.
>
> And even if Arab birth rates slow, Dov Friedlander and Calvin Goldscheider of Hebrew University of Jerusalem, estimate the Jewish population of Greater Israel — including the West Bank — at only 62 percent Jewish by that year.[7]

The survival and identity of the Jewish people is believed by many to be unique and a token of God's divine favor. Are they unique? Do we not find other nations and people in existence today as old and older than the Jewish people who have not lost their identity? For example: the Chinese, the Egyptians, the American Indians, the Africans, and others have not lost their identity. Are they not under the providence of God too? Is God any less concerned for other nations and people? Must we not ask in the words of the Apostle Paul, "Is He the God of the Jews only? Is He not also of the Gentiles? Yes, of the Gentiles also" (Romans 3:29).

The continuance of Jewish identity and a pure blood line can be two different things. One may be identified as a Jew and yet not be the pure stock of Abraham. Many of the black people in the United States are no longer "black" but "brown." A mixture of white and black genes produce an in-between race that is neither black nor white. Most of the "brown" people still have black characteristics and are classified as "black." By the same token, Jewish people can possess Gentile blood and still be identified and classified as Jews.

It is a matter of record that the New Testament is not concerned with the continuance of Jewish genealogies as found in the Old Testament Scriptures and the beginning of the New. The primary reason for the

6. *Christianity Today,* October 6, 1978, Vol. XXIII, No. 1, 29 .

7. *The Daily Times,* Maryville, Tennessee, April 10, 1984

preservation of a genealogical record was to identify and confirm the promise made to Abraham — which was Christ. After Jesus came in the flesh all genealogical records were discontinued. But old habits die hard. Some of the Jews quarreled over the merits of Jewish extractions and created problems within the church. It was for this reason that Paul exhorted Timothy to avoid "...fables and *endless genealogies,* which minister questions, rather than godly edifying" (1 Timothy 1:4; see also Titus 3:9). A continued emphasis on Jewish genealogies could have been the death of Christianity — especially among the Gentiles. Jewish "genealogies," Jewish "nationalism," and Jewish "tribalism" find no importance after Jesus was born. A revival and restoration of the twelve tribes of Israel in the so-called millennial kingdom as believed by the futurists is a "yellow brick road."

Several millennia have passed since Abraham's day. Will another millennium come and go before Jesus returns? If blood ties with Abraham are questionable today, what can we expect if the world continues another thousand years? We raise the question again: What percentage of Jewish blood in the human body is required for one to be classified as a descendant of Abraham? Dare we structure a theology on the basis of Jewish blood? Must we deceive ourselves and disillusion them (Jews) with such a groundless hope?

If the Jewish people of today took seriously some of the popular theology on the millennial theory, it would not be to their salvation but damnation. Any doctrine that leaves the slightest loophole for the neglect of one's salvation is to be deplored. Millennial teaching offers men a second chance *after* Jesus comes for His elect. "Behold, *now* is the acceptable time; behold, *now is the day of salvation*" (2 Corinthians 6:2). "How shall we escape if we *neglect so great salvation?*" (Hebrews 2:3).

Many premillennialists have a Jewish syndrome for which there is no antidote. Everything in Scripture revolves around "Israel." "Jewish-ness" is the touchstone of the past, present, and future. The Hebrew people are God's timetable. If one wants to know the time of day on the prophetic clock, then he must "look at Israel." Almost every passage of Scripture is to be understood in its relationship to the Jewish people. Jewish pre-eminence overshadows the pre-eminence of Christ in the theology of many futurists.

Premillennialism, with its Jewish mania, is making new inroads into the church every day. Since it has met with little or no opposition, its strength seems to know no end. Will God's people continue to cower and tolerate this Goliath that seeks to usurp the power and glory that belongs to Christ and His elect? Is there no David within our ranks to challenge this unorthodox giant? Dare we sit passively by and allow the blood of Jesus to be trampled on by those who defy and reject Him on every hand? Should we not stand with the Prophets of the Old Testament and the Apostles of the New Testament — even if it means death?

Because of its popularity, thousands of people have been attracted to premillennialism, unaware of the sleazy foundation on which it is built. Scores of people give lip service to its "doctrines" without knowing its innermost teachings. I refuse to walk down this dark path when so many glaring signs point in another direction.

I consider myself a far greater friend to the Jewish people than some of the advocates of the millennial theory. If a patient visited his doctor with pain in his body and the physician discovered that he had cancer and refused to make it known and treat it, the patient would have no further use for the doctor. In like manner, the Jewish people without Christ have a malignancy just like the Gentiles and that malignancy is *sin* and *death*. If they do not repent and believe on Christ, the Great Physician, they will die in their sin. As it is written, "All have *sinned* and come short of the glory of God" (Romans 3:23).

The "Israel" that is being imposed upon the church today is a counterfeit Israel. It has no demonstrable strength or glory but is contrived in the minds of men. This pseudo Israel is always in the future — always exceeding our grasp. It has emerged from a hodgepodge of Scriptures with endless ambiguities and inconsistencies. It is an isolated Israel with a mysterious two-thousand-year void. It is an Israel that has been written off God's calendar for an indefinite period of time — it is completely detached from God's elect in this age. The Israel of the futurists is a monstrosity — a two-headed Israel — an Israel of today and an Israel of some uncertain future — all of which leaves us in a state of consternation.

However, there is an Israel with which men must reckon — an unassuming Israel that derives its strength and glory from the face of Jesus Christ. This Israel was conceived in the heart of God before Abraham was born. This Israel has never gone into hiding — it has never disappeared from the earth. This Israel reigns and rules with her Lord at the present time and will throughout eternity. This Israel is the "apple of His eye" — the jewels in His royal diadem. Millions of people have been "blessed" and will continue to be "blessed" by this Israel until Jesus returns. Millions more have been "cursed" because they have refused to identify themselves with the true Israel of God. We have a mandate from the Lord to delineate between the true Israel and the false. This book is written to that end.

Chapter 2

ISRAEL vs. ISRAEL
Two Israels

Jewishness is stamped on practically every page of Scripture. The newcomer to the Bible, if he begins with the book of Genesis, will read only a few chapters until he is confronted with Abraham, the father of the Jewish race. From the twelfth chapter of Genesis to the closing chapter of Revelation the Bible student is faced primarily with one race of people — the Jewish people.

But the above statement is the discovery of the novice. Those who have "eyes to see" will see another people — a people within a people — that constitute the children of God. This is one of the mysteries of godliness that had its origin in the mind and heart of God before the foundation of the world.

My knowledge of the Jewish people was almost nil before I was converted. Shortly after my conversion I began to hear and read a good deal about the descendants of Abraham, the millennium, and related doctrines. Being new in the faith and unfamiliar with the Scriptures, I had little recourse but to accept those teachings to which I was exposed. These views were coming to me from individuals whom I considered "sound in the faith" and I had few qualms about them. However, the more I studied the New Testament the more I began to see that certain Bible teachers, preachers, and writers were making claims for the Jewish people that could not be substantiated by the Scriptures.

One of the most fallacious allegations for the Jewish people centered around the "Kingdom of God." The disciples of premillennialism contend that when Christ came in the flesh He would have established an earthly kingdom had the Jewish people received Him, but since He was rejected by so many, He went to the cross and the setting up of the kingdom was postponed to some future date. By clinging to this false premise the premillennialists insist that Israel, as a nation, has been *cast aside* during the "church age" but God will deal with the Jewish people again and the earthly kingdom of a thousand years with Jewish overtones will be established.

The establishment of an earthly kingdom was altogether foreign to the mind of God when Christ came two thousand years ago. Jesus

Himself said: "My kingdom is not of this world" (John 18:36a). When Jesus came face to face with His impending death He was not caught by surprise. He was undaunted in His desire to do the will of the Father: "Now is my soul troubled; and what shall I say? Father, save me from this hour: but *for this cause came I unto this hour*" (John 12:27). Had the cross of Jesus been averted, God would have forfeited the greatest display of His love, nature, and glory that the world would ever know. Christ's first mission on this planet was to die for the sins of the world and He fulfilled it to the letter.

It is implied by some premillennialists that the rejection of Christ by the Jewish people aborted the plan of God in setting up an earthly kingdom (see Scofield's notes, p. 998, 1010-1011). Such an implication is preposterous. The Apostle Paul settles forever the dust that the premillennialists have raised relative to such a miscarriage in the plan of God. Admittedly, the Jewish people had many advantages in the Old Testament era but God is not bound to man by virtue of His past goodness. God's goodness only enhances man's responsibility (see Romans 2:1-11). Paul is horrified at the very thought of God being bound by Jewish behavior:

> What advantage then hath the Jew? Or what profit is there in circumcision?
> Much every way: chiefly, because that unto them [Jews] were committed the oracles of God.
> *For what if some did not believe? Shall their unbelief make the faith* [or faithfulness] *of God without effect?*
> *God forbid:* yea, let God be true, but every man a liar; as it is written ... (Romans 3:1-4a).

The same truth is reiterated in the ninth chapter of Romans where Paul affirms that God's promise to Abraham did not fail when Christ came in the flesh. The Jewish argument for the Word of God failing would run like this: "Since the promises of God were made to them — and since they were an advantaged people throughout their history — and because so many of the Jewish people rejected Christ — the Word of God failed." The Apostle Paul says, "not so!"

> Now this does not mean that God's word to Israel *has failed.* For you cannot count all "Israelites" as the true Israel of God.
> Nor can all Abraham's descendants be considered truly children of Abraham. The promise was that "in Isaac shall thy children be

called." That means that it is not the natural descendants who automatically inherit the promise, but, on the contrary, that the children of the promise (that is, the sons of God) are to be considered truly Abraham's children. For it was promised when God said: "About this time I will come and Sarah shall have a son." (Romans 9:6-9, Phillips translation).

In the above passage Paul wishes to show that the promise made to Abraham *did not fail* (verse 6). The Word of God, which was spoken to Abraham in the form of a "promise," was not delayed one second when Christ came in the flesh. The success or failure of the "promise" is judged by the Apostle on the basis of those *who are* and *who are not* the "children of God." If the natural descendants of Abraham are God's children then the "promise" failed because many of the Jewish people did not believe on Christ. Paul is very bold when he says: "For you cannot count all 'Israelites' as the true Israel of God."

There is an "Israel" to which the Word of God was fulfilled but it was not the natural descendants of Abraham per se. The promise to Abraham embraced more than the Jewish people. The truth of the matter is that the Word of God would have failed had not the Gentiles believed on Him. "In thee shall *all the nations of the world be blessed,"* was the divine decree. A close examination of the Scriptures will reveal "another Israel" that is quite different from the carnal descendants of Abraham.

The Word of the Gospel was received by both Jews and Gentiles and it is very evident that the unbelieving Jews did not frustrate God's purpose in Christ. Jesus was a "Lamb slain before the foundation of the world" and the setting up of an earthly kingdom would have prevented the cross of Calvary. To speculate on an earthly kingdom that would exclude the death of Jesus is spiritual bedlam. *An earthly kingdom without a cross would undermine the entire tone of Scripture.*

The cross of Jesus has had its opponents from the beginning. The idea of an earthly kingdom that would preclude the death of Jesus has its conception and perpetuity in Satan and in the carnal minds of men. The tempter offered Jesus a "cop out" from the Calvary experience in the very outset of His public ministry. Satan promised Jesus all the "kingdoms of the world and the glory of them," if He would worship him. Jesus refused the rulership of the world in its *present state* for more reasons than one (2 Peter 3:13; Revelation 11:15; 21:5). His reply to the archdeceiver was: "Get thee behind me Satan ..." Jesus shall reign over "all things" but it will only be after He has "reconciled all things unto Himself by the blood of His cross" (Colossians 1:20).

Peter could not have played the Devil's game with more skill than when he protested the death of Jesus (Mark 8:31-32). Jesus refused to condone, even for a moment, Peter's suggestion that He avoid His passion. This impulsive disciple could claim no direction from God in this matter — a remonstration of this nature has its origin in men and Satan. Jesus used the same language to rebuke Peter that He used to resist Satan:

> *Get thee behind me, Satan:* for thou savourest not the *things that be of God,* but the *things that be of men* (Mark 8:33b).

The premillennialists, like Peter, are constrained to disapprove of Christ's humiliation. They are simply echoing the words of Peter when he said, "Be it far from thee, Lord: this shall not be unto thee" (Matthew 16:22). When it comes to the actual hour of His death they are forced to take their sword — and instead of cutting off a man's ear as Peter did in protest of Jesus' arrest — they must cut the entire episode of His sufferings from the Scripture. This is not an unjust criticism of premillennialism. *Premillennialism is founded upon a crossless theory.*

The establishment of an earthly kingdom without the death of Jesus has no sanction from God and arises only from the carnal minds of men. The slightest hint of an earthly kingdom over which Christ would reign, rather than a redemptive mission, was opposed by our Lord Himself. The kingdom of God was not postponed due to the rejection of Jesus by the Jews and therefore cannot be resumed in some future millennial age.

My bewilderment increased as I heard and read of a temple that is to be built in Jerusalem in conjunction with the millennial reign. According to premillennial views, animal sacrifices will be offered again as in the Old Testament dispensation. The priesthood, with all its paraphernalia, will be in vogue as in former days. "Shock" and "amazement" are the only words that could describe my first reaction to this teaching. I was "shocked" that men could believe it and "amazed" at the lack of Biblical knowledge within the church to expose and refute it.

A return to the sacrificial system of the Old Testament era would be like an adult man returning to the schoolroom of his childhood to begin his learning process all over again. Why would an astronaut want to return to the lecture room and the various assimilated programs while he is traveling in outer space beholding the wonders of God's creation?

What sane person would prefer the shadow figure of a house for the house itself? To revert to the Old Testament temple, sacrifice, and priesthood would be like turning back the clock. Jesus is the sacrificial Lamb — Jesus is the Great High Priest — and Jesus is the Temple.

Also, there will be at least three "kinds" of people living on the earth during the so-called millennial age. The saints who are raptured at the first appearing of Christ will return with Him (at the end of a seven-year period) in their glorified bodies and co-exist with believing and non-believing people (Jews and Gentiles) in their natural or physical bodies. Such a conglomeration as this is not to be found in Scripture. This, too, is in the category of theory and I must "lay it to rest" along with many other things the premillennialists teach.

Another thing that disturbed me was the enormous gap that the premillennialists place between the Old and New Testament saints. For them, the church is only a "parenthesis" in the over-all plan of God. The church is more or less a side issue. According to the premillennialists, the Jewish nation has been "cast aside" temporarily but God will deal with Israel again when the "church age is fulfilled." In the words of Dr. William Hendriksen the "parenthesis" theory is like a scheduled Jewish train that has been side-tracked temporarily until the "unscheduled Gentile-Special has passed through:"

> There are those who maintain that the church is a mere parenthesis, an afterthought in God's program of redemption, a valley invisible to Old Testament prophets who never even dreamed about it; that, in dealing with the church, history has left the main highway and is making a detour; and that God ignores the flight of time until He deals again with the Jews. In the sight of God, so runs the argument, the Jews are all-important. Hebrew time is the Lord's time. Israel is like a scheduled train which has been put on a side-track temporarily but will be put back on the main track again as soon as the *unscheduled* (!) Gentile-Special has passed through.[1]

According to the Apostle Paul, the church age will *not* be interrupted by a period of Jewish grandeur. The book of Ephesians declares that the glory of Christ is to be reflected in the church "throughout all ages world without end" (3:21). The premillennialists are determined to

---

1. Loraine Boettner, *The Millennium,* (Presbyterian and Reformed Publishing Company, Philadelphia, Pa., 1957), 229.

interrupt this ageless glory to make room for a Jewish millennium. In the minds of many futurists, Jewish glory will obliterate that of the church. The phrase just quoted from Ephesians 3:21 literally means that the glory of Christ will continue in the church "unto all the generations of the ages of the ages."

If there is no organic link between God's elect in the two dispensations, then why are the Old Testament saints held up as an example of faith for the New Testament saints? Over and over again the New Testament believers are admonished to follow the example of their predecessors (Hebrews 6:12ff). The Old Testament saints were the only recorded examples of faith that the first century Christians possessed (Hebrews 11). In the people of the old dispensation, there are to be seen both good and bad behavioral patterns that are very beneficial to the New Testament generation. It is impossible to create a generation gap between the saints in the two dispensations (Jude 3).

Some of the things I have read and heard in connection with the millennial theory bypass the laughing stage and reach the ridiculous. There is a pamphlet being circulated nowadays entitled: "Why All The Vultures?" It is written by Joel Darby and has to do with a new breed of vultures multiplying in Israel that will devour the slain after the Battle of Armageddon. Some premillennialists thrive on this tabloid-type theology. "Dispensationalism" has become "sensationalism." William E. Blackstone, who wrote *Jesus Is Coming,* 1878, literally had cases of Bibles hidden in the Palestinian area for the Jews to find during the Great Tribulation.[2]

These are only a few of the unfounded claims for the Jewish people that puzzled my mind. There are many more but we shall not belabour them at this point. A good deal of futuristic teaching is a return to the infantile stages of God's revelation to man. These people are floundering in the shadows of the Gospel rather than glorying in its substance.

The book of Romans gives the most elaborate and detailed analysis of the Jewish situation of any single book in the New Testament. This epistle has become my threshing floor for winnowing the truth regarding the "two Israels" found in the Scriptures. When the book of Romans is properly understood the chaff will be separated from the wheat.

Paul begins his discussion of the Jewish people by declaring that all

---

2. Boettner, 182

the natural descendants of Abraham are sinners (Romans 3:9) and ends by saying that God hath "concluded them all (Jews) in unbelief (or disobedience) that He might have mercy upon all" (Romans 11:32). The universality of sin, the necessity of faith, and God's mercy (atonement) in Christ are three foundational truths throughout the book of Romans. Any premise that violates these basic truths must be considered as unsound.

Most of the confusion today arises out of a misunderstanding of the "Israel of God." In my search for truth, I began to see that the New Testament speaks of *two kinds of Jews or two Israels*. In Romans two the Apostle Paul describes an "outward Jew" and an "inward Jew:"

> For he is not a Jew, which is one *outwardly:* neither is that circumcision, which is *outward* in the flesh:
> But he is a Jew, which is one *inwardly;* and circumcision is that of the *heart,* in the spirit, and not in the letter; whose praise is not of men, *but of God* (Romans 2:28-29).

In one brief statement, Paul gives both the negative and positive side of Jewishness. "For he is not a Jew ... but he is a Jew." If we were true to Paul's theology and the rest of Scripture we would completely disassociate the name "Jew" from the natural descendants of Abraham. Jewishness is not outward; it is not a race of people with certain physical characteristics. Jewishness is a condition of the heart. Jewishness does not consist in circumcision of the flesh ... performed by the hands of men. Jewishness is inward; it is a "new creation;" it is circumcision of the heart, performed by the Spirit of God whose praise is not of men but of God.

It is quite obvious from the above passage that portions of the Scriptures sound like double talk. They appear contradictory. One may be a Jew and not a Jew or he may not be a Jew and yet be a Jew. The same kind of language is repeated by the Apostle Paul in the ninth chapter of this epistle when he states that "all Israelites are not Israelites:"

> ...For they are not all Israel, which are of Israel: Neither, because they are the seed of Abraham, are they all children; but, in Isaac shall thy seed be called.
> That is, they which are the children of the flesh, these are not the children of God: but the children of the promise are counted for the seed (Romans 9:6b-8).

In the above passage the Apostle uses three very comprehensive statements to prove that the natural descendants of Abraham are not the children of God. (1) They are not all Israel which are of Israel (verse 6); (2) Being Abraham's seed does not make them children of God (verse 7); and (3) The children of the flesh are not the children of God (verse 8). Such clear, concise language ought to convince anyone that the Jewish people (in unbelief) are not the children of God.

Over the past several years, the premillennialists have created a mystical aura around the name "Israel" that confounds many people. It has become a mega-name that can by-pass all areas of theology. For the futurists, the name "Israel" needs no qualifying adjectives or words — it is able to stand on its own two feet. Such words as righteous, holy, justified, sanctified, redeemed, ransomed, etc., that describe the people of God in both the Old and New Testaments can be laid aside with the wink of an eye. The name "Israel" needs to be stripped of some of the false connotations that have been imposed upon it by the millenarians.

From the very beginning it has been the work of Satan to pervert the ways of God. Jesus said that Satan is come to "steal, destroy, and kill" (John 10:10). One of Satan's chief tactics is to steal, distort, and corrupt the Word of God. Thus Satan has a way of perverting the original plan or intention of God. Satan, in conjunction with the minds of men, seeks to invalidate God's Word. The Scriptures abound with warnings to those who would distort or abuse God's written revelation to man.

It is the responsibility of the interpreter of the Bible to see things from God's perspective and not from a fallen or corrupt state. *Oftentimes the fallen, corrupt state of things reflect the good, the original which has its source in God.* In other words, the fact that men and Satan try to imitate the true and genuine is proof of their existence. As pertaining to Israel, we must not mistake the fallen, sensual, corrupt state of Abraham's descendants for the original plan of God — they are not His children. Very frequently the fallen and original become fused, resulting in everlasting confusion.

God has an "Israel" but it is not a fleshly, sensual, carnal Israel. Men have taken the original plan of God — the "Israel" that God decreed — and have "cheapened" it and "created" an "Israel after the flesh" that was never in the mind of God. Abraham's descendants, if they were to claim a fatherhood with God, were to have been a God-centered people, a faithful people, a people *ruled by God* and not governed by the flesh.

According to *Strong's Exhaustive Concordance to the Bible,* the name "Israel" appears 2,539 times in the Scriptures. It is found 2,465 times in the Old Testament and 74 times in the New Testament. Derivatives of the name are used 35 times in both testaments, making a total of 2,574 times. Its first usage is in connection with the changing of Jacob's name (Genesis 32:28). It is no coincidence that the descendants of Abraham and Jacob were by and large called "Israelites" rather than "Jacobites." Generally speaking, names in the Scripture are very significant.

According to Dr. G. Campbell Morgan, a very excellent Bible scholar, the word "Israel" in the Hebrew language literally means "ruled by God." In his sermon, "The Healing Of Life," Dr. Morgan says concerning the changing of Jacob's name:

> Thy name shall be called no more Jacob, but *Israel;* no more trickster but one under the *mastery of God.* It is of equal importance that we should remember that Israel does not mean prince; the word "prince" has really no connection with the word at all. Thou shalt be called Isra El, *one ruled by God.* That is what the Wrestler said to him.[3] (Emphasis added.)

Some Bible scholars would disagree with Dr. Morgan's thoughts on the name "Israel." However, Dr. Morgan does not stand alone in his views. The *Harper's Bible Dictionary,* while objecting to the traditional opinions on the name, adopts a position very similar to that of Dr. Morgan's:

> The meaning of the word (Israel) in Jacob's time, to which it goes back, is not definitely known, and will not be, until the verb is found in some early inscription. The best guess thus far is: "May God strive, contend, or *rule,*" not "he strives or contends with God," as suggested by Genesis 32:28 and Hosea 12:4.[4] (Parenthesis and italics are the author's.)

The precise meaning of the name "Israel" may never be known, but there is one thing certain — Dr. Morgan's views in no way violate the Scriptures. Obedience to God's Word is the hallmark of God's people. If Jacob's descendants were to be true to his name, then they must be under the "mastery of God" or be *ruled by God.* However, disobedience, rebellion, and anarchy characterized the Hebrew people throughout much of their history. Their murmuring and complaining under the

---

3. G. Campbell Morgan, *The Westminster Pulpit,* Vol. IX, Fleming H. Revell, — a division of Baker Book House, p. 116.
4. *Harper's Bible Dictionary,* Harper & Brothers, Publishers, New York, 1956, 289.

leadership of Moses set in motion an insurgent spirit that emerged in every generation. They refused to be *ruled by God* by rejecting His Word on every hand. God's rule over Israel has both positive and negative factors. This is why the name "Israel" has taken on a double meaning.

The gravitation of the Hebrew people toward an earthly king rather than an invisible Ruler appeared shortly after their debut in the Land of Canaan. The flush of victory by Gideon and his 300 warriors, in the days of the Judges, was so spectacular that the men of Israel immediately wanted to make him their king. Along with this impromptu decision, they were willing to make Gideon's posterity a perpetual kingship for the nation. The providence of God, which was responsible for Gideon's success, was completely ignored by these zealous Israelites. Gideon refused this honor with these words:

> I will not rule over you, neither shall my son rule over you: *The Lord shall rule over you* (Judges 8:23).

The Hebrew people were unaffected by Gideon's firm rebuke. Their desire for an earthly king surfaced again in the days of Samuel. A showdown was inevitable — a choice must be made between a theocratic (God-ruled) form of government and a monarchial (earthly king) form of government. Their decision was very apparent; they preferred an earthly rule to the *rule of God*. The Lord instructed Samuel to honor their choice without taking personal offense:

> ... Hearken unto the voice of the people in all that they say unto thee: for they have not rejected thee, but *they have rejected me,* that *I should not reign over them* (1 Samuel 8:7).

God not only expected *His rule* in the lives of the common people but also in the personal conduct of all national leaders ... including the king. God's concepts of a king and kingdom were altogether different from the other nations of the world. Guidelines for the selection of a king were given to Moses before the Israelites came into the Land of Canaan. No man was to rule over Israel unless he met the qualifications that are set forth in the seventeenth chapter of the book of Deuteronomy (verses 15-20). According to this Scripture, the man who reigned over Israel was to know, love, and practice the Word of God. He was to know and adhere to the Word of the Lord as well as the heads of the religious order — the priests and Levites.

There can be no doubt that his rule was to be one of "righteousness" from the beginning to the end. He was not to dote upon a kingdom with military grandeur or accumulated wealth of silver and gold; nor was his heart to be distracted from the Lord by many wives, as was common with Eastern monarchs. The Hebrew king was to wield a scepter of "righteousness" over his subjects. It is inconceivable that any other nation of the world would follow such rules in the selection of a king.

God's concern for a "righteous" rule on the part of kings can be seen in Jeremiah's words to Jehoiakim, one of the kings of Judah. Jehoiakim was far from being an exemplary king. He had ruled his people with a good deal of cruelty and oppression. Jeremiah leaves the king with a ray of hope if he will give heed to God's Word:

> ... Hear the *Word* of the Lord, O king of Judah, that sittest upon the throne of David, thou, and thy servants, and thy people that enter in by these gates:
>
> Thus saith the Lord; Execute ye *judgment* and *righteousness,* and deliver the spoiled out of the hand of the *oppressor:* and *do no wrong, do no violence to the stranger,* the *fatherless,* nor the *widow,* neither *shed innocent blood* in this place (Jeremiah 22:2-3).

The Lord delegated kingly authority to the Hebrew kings, but it was always in the context of a "righteous" rule. Judgment, righteousness, and the treatment of strangers, widows, and the fatherless took precedence over every other aspect of their kingly duties. The "Word of righteousness" was to be exemplified both in their personal conduct and in their rule. King and people were to be a "holy nation" overshadowed by the *rule of God* in their lives:

> Now therefore, if ye will *obey my voice* indeed, and *keep my covenant,* then ye shall be a peculiar treasure unto me above all people; for all the earth is mine:
>
> And ye shall be unto me a kingdom of priests, and an *holy nation.* These are the *words* which thou shalt speak unto the children of Israel (Exodus 19:5-6).

God's kingdom has always been, and always will be, a "kingdom of righteousness." Whether in the Old Testament dispensation or in the New — whether present or future — it will forever remain a "kingdom of righteousness" (Hebrews 1:8-9).

Let us say parenthetically that an interruption of the "Kingdom of God" at the beginning of the church age and resuming after the rapture of the church, as the millenarians teach, is out of the question. The Kingdom of God has never been sidetracked by the unbelief of the Jews or anyone else. The Kingdom of God is the *rule of God* in the hearts of men, regardless of the dispensation. The whole matter is shelved in the words of Paul:

> For the *Kingdom of God* is not meat and drink [satisfying carnal appetites]; but *righteousness* and *peace,* and *joy* in the *Holy Ghost* (Romans 14:17).

It is very apparent that Israel's choice of an earthly monarch in the days of Samuel did not replace the divine government of God; nor did it eliminate God's role as "King" over the nation. God was Israel's King before Saul's day (1 Samuel 12:12) and He remained Israel's King throughout her history. Dr. Dale Moody, in his book *The Word of Truth,* says that the Hebrew kings were "representative" kings but not "absolute monarchs." Dr. Moody's comments are as follows: "Out of theocratic kingship came *representative kingship,* but belief in the Lord as the invisible sovereign never vanished. There was not absolute monarchy in Israel, for the Lord alone was the absolute sovereign." [5]

Many of the Old Testament seers spoke of God as King over His people. Isaiah's lucid vision of the Lord sitting upon a throne causes us to stand in awe as we come face to face with God's Kingly nature (Isaiah 6:1-5). Jeremiah speaks of God as "King of nations" (Jeremiah 10:7) and uses the words "Lord" and "King" synonymously (Jeremiah 46:18; 51:57). Also Daniel, Zechariah, and Malachi ascribe to God the title "King." (See Daniel 4:37; Zechariah 14:16-17; and Malachi 1:14).

If any voice from the past should be heard regarding God's role as "King" over Israel, it should come from the model king of Israel, David. David's zeal for the Lord and his forty years' experience as ruler over his people should qualify him to speak with a good deal of credibility. David acknowledged God as his *own* "King" (Psalms 44:4) and sees Him as "King," not only over Israel, but "over all the earth" (Psalms 47:2).

When David's age and health constrained him to turn his throne over to Solomon, he wanted the people of Israel to know that Solomon was *God's choice of a king* and not his (1 Chronicles 29:1). This transfer

5. Dale Moody, *The Word of Truth,* William B. Eerdmans Publishing Co., Grand Rapids, MI, 1981, 516

of rulership from David to Solomon was a momentous event in the history of the Hebrew nation. On this special day, David made it known to the people that Solomon was *more* than God's choice of a king—God was to be Solomon's strength, might, wisdom, and glory throughout his reign. The people need not be anxious over Solomon's young manhood. The following statement was made, not only for the congregation of Israel, but for Solomon and all Hebrew kings who would follow him:

> Thine, O Lord, is the greatness, and the power, and glory, and the victory, and the *majesty:* for all that is in the heavens and in the earth *is thine; Thine is the kingdom,* O Lord, and thou art exalted as *head above all.* Both riches and honor come of thee, and thou *reignest over all;* and in thine hand is *power* and *might,* and in thine hand it is to make great, and to give strength unto all (1 Chronicles 29:11-12).

Hebrew kings were always subordinate to the Lord. God had no rival. Greatness, power, glory, victory, majesty, and all that is in the heavens belong to the Lord. The "kingdom," whether the "kingdom of Israel" or the "Kingdom of God" in general, belong to the Lord. God owns all, is exalted above all, and reigns over all.

Israel was never permitted to be a freewheeling, independent "nation" that would exclude the *rule of God.* The righteous government of God was to have permeated every facet of the Hebrew regime. Even Israel's most glorious era, the reign of David, was overshadowed by a theocratic rule. The eyes of the Lord were always upon the Hebrew kings and their subjects. When the over-all character of a king is described in the Old Testament, it is generally with this phrase: "And he [name of king] did that which was evil (or good) in the *sight of the Lord.*" Hebrew kings were allowed to reign, but only under the scrutiny of the Lord.

One of the evils that hastened the downfall of both Israel and Judah was the appointment of kings without God's approval. According to Hosea, it was a serious offense:

> They have *set up kings,* but *not by Me:* they have *made princes,* and *I knew it not* ... (Hosea 8:4).

It is very obvious that God expected a righteous *rule* on a "national" level but Israel blighted this expectation in every period of her history. More importantly is the *rule of God* on an "individual" level. The premillennialists make much ado over the Jewish people as a "nation" as opposed to "individuals." In my opinion, there is as much written on

individual relationships to God in the Old Testament as there is on
national relationships — and perhaps more so. The ideal citizen of any
nation at any given period of history is one who obeys God and loves his
fellow man (1 Peter 2:13-15). Israel failed as a nation in every age and
generation because thousands of individuals failed in every age and
generation. This is why the name "Israel" has acquired a twofold
meaning.

The name "Israel" was used so loosely in New Testament days that
Jesus and the Apostle Paul found it necessary to redefine it. Its original
meaning had become lost in the quagmire of Israel's sin. Jesus'
explanation, along with the Apostle Paul's, is an index to its original
meaning. The name "Israel" had such excellent connotations that
neither man could abandon it and both men refused to associate it with
the *faithless* decendants of Abraham (John 1:47; Romans 9:6). Since the
name has been redefined by two of the most prominent men in Scripture,
the distinction between a "true Israelite" and a "pseudo-Israelite"
should always be maintained. The line between the two groups has been
drawn for time and eternity. God forbid that this distinction should ever
be muddled again. To do so would be an insult to our Lord and the
Apostle Paul.

When the full particulars of Jesus' and Paul's remarks on the name
"Israel" are carefully considered, it will be noted that the name implies
a people who would be subject to the will of God. For this reason, it is
possible, in good faith, to accept Dr. Morgan's views on the name
"Israel." The *rule of God* in the lives of men is insisted upon from the
creation of man to the consummation of all things. The Hebrew people
were no exception. *God's desire to rule over the Israelites transcends
every other truth in the Old Testament.* The heads of state were to be
subject to the Word of God as well as the common people. Abraham's
descendants, including the king, were to be the embodiment of the name
"Israel" — one *ruled by God.*

But over the centuries the "ideal Israel" did not always materialize.
Instead, Israel became apostate Israel, *yet retaining her name.* This is
confirmed over and over again in the writings of the prophets where
Israel is portrayed as a "harlot" or "whore." (See Jeremiah 2:20; 3:1, 6,
7, 8, 9; 13:27; Hosea 2:2, 4, 10, 13, and Ezekiel 16:15-41). Thus the
name "Israel" became perverted. There arose the need to distinguish
between the "true Israel" and the "false Israel." "He is a Jew ... He is not
a Jew" or "they are not all Israel which are of Israel;" again, "they which

are the children of the flesh, these are not the children of God." Many of the Jewish people refused to be "ruled by God" and for this reason we cannot call them "true Israelites."

Names seldom, if ever, retain their original meaning. Man's evil propensities demand qualifying terms for practically everything with which he is associated. The concepts of "good" and "evil" have their influence upon every area of man's life. It is for this reason that most names, places, eras, etc., must be described with qualifying terms. Circumstances, conditions, and time result in change. History is not static. Qualifying adjectives, whether good or bad, oftentimes say more than the original name, place, era, etc. It is for this reason that the name "Israel" has both negative and positive connotations.

The Apostle Paul knew what the name "Israelite" meant to his own kin. This term designated them as the "children of God" in their own eyes, but their life style did not coincide with the name they bore — their character betrayed its true meaning. *The Apostle retained the original name for God's people but distinguished between those who were entitled to bear the name and those who were not.*

We see the same pattern throughout the history of the church. God's original plan was a pure church with singleness of mind and heart (Acts 2:46). God is not the author of all that happens under the name and guise of "church." Very frequently we must distinguish between the "true church" and the "spurious." This principle is no less true with the name "Israel." Over a period of years words and names have a way of degenerating. The "ideal Israel" gave way to "fleshly Israel."

The name "Israel" was given a dual meaning by our Lord. When Jesus describes the godly character of Nathanael, He distinguishes between an "Israelite" and an "Israelite *indeed*" (John 1:47-51). The Greek word for "indeed" *(alethos)* is oftentimes translated "true" or "in truth" in the New Testament. The same Greek word is used in Jesus' comments on the True Vine. "I am the true (indeed) vine." Jesus is saying that Nathanael was a *true Israelite.*

Jesus also describes Nathanael as an Israelite indeed in whom is *no guile.* According to Dr. G. Campbell Morgan, it is permissible to say that Nathanael was a *true Israelite* in whom was *no Jacob.* The Greek word for "guile" as found in the King James Version is also translated "Jacob" in the Septuagint, which is a Greek version of the Old Testament. Dr. Morgan's insight into the two Greek words (guile and Jacob) adds a new dimension to Jesus' statement:

> I do not need to describe Nathanael. Our Lord did it. "Behold, an
> *Israelite indeed,* in whom is *no Jacob."* That is exactly the signifi-
> cance of "no guile." Certainly Jacob was in the mind of our Lord,
> because He made another reference to him presently, about a ladder
> set up on earth, and reaching to the heavens.[6] (Author's emphasis.)

The old "Jacob" whose name means "supplanter" or "trickster"
should never be seen in a *true Israelite.*

There should be no misapprehension about the "two Israels" that
are so obvious in the Romans epistle. One of the cardinal teachings of
the premillennialists is that God has set the Jewish nation aside temporarily, but will deal with it again at some future date. Romans 11:1-2 is
oftentimes quoted by the futurists as referring to this future restoration
of Israel:

> I say then, Hath God cast away His people? God forbid. For I also
> am an Israelite, of the seed of Abraham, of the tribe of Benjamin.
> God hath not cast away His people which He foreknew (Romans
> 11:1-2).

When the Apostle Paul raises the hypothetical question "Hath God
cast away His people?" and answers it with a "God forbid," he is not
speaking of the rejection and restoration of the Jewish nation. He is not
implying that Israel has been put on "hold" until some future millennial
age. How can the millenarians contend that the Jewish people have been
"cast away" to be gathered again in some future millennial age when the
Apostle clearly states that "God hath not cast away His people?"

The people who have not been "cast away" in the above passage are
"His people" (God's). As we have already shown, a Jew can be an
"Israelite" and be "His people" or he may be an "Israelite" and *not* be
"His people." "God's people" come from an entirely different mold than
that of the natural descendants of Abraham.

The Apostle Paul has written ten chapters in the book of Romans
to show conclusively that natural Israel cannot be "His people." The
futurists are forced to ignore these ten chapters in order to say that
Romans 11:1-2 is speaking of the Jews as "God's people." If the Jews
are "His people" as the futurists claim, then the Scriptures as we know

---

6. G. Campbell Morgan, *The Gospel According to John,* Fleming H. Revell — a division
   of Baker Book House, p. 43

them now must be supplanted by a new book of theology before the so-called millennial kingdom occurs. Paul's views on the doctrine of sin, justification by faith, regeneration, Christ's atoning work, God's impartiality, etc., must be replaced by a new revelation. This precious gem (Romans 11:1-2) that seems to glitter so brightly in the theological coffers of the premillennialists turns into a rhinestone when properly interpreted.

The key word in Romans 11:2 is "foreknew." From the beginning, even before man was created, God knew the "kind" of people that would make up His family and that decree has never changed. As we shall see, God's people are those who are begotten by Him and bear His image and character. Those who know only the "physical birth" have never been, nor will ever be, "His people."

This is not to deny the choice of God in giving the Hebrew people the law, the prophets, the ordinances, and the fact that it was through the natural lineage of Abraham that Christ came. With all of these privileges, they are still "Israel according to the flesh" and with no more advantages than the Gentile world unless they believe the Word of the Gospel.

Paul's interrogatory statement, "Hath God cast away His people?" is answered by his own personal testimony. He considered himself as being one of "His people" and one of those whom God "foreknew." If any descendant of Abraham had reason to trust in Jewish blood or heritage, it was the Apostle Paul. His Jewish lineage was untainted by outside sources, but the confidence he once cherished became as a dunghill in the light of the glorious Gospel of Christ. Such sentiments are expressed in his epistle to the Philippians:

> For we are the circumcision, which worship God in the spirit, and rejoice in Christ Jesus, and *have no confidence in the flesh.*
> Though I might also have *confidence in the flesh.* If any other man thinketh that he hath whereof he might *trust in the flesh, I more:*
> Circumcised the eighth day, of the stock of Israel, of the tribe of Benjamin, an Hebrew of the Hebrews; as touching the law a Pharisee;
> But what things were gain to me, those I counted loss for Christ.
> Yea doubtless, and *I count all things but loss* for the excellency of the knowledge of Christ Jesus my Lord: for whom I have suffered the *loss of all things,* and *do count them but dung* (manure), that I may win Christ (Philippians 3:3-8).

What present day Jew or Jew of the future can boast of a Jewish heritage as described above? If blood ties with Abraham were meritorious in matters of redemption, surely the Apostle Paul would have been ushered into the Kingdom of God in grand array. "Confidence in the flesh" was a no-no for the Apostle and should be for all Jews, past, present, and future. It could well be that God, in His providence, chose a man with such an untarnished blood line as the Apostle Paul to discourage any and all trust in Jewish flesh. Paul, like Elijah, was a part of the remnant of his day.

The two Israels are also expressed in the Scriptures by the concept of a "remnant," and "His people" (God's) emerge with unmistakable clarity. There have been times in the course of history when it would appear that God had not maintained a witness for Himself in the world. There have been seasons when sin and wickedness seemed to have obliterated all light and hope in God. Such were the days of Elijah. Elijah was truly a prophet of God but he felt that he stood alone in his dedication. Paul uses this despondent experience of Elijah to show that *"God hath not cast away His people whom He foreknew."* Elijah's intercessory prayer runs like this:

> Lord, they have killed the prophets, and digged down thine altars;
> and I am left alone, and they seek my life (Romans 11:3).

The reader will observe that Elijah's prayer is against a people (Jewish people, mind you) who have "killed the prophets, and digged down God's altars, and are seeking the life of the prophet himself." Can the "Israel of God" be characterized by such an image as Elijah gives us? Are these "His people?" Does the Lord rule over them? Surely not! But the Lord assures Elijah that He has a people, but it is not Israel, "according to the flesh," — it is a "faithful" Israel — a *remnant* within the nation that has not bowed its knee to Baal:

> But what saith the answer of God unto him [Elijah]? I have reserved *to myself* seven thousand men, who have not bowed the knee to the image of Baal.
> Even so then at this present time also there is a *remnant according to the election of grace.*
> And if by grace, then it is no more of works; otherwise work is no more work.
> What then? Israel [according to the flesh] hath not obtained that which He [God] seeketh for; but the *election* hath obtained it, and the

rest were blinded (according as it is written, God hath given them the spirit of slumber, eyes that they should not see, and ears that they should not hear;) unto this day. (Romans 11:4-8).

The phrase "Even so then" in verse five literally means "as it was then, so is it now." Paul implies that some of the Hebrew people were not God's people in Elijah's day. He says that "Israel *hath not obtained that which He* [God] *seeketh for;* but the *election hath obtained it* and the *rest* [of the Israelites] *were blinded."* What was it that some of the Hebrew people did not obtain? It was God's grace (or righteousness) through faith.

Paul is not introducing a new field of theology in the Romans epistle. He is writing in retrospect as well as for New Testament days. He is saying: "This is the way it has always been." Faith in God's Word has been the means of salvation from the beginning (Hebrews 11). If the natural descendants of Abraham are not "His people" in Romans nine and eleven, neither are they in Isaiah, Ezekiel, Daniel, or any other portion of Holy Scripture. God is not a capricious God changing His mode of redemption from one chapter of the Bible to another.

The last statement in the above paragraph is not sustained by some millenarians. A red flag must be raised before those who would give serious study to premillennial teachings. Any "change" in God's insistence upon "faith" as the sole means of justification must be rejected. "Imputed righteousness," which translates into the "children of God," is received by faith and by no other means. This truth is confirmed in both the Old Testament (Genesis 15:6) and in the New (Romans 4:3).

Theological views, such as J. Dwight Pentecost holds on the "physical" seed of Abraham, must be exposed and disclaimed without apology. Following the death and resurrection of Jesus (according to Dr. Pentecost), the Lord established a "new relationship" with the "physical" seed of Abraham, based on "faith." While commenting on the twelfth chapter of Matthew's Gospel, he writes:

As the chapter closes (12:46-50) the Lord indicates that He is *setting aside all natural relationships,* such as Israel sustained to *Him* and to the *covenant promises* by a *physical birth,* and *establishes a new relationship, based on faith.*[7] (Author's emphasis.)

---

7. J. Dwight Pentecost, *Things To Come,* Zondervan Publishing Co., Grand Rapids, Michigan, 1958, 141.

It should be stated unequivocally that the Lord did *not* begin a "new program" with the "physical" seed of Abraham "based on faith." Such views on the "physical" seed of Abraham are diametrically opposed to the "remnant" concept that dominates the Old Testament Scriptures. By using the phrase "setting aside all natural relationships," Dr. Pentecost is implying that such a "relationship" with the "physical" seed of Abraham will be resumed at the beginning of the quasi-millennial age. On page 133 of the same book, he states that "After the death of Christ, God instituted a *new program, not to replace* the program for Israel, but to *interrupt* that divinely covenanted program" (emphasis mine). Thus God alternates between "one program" and the "other" — first, the Jews' relationship to God is "physical" — next "faith" — and then a return to "physical." This one statement by Dr. Pentecost should be sufficient to alert every earnest Bible student to some of the controvertible views of premillennialism. Dr. Pentecost *cannot* be true to New Testament doctrine and hold to the above quote. (See addendum at the end of this chapter for further comments on Dr. Pentecost's interpretation of Matthew 12:46-50).

The Jewish people were not saved in the Old Testament era because of their "physical" ties with Abraham — neither will they be saved in this manner in the future. There was a "remnant according to the *election of grace*" in Elijah's day as well as Paul's. Elijah, along with the seven thousand, make up the "true Israel" of God.

C. I. Scofield implies that the "remnant" in Romans 11:5 is composed only of "believing Jews" of the church age.[8] I must disagree with Mr. Scofield. The remnant has its origin in the "election of grace" and not in a certain nationality of people. Before the foundation of the world, God elected grace as the means of man's salvation — for Jew and Gentile. There will be no unconditional, wholesale salvation for the Jews *after* Christ returns for His church.

The two Israels become apparent also in Paul's exegesis on the births of Ishmael and Isaac/Esau and Jacob as found in the ninth chapter of Romans. In our consideration of these stories we are going to begin at the summit of God's revelation and look downward rather than stand in the valley and look upward. In other words, we are going to begin with God's ultimate and sovereign purpose in Christ as we review the

---

8. *The Scofield Reference Bible*, 1205.

narratives of Ishmael and Isaac/Esau and Jacob rather than *vice versa.* This method of interpretation is less likely to end in error than any other method.

In the New Testament, especially in the Colossians and Ephesians epistles, God's ultimate and sovereign purpose in Christ can be summed up in two concepts: (1) All things were created for Christ and by Christ; (2) Christ is Lord over all things. The ideas of "creativity" and "Lordship" seem to be the most distinctive features in God's purpose in Christ. This truth stands out very clearly in the Christology of the aforenamed epistles:

> For by Him (Christ), were *all things created,* that are in heaven, and that are in earth, visible and invisible, whether they be thrones, or dominions, or principalities, or powers: *all things were created by Him and for Him:*
> And He is *before all things,* and by Him *all things consist.*
> And He is the *head of the body,* the church: who is the beginning, the firstborn from the dead; that *in all things He might have the preeminence* (Colossians 1:16-17). See also John 1:3.

The resurrection is proof of Christ's "Lordship" over all things. Paul's prayer for the Ephesians was that they might understand this all-important truth. They were to know and share in the mighty power,

> Which He (God) wrought in Christ, when He raised Him from the dead, and *set him at his own right hand* in the heavenly places,
> *Far above all principality,* and *power,* and *might* and *dominion,* and *every name that is named, not only in this world, but also in that which is to come:*
> *And hath put all things under His feet,* and *gave Him to be the head over all things to the church,*
> Which is His body, the fulness of Him that filleth all in all (Ephesians 1:20-23).

It was *by Him* and *for Him* that *all things were created* and He has been given *Lordship over all things.* God's children are created to this end — to have their being and existence in Him and to reign with Him eternally. God's "creativity" and "Lordship" should be seen in juxtaposition with the narratives of Ishmael and Isaac/Esau and Jacob.

The divine activity that surrounds the stories of Ishmael and Isaac/ Esau and Jacob is God's "calling" and "election." *These two ideas are inherent in Christ's "creativity" and "Lordship."* God's "calling" and "election" should be considered in conjunction with the Incarnation (or God's purpose in Christ).

It is very apparent that God's "calling" and "election" are the distinguishing factors in the "children of the flesh" and the "children of God" as set forth in this chapter. Paul is not introducing a new concept — this fact was established in the Genesis story. When Sarah, Abraham's wife, thrust Hagar and Ishmael from her household, Abraham showed a degree of anxiety (Genesis 21:9-12). Since Ishmael was his firstborn son, Abraham felt that he would be hard pressed for an heir, but the Lord admonished the Patriarch to accept what Sarah had done and calmed his fears with these words: " ... for in Isaac shall thy seed be *called"* (Genesis 21:12b). The idea of "calling" is very important throughout Paul's epistles and is the most prominent feature in the births of Ishmael and Isaac/Esau and Jacob.

The Apostle Paul has used the word "calling" two or three times previously in the book of Romans. In chapter four, it is said of Abraham that "he believed, even God, who *quickeneth* the dead, and *calleth* those things which be not as though they were" (Romans 4:17b). The "quickening" and "calling" of God are correlatives — both have to do with His "creativity" by the spoken Word. In the creation narrative, as given in the Genesis account, God simply spoke the Word (or called) and the material world appeared. Hebrews 11:3 says: "Through faith we understand that the worlds were *framed of the Word of God,* so that things which are seen were not made of things which do appear." This is an echo of Romans 4:17. *The "Word" by which God "calls" is also the source of His creativity.*

Isaac was born, not as a consequence of his own faith, but Abraham's. God's Word (or promise) to Abraham was that he would have a son from his own loins to be his heir (Genesis 15:4). The "Word" was spoken many years *before* the dead bodies of Abraham and Sarah were quickened. God's Word does not always materialize the moment it is spoken. At God's appointed hour, the Word became active; its "quickening" and "creative" powers became operative, and Isaac was conceived. "I will come" and you shall have a son, was God's Word to Sarah. The book of Hebrews informs us that "Sarah *received* strength to conceive seed" (Hebrews 11:11). It was not her own strength — she received it. The word "strength" in this passage is the same Greek word (dunamis) that is used for "power" elsewhere in Scripture. The "strength" or "power" was no doubt the Holy Spirit and the Word.

Without the quickening and creative energy of the Word and Spirit (Galatians 4:29), Isaac would have never come into being. Both *flesh* and *Word* were involved in Isaac's birth, but the Word is superior to the flesh. The Word does what the flesh can never do, i.e., "quickeneth the dead and calleth those things which be not as though they were."

By God's calling (or creativity by His Word) Isaac was born. This is why Isaac was called a "child of the promise," or better still, a child of the "Word of Promise." Note Paul's emphasis upon the Word in this passage:

> Not as though the *Word of God* hath taken none effect [meaning that the "Word" was effectual]. For they are not all Israel, which are of Israel:
>
> Neither, because they are the seed of Abraham, are they all children; but, in Isaac shall thy seed be *called*.
>
> That is, they which are the children of the flesh, these are not the children of God: but the children of the promise [or "Word of Promise"] are counted for the seed.
>
> For this is the *Word [9] of Promise,* at this time will I come, and Sarah shall have a son (Romans 9:6-9).

Let it be pointed out again that God's "calling" and "election" are always in conjunction with the Incarnation. Isaac's birth set in motion the "promise" or "word" that would culminate in Christ.

The Apostle is explaining to the Roman church that God's people come into being by the same process; i.e., they are the "called"; they are the "created"; they are quickened by God's Word and Spirit. God decreed that His children be sired in this manner. Romans 9:8 and Romans 4:17 have everything in common. We, like Abraham, believe in "God, who *quickeneth* the dead, and *calleth* those things which be not as though they were" (Romans 4:17). The natural descendants of Abraham (in unbelief) can never be the children of God.

An act of "creation" is indispensable for those who are in Christ. Human works, as a means of becoming God's child, is futile. Man can *procreate,* but he cannot *create.* Any kind of "person" or "being" that man attempts to make is at best a *self-made* creature. In this case, man becomes his own "saviour" and such an endeavor would result in selfish

---

9. Many modern day versions of the Scripture are incorrect in their translation of this passage. The phrase "Word of Promise" is translated by a single word "promise" in most versions. This is a serious mistake. The Greek word λόγος is included in the phrase ἐπαγγελίας γὰρ ὁ λόγος οὗτος. The King James Version is the proper rendition.

"boasting" (Ephesians 2:9). In the act of redemption, God is portrayed as both a "workman" and as a "creator." Those who are in Christ are not a product of their own invention but are God's *"workmanship created in Christ Jesus unto good works"* (Ephesians 2:10).

The above truth finds support also in Paul's second letter to the Corinthians. The Apostle wanted this church to understand every aspect of their new relationship in Christ. Christ, along with all mankind, must be seen from a new point of view. To be "raised with Christ" means *life* on a different level. A paraphrase of 2 Corinthians 5:15b-16 will help in establishing this fact:

> ... once we die with Christ and are raised together with Him, we henceforth do not see others through carnal or fleshly eyes; and though we once understood Christ solely from a human perspective; we no longer do so ...

It is in conjunction with the above conclusion that Paul writes: "Therefore if any man be in Christ, he is a *new creation:* old things are passed away; behold, *all things are become new"* (2 Corinthians 5:17). The "creativity" of God in man's redemption is irrefutable. The Gospel (or Word) is the power *(dunamis)* of God unto salvation to everyone that believeth" (Romans 1:16). The Gospel that "calls" men to faith in Christ is also the means of God's "creativity."

God's role as Creator and its importance is well documented in the first chapter of the Romans epistle. Even the heathen world who knew nothing of the Scriptures could not escape God's role as Creator. The first indictment brought against the Gentiles by Paul was their denial of God's power, wisdom, intelligence, love, etc., that are clearly discerned from the *creation* (Romans 1:19-20). God and His creation are not the same, but the creation is a witness to His existence and attributes in every age and generation. There is a universal language and revelation associated with the heavens and the earth (Psalms 19:1-6). They speak of God's infinite power to "quicken" and "create." If the heathen world has a certain accountability to God because of His created universe, then surely those who are familiar with His Word have a greater accountability. The community of faith is constrained to believe in Him "who *quickeneth* the dead, and *calleth* those things which be not as though they were" (Romans 4:17).

This unique role of God as the Creator and Lord of life can be seen in the births of Esau and Jacob. The *Word* was not directly involved in the conception of Esau and Jacob as it was in the birth of Isaac; therefore, another aspect of God's "calling" and "election" must be considered.

Before the twin sons were born, God said to Rebecca, "the elder shall serve the younger." The key concept given in conjunction with the "elder" and "younger" is "serve." This was God's *Word* to Rebecca — actually, it was His "calling" and "election." To put it another way, it was God's *Word* and *choice*. The idea of "servitude" was set in concrete and when properly understood will never change. God "elected" it to be this way and He established it by the spoken Word (calling):

> (For the children being not yet born, neither having done any good or evil, that the purpose of God according to *election* might stand, not of works [human efforts], but of Him that *calleth:*)
>
> It was said [Word] unto her, the *elder shall serve the younger* (Romans 9:11-12).

God's "calling" or creativity by His Word most naturally involves His Lordship or "rulership." His sovereign "rulership" comes into prominence in the lives of Esau and Jacob. If the "natural" order of births had been followed Jacob, the younger, would have been subservient to Esau. Esau was the *firstborn* — occupying the highest position in the Jewish family. The Old Testament Scriptures reveal that the firstborn, according to the flesh, was to play a very important and significant role in the Jewish household. Dr. Dale Moody's comments on the role of the firstborn in the Jewish family are worthy of note. In his book, *The Word of Truth*, Dr. Moody writes: "In Israel all the inheritance and authority of the father belonged to the firstborn."[10]

Had the progenitorship of the Jewish stock, and the eventual birth of Christ, been allowed to proceed through Esau without interruption, the descendants of Abraham would have had all the more reason to "glory in the flesh." But the fleshly birth, which has its highest expression in the role of the firstborn, was to carry no weight whatsoever in the divine family. Neither Ishmael nor Esau, the firstborn of Abraham and Isaac respectively, was allowed to be the source of God's "calling" and "election."

This switch in the rights of the firstborn from Esau to Jacob would be unique and have everlasting consequences. It would make the divine Word and Mind conspicuous. The "rights of the firstborn," in the case of Esau and Jacob, are compounded with several spiritual implications.

---

10. Moody, 504.

The Patriarchal blessing that by-passed the firstborn of Abraham and Isaac was to be reserved for God's *Firstborn*, even Jesus, who was to be the "firstborn among many brethren" (Romans 8:29). Dr. Dale Moody's statement on the *authority* and *inheritance* of the firstborn in Israel becomes very clear when we consider God's *Firstborn*. All authority has been given to Jesus (Matthew 28:18 NIV) and He is "heir of all things" (Hebrews 1:2). All creatures, great and small, Jew and Gentile, must be *subservient* to God's FIRSTBORN (Philippians 2:10-11).

According to Paul, the moral aspects of Esau and Jacob's behavior are not to be taken into consideration. The prediction "the elder shall serve the younger" was made before they were born — before either had done "good or evil." *God intended for Jacob to be the one through which the PROMISE would be fulfilled, but not by deception.* Jacob's actions approximate that of Abraham who prematurely fathered a child by Hagar in order to have an heir. The misgivings of both Abraham and Jacob became a means of magnifying God's sovereign grace and election. The clever devices of these two Patriarchs reveal a clear distinction between the "children of the flesh" and the "children of God." The record of their carnal behavior was preserved for our profit. God forbid that any man should ignore this floodlight of truth coming from both the book of Genesis and Paul's letter to the Romans.

God uses the actions of men, both good and evil, to fulfill His divine purpose. Pharaoh is a case in point (verses 15-18). Can we accept any less concerning Esau and Jacob? Whether or not God's actions always precede those of Esau and Jacob in the unfolding of this drama or *vice versa* is not known. Where God's sovereignty begins and man's freedom ends is an age-old problem. We can only agree with Paul when he writes: "...how unsearchable are His judgments, and His ways past finding out!" (Romans 11:33b).

Again, it should be noted that God's "calling" and "election" are always in conjunction with the "promise" that was to be fulfilled in Christ. As pertaining to the births of Esau and Jacob, God's "calling" and "election" would include two things: (1) God must show that the "natural process" of birth is not His means of calling and electing His children; and in connection with this, (2) He must choose one of the twins through which Christ would come. He accomplished this by rejecting Esau, who represents the highest position in the human family (the firstborn), and chose Jacob through whom His divine purpose would be realized. We must not deviate from the Apostle's position regarding "God's children" as we deal with the roles of Esau and Jacob, i.e., "they which are the children of the flesh, these are not the children of God" (Romans 9:8). The flesh line was never God's choice for His people.

The phrase, "the elder shall serve the younger," has an eternal echo to it — it is beset by eschatological overtones. It extends far beyond the relationships of Esau and Jacob. It would be consummated in the Lordship and "rulership" of Christ. Any servitude to Jacob on the part of Esau or anyone else would be to the degree that the *Word* and *Spirit* of God was in him. Jacob, himself, must be subdued and conquered. He, too, must be "ruled by God." This happened at Peniel when his thigh was moved out of joint, etc. (Genesis 32:24-30). This subjection of Jacob resulted in his name being changed to Israel — one *ruled by God.*

Paul does not comment on the full story surrounding the events of Esau and Jacob as given in the Genesis account. He only quotes enough of the narrative to express the sovereign "rulership" of God in the affairs of men. When Rebecca came to the Lord concerning her unusual and unfamiliar pregnancy, she was given these prophetic words:

> The Lord said unto her, two nations are in thy womb, and two manner of people shall be separated from thy bowels; and the one people shall be stronger than the other people; and the elder shall serve the younger (Genesis 25:23).

The above prophecy includes far more than the relationship of Jacob and Esau. It says:

Two nations are in thy womb ... *Two manner of people* shall be separated from thy bowels ... One people shall be *stronger than the other people* ... The ELDER (people implied) shall serve the YOUNGER (people) ...

The "people" in this passage involve more than the Israelites (the descendants of Jacob) and the Edomites (the descendants of Esau). We cannot say that Israel, according to the flesh, was a strong people and that the Edomites served them (except for one brief incident in the days of David, 1 Chronicles 18:12-13). Israel, as a nation, was dominated by stronger nations most of her history. Had not God intervened at intervals, she would have been destroyed as Sodom and Gomorrah (Romans 9:29). We cannot say that Jacob, personally, was a strong man. Neither can we say that Esau served him in the proper sense of the term.

The "two nations," the "two manner of people," and the "stronger people" is a prophecy concerning the "children of the flesh" and the "children of God."

The same truth is repeated again, but in different language, in Isaac's blessing that was unknowingly pronounced upon Jacob:

> Therefore God give thee of the dew of heaven, and the fatness of the earth, and plenty of corn and wine:
>
> *Let people serve thee,* and *nations bow down to thee: Be Lord over thy brethren,* and *let thy mother's son bow down to thee: Cursed be every one that curseth thee, and blessed be he that blesseth thee* (Genesis 27:28-29).

As has been suggested, the phrase "the elder shall serve the younger" involves God's calling and election. There is a divine principle in this statement that is orchestrated throughout the Word of God. *The sequence of births and events are important in the Scriptures.* Adam was the *first* man (he was flesh) and the eldest in time. Christ was the Second Man (He was Word), the youngest in time. The "old man," which represents man's sinful nature (flesh), must yield to the "new man" or the second birth, which is from above. Concerning the "old" covenant (or first) and the "new" covenant (second), the writer of the epistle to the Hebrews says: "He taketh away the FIRST, that He may establish the SECOND" (Hebrews 10:9). The same truth is expressed in the "old" (or first) creation and the "new" (or second) creation (Revelation 21:1). Examples of this truth are too numerous to mention, but it is expedient that one more example be given to support the thesis of this work: The "old" Israel (or first according to the flesh) must yield to the "new" Israel (according to the Word and Spirit), and this includes both dispensations.

Paul is not just uttering some theological prattle when he says, "the elder shall serve the younger." He is setting forth a divine principle, inherent in God's calling and election, that is applicable to this day. The Apostle never alters his original thesis as set forth in the ninth chapter of Romans: "They which are the *children of the flesh, these are not the children of God"* (Romans 9:8).

The fact that Isaac and Rebecca had twin sons was no "coincidence" or "accident." It was to be a theological lesson for future generations. The little ripplet of God's "calling and election" which began with the births of Isaac and Ishmael/Esau and Jacob becomes a mighty wave as it reaches New Testament days. God has the sovereign right to choose the "kind" of people that will make up His kingdom. He did not choose the "flesh line" of either Jew or Gentile. Only those who are born of His Word and Spirit and those who are ruled by His Word and Spirit comprise His children. *"Israel, according to the flesh, are not the children of God."*

The "lump of clay" imagery in Romans 9:21 is another building block in the theological structure that Paul has been erecting throughout the Romans epistle. It fits perfectly into his over-all presentation of the Gospel and its relationship to both Jews and Gentiles. The "lump of clay" is the whole of humanity stemming from Adam. Paul suggests only two types of vessels coming from this coarse piece of clay — "vessels of wrath" and "vessels of mercy." All men become one or the other. A potter does not make two vessels at the same time. He can destroy a vessel that is being formed and redesign it, but generally speaking, he molds one vessel at a time.

Several words and phrases are used in the Scriptures to describe these two vessels. Our major concern at this point is to focus our thoughts on the "vessels of wrath." Jesus involves all men in His statement when He said: "He that believeth on Him (Son) is not condemned; but he that believeth not is *condemned already*" (John 3:18; see also Romans 8:1-3). In the same chapter and in a similar tone John writes: "He that believeth on the Son hath everlasting life: and he that believeth not the Son shall not see life; but the *wrath of God abideth on him*" (verse 36). Before their conversion, Paul speaks of himself and the Ephesian church as "children of wrath" (Ephesians 2:3). In warning the same church against certain sins, the Apostle wrote: "... for because of these things (sins) cometh the *wrath of God* upon the children of disobedience" (5:6). An identical statement can be found in his epistle to the Colossians: "For which things' (sins) sake the *wrath of God* cometh on the children of disobedience" (3:6). While writing about the wicked deeds of the Jews and their hatred for the Gentiles, Paul affirms: "For the *wrath* is come upon them to the uttermost" (1 Thessalonians 2:16). God's wrath is both present (Romans 1:18; 2:8) and future (1 Thessalonians 1:10; 5:9; Romans 2:5). Unregenerate man is also described as "children of darkness" (1 Thessalonians 5:5), "children of *Satan*" (John 8:44), *Dead* in trespasses and sins (Ephesians 2:1), etc.

The above statements describe ALL men who are born of woman. There are no exceptions (Jew or Gentile). Man is born a "sinner" and subject to God's "wrath" both now and in the future. Man has to be oblivious to human nature, the Scriptures, and history to deny his plight and God's anger at sin (Romans 1:18).

Men are *what* they are because God was willing to allow sin to enter the human race, which in turn affected all mankind. Men can deny this fact, ignore this fact, protest this fact (as in the case of the hypothetical man in verse 19), etc., but *this does not change the fact.* It is God's prerogative to do as He wills (verse 20). Men can shout at God until they fall on their faces but this does not alter their situation — the potter still has authority over the clay — men are subject to become "vessels of wrath fitted to destruction."

But all is not ruined. It is possible for the "vessels of wrath" to become "vessels of mercy" — and not without Infinite design. Men could never know the ultimate of God's "mercy" and "glory" until they first tasted the dregs of sin and death. It is not until men have been "delivered from the power of darkness and translated into the kingdom of his dear Son" (Colossians 1:13) that they can begin to understand and appreciate (to a limited degree) the eternal purpose of God. The contrast between the "vessels of wrath" and the "vessels of mercy" is the crux of Paul's analogy.

It is difficult to arrive at the above truth from the King James Version alone. The critical key that unlocks the imagery of the "lump of clay" is to be found in verse 23 and that from the Revised Standard Version. The RSV is nearer the Greek text than most translations. Notice the capitalized words in the RSV as compared to the KJV. Verse 23 is quoted in the context of verses 22 and 24:

> 22 What if God, desiring to show His wrath and to make known His power, has endured with much patience the vessels of wrath made for destruction, 23 IN ORDER to make known the riches of His glory for the vessels of mercy, which He has prepared beforehand for glory, 24 even us whom He has called, not from the Jews only but also from the Gentiles? (Romans 9:22-24). RSV

Paul is saying that God was willing for sin to enter the world, which resulted in "vessels of wrath," *in order* that He might make known His "glory" on "vessels of mercy." According to verse 23, these "vessels of mercy" were determined (or prepared) before the foundation of the world. Of course, this "mercy" was predetermined in the death and resurrection of Christ.

The Apostle is not struggling with a "national" issue per se in

Romans nine. He mentions several "individuals" in this chapter and
their particular role in establishing certain spiritual truths. Our attention
is drawn to Abraham, Isaac, Sarah, Rebecca, Esau, Jacob, and Pharaoh.
The hypothetical man in verse 19ff is an "individual." Paul's introductory remarks on the "lump of clay" may be somewhat unclear, but there
can be no doubts about his conclusions. A comparative diagram of
Paul's terms should be very helpful:

Same Lump of Clay

Vessels of Wrath	Vessels of Mercy
Jews and Gentiles (vs. 24)	Jews and Gentiles (vs. 24)
Vessels of Dishonor	Vessels of Honor
Not My People	My People
Not Beloved	Beloved
Like Sodom and Gomorrah	Children of the Living God
Did not Attain unto Righteousness	Attained Righteousness
Sand of the Sea (Many Israelites)	Remnant
Stumblingblock/Rock of Offense	Unashamed
Works of the Law	Faith

   Paul anticipated a strong objection from his own kin relative to what
he had written. The Jews would be repelled at the idea of God's wrath
being upon them. Paul confirms what he has written by quoting from
their own prophets; namely, Hosea and Isaiah. Many years earlier
Hosea, while speaking for the Lord, wrote: "I will call them *my people,*
which are *not my people* and her *beloved,* which was *not beloved.* And
it shall come to pass, that in the place where it was said unto them, ye
are *not my people;* there shall they be called the *children of the living
God"* (verses 25-26). Paul and Hosea are writing primarily about the
Jewish people. This fact is proven as the Apostle ties Hosea's and
Isaiah's words together. Paul says that "Isaiah *also* crieth *concerning
Israel,"* etc., (verse 27). The word "also" means that both prophets had
the Jewish people in mind when they penned their words.
   A detailed and elaborate exegesis on the "lump of clay" is not
necessary. The comparative diagram above tells the whole story of the
book of Romans. If all Jewish people are sinners as depicted in the early
chapters of Romans, and if some of them "despised the riches of God's
goodness and forbearance and longsuffering," which should have led
them to repentance (Romans 2:4), then they became "vessels of His
wrath" (Romans 2:5-9). God's patience and longsuffering are key
factors in both Romans two and Romans nine (Romans 2:4; 9:22). When

men continue to suppress, ignore, and reject the light that God has given them (Jew and Gentile), they become a "vessel of His wrath" (Romans 1:18). The other side of the coin is found in Romans 2:10: "But *glory, honor,* and *peace,* to every man that *worketh good,* to the Jew first, and also to the Gentile." Two vessels are possible from the "same lump of clay."

When faith is exercised in the atoning work of Christ, the Divine Potter is able to create a "vessel of mercy" (2 Corinthians 5:17). The "mercy" of God, that was displayed in the agonies of Calvary, is like the hub of a wheel to which all the spokes are anchored. All facets of redemption are anchored in the mercy of God. Since Jesus was a Lamb slain before the foundation of the world, the mercy of God is to be understood as past, present, and future — it covers time and eternity. It flows from Paul's pen as it did from the wounds of Jesus. God's mercy in Christ is also a prime factor in Paul's "olive tree" imagery.

Paul's analogy of the olive tree in the eleventh chapter of Romans provides another lesson on the *two Israels* with which we are dealing. It will be helpful if we begin with Paul's summary of this analogy and work from this direction rather than *vice versa.* Of course, a summary is simply a condensation of all that has been previously written. The central truth in Paul's summary is that "God hath concluded them all (Jews and Gentiles) in *unbelief,* that He might have *mercy* upon all" (verse 32). If we arrive at any other conclusion than this, we have missed the main lesson in this analogy.

Before the Apostle begins his olive tree analogy, he declares that something unusual has happened to the Jewish people. He speaks of

the fall of them ... (vs. 12)

the diminishing of them ... (vs. 12)

the casting away of them ... (vs. 15)

This seems to be a contradiction of what he says in the beginning of this chapter. In verses 1-2 of chapter eleven, Paul states that "God has not cast away His people," but in verses 12-15, he uses three expressions to assert that some drastic thing has happened to the Jewish people. Paul is not speaking with a forked tongue. He is telling us that Israel, according to the flesh, has been cast away because of unbelief. It has already been shown that all Jewish people are not "His people."

Let it be pointed out that the "casting away" or "rejection" of Israel, according to the flesh, is not confined to the church age. Paul quotes passages from Moses, Isaiah, and Hosea, and gives the experience of

Elijah to say that the natural descendants of Abraham per se were never God's people. The unbelieving Jew was "cast away" long before Paul's day. The "casting away" that Paul writes about is the grand finale of this ancient truth. That which was only stalk and blade in the Old Testament period comes to full fruition in the days of our Lord. *The Jews' rejection of Christ resulted in the ultimate revelation of God's rejection of them.*

We may ask, is God excluding the Jewish people from His covenant of grace by "casting them away?" Is He writing them off completely? We must resort again to Paul's familiar expression, "God forbid!" He is doing them a favor. The "casting away" of the natural seed of Abraham is just another way of saying that "God hath concluded (shut together) them all in unbelief that He might have mercy upon all." God *must* reject every carnal aspect of Jewish confidence if they are to know His mercy.

When a natural descendant of Abraham comes to Christ he must "cast away" his carnal Jewishness as a means of salvation. In the words of Paul, "old things are passed away and behold *all things are become new*" (2 Corinthians 5:17). He emerges as a "new creation." It is then, and then only, that he is entitled to bear the name "Jew" or "Israelite" in the proper sense of the terms. He is a son of Abraham in a manner heretofore unknown. His Jewish heritage, such as circumcision in the flesh, carnal ties with his forefathers, and the good works of the law, become as refuse in the light of his inheritance in Christ.

The unbelief of the Jewish people must not go unnoticed. It served a multiple purpose in the providence of God. Their unbelief was responsible for the death of Jesus resulting in "riches" and "reconciliation" for the world (verses 12-15). It also opened the door for a potential "receiving" and "fulness" for themselves if they believe (verse 12). If the Jewish people believed on Christ, it would be like "life from the dead" (verse 15).

Here again is the great paradox of Scripture — God *has* cast the Jewish people away, but He *has not* cast them away. The Lord will save any Israelite that will turn to Him in faith and receive His mercy offered to all men through Jesus Christ our Lord. God has left no stone unturned for their salvation. Even the inclusion of the Gentiles was designed to provoke them to believe. God pitted the Gentiles against the Jews (and *vice versa*) to "provoke them to jealousy that they might be saved." The spiritual rivalry between the two groups — the provocation and jealousy — and the display of God's mercy — is the crux of the good olive tree.

The Apostle begins his analogy by saying, " ... if the root (of the tree) be holy, so are the branches" (verse 16). By using this expression, he is not saying that all the Jewish people are "holy." He is stating a *matter of fact.* He is implying that if the root of the tree is "holy," the branches *must* be holy. In other words, the branches are to be of the same quintessence as the root and trunk. Many of the Jewish people were not of the same quintessence as their believing forefathers. Therefore they were "cut off." They were "cast away." Had they believed, they would have remained a "branch" in the good olive tree.

What does Paul mean by the term "natural branches?" It is the same lesson that he has been teaching throughout the book of Romans. As we shall learn in chapter four, the "true Israelite" is both a "natural descendant" of Abraham and a "faithful descendant" of Abraham (Romans 4:11-12). Abraham is a twofold father. The "good olive tree" consists of Abraham and his "faithful children." The "natural descendants" of Abraham who reject the Word of the Gospel are "broken off" from the "true stock of Israel" — or the good olive tree. Paul plainly says that it was unbelief on the part of some Jews that caused them to be broken off (Romans 11:20). On the other hand, if they believed, they would be grafted into the good olive tree. This cleavage within the Jewish race is far more serious and dramatic than is commonly acknowledged.

The "broken branch" in the analogy must be seen in relationship to both Abraham and Christ. There is an eternal, everlasting link between Abraham and Christ that consists of more than physical descent. Jesus Christ was the Son of Abraham according to the flesh (Matthew 1:1; Romans 1:3), but He was also the Son of God according to the "spirit of holiness, by the resurrection from the dead" (Romans 1:4). Abraham shared in the righteousness of Christ by *faith* in the "Word of promise" that would in time become the Word Incarnate. This inexplicable, mystical union between Christ and Abraham cannot be shared by unbelieving Jews. Sharing physical descent with Abraham is one thing, but sharing in the union of Abraham and Christ is another.

This sacred union between Christ and the believer (whether Jew or Gentile) is a real, organic relationship. Several analogies were used by our Lord to describe this union. The parable of the vine and branches, which essentially has to do with the "Word abiding in the believer," is a beautiful illustration of this bond between Christ and His elect (John 15:1-10). Paul's olive tree analogy is a reverberation of the lesson taught by Jesus in the "vine and branches."

The same truth is to be found in Jesus' intercessory prayer in the seventeenth chapter of John's Gospel. In this notable prayer, Jesus prays for *perfect oneness* between Himself, the Father, and those who would believe upon Him:

> And the glory which thou gavest Me I have given them; that they may be *one,* even as We are *one:*
>
> I in them, and Thou in Me, that they may be made *perfect in one;* and that the world may know that Thou hast sent Me, and hast loved them, as Thou hast loved Me (John 17:22-23).

This union between Christ and those who believe upon Him is possible only through the Word and Spirit of God. A Jew may be able to trace his carnal lineage to Abraham, but if he rejects the Word of the Gospel, he is literally broken off from Abraham and all other faithful Israelites.

The unbelieving Jew is not only broken off in spirit but also in body. There is no way of isolating the role of the physical body in matters of redemption. The Gospel of Jesus Christ creates a great chasm between the physical body of the faithful Jew and the unregenerate Jew — not in composition — but in use and destiny. The physical body of the faithful Jew is the temple of God — it belongs to God — it is bought with a price, and it glorifies God (1 Corinthians 6:20). This is impossible in the case of the unbelieving Jew.

When the above truth is carried to its ultimate conclusion (assuming we believe in the resurrection of the body), we will discover this "break" in the Jewish race to be even greater. There will be a "great gulf" between the bodies of the faithful Jew and the unfaithful Jew in the resurrection. The body of the believing Jew will be raised incorruptible — the other will not. The body of the believing Jew will be glorified and be like the body of Christ — the other will not. The body of the believing Jew will share in the heavenly inheritance while the body of the unbelieving Jew will be cast into the regions of the damned (Matthew 10:28; Luke 16:19-31).

The Gentile who is grafted into the good olive tree (or becomes a member of the household of faith) has everything in common with the believing Jew. Their bodies are the temple of God. Both are purchased with the blood of Christ. Both glorify God in their bodies. In the resurrection both will share in the heavenly inheritance. The believing

Jew and the believing Gentile become one in the body of Christ (Galatians 3:28).

We are not out in "left field" when we make a distinction between the physical body of the Christian and non-Christian (whether Jew or Gentile) in matters of redemption. This is why Paul implores both Jew and Gentile to present their *bodies* a "living sacrifice" unto God:

> I beseech you therefore, brethren, by the mercies of God, that ye present your *bodies a living sacrifice, holy, acceptable unto God,* which is your reasonable service.
>
> And be not conformed to this world: but be ye transformed by the *renewing of your mind* (which is a part of the body), that ye may prove what is that good, and acceptable, and perfect, will of God (Romans 12:1-2).

The Gentile, who believes the "promise" made to Abraham, becomes an "Israelite" in the true sense of the term. By imitating Abraham's faith, he becomes both a "child of Abraham" and a "child of God." But the Gentile has no ground for boasting. According to Paul's analogy, the Gentile branch is borne of the "root" and not *vice versa* (verse 18). In other words, the Gentile is indebted to the Patriarchs of old who "believed" and through whom Christ, according to the flesh, was to come.

Paul assures us that the Israelites are not out of the pale of God's mercy. If they turn to Him in *faith,* they can still be grafted into the good olive tree (verse 23). Because of their religious heritage, and because of the promise made to their Jewish forefathers, it is all the more reason that God is "able to graft them in again" (verse 23).

After Paul's discourse on the olive tree analogy, he gives us an addendum in conjunction with it. This addendum is found in Romans 11:25ff. Verses 25-26, in particular, have become a strong bastion for the futurists. These two verses are their Mount Nebo of the New Testament from which they behold the so-called thousand years reign for the Jews:

> For I would not, brethren, that ye should be ignorant of this mystery, lest ye should be wise in your own conceits; that blindness in part is happened to Israel, until the fulness of the Gentiles be come in.
>
> And so all Israel shall be saved: as it is written, There shall come out of Sion the Deliverer, and shall turn away ungodliness from Jacob

(Romans 11:25-26).

The premillennialists interpret the above passage to mean that a partial blindness has happened to Israel until a certain number of Gentiles come into the church. When this happens (or when the "fulness of the Gentiles come in"), all Jews will be gathered together as a nation during the millennial reign, and "all Israel shall be saved."

Suppose we interpret the phrase, "And all Israel shall be saved," literally, as the premillennialists are prone to do. This would mean that "all Israelites," from the days of Abraham to the coming of Christ, would be saved. If this were true, Paul's energies and prayers for his own countrymen would be thrown to the wind (Romans 10:1). His hardships and sufferings would be kin to a mock suicide. In addition to this, the Apostle would be guilty of contradicting himself throughout the Romans epistle. Can he be guilty of such a travesty as this?

Paul's thoughts on the phrase, "And all Israel shall be saved," must be understood in conjunction with Israel's partial blindness as given in verse 25. Israel's partial blindness is a "mystery" until the "fulness of the Gentiles be come in." The term "mystery," as used here and elsewhere in Paul's works, has to do with something that is not fully known or understood. Most of the Jewish people did not know that they were blind — quite the contrary.

Actually, there were two blind spots in Israel's religious beliefs that need to be considered side by side: (1) They were blind to their own spiritual condition; and (2) They were blind to the "inclusion of the Gentiles" that was revealed to the Apostle Paul. These two ideas unfold concurrently with each other. Paul suffered very much at the hands of his own Jewish kin while trying to convince them of their blindness. He also went to great lengths to make them cognizant of the "inclusion of the Gentiles." How else can they be "provoked to jealousy" (as given in the olive tree analogy) if these two facts are not known? "Israel's partial blindness" and the "inclusion of the Gentiles" are two crucial concepts for Paul's theology.

The "inclusion of the Gentiles" is not a "mystery" per se as taught by the futurists and other exponents of the Scriptures. Jesus Christ is the "mystery" that is discussed in the third chapter of Ephesians and not the "inclusion of the Gentiles." The first time Paul mentions the word "mystery" in the book of Ephesians is in conjunction with God's "will." The revelation of God's "will" was that He might "gather together *in one* all things *in Christ,* both which are in heaven, and which are on earth; even *in Him."* Christ was God's "will" or "good pleasure" from the beginning to the end. So, the "mystery" in Ephesians 1:9 is the "gathering together *in one* all things *in Christ"* (verse 10). This "gathering together in one" or the "reconciling of all things unto Himself" must be preceded by His death on the cross (Colossians 1:20). Again, a death blow is struck at the setting up of an earthly kingdom at Christ's first appearance.

The "gathering together *in one"* deals primarily with the *oneness* of the Jews and Gentiles in Christ. All of chapter two in the book of Ephesians is devoted to explaining this *unity* between the two groups. Paul uses such pronouns as "us," "we," and "our" to prove that both Jews and Gentiles are to be *one body* in Christ. In the last three verses of chapter two, Paul uses the imagery of a "building" to illustrate this oneness in the body of Christ (verses 20-22). Jesus had only *one body* to offer for the sins of the world (Hebrews 10:12, 14) and only one body was resurrected from the grave. His *body,* which is the *church,* can never be *two separate bodies* — either now or in the future. The New Testament never speaks of *two entities* (church and national Israel) arising out of the body of Christ.

The next time Paul uses the word "mystery" in the book of Ephesians is in conjunction with "his knowledge in the *mystery of Christ"* (3:3-4). It is very obvious that Christ *is* the *mystery.* Paul was given "knowledge" or "revelations" *within* that mystery. A part of that "knowledge" or "revelations" was that the Gentiles were to be *"fellow-heirs,* and of the *same body,* and partakers of his promise in *Christ* by the gospel" (verse 6). The "inclusion of the Gentiles" was not a "mystery" per se; it was only a *part* of the mystery of Christ.

If we omit verse 5, which has to do with the "mystery of Christ" that was not known in ages past, and read verses 3, 4, and 6 together, Paul's mind will become very clear. Notice the context in which the words "known" and "knowledge" are used in this passage:

> How that by revelation He [God] made *known* unto me the *mystery;* (as I wrote afore in few words, Whereby, when ye read, ye may understand my *knowledge* in the *mystery of Christ*)... That the Gentiles should be *fellowheirs,* and of the *same body,* and partakers of His *promise in Christ* by the gospel (Ephesians 3:3, 4, 6).

Paul's "knowledge" in the *mystery of Christ* was that the Gentiles should be as much a part of Christ's body, the church, as the believing Jews. The same truth is expressed in Paul's letter to the Colossians. Paul wanted this church to come to the full understanding and "acknowledgement of the *mystery of God,* and of the Father, and *of Christ;* In whom are *hid* all the treasures of *wisdom* and *knowledge"* (Colossians 2:2-3); (see also 2 Timothy 1:9-10). So, Christ *is* the "mystery" and the "inclusion of the Gentiles is only a *part* of that mystery.

The above truths are affirmed again in the closing verses of Paul's letter to the Romans. Paul wanted the Roman church to be established according to his *knowledge* of the Gospel, which was "the preaching of Jesus Christ, according to the *revelation* and *mystery,* which was kept secret since the world began (Romans 16:25). The "Gospel," the "revelation," and the "preaching of Jesus Christ" compose the "mystery" that was not fully known until Christ came in the flesh. Christ *is* the "mystery."

The premillennialists are happy to tell us that the "church age" was not revealed to the Old Testament prophets. In their views, the only thing that God made known to the prophets was God's dealings with the Jews, in their respective day and in the future. It is oftentimes illustrated by the prophets, standing on the peak of one mountain and looking to the peak of another mountain. The church is like a "valley" between the two mountains and is never "seen" by the Old Testament prophets. If Christ was a "mystery" that was not fully revealed to the prophets, and if the church is His *body,* then it is very conclusive that *God did not intend for the prophets or anyone else to understand the full scope of Christ's mission and its ultimate outcome.* The futurists are not telling us anything new or novel. Of course, this theological arrangement fits perfectly into their "postponement" theory on the Kingdom of God.

The most outstanding "prophets" and "kings" of the Old Testament era were very limited in their knowledge of the coming Messiah. According to Jesus, such men would have welcomed the opportunity to be living when He came in the flesh, but were not given this spiritual luxury. Jesus assured His disciples that they were a privileged and honored group: "Blessed are the eyes which see the things that ye see: For I tell you, that *many prophets* and *kings* have desired to see those things which ye see, and *have not seen them;* and to hear those things which ye hear, and *have not heard them"* (Luke 10:23-24). Although the disciples "saw many things" and "heard many things" prior to Jesus' passion and resurrection, they did not understand the true significance of His mission until after Pentecost and the coming of the Holy Spirit (John 16:12-15).

Jesus gave His disciples many hints and clues regarding His death and resurrection, but for the most part they fell on deaf ears. In fact, Jesus explained to His disciples, in very clear language, that He must suffer, die, and be resurrected from the dead (Luke 18:31-33). But in the next verse (34) it is said: "And they *understood none of these things,* and this saying *was hid from them, neither knew they the things which were spoken.*" If the New Testament disciples were not permitted to understand Christ's mission and the subsequent "church age" until *after* His death and resurrection, then it is very feasible that the prophets of the Old Testament period would not be allowed to "see" the church age.

The Lord followed a strict timetable as He unveiled the story of redemption and the world was not ready for the revelation of Christ and the "church age" until God's determined hour (Romans 3:26; Galatians 4:4; 1 Timothy 2:6 NEB; 2 Timothy 1:9-10; Titus 1:1-3). According to the book of Hebrews, "...the way into the holiest of all *was not yet manifest"* until after the death and resurrection of Christ (Hebrews 9:8). Notwithstanding this fact, men try to rearrange God's schedule in a way that will accommodate *their* "theological calendar."

No "prophet" or "king" of the old economy was monitored for his knowledge of God as was the Apostle Paul. Paul's knowledge and revelations of Christ were so great that he was given a "thorn in the flesh" to prevent him from boasting of such things (2 Corinthians 12:7). This severe disciplinary measure is proof that God did not intend for just anybody and everybody to be entrusted with the revelations of Christ and His church. This well-guarded "mystery" was given to a "special" person at a "special" time in history (Galatians 1:15ff; Acts 9:15).

If Paul's revelations of Christ and His church were so profound that he was given a "thorn in the flesh" to keep *him* from boasting, then we can be sure that God is not going to reveal Paul's theology to every Tom, Dick, and Harry today. Even Peter acknowledged the difficulties in understanding Paul's epistles and gave a warning to those who might interpret Paul's works to their own destruction (2 Peter 3:15-16). The Scriptures are capable of having a twofold effect upon mankind—death and destruction or life and peace.

The church is the depository of the "mystery" of Christ and has a mandate from the Lord to keep it pure and free from any and all perversions (1 Timothy 3:1-9; 15; see especially verses 9 and 15). An "unfeigned faith" and a "pure love" are key factors in the preservation and understanding of the "mystery" of Christ. The entire epistle of First Timothy should be studied with these two concepts (faith and love) in mind. "Faith" is so conjoined with the "mystery" of Christ that Paul speaks of it as the "mystery of the faith" (1 Timothy 3:9). The "mystery of the faith" is no less than Christ's having come in the flesh: "...great is the *mystery of Godliness:* God was *manifest in the flesh,* justified in the Spirit, seen of angels, preached unto the Gentiles, believed on in the world, received up into glory" (1 Timothy 3:16). "Unfeigned faith," "pure love," and the "flesh and blood" of Christ complement each other. Any diversion from these three concepts results in all manner of sin (1 Timothy 4:1-3).

Most of the "mystery" pertaining to Christ continues to be a "mystery" to the masses of people within the church. However, this was not God's intention. Genuine faith and a pure love will open a storehouse of wisdom and knowledge for those who are in Christ. Paul had a passionate desire for the church to abound in such wisdom and knowledge (Ephesians 1:17). While Paul wanted the church to have its understanding enlightened and know the "riches of the glory of His (God's) inheritance in the saints and the exceeding greatness of His mighty power that raised Christ far above all principalities and powers, and might, and dominion, and every name that is named, not only in this world, but also in that which is to come," the premillennialists want the church to be enlightened about "national" Israel. If the church had followed Paul's advice over the centuries, it would continue to "turn the world upside down" for Christ.

The futurists are in error regarding the "fullness of the Gentiles" as much so as their views on the "mystery of the Gentiles." The "fullness of the Gentiles" is not an "X" number of Gentiles that will be saved before the so-called millennium occurs. It is an indefinite period of time, after the death and resurrection of Christ, in which their inclusion will be *fully known* to both the Jews and themselves (Acts 28:28). Paul was a minister to the Gentiles for this very purpose. He experienced all manner of hardships in order that his,

> ...preaching might *be fully known,* and that *all the Gentiles might hear;* and I was delivered out of the mouth of the lion (2 Timothy 4:17). See also Romans 16:25-26; Acts 19:10).

The "partial blindness" of Israel *must* be known and the "inclusion of the Gentiles" *must* be known. The darkness that shrouded both has dissipated. Israel's "partial blindness" is announced on almost every page of the New Testament for all to read and acknowledge — the "mystery" is past. The "full inclusion of the Gentiles" is an established fact. There is no way of pin-pointing the exact day and hour for the "full inclusion," but Paul's ministry and theology removes every trace of doubt. The "wall of partition" has been broken down — in matters of redemption, the Jew and Gentile are on the same level — in this sense "all Israel will be saved." Both Jew and Gentile will comprise the "true Israel" of God.

The New English Bible translation supports the above interpretation to the letter:

> For there is a deep truth here, my brothers, of which I want you to take account, so that you may not be complacent about your own discernment: this partial blindness has come upon Israel *only* until the Gentiles have been admitted in *full strength:* when that has happened, the *whole of Israel will be saved,* in agreement with the text of Scripture:
> "From Zion shall come the Deliverer; He shall remove wickedness from Jacob. And this is the covenant I will grant them, When I take away their sins" (Romans 11:25-27).

Paul is not writing about a *future* Deliverer for Israel or a *future* covenant with Israel in the above passage. He is dealing with the situation at hand and things that pertain to the New Testament era. Verses 26-27 are a composite quote from Isaiah and Jeremiah. Neither prophet is quoted verbatim; nor does Paul give the full prophecy in either case. The *future tense* is used by the Apostle because he sees the Deliverer and covenant from the eyes of the prophets rather than his own.

The full prophecies from Isaiah and Jeremiah have very much in common when considered together, and according to the book of Hebrews were fulfilled when Christ came in the flesh. Isaiah writes:

> And the Redeemer *shall come to Zion,* and unto them that *turn from transgression in Jacob,* saith the Lord.
> As for me, this is *my covenant* with them, saith the Lord; My *Spirit* that is upon thee, and my *words* which I have put in thy mouth, shall not depart out of thy mouth, nor out of the mouth of thy seed, nor out of the mouth of thy seed's seed, saith the Lord, from henceforth and forever (Isaiah 59:20-21).

The "Redeemer" is not mentioned in Jeremiah's prophecy, but in the light of the book of Hebrews and other portions of Scripture the Redeemer is implied. Compare Jeremiah's thoughts on the covenant with that of Isaiah's:

> But this shall be the *covenant* that I will make with the house of Israel (future tense): After those days, saith the Lord, *I will put my laws in their inward parts, and write it in their hearts;* and I will be their God and they shall be my people.
>
> And they shall teach *no more every man his neighbor* and *every man his brother, saying, know the Lord: For they shall all know Me,* from the least of them unto the greatest of them, saith the Lord: for I will *forgive their iniquity,* and I will *remember their sin no more* (Jeremiah 31:33-34).

In writing about the Priesthood of Christ and the *New Covenant* that was initiated by His death, the writer of the epistle to the Hebrews quotes almost word for word from Jeremiah:

> For this is the *Covenant* that I will make with the house of Israel after those days, saith the Lord; I will *put my laws in their minds,* and *write them in their hearts:* and I will be to them a God, and they shall be to me a people:
>
> And they shall *not teach every man his neighbor,* and *every man his brother,* saying, Know the Lord: for *all shall know Me from the least to the greatest.*
>
> For I will be merciful to their unrighteousness, and their *sin* and their *iniquity* will I *remember no more* (Hebrews 8:10-12).

Paul's thoughts in Romans 11:26-27 are in perfect agreement with Isaiah 59:20-21, Jeremiah 31:33-34, and Hebrews 8:10-12. All of these passages speak of a Deliverer, a covenant, and the problem of sin and its solution — the *only* solution being God's *mercy* that came in the death and resurrection of Christ. The Apostle is concerned with the *sins* of the Jews *here* and *now* and not an "unconditional" take-over of Palestine in the future. To smuggle the Land of Canaan into the covenant of Romans 11:26-27 is out of character with all that has been previously written in the Romans epistle.

It was God's *mercy* that Israel forfeited, because of her unbelief, and not the Land of Canaan. The most important thing that the Gentiles received, as a result of Israel's unbelief, was God's *mercy* (verse 30). *The ultimate for both Jew and Gentile is God's mercy.* God's wrath, which is upon every Jew in every age (Romans 2:8-9), insists upon God's *mercy* for every Jew in every age. The "obedience" of the Gentiles and the corresponding "mercy" for the Jews was not to be postponed to some future millennial age. God's mercy for the Jews was anticipated in Paul's day and was to continue until Christ returns for His elect. Note carefully the Apostle's emphasis on the word "now" in his concluding remarks on the Jews and Gentiles:

> For as ye [Gentiles] in times past have not believed [obeyed] God, yet have *now* obtained *mercy* through their [Jews] unbelief [disobedience]:
> Even so have these [Jews] also *now* not believed [obeyed] that *through your* [Gentile] *mercy* they [Jews] *also* [to the same degree and manner] *may obtain mercy* (Romans 11:30-31).

If the Gentiles were to "show mercy" to the Jews in Paul's day and thereafter, then the Jews were expected to receive God's mercy *then* and *thereafter*, and not in some imaginary millennial age. The Apostle's thoughts in verse 31 will bear repeating: "...through your [Gentile] *mercy* they [Jews] *also may obtain mercy*." In other words, the Jews were expected to receive God's mercy *then* and *there*, as much so as the Gentiles.

The channel to God's *mercy* is through an awareness of "disobedience" or a recognition of one's sinful nature (Romans 7:7ff). The discovery and acceptance of this truth on the part of some Jews, and the refusal on the part of others, is the distinctive feature by which the two Israels are so well defined in the Scriptures.

The first step in man's approach to God is through His *mercy* (or grace) that came in the death and resurrection of Christ. In fact, man's *only* approach to God is through His *mercy*. It is unthinkable that God would establish an earthly kingdom in lieu of the cross of Christ. *The most important ingredient in the covenant made with Abraham was God's mercy that is offered to all men through the Gospel*. It can be proven many times over that the covenant made with Abraham was primarily a covenant of *mercy* and not a national Jewish state. Generally speaking, God's covenant and mercy are spoken of in connection with the problem of sin and man's obedience, or lack of obedience, to His commandments. God's *mercy* is associated with the Abrahamic covenant in both the Old and New Testaments. Moses describes God as a "faithful God, which keepeth *covenant* and *mercy* with them that love

Him and keep His commandments to a thousand generations" (Deuteronomy 7:9). A follow-through of Moses' thoughts from the same chapter (verse 12) will show conclusively that he is writing about the covenant made with Abraham: "...if ye hearken to these judgments, and keep, and do them, that the Lord thy God shall keep unto thee the *covenant* and the *mercy* which He *sware* unto thy *fathers*." The Sinaitic covenant, for which Moses is famous, contains *no mercy* whatsoever! It insists upon perfect obedience for God's favor and blessing.

God's *mercy* is more than an asterisk in the promise made to Abraham; it is the very heart and soul of the promise. The superb language that is used in conjunction with God's faithfulness to His *covenant* and *mercy* speaks volumes to those who have ears to hear, and there are very few exceptions to the use of such elevated language. When Solomon dedicated the first temple, he used a chain of simple words to speak of God's faithfulness to His *covenant* and *mercy,* but their arrangement does not leave the reader guessing as to God's exalted character and commitment thereto:

> ... there is no God like thee, in heaven above, or on earth beneath, who keepest *covenant* and *mercy* with thy servants that walk before thee with all their heart, etc., (1 Kings 8:23).

The above prayer is a recapitulation of God's promise to David (see verses 24-25). The essence of Solomon's prayer is a display of God's *mercy* in forgiving Israel's transgression when she sins against Him (see verses 31, 35, 39, 46, 47, 50). Whether the Israelites are "in the land" or "out of the land," Solomon's primary concern is God's *mercy* in forgiving Israel's sin (verses 46-50). Both the *temple* and the *land* count for naught if the people are void of God's *mercy.*

The most significant feature in God's *promise* to David is His *mercy* that came in the death and resurrection of Christ. This fact is clearly established in the book of Acts. While Paul and Barnabas were in Antioch of Pisidia, the Apostle tried to convince his Jewish brethren that Jesus was the fulfillment of both the *promise* to David and the *promise* to the "fathers," i.e., Abraham, Isaac, and Jacob. Paul begins his brief recall of Jewish history with the Egyptian bondage and concludes with the death and resurrection of Christ. When Paul makes reference to David's role in the Jewish chronicles, he says that Saul, the king of Israel, was removed from his throne and that God "raised up unto them (Israelites) David to be their king ... and of this "man's seed (David's) hath God according to His *promise* raised unto Israel a *saviour, Jesus*" (Acts 13:22a-23).

Paul's survey of Jewish history jumps from David's day to two events nearer his own period and time, the preaching of John the Baptist and the death and resurrection of Jesus. These two events are followed by the Apostle's personal ministry. Notice the content of Paul's message to his Jewish kin:

> And we declare unto you *glad tidings,* how that the *promise* which was made to the *fathers,*
>
> God *hath fulfilled the same* unto us *their children,* in that *He hath raised up Jesus again;* as it is also written in the second Psalm, Thou art My Son, this day have I begotten Thee.
>
> And as concerning that He *raised Him up from the dead,* now no more to return to corruption, he said on this wise, *I will give you the sure mercies of David.*
>
> Be it known unto you therefore, men and brethren, that through this man (Jesus) is preached unto you the *forgiveness of sins* (Acts 13:32-34, 38).

The *promise* to the "fathers," the *promise* to David, and the *sure mercies of David* were fulfilled in the *death* and *resurrection* of Christ. It is very obvious that the *promise* and the *sure mercies* of David are related to the *forgiveness of sins* and not to the Land of Canaan.

According to Isaiah, the *sure mercies of David* are a vital part of God's *everlasting covenant.* Isaiah, in a well-known prophecy of the coming Messiah, addresses his generation and future generations with these words:

> Incline your ear, and come unto me: hear, and your soul shall live; and I will make an *everlasting covenant* with you, even the *sure mercies of David* (55:3).

The *mercy* of God is coupled with the *covenant* made with *Abraham* in practically every major period of Jewish history. Daniel's *seventy weeks prayer* is related to God's *covenant* and *mercy.* Daniel, like Moses and Solomon, magnifies the greatness of God as he speaks of His *covenant* and *mercy:* "And I prayed unto the Lord my God, and made my confession, and said, O Lord, the great and dreadful God, keeping *covenant* and *mercy* to them that love Him, and to them that keep His commandments" (Daniel 9:4). It should be observed that Daniel's confession is uttered in conjunction with the "sins of his people" (verse 5).

While Isaiah prophesies against the evils of Moab, he is interrupted with a Messianic vision of the future. The "throne" that is established by the Messiah is mentioned in conjunction with God's *mercy:*

> And in *mercy* shall the *throne* be established: and He [Messiah] shall sit upon it in truth in the tabernacle of David, judging, and seeking judgment, and hasting righteousness (Isaiah 16:5).

The "throne" of the Messiah is first and foremost a throne of *mercy* and not a literal throne in Jerusalem. The writer of the Hebrews epistle speaks of a *"throne* of grace" whereby the believer "may obtain *mercy,* and find grace to help in time of need" (Hebrews 4:16).

There is no greater portrayal of God's love for the sinner in the Old Testament than the words of Micah — and His love is conjoined with the *oath* made to *Abraham* — which in turn involves God's *mercy.* Micah's description of God's love for the sinner is almost unparalled:

> Who is a God like unto thee, that pardoneth iniquity, and passeth by the transgression of the remnant of His heritage? He retaineth not His anger for ever, because He *delighteth in mercy.*
>
> He will turn again, He will have compassion upon us; He will subdue our iniquities; and Thou wilt cast all their sins into the depths of the sea.
>
> Thou wilt perform the *truth* to *Jacob,* and the *mercy* to *Abraham,* which Thou hast *sworn* unto our *fathers* from *days of old* (Micah 7:18-20).

Whenever a crisis arose in Israel there was always an appeal to God's *covenant* and *mercy.* Nehemiah's grief for his people and land is prefaced with such an appeal. His prayer follows the same pattern as his predecessors: "I beseech thee, O Lord God of heaven, the great and terrible God, that keepeth *covenant* and *mercy* for them that love Him and observe His commandments" (Nehemiah 1:5). Again, Nehemiah's prayer is a confession of the sins of his people.

The Levites of Ezra's day made a similar appeal to God. After a brief review of Israel's history, these religious leaders concluded that it was God's *mercy* that had preserved the Israelites from extinction. Notice their insight into God's *grace* and *mercy:*

> Nevertheless, for Thy great *mercies'* sake Thou didst not utterly consume them, nor forsake them; for Thou art a *gracious* and *merciful* God.

Now therefore, our God, the great, the mighty, the terrible God,
who keepest *covenant* and *mercy,* let not all the trouble seem little
before Thee … (Nehemiah 9:31-32a).

The same truth is echoed in the New Testament. Mary, the mother
of Jesus, perceived the role of her Son in the world as a mission of *mercy*
and the fulfillment of the Abrahamic covenant. Mary emulates the Old
Testament writers by magnifying the greatness of God in conjunction
with His *covenant* and *mercy.* A description of God's majesty by Mary
is followed with these words:

And His *mercy* is on them that fear Him from generation to
generation…
He hath holpen His servant Israel, in remembrance of His *mercy;*
As He *spake* to our *fathers,* to *Abraham,* and to his seed for ever
(Luke 1:50, 54-55).

Zacharias, the father of John the Baptist, makes a significant
contribution to the subject under consideration. Zacharias, while under
the inspiration of the Holy Ghost, declares that God

… hath visited and redeemed His people,
And hath raised up an *horn of salvation* for us in the house of David;
As He *spake* by the mouth of His *Holy Prophets, which have been
since the world began:*
That we should be *saved* from our enemies, and from the hand of
all that hate us;
To perform the *mercy* promised to our fathers, and to remember His
holy covenant;
The *oath* which He *sware* to our father *Abraham* (Luke 1:68-73).

Deliverance and redemption from *sin* through God's *mercy* in
Christ are the essence of Zacharias' prophecy. According to Zacharias,
a "knowledge of salvation" cannot be possible until there is "remission
of sins" (Luke 1:77). *Sin* is the great barricade between man and God.

The real clincher to all that has been written on the mercy of God
is to be found in the words of Peter. Peter establishes a relationship
between God's mercy and the death and resurrection of Christ that
cannot be disclaimed. For Peter, it is more than "mercy" — it is
abundant mercy: "Blessed be the God and Father of our Lord Jesus
Christ which *according to His abundant mercy* hath *begotten us again*
unto a lively hope by the *resurrection of Jesus Christ from the dead*" (1
Peter 1:3). According to Peter, this was *not* an afterthought in the eternal

plan of God. It was in the "foreknowledge" of God from the beginning (verse 2). In addition to this, the elect of God are not "begotten" to an inheritance in the "Land of Canaan" for a thousand years, but to an "inheritance incorruptible, and undefiled, and that fadeth not away, reserved in heaven" (verse 4).

In three brief verses Peter describes God's eternal plan of redemption from the beginning to the end. The entire episode is "according to His *abundant mercy*" that was displayed in the death and resurrection of Christ. Peter begins his discussion with the "foreknowledge of God" and ends with an "incorruptible inheritance." Sandwiched between these two concepts is the phrase, "according to His *abundant mercy*." There is not a smattering of premillennial doctrine in Peter's remarks.

One concise word from our Lord should resolve forever the relationship between the *new covenant* (God's mercy) and the *problem of sin.* When Jesus initiated the Lord's Supper, He said to His disciples: "This is my blood of the *New Testament* (covenant), which is shed for many for the *remission of sins*" (Matthew 26:28). In both the Old and New Testaments, the "shedding of blood" is always associated with the problem of sin and God's mercy and not the Land of Canaan.

The above statements (from Moses, Solomon, Daniel, Isaiah, Micah, Nehemiah, the Levites of Ezra's day, Mary, Zacharias, Luke, Peter, and Jesus), on the *covenant* and *mercy* of God, are cited to show that Paul is writing in the same vein in his Romans epistle. Paul quotes a prophecy from Isaiah that was fulfilled in the death and resurrection of Christ: "For this is my *covenant* with them when I shall take away their *sin*" (Romans 11:27). The only answer to man's sin (Jew and Gentile) is the blood of Christ (Hebrews 9:22). The premillennialists have taken Paul's comments on the covenant and tried to squeeze ten pounds of theology into a one-pound bag. The Romans epistle, along with the rest of the New Testament, is *never* concerned with the "Land of Canaan" as the fulfillment of the covenant made with Abraham. God's promise and covenant are related first and foremost to His mercy that was foretold and fulfilled in the death and resurrection of Christ.

The human equation of "sin and death" can scarcely compare to a jubilant one thousand years in the "Land of Canaan." The human race has been, and still is, in the throes of "sin and death." God's mercy in Christ was designed to deal with this monumental problem. That all mankind is "dead in trespasses and in sins" is irrefutable Biblically (Ephesians 2:1), but this "dead state" of man must be brought to his attention before he can be delivered from it. This is the role of God's holy law (Romans 7:7). According to the Apostle Paul, sin must be magnified in man; it must become "exceeding sinful" before death can be experienced in the sinner (Romans 7:13). When sin is "revived" or awakened in the sinner, the end result is an inward death (Romans 7:9). After sin has become full-blown and produced a spiritual death in the transgressor, there is no alternative but the mercy of God. No military force, no doctor, no psychiatrist, no educator, or any other mortal man can lift the sinner out of this "state of death." This is accomplished by faith in the death and resurrection of Christ (Romans 10:9-10). As the bitten Israelites looked at the brazen serpent in the wilderness and lived, so must the sinner look at the One who was lifted upon the cross for his sin (John 3:14-15). The sinner is brought from "death" unto "life." The Scriptures describe this as an inward, spiritual resurrection (Ephesians 2:4-6). Only God can raise the dead. God's covenant and mercy is the point of issue in Romans 11:26-27 and not the "Land of Canaan."

Men who are in desperate straits see Christ's mission in the world very differently from many modern day prophets who sit behind their mahogany desks and dream about a misty, millennial kingdom. When men are afflicted and take sin seriously, they begin to cry for God's mercy rather than an inheritance in the "Land of Canaan." One of the common cries of the troubled soul in Jesus' day was: "Thou Son of David, have mercy on us" (Matthew 9:27; 15:22, 20:30-31; Mark 10:47). The broken in heart did not look upon David's Son as one who would "rule with a rod of iron" upon a literal throne in Jerusalem, but one who would show *mercy* and *compassion* without favor. Matthew uses two very common analogies of his day to describe the tenderness of our Lord: "A bruised reed shall He not break, and smoking flax shall He not quench, till He send forth judgment unto victory" (12:20).

When the rich man lifted his eyes in hell, he cried "Father Abraham, have mercy on me, and send Lazarus, that he may dip the tip of his finger in water, and cool my tongue; for I am tormented in this flame" (Luke 16:24). Such will be the cry of all men who reject God's covenant and mercy that is clearly revealed in the death and resurrection of Christ. God's mercy received by faith or God's mercy rejected through unbelief creates two classes of people within the Jewish race — faithful Israel and natural Israel.

There are two major strains of thought running throughout the book of Romans. These two lines of thought consist of God's *mercy* (grace) and God's *wrath*. These two outstanding characteristics in God's nature are related to a variety of other terms and phrases that implicate the Jewish people. For example, the word "belief" coincides with God's mercy. The word "unbelief" coincides with God's wrath. Paul was a great artist with words, and he writes from the same inkwell in Romans nine, ten, and eleven that he does in the introductory chapters of this epistle. His language may fluctuate from one thought to another, but he never contradicts himself. After a lengthy discussion on the pros and cons of the Jewish people, he still maintains that "God hath concluded them all in *unbelief*, that He might have *mercy* upon *all*" (Romans 11:32). For the candid Bible student, Paul's statement can mean only one thing — *all* Jewish people fall into the category of "unbelief" which results in the "wrath" of God and the only avenue to God's mercy is for each one to believe the Word of the Gospel. The Apostle uses a catalogue of words and phrases in the "olive tree" analogy that reveal this truth. If we consider the positive and negative aspects of the analogy along with the comparative diagram on the "lump of clay," we will see that both imageries tell the same story. The great paradox in the Romans epistle is set forth in glowing language:

ISRAEL

All in Unbelief (natural Israel)	Mercy upon all (Faithful Israel)
Disobedient	Obedient
Children of the Flesh	Children of the Promise
The diminishing of them	Their fulness
Works of the Law	Grace (by faith)
Casting Away	Life from the Dead
Rest Blinded	Remnant (or election)
Broken off	Grafted in
Severity of God	Goodness of God

Same Lump of Clay

Vessels of Wrath	Vessels of Mercy
Jews and Gentiles (vs. 24)	Jews and Gentiles (vs. 24)
Vessels of Dishonor	Vessels of Honor
Not My People	My People
Not Beloved	Beloved
Like Sodom and Gomorrah	Children of the Living God
Did not attain the	

righteousness of God	Attained the righteousness of God
Sand of the Sea (Many Israelites)	Remnant
Stumblingblock and Rock of Offense	Unashamed
Works of the Law	Faith

There have always been two groups of people within the Jewish race and Paul's documentary of this fact is almost inexhaustible. In Romans 11:28 he describes them as "enemies of God" and "beloved of God." The "enemies of God" are those who reject the gospel message and the "beloved of God" are those who believe the Gospel message:

> As concerning the Gospel, they [Jews] are enemies for your [Gentile] sakes: but as touching the election they are beloved for the Father's sake (Romans 11:28).

The "election" in the above verse is no less than the grace that was promised to the Patriarchs in the form of a *covenant* and fulfilled in Jesus Christ (Romans 11:5). God's "election" has to do with the *manner* in which He chose to redeem mankind (Jew and Gentile) and not the election of the Jewish people per se. God "elected" that man be saved by "grace through faith" before the foundation of the world.

The Jews' rejection of the Gospel did not lessen or diminish God's love for them one iota. God never changes (Hebrews 13:8). Only men change. The Jews' enmity toward the Gospel, which became an occasion for Gentile prominence in the household of God, redounded to their good. The miraculous "change" in the faithful Gentile was meant to send an important message to all Jews. Gentile "obedience" was to reveal Jewish "disobedience." The Gentile was to "show mercy" toward the Jew and this in turn would awaken the Jew to his disobedience (or unbelief) and draw him to the mercy of God in Christ. The godly conduct of the Gentile served the same purpose as the law of Moses. The law was given that "...every mouth may be stopped, and all the world may become guilty before God" (Romans 3:19b). In addition to this, the Gentiles' mercy toward the Jew revealed that the Jew was *not* out of the scope of God's grace. God chose to reveal His mercy (to a certain degree) to the Jews through Gentile believers — which was another plus for the Jews.

That which was decreed before the foundation of the world poses no redress for God. The covenant made with the fathers of old and fulfilled in Christ is immutable. God's "gifts of grace" and "call" to mankind require no recantation on His behalf. His impeccable love for the Jewish people (as well as the Gentiles) was as steadfast in Paul's day as in any age. The only way the Apostle can express this profound truth is by using anthropomorphic language:

> For the *gifts of grace* and *call* of God are without repentance (Romans 11:29).

Only the disobedient (or unbelieving) Jew was denied God's mercy in the Gospel. The mercy of God is the meridian of Romans nine and eleven. It is man's only recourse. It doesn't matter how many dispensations, programs, fleshly claims, theories, diagrams, or prophecies the premillennialists invent for the Jews; the only legitimate approach to God is through His mercy. When all the smoke from the prophetic books on the Jewish people is cleared away, it will still be God's mercy. When all the hoopla on the millennial kingdom for the Jews is absorbed by the hallelujahs of heaven, it will continue to be the mercy of God. When the last chapter in the book has been written, it will conclude with the mercy of God.

In studying the Word of God we must delineate between the two Israels or we will make the same error as multitudes have done. Just because the natural descendants of Abraham are called "Israelites" does not mean that they are the "true Israel" of God. There are a variety of names given to God's people in the Old Testament other than "Israelites." We find such designations as: "chosen generation," "peculiar treasure," "holy people," "holy nation," "called," "sons," "daughters," "servants," "saints," "remnant," "righteous," "chosen," "just," "priests," "strangers," "sojourners," "holy seed," etc.

The counterpart of the above terms can also be found in the Old Testament. The following words and phrases are frequently used to describe "Israelites:" "perverse and crooked generation," "children in whom is no faith," "sinful nation," "rulers of Sodom and people of Gomorrah," "uncircumcised," "children of iniquity," "children of whoredoms," "impudent children and stiffhearted," "seed of evildoers," "rebels," "children that are corrupters," "scorpions," etc.

It is very apparent that there are two "kinds" of people in the Old Testament Scriptures bearing the name "Israel." There are two Israels and we have the responsibility of making the distinction. This is a part of "rightly dividing the Word of Truth."

When distinguishing between the two Israels many Bible students use the terms "spiritual Israel" and "carnal Israel." I prefer the term "faithful Israel" rather than "spiritual Israel." The term "spiritual Israel" suggests some vague, invisible people, detached from this present world order. Such is not the case. In both the Old and New Testament periods God's people are "for real." Their faith in God is reflected in their everyday conduct. God is glorified in their bodies and in their spirit. God's people are individuals you can see, touch, and hear. The designation "faithful Israel" covers both dispensations of the Bible.

Some interpreters of the Scripture maintain that the church is the "new Israel." I am inclined to believe that the church is a continuation of the "faithful Israel" that is so apparent in both Testaments. From the beginning, God ordained that man should be saved by "faith" and faith alone. This is why I prefer "faithful Israel" as distinguished from "carnal Israel." This term will be used throughout the remainder of this work.

Paul's lengthy exegesis on the Jewish situation in the book of Romans does not mean that the Jews are "better" than the Gentiles in any way. This fact is stated in very clear language throughout this epistle (See Romans 2:11; 3:9; and 10:12). The Jewish mentality in matters of religion was much more complex than that of the heathen world. Their distorted views of themselves and their relationship to God required a thorough investigation of the Old Testament Scriptures. The amount of time, thought, and space given to their peculiar need in no way minimizes God's love and concern for the Gentiles.

Addendum

Confrontations within the community of faith are inevitable, but ultimately they serve a good purpose. They have been the means of maintaining sound doctrine from one generation to the next. Differences of opinion are oftentimes painful to those involved and should be handled with a good deal of wisdom and tact. It is with these thoughts in mind that we approach Dr. Pentecost's views on Matthew 12:46-50. Dr. Pentecost's interpretation of this passage is another example of exaggerated premillennial views being imposed upon certain texts of Scripture. In this passage someone informs Jesus that His mother and brethren wish to speak to Him. According to Luke's Gospel, His mother and brethren could not come near Him because of the "press" or crowd of people (8:19).

We can only guess as to how Dr. Pentecost came to his conclusions on Matthew 12:46-50. Does the plight of Jesus' family to speak to Him mean that He is renouncing all "physical" ties with them and the Jewish nation? Is it possible for Jesus' family to *represent* or *act for* the entire Jewish nation? When Jesus stretched His hand toward His disciples and said, "Behold my mother and my brethren," did He initiate a "new program based on faith?" This seems to be what Dr. Pentecost is saying (See also page 463 of Dr. Pentecost's book).

It is impossible to avoid a confrontation when faced with an interpretation of Matthew 12:46-50, as given by Dr. Pentecost. Jesus is not dealing with a "national" issue in this passage of Scripture. Nor is Matthew 12:46-50 a lesson on "faith" versus "physical" ties. "Physical" relationships are necessary in any family, but the family of God takes precedence over "natural" ties in every age and generation. This does not mean that we *must* deny or renounce our physical lineage because we are in the household of God. Jesus is saying that the family of God fulfills the role of a natural mother and natural brothers on a different level. It is the same lesson that Jesus taught His disciples in Mark's Gospel:

> There is no man that hath left house, or brethren, or sisters, or father, or mother, or wife, or children, or lands, for My sake, and the Gospel's,
> But he shall receive an hundredfold now in this time, houses, and *brethren*, and *sisters*, and *mothers*, and *children*, and lands, with persecutions; and in the world to come eternal life (Mark 10:29-30).

The unnecessary problem that Dr. Pentecost has created from this passage of Scripture is resolved in the last verse of the same text: "For *whosoever* (Jew or Gentile) shall *do the will of My Father* which is in heaven, the *same* is My brother, and sister, and mother" (verse 50). "Obedience" to God's will (or Word) has been the rule of thumb for the household of God from the beginning (Exodus 19:5). The "remnant" that arises out of "faith" in God's Word existed long before New Testament days. Luke, while writing about the same incident quotes Jesus as saying: "My mother and my brethren are these which *hear the Word of God, and do it*" (Luke 8:21). Moses taught the same truth many centuries earlier. Notice the similarities between Moses' words and that of Jesus:

> For this commandment [Word] which I command thee this day, it is not hidden from thee, neither is it far off.

It is not in heaven, that thou shouldest say, Who shall go up for us to heaven, and bring it [Word] unto us, that we may *hear it, and do it?*

Neither is it [Word] beyond the sea, that thou shouldest say, Who shall go over the sea for us, and bring it [Word] unto us, that we may *hear it, and do it?*

But the *Word* is very nigh unto thee, in thy mouth, and in thy heart, that thou mayest *do it* (Deuteronomy 30:11-14).

"Hear the Word of God and do it." Moses made this statement three times and Jesus repeated the same truth: "My mother and brethren are these which *hear the Word of God, and do it.*" Paul quotes Moses' words almost verbatim and says that "faith cometh by *hearing,* and *hearing* by the Word of God" (Romans 10:17). Faith was the media by which men were saved in Moses' day and will be as long as time endures. Matthew 12:46-50 is not a case *for* premillennialism, but *against* premillennialism.

Chapter 3
Abraham vs. Abraham
Abraham — A Twofold Father

In the course of divine history God has chosen men to fulfill special roles that are never duplicated in succeeding generations. Such was the unique role of Abraham. Abraham was called to be a "father" in a manner that has not been repeated. Abraham was chosen to be a twofold father. This double role as a "father" has been a stumblingblock to countless people.

Even Abraham's name reflects this unrivaled role as a father. The Hebrew word "Abram" literally means *high* or *exalted* father. Later, the name "Abram" was lengthened to "Abraham" which means *father of a multitude* or *father of many nations*. The promise of God to Abraham, as given in the King James Version, was that He would "make him a father of many nations " (Genesis 17:4).

The book of Romans is the classical exposition on this dual role of Abraham. The role of "fatherhood" must be seen in the light of some other crucial matters in this epistle — namely, the universality of sin and the righteousness of God.

Before Abraham was born, something happened to the human race that affected all mankind — including Abraham. That something was the entrance of sin and death through Adam's transgression (Romans 5:12). Man became alienated from God and no longer stood in a "right" relationship to his Creator. The first three chapters of Romans are devoted to this truth. Without question, both Jew and Gentile are in this sinful state (Romans 3:9-10; 23). Being a sinner bears certain objectionable consequences, the summation of which is the "wrath of God" (Romans 1:18; 3:5-9).

But there is good news — God has not left mankind without hope — there is a way of escape. It is possible for man to be delivered from this unrighteous state, to be acquitted, and to be "made the righteousness of God." The New Testament speaks of this change of position as "imputed righteousness," i.e., the sinner is counted righteous as God is righteous (2 Corinthians 5:21). This act of "imputed righteousness" is to be equated with such terms as justification, born again, new creature, children of God, and sons of God. But the most intimate terms to describe this "imputed righteousness" are "children of God" and "sons of God."

The big question is — how does one experience this "imputed righteousness" — how is one justified — or how does one become a "child of God"? The majority of the Jewish people would argue that it is a combination of things: circumcision, keeping the law, and blood ties with Abraham. Paul's theology runs counter to all of these cherished beliefs.

No individual could speak to the above question as Abraham. Several centuries before his descendants became trapped in a labyrinth of religious practices, Abraham was made righteous. Abraham's unwavering faith in God's promise established a precedence that would have a profound impact upon the rest of mankind.

Largely for the benefit of the Jewish people, Paul proves from their own Scriptures that Abraham was not born a righteous man; nor was he "counted righteous" through the covenant of circumcision (Romans 4:9-10). Also, the law of Moses played no part in Abraham's righteous standing before God. (The law was not given until several hundred years after Abraham's day.) Neither did Abraham claim any special kind of blood or genes in his body for his acceptance before God. Abraham was "counted righteous" through *faith* in God's promise. Abraham *believed* God's Word. Genesis 15:6 reads, "...he (Abraham) believed in the Lord and He (Lord) counted it to him for righteousness." From a theological point of view, we might say that this is the "golden passage" of the Scriptures. The "faith principle," set forth in this verse, is the sole foundation for man's hope in God.

Abraham displayed a "pre-resurrection faith" which all New Testament believers have in common with him (Romans 4:20-25). Abraham believed in "God ... who quickeneth the dead, and calleth those things which be not as though they were" (Romans 4:17). *In matters of redeeming faith, Abraham became a pattern for succeeding generations.* This is why the Apostle Paul designates him as the "father of the faithful" or the "father of all them that believe" (Romans 4:11-12). Abraham is a twofold father: he is the father of the natural born Jew and he is also the "father of them that believe" (Jew and Gentile).

All men (Jew and Gentile), from Abraham's day to this present hour, if they are to be "counted righteous" (i.e., saved, justified, redeemed, children of God, etc.), must follow the example of Abraham. In the natural order, children are prone to "follow in the steps of their father." This is the picture that Paul gives in the fourth chapter of

Romans relative to Abraham's "fatherhood:"

> And he (Abraham) received the sign of circumcision, a seal of the righteousness of the *faith* which he had yet being uncircumcised: that he might be the *father of all them that believe,* though they be not circumcised: that *righteousness might be imputed to them also:*
>
> And the *father* of circumcision to them who are not of the circumcision only, but who also *walk in the steps of that faith of our father Abraham,* which he had being yet uncircumcised (Romans 4:11-12).

The babyish language used in the above passage speaks very clearly. As a small child walks in the steps of its father, so must every believer (past and present — Jew and Gentile) walk in the steps of Abraham; i.e., they must exercise a faith in God's promise similar to that of the Patriarch.

This is why Jesus could refute the claim of many Jews who considered themselves "children of Abraham." The Gospel of John records a conversation between Jesus and certain Jews that is very revealing. In the dialogue, Jesus points out quite a discrepancy between their attitude toward Him and their attitude toward Abraham. The discussion begins with Jesus encouraging the Jews to continue in His Word if they would be His disciples, but it leads into the subject of "fatherhood" — the fatherhood of Abraham and the fatherhood of God. The Jews claimed both God and Abraham as their "father," but in paradoxical language Jesus shows they lose on both counts. Jesus said to the Jews:

> I know that ye are *Abraham's seed:* but ye seek to kill me, because my *Word* hath no place in you.
>
> I speak that which I have seen with *My Father:* and ye do that which ye have seen with *your father.*
>
> They answered and said unto Him, *Abraham is our father.* Jesus said unto them, if ye were *Abraham's children,* ye would do the *works of Abraham.*
>
> But now ye seek to kill me, a man that hath told you the truth, which I heard of God; *this did not Abraham.*
>
> Ye do the deeds of *your father.* Then said they to Him, we be not born of fornication; we have one Father, even God.
>
> Jesus said unto them, *If God were your father, ye would love Me;* for I proceeded forth and came from God; neither came I of myself, but He sent Me.
>
> Ye are of *your father the devil,* and the lusts of *your father* ye will

do, etc. (John 8:37-44).

Jesus admits that the above Jews were "Abraham's seed," but in the same breath He declares they are not. This is not a contradiction. They were Abraham's seed, "according to the flesh," but they did not imitate him in believing the Word of God. Thus, they refused to "walk in the steps of Abraham." The same Voice that spoke to Abraham was speaking to them but they believed Him not. Their rejection of the *living Word* disqualified them as "children of Abraham" and "children of God." Jesus called them "children of the devil."

To refer to the Jewish people as "children of the devil" would amount to the unpardonable sin in the eyes of many people in our day. It would excite the adrenal glands of the futurists because it controverts some of their cherished doctrines on the Jews. Jesus does not leave us in doubt about their progeny and E. W. Kenyon's thoughts on the subject are very illuminating. Mr. Kenyon is not writing directly on the Jewish people but his remarks on man's nature would certainly include them:

> Man was actually BORN AGAIN when he sinned. That is, he was BORN OF THE DEVIL. He became a partaker of Satan's nature just as man today becomes a partaker of divine nature when he is born of God by accepting Jesus Christ.[1] (all caps mine)

Let us restate and enlarge upon the dominant features in Abraham's faith that earned him the title "father of the faithful." It is written of Abraham that he "believed God, who *quickeneth* the dead, and *calleth* those things which be not as though they were" (Romans 4:17). In a word, Abraham believed that God was able to bring the dead to life again and to call into being that which did not exist. Although the words "quickeneth" and "calleth" are sometimes used independently of each other in Paul's works, the one implies the other. They are correlative terms. The same method will be followed as we examine the two ideas.

We have not begun to fathom Abraham's faith. Since his body (and Sarah's) was dead, he believed for a Seed that only God could generate (Genesis 15:4). The Seed, for which Abraham believed, had to be divine

1. Kenyon, E. W., *The Father and His Family,* Kenyon Gospel Publishing Society, copyright 1964, 48.

in origin if "all the families of the earth were to be blessed." "All the families of the earth" is a concept that involves century upon century and family upon family. Such a feat could only be accomplished through a Seed that was on an equality with God.

Also, the idea of "blessing" as given in the promise to Abraham meant the "ultimate in blessing" that only God could bestow. As all Scripture attests, it meant the gift of eternal, everlasting life that would be offered through the Gospel of Jesus Christ (Galatians 3:8).

And in conjunction with this One Seed, Abraham believed for a posterity beyond the natural powers of procreation. The "blessing," which was divine in nature, must be associated with a "family" (or nation) that would be divine in nature. Abraham believed for a people whose *origin* and *being* would be in God.

If Abraham was to be the "father of the faithful," as described in the words of Paul, and if the concepts of "quickening" and "calling" are inherent in his faith, then he must have a generation of people who would have this in common with him. Abraham's faith included a multitude of people, that no man could number, who would be quickened and called by the same power.

Both the Incarnation and resurrection principles of Christ are embodied in Abraham's faith. Paul is more concerned with the death and resurrection of Christ, since this is the heart of the Gospel. The God that quickened the dead bodies of Abraham and Sarah is the same God that quickened the dead body of Christ and raised Him from the dead. The Apostle establishes a direct relationship between the two works of God.

Faith in God's ability to quicken his dead body (and Sarah's) resulted in God's imputed righteousness to Abraham. In like manner, faith in God's power to quicken and raise Christ from the dead results in imputed righteousness for the New Testament believer:

> He (Abraham) staggered not at the promise of God through unbelief; but was strong in the faith, giving glory to God;
>
> And being fully persuaded that, what He had promised, He was also able to perform.
>
> And therefore *it was imputed to him for righteousness.*
>
> Now it was not written *for his sake alone,* that it (righteousness) *was imputed to him;*
>
> *But for us* (New Testament believers) *also, to whom it* (righteousness) *shall be imputed, if we believe on Him that raised up*

Jesus our Lord from the dead;
     Who was delivered for our offences, and was *raised again* for our
     justification (Romans 4:20-25).

There is an unbroken link between the faith of Abraham and the
New Testament generation. In fact, the fourth chapter of Romans shows
conclusively that Abraham's example is to be imitated by the followers
of Christ. Those who delineate between the Old and New Testament
saints must reject a good deal of Pauline theology.

When Christ was raised from the dead, myriads of people were
quickened and *raised* with Him. This does not mean that all believers
were quickened the very hour that Christ came forth from the tomb, but
it does mean that all men of all ages (Jew and Gentile) must identify with
the same *quickening power* when they believe and "walk in the steps"
of Abraham.

This truth is beautifully illustrated in Paul's letter to the Ephesians.
We are given a picture of what these people were like *before* and *after*
their reception of the Gospel. Before their conversion they are described
as "walking" and as "children," but they are the very opposite of the
children of God:

     "...ye *walked* according to the course of this world, according to
     the prince of the power of the air, the spirit that now worketh in the
     children of disobedience.
     Among whom also we all had our conversation in time past in the
     lusts of our flesh, fulfilling the desires of the flesh and of the mind; and
     were by *nature the children of wrath,* even as others (Ephesians 2:2-
     3).

In short, the Ephesians, prior to their regeneration, are described as
"dead in trespasses and in sins." But this dead state of existence only
enhances the love and mercy of God. The Ephesians, like Abraham,
believed in "God who quickeneth the dead and calleth those things
which be not as though they were." Their faith in the risen Christ
resulted in their being "quickened with Him." The "quickened" Christ
and the "quickened" believer share a common experience together:

     But God, who is rich in mercy, for His great love wherewith He
     loved us,
     Even when we were *dead in sins,* hath *quickened us together with
     Christ,*
     And hath raised us up together, and made us *sit together* in
     heavenly places in Christ Jesus (Ephesians 2:4-6, see also Colossians

3:1-4).

The Ephesian church, made up of Jews and Gentiles, would qualify to be called the "children of Abraham" and the "children of God" because they believed in the One "who is able to quicken the dead," as did Abraham. The quickening of Abraham's (and Sarah's) dead body, the quickening of Christ from the dead, and the quickening of those who are "dead in trespasses and in sins" are a theological triad that complement each other.

What is written of the Ephesian church must be said of all New Testament believers. The same terminology that is used to describe Abraham's faith is used to describe those who are in Christ. The New Testament Christians are "quickened" and "called" by the Word and Spirit of God.

As we have already shown in chapter one, the word "calleth" has to do with God's "creativity" by the spoken Word. Abraham knew nothing of fatherhood when the Word was given to him that he would be the "father of many nations." The fulfillment of the promise was delayed until Abraham and Sarah were beyond the childbearing years. Their old age (or dead bodies) would prohibit such a thing, but Abraham believed that God could "quicken" and "call" into being (or create) that which did not exist. Other translations of Scripture bring this truth out more clearly:

The *Revised Standard Version* reads: "...who gives life to the dead and *calls into existence* the things that *do not exist.*"

Phillips Translation states: "...who can *make the dead live, and speak the Word to those yet unborn.*"

From the *Modern Language Translation:* "who makes the *dead live* and *calls into existence what has no being.*"

Isaac was born as a result of God's Word and Spirit. God had promised Abraham a son (by the spoken Word) and Isaac's birth would follow as surely as the creation followed the spoken Word. Isaac's birth marked the beginning of a people (or nation) that God would beget by the same method. Abraham believed that God, by His Word, would *quicken* and *call* into being (or create) a people that at one time were "not a people." This is the very truth that Peter wishes to impress upon us in his first epistle as he describes those who have been *called* by God:

> But ye are a *chosen generation, a royal priesthood, an holy nation, a peculiar people:* that ye should show forth the praises of *Him who*

hath called you out of darkness into His marvelous light:
   Which in time past *were not a people,* but are *now the people of God:* which had not obtained mercy, but now have obtained mercy (1 Peter 2:9-10).

A "chosen generation," a "royal priesthood," a "holy nation," and a "peculiar people" are a chain of ideas taken from the Old Testament to describe God's people. These terms distinguish His people in both dispensations. Peter connects Hosea's words (verse 10) with the above characterization of God's people and says that "in time past *were not a people.*" In both the words of Hosea and Peter, the Jewish people, apart from God's mercy, are "not a people." This is the great paradox of Scripture. They are a "people" but they are "not a people" — i.e., they are not the people of God. (We have already shown that Jesus refused to call them either the "children of Abraham" or the "children of God.") God's people are both a "called" people and a "created" people. They owe their existence and being to the "Word" of God and the "Spirit" of God.

One of the most common designations for New Testament believers is "the called." When Paul writes his letter to the church at Rome, the first title given to the Christians there was not "believers" or "saints" or "brethren," etc., but "the called:"

   Among whom are ye also *the called* of Jesus Christ: To all that be in Rome, beloved of God, *called* to be saints: Grace to you and peace from God our Father, and the Lord Jesus Christ, etc. (Romans 1:6-7).

Also, we learn how meaningful the term "called" is as we see it in a cluster along with three other giant words in the eighth chapter of Romans. Predestination, justification, glorification and "calling" are a foursome of equal importance. Although each of the four terms has its own special meaning, they are a part of the whole work of redemption:

   And we know that all things work together for good to them that love God, to them who are the *called* according to His purpose ...
   Moreover whom He did predestinate, them He also *called:* and whom He *called,* them he also justified, and whom He justified, them He also glorified (Romans 8:28-30).

The above passages are only two among many verses that refer to the people of God as the "called." Many more New Testament Scriptures could be cited: (Romans 1:7; 9:24; 1 Corinthians 1:2; 9, 24, 26;

7:15; Galatians 1:6; Ephesians 4:1,4; Colossians 3:15; 1 Thessalonians 2:12; 4:7; 2 Thessalonians 2:14; 2 Timothy 1:9; Hebrews 9:15; 1 Peter 1:15; 3:9; 5:10; and Jude 1). The New Testament does not stand alone in using this title for God's elect. Isaiah goes to the very fountainhead of the Jewish race and says that Abraham was "called." *The prophet admonished his generation to imitate Abraham's example long before Paul gave him the title "father of the faithful."* Abraham's divine "blessing" and "increase" are related to God's "call:"

> Look unto Abraham your father, and unto Sarah that bare you: for I *called* him alone, and blessed him, and increased him (Isaiah 51:2).

The same word (called) is used to describe God's people in the forty-eighth chapter of Isaiah. Its usage here is idealistic. "Israel" and "Jacob" (two names used for the same purpose) are also the "called" of God:

> Hearken unto me, O Jacob and Israel, *My called,* I am He; I am the first, I also am the last (Isaiah 48:12).

If the word "called" is generally understood in conjunction with God's "creativity," then the above names "Israel" and "Jacob" cannot include the entire Jewish nation. We must look beyond one passage of Scripture to understand Isaiah's views on God's people. Isaiah uses terms to express God's "creativity" that are comparable to those used in the New Testament. The forty-third chapter is remarkable for its use of such words as "created," "formed," "made," and "redeemed" to describe a people who are "called by God's name." He also looks into the future and contemplates "other seed" that will originate from the witness of those whom God has "created," "formed," and "made" (verses 12, 21). God's "sons" and "daughters" will come from the "ends of the earth" (verse 6). In all probability, these will be Gentile nations. Notice the "individual" emphasis in the last verse of the following quote:

> Fear not: for I am with thee: I will bring thy seed from the East, and gather thee from the West; I will say to the North, give up; and to the South, Keep not back: bring My sons from far, and My daughters from the ends of the earth.
>
> Even *every one* that is *called* by My name: for I have *created* him for My glory, I have *formed* him; yea, I *have made him* (Isaiah 43:5-7).

God's creativity by His "Word" and "Spirit," the like of which is expressed in the word "called," can be refused. Men can spurn God's call and thereby deprive themselves of this wonderful work of the "Spirit" and "Word" in their lives:

> Turn you at My reproof: behold, I will pour out My *Spirit* unto you, I will make known My *Words* unto you. Because I have *called,* and ye refused; and I have stretched out My hand, and no man regarded; But ye have set at nought all my counsel (Word) and would none of My reproof (Proverbs 1:23-25).

It should be noted that the above passage is quoted from the Old Testament, the truth of which parallels that of the New. To reject God's "call" is to be denied His "Word" and "Spirit." It is to forfeit His "creativity," by which men become the "children of God."

Isaiah describes a generation of people in his day who had no ear for the voice of God. When God "called," they deliberately walked contrary to His ways. Their relationship to God was decided by their *reception* or *rejection* of His "call" or Word:

> I also will choose their delusions, and will bring their fears upon them; because when I *called,* none did answer; when I *spake,* they did not hear; but they did evil before mine eyes, and chose that in which I delight not (Isaiah 66:4).

The synonymity of God's "call" and "Word" is very obvious in the above passage. A positive response to God's "call" or "Word" would have resulted in a "people" in whom God could delight.

The same term (call) is to be found in one of the most familiar Old Testament prophecies. When Joel writes about the coming of the Holy Spirit and the beginning of the New Testament era, the remnant is spoken of as the "called:"

> And it shall come to pass, that whosoever shall call on the name of the Lord shall be delivered: for in mount Zion and in Jerusalem shall be deliverance, as the Lord hath said, and the *remnant* whom the Lord shall *call* (Joel 2:32).

The "remnant" and those "whom the Lord shall *call*" are identical concepts. Paul declares that the remnant is made up of those who are saved by God's grace (which is received by faith), and not by works (Romans 11:5-6). We can say very candidly that God's people are *the called* in both the Old and New dispensations.

The "calling" of God is more than just an invitation to the Gospel. There is a "general calling," which includes all men, and there is an "effectual calling" which involves the creativity of God in effecting a new creation in those who respond to the Gospel in faith:

> Therefore if any man be in Christ, he is a new creature (or *creation*); old things are passed away and behold *all things are become new* (2 Corinthians 5:17).

Those who imitate Abraham in believing "God, who quickeneth the dead and *calleth* those things which be not as though they were," are a product of God's creativity. They are a people unto themselves. By their faith they are counted righteous and bear the title, "children of God," and the "children of Abraham:"

> For ye are all the *children of God* by *faith in* Jesus Christ ... And if ye be Christ's then are ye *Abraham's seed* and heirs according to the promise (Galatians 3:26, 29).

There is a very interesting relationship between the words "called" and "church" in the Greek language. We learn something from the Greek that is not brought to light in the English translations. The English word "called" is translated from a Greek verb known as *kaleo*. However, the Greek word *klesis*, which is the noun form of the verb *kaleo,* is used in conjunction with our English word "church." The Greek word for "church" is *ekklesia. Ekklesia* is a combination of two Greek words, one of which is directly related to *kaleo* (i.e., *klesis*). The other Greek word is *ek* which, according to *Strong's Greek Lexicon,* means "from" or "out." Combining the two Greek words (*ek* and *klesis)* we have *ekklesia* or the "called out." Thus, the "church" and "called" are one and the same thing.

God's people have always been the "called" or "church." According to George E. Ladd, "The Greek word *ekklesia,* is the word most commonly used in the Greek Old Testament to refer to Israel as the people of God."[2] Those who attempt to erect a wall between the Old Testament saints and the New Testament saints error exceedingly. God's people are those who "walk in the steps of Abraham" and believe

---

2. George E. Ladd, *The Gospel of the Kingdom,* Wm. B. Eerdmans Publishing Company, Grand Rapids, Michigan, 1959, 112.

in "God who *quickeneth* the dead, and *calleth* those things which be not as though they were."

The "calling" of God is associated with the most transforming event in the chronologies of eternity, namely, the cross of our Lord Jesus Christ. There is no event in all of God's activities comparable to the death and resurrection of Jesus. The carnal opinions of men are laid aside by those who are "called" and the cross becomes both the "power" of God and the "wisdom" of God. To the Jew, the cross of Christ was a "stumblingblock" and to the Greek "foolishness," but the "creativity" of God that is inherent in the word "called" results in regeneration for both Jew and Gentile. This is no less than a supernatural work of God. Those who are "called" do not "change" the cross, rather the power of the cross changes them (Romans 1:16). Paul's "one new man" concept that is written in the Ephesians letter (2:15) is also implied in his remarks on the cross of Jesus as given in one of his letters to the Corinthians:

> But unto them which are *called* both Jews and Greeks, Christ (crucified) the power of God, and the wisdom of God (1 Corinthians 1:24).

A secondary term that is used for the Holy Spirit in the King James Version is also related to the word "called." The Greek word *parakletes*, that is translated "Comforter," is a combination of two Greek words which are *para* (meaning "to be near") and *kaleo* (meaning "to call"). The Greek word *parakletos* literally means to "call near" or "in the vicinity of." Thus the Spirit of God, along with the Word of God, become the media by which men are called to Christ. The word "called" is a very important concept in both dispensations.

It should be added that the "calling" in the New Testament is always a "heavenly" calling rather than an "earthly" one. The author of the Hebrews epistle describes the believer as a "partaker of the *heavenly calling*" (Hebrews 3:1). Peter states that those who are in Christ are called "to glory and virtue" (2 Peter 1:3). Paul confirms the same truth when he writes to the Thessalonian church: "God...hath *called* you unto His *kingdom* and *glory*" (1 Thessalonians 2:12. See also 2 Thessalonians 2:14; and Ephesians 1:18). Nowhere in the Scriptures do we find that God has *called* mankind to an earthly inheritance such as the land of Palestine.

From the book of Genesis to the book of Revelation, God's people are known and designated by the word "called." When the "beast" of

Revelation is overcome by Christ, it is stated that those who are with the Lord of lords and King of kings and share in His victory are the *"called, and chosen, and faithful"* (Revelation 17:14). These three concepts (called, chosen, and faithful) dovetail into an impervious theological wall throughout the Scriptures. This impenetrable stronghold secures the "faithful" seed of Abraham while shutting out the "natural" seed of Abraham. Only those who have responded to the Gospel, in *faith*, and are known as the *called* (as a result of the creativity of God's Word and Spirit), can be the true "children of Abraham" and the true "children of God."

Abraham is never portrayed as being more than *two fathers*. He is the father of the "physical" Jew and the father of the "faithful" Jew. Since Abraham is called the "father of *all them that believe,"* he is the father of the "faithful" Gentile as much so as to the "faithful" Jew (Galatians 3:7). There are no physical barriers, especially blood ties, in the concept and exercise of faith. To impose a third role upon Abraham as a father would create a theological impasse. Any attempt to skirt or manipulate the two roles of Abraham will end in chaos.

There is a very subtle duplicity that is used by the premillennialists to foster the physical seed of Abraham. The dubiousness of their tactics come to light when they try to prove that God gave the Promised Land to Abraham's physical seed on an unconditional basis. In the final analysis, the physical seed are left high and dry unless they become the spiritual seed of Abraham. If a prize was given for "confounding the seed of Abraham," the millenarians would certainly win it. They have "run off the chart" in trying to sell the church on the "unconditional" promise made to Abraham's physical seed.

Regrettably, Dr. John F. Walvoord falls into the above characterization of the futurists. His illusive temperament can be seen in his book, *Israel in Prophecy,* as he tries to delineate between *three* categories of Abraham's seed. In brief, they are: (1) The "natural" seed of Abraham; (2) The "spiritual" seed of Abraham; and (3) The Gentiles who are related to the spiritual seed of Abraham.

The "three seeds" will be discussed in the same order that is given in Dr. Walvoord's book. Concerning the "natural" descendants of Jacob (or the twelve tribes), he writes: "To them God promises in a special sense to be their God. To them was given the law of Moses, and the perpetual title to the Promised Land is given to them."[3] Please keep in mind that Dr. Walvoord is writing about the "natural" seed of Abraham and Jacob or the twelve tribes.

It should be noted that there are no qualifying terms or conditions in the above statement by Dr. Walvoord. Three specific things are promised to the "natural" seed of Jacob: (1) God promised in a "special sense" to be their God; (2) To them was given the law of Moses; and (3) To them was given the "perpetual title" to the Promised Land. This blanket statement on the "natural" descendants of the twelve tribes is given a different twist when Dr. Walvoord deals with the "spiritual" seed of Abraham.

When Dr. Walvoord presents his thoughts on the "spiritual" seed of Abraham, we discover that *not all* the "natural" seed of Abraham will share in the Promised Land. He writes that "all Israelites do not actually inherit the land and that only spiritual Israel will enter the future millennial kingdom and fulfill the promise" (page 36). To be the "spiritual" seed of Abraham, according to Dr. Walvoord, an Israelite must "trust in God", "keep the law" and "qualify for many of the blessings of the covenant." We are unable to reconcile how God, in a "special sense," could be the God of the "natural" seed of Jacob and give them a "perpetual title" to the Promised Land and yet not allow *all* Israelites to share in the land. On page 38 of the same book he writes: "Upon *natural Israel* in *unbelief* God has *heaped His judgment* and *divine discipline*" (emphasis mine). Dr. Walvoord makes a big commotion over the "physical" seed of Abraham but they do not have a leg to stand on unless they become the "spiritual" seed of Abraham.

It seems that Dr. Walvoord has presented us with both a "conditional" and "unconditional" promise — an "unconditional" promise to the "natural" seed of Jacob and a "conditional" promise to the "spiritual" seed of Jacob or Abraham. In the light of eternal verities, it would have been helpful if Dr. Walvoord had explained in what "special sense" God would be the God of the "natural" seed of Jacob. Along with this, it would have been interesting to know how the twelve tribes of Jacob could be given a "perpetual title" to the Promised Land, but only the "spiritual" seed would be allowed to possess it. This irregularity in the promise to the "natural" seed of Abraham and the promise made to the "spiritual" seed of Abraham should not come as a surprise to those who have given serious study to premillennialism. This double standard for

---

3. John F. Walvoord, *Israel in Prophecy*, Zondervan Publishing House, Grand Rapids, Michigan, 1962, 36.

the Jews is the only way the millenarians can maintain their "unconditional" promise to the descendants of Abraham.

The third group that belong to the "seed of Abraham" are the believing Gentiles. In this group, Dr. Walvoord makes a distinction between the *promise* given to the Gentiles and the *promise* given to the "physical" seed of Abraham. According to Dr. Walvoord, the Gentiles cannot share in the *promise* given to the "physical" seed of Abraham. He writes: "Gentiles who are recognized as the children of Abraham come under the promise given to the Gentiles and not under the promise given to the physical seed of Abraham" (page 37). It should be observed that Dr. Walvoord is differentiating between the promise made to the Gentiles and the promise made to the "physical" seed of Abraham. Why would Dr. Walvoord contrast the Christian Gentile with the "physical" seed of Abraham? By his own pen he has pronounced God's "judgment" and "divine discipline" upon the "natural" seed of Abraham unless they "trust in God," "keep the law," and "qualify for many of the blessings of the covenant."

We must not be led astray by such catchy statements by Dr. Walvoord. A promise *made* and a promise *realized* are two different things. Without a redemptive faith, the physical seed of Abraham do not share in anything of eternal consequence.

Dr. Walvoord has a real problem in identifying believing Gentiles with Abraham and the subsequent *promise*. Notice his statement: "A Gentile Christian therefore becomes the seed of Abraham not because of any physical lineage with Abraham himself, *nor simply by imitation of Abraham's faith,* but because he is regarded by God as *in Christ* who is indeed a physical descendant of Abraham" (page 37 - emphasis mine). Again, Dr. Walvoord makes a big fuss over the physical lineage of Abraham. He is trying to tell us that the Gentiles cannot share in the full promise to Abraham because they have no physical ties with him.

Dr. Walvoord is very adept at chopping the promise to Abraham into bits and pieces. He writes about the "more particular promises," "most of the promises," "all the promises," and the "full promise." These are ideas that have been conjured up in the mind of Dr. Walvoord and serve only to distract from the *one promise* who is Jesus Christ. All promises, of whatever nature they may be, are subordinate to this *one promise* (2 Corinthians 1:20). Dr. Walvoord provides us with a good deal of premillennial hype that leaves us guessing and running in circles. It is like trying to find the proverbial pot of gold at the end of the rainbow.

What more does a Christian Gentile need than to be *in Christ?*
Christ existed *before* Abraham's name was recorded in Scripture. All
the promises of God are *made to Christ* (Galatians 3:16). All the fulness
of the Godhead is *in Christ* (Colossians 2:9). All believers are *complete
in Christ* (Colossians 2:10). In Christ are hid *all the treasures of wisdom
and knowledge* (Colossians 2:3). Christ is the *Alpha* and the *Omega,* the
beginning and the *end* (Revelation 1:8). Christ has been given the
preeminence in all things (Colossians 1:18). Christ is *heir of all things*
(Hebrews 1:2). Is it possible to add to or enhance Paul's words to the
Corinthian church?: "For all things are yours; Whether Paul, or Apollos,
or Cephas, or the world, or life, or death, or things present, or things to
come: all are yours: and ye are Christ's: and Christ is God's" (1
Corinthians 3:21b-23).

The Corinthian church was made up largely of Gentile Christians.
Is Dr. Walvoord, along with all other millenarians, trying to tell us that
the Gentiles are going to "miss something" because they are not the
physical seed of Abraham?

All the elect of God, whether Jew or Gentile, have their origin in
Christ. When Galatians 3:29 is properly interpreted, there can be no
doubt about this truth. The Apostle Paul writes: "If ye be Christ's, then
are ye Abraham's seed, and heirs according to the promise" (Galatians
3:29). These words are written, as it were, with an iron pen and can never
be changed to read: "If ye be Abraham's seed, then are ye Christ's, and
heirs according to the promise." All men must be *in Christ* before they
can be the everlasting seed of Abraham. This excludes all the seed of
Abraham except those who are of faith. A paraphrase of Paul's words
in Galatians 3:29 would read like this: "If you are *in Christ,* who is
Abraham's *one significant seed,* then *you are Abraham's seed* as surely
as Christ is Abraham's seed, and this entitles you to be an heir according
to the promise." It is the same truth that Paul is teaching in Galatians
3:16. All the *promises* of God are *made to Christ* and there is no way of
sharing in those promises except to be *in Christ.*

No effort is made on the part of Dr. Walvoord to tell us how the
Christian Gentile arrives at his state of being *in Christ.* The Christian
Gentile finds himself in Christ the same way that Abraham did, i.e., *by
faith.* The common denominator by which all men are to realize the
promise of God is faith. Faith is a concept that is catholic in nature and
permeates the entire Bible. In other words, it can be utilized by all
mankind — Jew, Gentile, black, white, rich, poor, educated, unedu-

cated, young, old, slave, master, blue collar, white collar, male or female. Faith can be appropriated at any given period of history — ancient or modern. Faith is not limited to a particular geographical location. From the depths of the ocean (as in the case of Jonah) to the highest mile in space, man can have access to God by faith. According to the Apostle Paul, there is only *one faith:*

> There is *one* body, and *one* spirit, even as ye are called in *one* hope of your calling; *One* Lord, *one* faith, *one* baptism; *One* God and Father of *all*, who is above *all*, and through *all*, and in you *all* (Ephesians 4:4-6).

Dr. Walvoord has taken a simple promise that was made to Abraham — a promise that was to be fulfilled in Christ — a promise that is to be realized by a childlike act of faith — and has created a theological King Kong that is out of step with the rest of Scripture and the experiences of men.

Faith was the sole means of pleasing God before Abraham's day. Abraham's response to God's call established a precedence that is to be emulated to this day. There are many noble and outstanding characters in the Scripture, but none can claim the unique role of Abraham. The titles "father of the faithful" and the "father of all them that believe" belong exclusively to him. The link between Abraham and his "faithful children" in both dispensations is the Word. Faith in the "Word of Promise" that was fulfilled in Christ is the common bond between "father" and "children." The carnal offspring of Abraham, who reject the Word and refuse to "walk in his steps," are neither the children of Abraham nor the children of God.

Addendum

When Dr. Walvoord writes about the "spiritual" seed of Abraham and their occupancy of the Promised Land, he *fuses* the "millennial period" of the Jews with the "eternal state" of the Jews. In other words, the Jews who "qualify" to enter the "millennial age" are eligible to enter the "eternal state." Dr. Walvoord believes that the "strongest kind of promises are related to the possession of the land, in that not only the nation Israel is promised *eternal continuity,* but the land is promised as an *everlasting possession*" (page 77 - emphasis mine). One wonders if Dr. Walvoord has read the New Testament when he says that the "strongest kind of promises are related to the possession of the land."

The promises in the New Testament are *never* related to the Promised Land — they are related to Christ, to everlasting life, and to a "heavenly inheritance."

Dr. Walvoord believes that the people of Israel will "retain their identity as Israelites even as the Gentiles retain their identity as Gentiles in the eternal state" (page 99). The *oneness* that is to exist between the Jews and Gentiles, by the blood of Christ, is laid aside by Dr. Walvoord and the wall of partition is erected again (Ephesians 2:12-19). Our curiosity overwhelms us as we reflect on the above statement by Dr. Walvoord. We are made to wonder which group Timothy, Paul's spiritual son in the faith, will decide to identify with in the eternal state — Jew or Gentile? Timothy's mother was of Jewish descent and his father was a Greek (Acts 16:1). Timothy is only one believer among many thousands who come from a racially mixed background. Our curiosity is further aroused by wondering if the black Gentiles, the Chinese Gentiles, the Indian Gentiles, the English Gentiles, etc., will retain their identity in the eternal state?

It seems that some of the millenarians know more about what people will be like in the eternal state than those who wrote the Scriptures. Tradition has it that John wrote the book of Revelation, one of the four Gospels, and three epistles, but John was uncertain as to what people would be like in the eternal state. John writes: "...what we shall be *has not yet been disclosed,* but we know that when it is disclosed we shall be like Him (Jesus), because we shall see Him as He is" (1 John 3:2, N.E.B.). John follows the same example as the Psalmist who said: "I shall be satisfied, when I awake with *Thy likeness"* (Psalm 17:15b). John and the Psalmist were content to know that they would be *like Jesus* and that should satisfy everyone who names the name of Christ.

Chapter 4

Seed vs. Seeds?

Communication gaps or breakdowns in language are not peculiar to modern man. They have always existed and language barriers can sometimes be very costly. Frequently, they are the source of strife, division, wars, and can make the difference between life and death. The greatest danger in this lack of communication lies in the eternal realm — between man and God. The Babel experience is repeated in every generation, even among men with a common language.

Many language barriers arise out of the Scriptures, but most of them are self-imposed. It is not uncommon for men to "read into" the Scriptures, i.e., make them say something that is altogether foreign to their true meaning. When interpreting the Bible, men will "grab at straws" in order to make the Scriptures conform to their preconceived ideas. The Scriptures are to be studied very carefully — even the "corners of the field" are to be gleaned by someone. The voice of Jacob and the hand of Esau will become confused if our ears are dull and our eyes dim.

It may come as a surprise to some individuals to learn that the *singularity* or *plurality* of a word in the Scriptures can create a theological revolution. In making a distinction between Abraham's *seed* (singular) and *seeds* (plural), the Apostle Paul dropped a bombshell in the religious world of the Jewish people. In the book of Galatians, the Apostle points out a difference in Abraham's *seed* that many people will not acknowledge to this day (Jews and Christians). Paul declares that the promises made to Abraham were not to his "seeds," but to a single "seed," and that One Seed was Christ (Galatians 3:16).

There are some Bible scholars who feel that Paul is not being true to the Hebrew language when he makes a distinction between the singular "seed" and plural "seeds" in Galatians 3:16. They feel that the original promise was to Abraham's "seeds" rather than "seed." I must admit that I am unable academically to debate either side of the issue. However, it seems that Paul, living two thousand years nearer Abraham's day, and knowing the Hebrew language (and mind) much better than the present generation, would be in a position to speak with far more credibility than modern day Bible scholars.

This unique promise of the Father to Christ is possible because of Christ's singular relationship to the Father — also, because the Father has exalted Him above every other being and thing (Philippians 2:9-11). These facts are to be seen throughout the New Testament. The epistle to the Hebrews speaks of Him as the *First Begotten* of the Father (Hebrews 1:6; see also John 1:14, 18; 3:16; 18, Acts 13:33; 1 John 4:9). The book of Colossians says that He is the "Firstborn of every creature" (1:15). Romans 8:29 describes Jesus as the "Firstborn among many brethren." Three books of the New Testament declare Him to be the "Firstborn from the dead" (Colossians 1:18; Revelation 1:5; 1 Corinthians 15:23). The book of Revelation refers to Him as the "Alpha and Omega, the First and the Last" (Revelation 1:8, 17). Finally, Jesus is affirmed to be the "Heir of all things" (Hebrews 1:2). While Christ is the "Firstborn" and "Heir of all things," man is totally bankrupt. In the words of Paul, man brought *nothing* into this world and he can carry *nothing* out (1 Timothy 6:7). Some of the above ideas will be expanded later on in this chapter. They are mentioned at this point to show that Paul's thoughts in Galatians 3:16 do not violate the tenor of Scripture.

A serious problem had developed within the Galatian church since its founding by the Apostle Paul. The Judaizers of that day were enticing this body of believers away from the Gospel of Christ into "another gospel" (Galatians 1:6-7). The "other gospel" that was being imposed upon them was the law of Moses and other facets of Judaism. This was not a new religious problem — it was almost as old as the Jewish nation. Over the centuries it had taken on different shapes and forms, but essentially it was the same in every generation.

In dealing with the Galatian problem, Paul exposes a double error in traditional Judaism. The Judaizers were not only wrong in their understanding of the law of Moses — they were in error as to whom the promises of God were made. The Apostle contends that the law of Moses was totally unrelated to the promise made to Abraham. Unwittingly, the exponents of the law were trying to blend two irreconcilable forces (law and grace) into one. It was like trying to ride two horses running in opposite directions. The law was given for the benefit of *man* — to reveal sin; the promises were made to Christ. The law was given that the sinner might feel his sin and drive him to the Saviour. *This truth alone indicates that the promises were made to Christ rather than the Jews.* Any attempt to be justified and share in the promises of God by keeping the law was folly to the nth degree.

Like the prophets of old, the Apostle Paul uttered a truth that would make all Jewish ears tingle. With divine illumination and authority, he states that the natural descendants of Abraham have no part nor lot in the promises of God — all the promises are made to Christ:

> Now to Abraham and his seed were the promises made. He saith not, and to *seeds* (plural), as of many; but as of *one,* and to thy *seed* (singular), which is *Christ* (Galatians 3:16).

There is no indication that the above passage is an exact quote from the book of Genesis. It is perhaps a free translation of the promise made to Abraham in the Old Testament and Paul's special insight into the Gospel of Christ (Galatians 1:11-12). The Apostle implies that *there is no direct promise, with eternal significance, to the descendants of Abraham.* It is true that God's providential care extends to all men — even in their sins — and God makes the sun to shine upon the unjust as well as the just. But the eternal promises and blessings of God belong to Christ and to those who are justified by faith in Him.

C. I. Scofield, in his attempt to distinguish between the Christian church and the Jewish nation, says that the Christian does not inherit the "distinctive Jewish promises" (page 1204; note 2). The truth of the matter is, there are no "distinctive Jewish promises." All the promises belong to Christ. Paul's comments in Galatians 3:16 are supported by similar thoughts in his second letter to the Corinthians:

> For *all the promises of God in Him* (Christ) are yea, and in Him Amen, unto the glory of God by us (2 Corinthians 1:20).

Paul's remarks on the "seed" of Abraham are nestled in the midst of four outstanding Old and New Testament concepts. These ideas are: (1) Gospel; (2) promise(s); (3) covenant; and (4) inheritance. Although differing somewhat in nature, these words have emerged from a common heritage. The Galatian church must have understood these terms without difficulty. The Apostle seems to move very gracefully from one idea to the other, with little or no explanation.

These four terms have been the source of much controversy and confusion among both Jews and Christians. From the beginning of their history, the majority of the Jewish people understand the "promise" and "covenant" to be made with Abraham's natural descendants; others have repeated their mistake.

From these concepts, the premillennialists and other religious

groups have developed the most subtle and systematized doctrines that
the human mind can conceive. Like the Bereans, though by-passing
much of the truth, they "search the Scriptures daily," to discover some
novel interpretation that will enhance their scheme. The very terms that
are used to describe the riches of God's grace in Christ are applied to a
piece of real estate in the Middle East. In an insidious manner, the
glorious Gospel, the precious promises, the everlasting covenant, and
the incorruptible inheritance have been reduced to a dunghill that would
provoke a resounding "God forbid" from the Apostle Paul.

Let us examine these four terms as they relate to the "Seed" and
"seeds" of Abraham:

In the epistle to the Galatians, as elsewhere in Paul's letters,
Abraham was like a prism, creating a spectrum of theology that would
serve his purpose. Abraham was not as far removed from the New
Testament Christians as some would have us believe. The Galatians
were to embrace the same gospel and promise that Abraham believed—
no more and no less:

> And the Scripture, foreseeing that God would justify the heathen
> (Gentiles) through faith, *preached before the Gospel unto Abraham,*
> saying, in thee shall all the nations be blessed.
> So then, they which be of *faith are blessed with faithful Abraham*
> (Galatians 3:8-9).

In the Greek language, the words "Gospel" and "promise" have
basically the same meaning. Both are designed to herald the good news
of Christ. The "promise" was fulfilled in the "Gospel." *To depart from
the "Gospel," as the Galatians did, meant a departure from the
"promise" made to Abraham.* No wonder the apostle rebukes this
church so strongly:

> O foolish Galatians, who hath bewitched you, that *ye should not
> obey the truth,* before whose eyes Jesus Christ hath been evidently set
> forth, crucified among you? (Galatians 3:1).

But the Galatians, in trying to be justified, were going beyond
Abraham's example. They were incorporating religious practices that
were altogether foreign to Abraham's faith. With these supererogating
acts of the law, they were actually bringing themselves into bondage
again (Galatians 5:1ff). Abraham's hope rested upon a Seed from his
own loins, even Christ, whom the ages would reveal (John 8:56;
Matthew 1:1).

We discover also that the blessings promised through Abraham's Seed, and confirmed to the Galatians by the gift of the Holy Spirit (verse 14), are in the form of a "covenant." If the "promises" of God were made to Abraham's One Seed, which was Christ, then so was the "covenant" made with Him. The "covenant" is but the guarantee of the fulfillment of the "promise." The one complements the other. Notice the interchange and mutuality of these two terms (promise and covenant) and to *Whom* they apply, as we combine verses sixteen and seventeen:

> Now to Abraham and his seed were the *promises* made. He saith not, And to seeds, as of many; but as of one, and to thy seed, which is *Christ.*
> And the law which came four hundred and thirty years after the *Covenant,* and was confirmed by God *in Christ,* cannot disannul or make the *promise* of none effect. (Galatians 3:16-17).

There is not the slightest hint that the "promise" and "covenant" were made with Abraham's natural descendants. Charles H. Spurgeon, one of the greatest preachers of the Gospel since the days of the apostles, and the theme of whose ministry was ever the cross and blood of Jesus, contends that the New Testament covenant was made with Christ. In his message, "The Blood of the Testament," he states that the covenant was in the mind of God before the world was made round. Knowing in advance that man would sin,

> *A covenant therefore was arranged between the persons of the Trinity.* It was agreed and solemnly pledged by the oath of the eternal Father that He would give unto the Son a multitude whom no man could number who should be His, His spouse, the members of His mystical body, His sheep, His precious jewels ... To show you that salvation is not by human merit, God was pleased to cast it entirely upon *covenant arrangements. In that covenant, made between Himself and His Son, there was not a word said about our actions having any merit in them* ... Oh, what grace it was that put your name and mine in the eternal roll, and provided for our salvation, *provided for it by a covenant, by a sacred compact between the Father and His eternal Son,* that we should belong to Him in the day when He should make up His jewels!
> ...But there was needed a seal to the *covenant,* and what was that? Jesus Christ in the fulness of time set the *seal of the covenant,* to make it valid and secure, by pouring out all His life's blood to make the

covenant effectual once for all.[2] (Emphasis mine)

To deny that Christ fulfilled the covenant for both man and God is to write "Ichabod" across the Old and New Testaments. It is to count the *blood of the everlasting covenant* an unholy thing and do despite unto the *spirit of grace* (Hebrews 10:29). The doctrine of substitution for man's redemption permeates both testaments and its rejection would annul the cross of Jesus.

The covenant that was made with Christ and confirmed by His death and resurrection is rooted and grounded in the Old Testament Scriptures. It is interlocked with the "shadow ministries" of that period and with those who shared in them. Every animal that was sacrificed in the old dispensation and every drop of blood that was sprinkled on the mercy seat in the Holy of Holies *foreshadowed* the death and resurrection of Jesus. The law of Moses was to have been a "shadow of *good things to come,* and not the *very image*" (Hebrews 10:1). Jesus was the *"very image."*

Jesus was the "real Israel" that emerged from the "shadow Israel" of the Old Testament dispensation. All the "shadow ministries," such as prophet, priest, sacrifice, temple, judge, king, etc., had their fulfillment in Jesus. The "shadow ministries," which had their origin and perpetuity in the Word of God, became the Word Incarnate.

The "shadow ministries," which were nevertheless real, were to function and interact with each other in a harmonious manner and within their prescribed boundaries; all were meant to serve the best interest of the community of faith. Ideally, the "shadow image" of Jesus should have appeared in every age and generation of the Hebrew nation. Every Israelite that believed God's Word and found his niche in depicting the "shadow image" can be called the "true Israel" of God and an heir of eternal life.

When Jesus came in the flesh and completed His mission, all the "shadow ministries" ceased to function. Jesus took the "shadow Israel" unto Himself. He fulfilled both her role and His — the "shadow" and "substance" merged into one. Every faithful Israelite who projected the "shadow of *good things to come*" was borne in the body of Christ in His death and resurrection. Jesus died for the B.C. generations of people as well as the A.D. generations.

One of the most profound and revelatory statements that I have read

2. Spurgeon, Charles H., *The Treasury of the New Testament,* Vol. IV, 121.

in the past thirty-eight years, in connection with the theme of this work, is to be found in the words of Robert D. Brinsmead, Editor of the *Present Truth* magazine. The following quote is neither an endorsement nor a censure of this magazine; it is cited because of its spiritual depth. Mr. Brinsmead is writing on the subject: "Eschatology in the Light of the Gospel." This author says that Christ was ...

> ... the One in whom all Israel was represented ... He would not only be the One through whom God would fulfill all His promise to Israel, but *He would be the One through whom Israel could fulfill all her promises to God.*
>
> We will say this again: God had entered into a covenant with Israel —He had covenanted to do certain things for them. On the other hand, the people had entered into covenant contract with God — they promised to do certain things for Him. Now we must see that Christ was not only the means of God's fulfilling His Word to Israel; He was the means of Israel's fulfilling her contract to God.
>
> Standing as "a covenant of the people," Christ fulfilled the promise of the people. "All that the Lord hath spoken we will do." This obedient, suffering Servant stood before God as Israel, to do for Israel — in Israel's name and on Israel's behalf — that which Israel was utterly unable to do ...
>
> Thus, Christ is the Mediator of the covenant. Through Him and in Him Israel fulfilled all her promises to God. All this was completed by Christ's death on the cross. Also, through Him and in Him God fulfilled all His promises to Israel. All this was accomplished in Christ's resurrection from the dead ...
>
> Thus, Paul declares to the Corinthians, "... all the promises of God find their Yes in Him," 2 Corinthians 1:20, R.S.V. That is to say, when God raised Christ from the dead, He fulfilled not only His promise to Israel but every promise which He ever made to the human family since time began. In Christ He has blessed us with every conceivable blessing (Ephesians 1:3).
>
> Unless we can take out our pen and write "Fulfilled" across every one of the three thousand promises of the Old Testament, we deny "the finished work of Jesus Christ." [3]

Several sacrifices were made each year in the Levitical priesthood. But only *one* sacrifice was made by our Lord. The sins of the Old

3. *Present Truth,* Verdict Publishers, Fallbrook, Calif., 92028-0904, September, 1974, Vol. 3, No. 4, pp. 5, 6, 7.

Testament saints were included in this *one* sacrifice. If this fact is not true, argues the book of Hebrews, Jesus would have had to suffer many times, not just since New Testament days, but since the *foundation of the world* (Hebrews 9:26). That is to say, Jesus would have had to die in every generation of the Old Testament dispensation.

Jesus fulfilled both the "covenant of law" (old) and the "covenant of grace" (new). This was a feat that no Israelite could perform. Jesus did for man (in both dispensations) what man could not do for himself (Jew and Gentile). The inclusion of the Old Testament saints in the death of Jesus is irrefutable:

> And for this cause He is the mediator of the *new covenant,* that by means of death, for the *redemption of the transgressions that were under the first covenant,* they which are *called* might receive the *promise of eternal inheritance* (Hebrews 9:15).

The "called" in the above text includes both the Old and New Testament believers who responded to God's Word in faith. Jesus' death sufficed for the "sins of the whole world" (1 John 2:2), but faith was the sole means of its efficaciousness.

In connection with his usage of "covenant" and "promise," Paul introduces another term of the same quintessence. The word is "inheritance:"

> For if the *inheritance* be of the law it is no more of *promise:* but God gave it (inheritance) to Abraham by *promise.*
> Wherefore then serveth the law? It was added because of transgression till the *seed* (Christ) *should come to whom the promise was made:* and it was ordained by angels in the hand of a mediator (Galatians 3:18-19).

And what is the inheritance? It is all the blessings included in the "promise," sealed by the blood of the "covenant," and proclaimed in the "Gospel." It is all that the Father hath bequeathed to Christ and those who believe upon Him. We can be sure that Paul includes all believers in the "promise" and "inheritance" made to Christ because this is the conclusion to which he brings us in the last verse of Galatians three:

> And if ye be Christ's then are ye *Abraham's seed* and *heirs according to the promise* (verse 29).

Paul's allegory of Hagar and Sarah in Galatians four is a follow-through of his remarks on the "promises" made to Christ and His elect in Galatians 3:16. None of the terms under consideration, (Gospel, promise, covenant, and inheritance), are used in the allegory but they are implied. The allegory is applicable to both Jews and Gentiles. Ishmael is portrayed as being "born after the flesh," while Isaac is a "child of promise" — born of the *Word* and *Spirit*. It is only an allegory, but the lesson is quite clear. Only those who by faith in Christ — born of the Word and Spirit — are *heirs* of God:

> Now we, brethren, as Isaac was, are the *children of the promise* (or "Word of Promise").
> But as then he that was *born after the flesh* persecuted him that was *born after the spirit,* even so it is now.
> Nevertheless what saith the Scripture? Cast out the bondwoman and her son: for the son of the bondwoman *shall not be heir with the son of the freewoman.*
> So then, brethren, we are *not children of the bondwoman* (flesh), but of the *free* (Spirit and Word). (Galatians 4:28-31).

The truth taught in Paul's allegory is valid to this hour and will be throughout eternity. Jewish flesh and blood are unavailing with regard to the "promises," the "covenant," and "heirship" of God — *everything belongs to Jesus.*

The premillennialists probably wish that Paul had not written his allegory on Sarah and Hagar and their respective sons, Isaac and Ishmael. It puts a chill on their "literal" interpretation of the Genesis story. The futurists see the clash between Isaac and Ishmael through a different set of eyes. While not denying the spiritual aspects of Paul's allegory, they would outwit Paul's real objective. The millenarians see the current conflict in the Middle East between the Jews and Arabs as an extension of this struggle between Isaac's descendants and those of Ishmael. There is much to be said in favor of this view, but the embroilment between Isaac and Ishmael, as described in Paul's allegory, is very different from the strife that is going on in the Palestinian area at this hour.

The combatants in Paul's allegory are completely alien to the struggle in the Middle East. There *is* a warfare between the descendants of Isaac and Ishmael today, but it is not a "carnal" conflict. As pointed out earlier, there are two classes of people issuing from Abraham and Isaac — the "carnal" Jew and the "faithful" Jew. The faithful Jew is analogous with Paul's "children of the promise" and "he that is born of the Spirit" (verses 28-29).

According to Paul's allegory, Ishmael, who was "born after the flesh," is representative of *all men* who know only the natural birth (Jew and Gentile). Every unregenerate Jew and every unregenerate Arab, whether in the Palestinian area or elsewhere, are in the same category as Ishmael. Those who are born of God's Word and Spirit are not involved in the Middle East crisis per se. The warfare in the Middle East is Jewish "flesh" against Arab "flesh" — it is Jewish Zionism against displaced Arabs and their supporters. It is orthodox Judaism against the Muslim religion. Neither the Jews nor the Arabs in that region are concerned with "fighting the good fight of faith" (1 Timothy 6:12), or putting on the "whole armour of God," or having their "feet shod with the preparation of the Gospel of peace," or taking the "helmet of salvation, and the sword of the Spirit, which is the Word of God" (Ephesians 6:13-17). It is a carnal vendetta from the beginning to the end — even a false religious feud can be classified as "carnal." In the main, the Gospel of Jesus Christ is not a concern of either Jew or Arab. In fact, the Israeli government has passed laws in recent years banning all Christian proselytizing in the state of Israel.

If the Jews become the victors in the Middle East brawl, what will they have gained? If the Arabs become the victors, what will they have gained? *Whoever wins it today will die and leave it tomorrow.* The occupancy of Palestine has nothing to do with eternal, everlasting life, as offered through the Gospel of Christ. Where is the church's sense of theological values today? Should the church adopt a *Ji' had* (Moslem holy war) or *kamikaze* mentality with regard to the Jews' possession of the Holy Land? Is the clash in the Land of Palestine today any different from the juggernaut, militant crusades of several centuries ago (1100-1300 a.d.)? We are forced to believe that the premillennialists live on the very edge of such a postulation. Why must we go over the same ground century after century? The New Testament should have ended the Palestinian obsession two thousand years ago, but we keep returning to square one. Will we leave the door open for future generations to mock our idiocy? Syncretizing the Land of Canaan with the Gospel of Christ leads only to embarrassment and confusion.

To take the terms "promise," "Gospel," "covenant," and "inheritance" and apply them to the natural descendants of Abraham and the Land of Palestine, as the premillennialists do, is a theological blunder of the highest magnitude. These concepts are the ultimate expression of God's love for fallen man (Jew and Gentile). They are the very essence of God's nature and character. They are the summation of God's plan for His Beloved Son and those who believe upon Him. And to twist, distort, and pervert the most significant truths in the Scriptures is to pour contempt upon the wisdom and power of God (1 Corinthians 1:18-31).

Properly speaking, there are only two representative men in the Scriptures: (1) the First Adam; and (2) the Second Adam or Christ. The first Adam lost everything in his disobedience — the Second Adam gained everything in His obedience (Romans 5:19). It would be necessary to create a *third representative man* if the Jews are going to claim anything apart from Christ. The premillennialists practically create a "third representative" in their zeal to promote futuristic doctrine. There is but One Seed issuing from Abraham to whom the promises are made. All others (Jews and Gentiles) share in these promises by faith. Jesus is a composite of all the aforementioned terms:

Jesus is the *Gospel* — the *Good News*
Jesus is the *Promisee* and the *Promisor*
Jesus is the *Covenantee* and the *Covenantor*
Jesus is *Heir of all things*

The controversy over the "promises" of God is beset by a long history. Premillennialism is just another subtle attack upon the entitlements of Christ. *"Heirship" comes first and foremost through "Sonship."* Jesus is the One significant Seed descending from Abraham and the One significant Seed coming from God. He is both the Son of Abraham and the Son of God — the God-Man. No other individual can make this claim. Jesus is the only one of His kind — He is in a class by Himself. He is the Son of Abraham "according to the flesh" and the Son of God "according to the spirit of holiness, by the resurrection of the dead" (Romans 1:1-4). The designation "the Only Begotten of the Father" belongs exclusively to Jesus.

In the beginning of Matthew's Gospel we are given a list of "seeds" coming from the loins of Abraham — including Jesus. But before a single seed is mentioned we are given an abridgment of Jesus' genealogy:

> The book of the generations of Jesus Christ, the son of David, *the son of Abraham* (Matthew 1:1).

It is very obvious that there is only one seed between Jesus and Abraham — David. David's name is mentioned to epitomize Jesus' fleshly nature and to touch base with the royal line through which He would come. Without doing harm to the Scripture we could omit David's name and the above passage would read thus:

The book of the generations of Jesus Christ ... the son of Abraham.

Jesus was the One august Son issuing from Abraham. The Jewish people have *nothing to claim by reason of their natural birth.* All the promises of God were made to Abraham's One Son who was *the Christ.*

The Lord went to great lengths to make His kinship with Jesus known. Neither before nor after the days of Jesus' flesh was the Voice of God heard speaking from heaven. The voice came on three different occasions; but only twice was it understood by those who heard it. The two messages were brief and to the point. They dealt solely with Jesus' "Sonship."

When Jesus was baptized by John the Baptist, the Spirit of God descended upon Him in the form of a dove,

And lo a *voice* from heaven, saying *This is My beloved Son,* in whom I am well pleased (Matthew 3:17).

Why this voice from heaven? The audibility of God's voice was to identify the "Sonship" of Jesus with the Father. Jesus' relationship to the Father must be seen as superior to all who had gone before Him. Even the unusual birth and ministry of John the Baptist must not rival that of Jesus.

The populace of John's day esteemed the Baptist very highly — and rightly so. He was regarded as a prophet of God, but in the words of Jesus, he was "more than a prophet," — John was the fulfillment of prophecy (Matthew 11:10). Jesus described him as the greatest man born of woman (Matthew 11:11). He was given the singular role of preparing the way for Jesus' mission. But John's relationship to the Father can never compare with that of Jesus. The seer was *a* "voice" *for* God "crying in the wilderness," but Jesus was *the* Voice of God. John and all the prophets that preceded him were only "servants" of God — Jesus was the "beloved Son of God."

The transfiguration of Jesus was meant to teach the same lesson. Peter, James, and John were chosen to accompany Jesus into a certain mountain. After arriving at their appointed place, Jesus was transfigured before their very eyes. His face shone with the brightness of the sun and His clothes became as white as light. While Jesus was in this fashion, Moses and Elijah appeared on the scene. A bright cloud overshadowed the group. Peter was overjoyed. While Peter spoke of plans to build three tabernacles he was interrupted by a Voice from heaven:

> While ye yet spake, behold, a bright cloud overshadowed them: and behold a *voice out of the cloud,* which said, This is *My beloved Son,* in whom I am well pleased; *Hear ye Him* (Matthew 17:5).

Moses and Elijah were two of the most prominent figures in the Old Testament. Moses represented the "law" and Elijah represented the "prophets" of that period. These key disciples must learn that the "Son" (along with the things He taught) was the ultimate revelation of God to the world. His "Sonship" gave Him a credibility with the Father that neither Moses nor the prophets could claim. It is this unique relationship that qualifies Him to be "heir of all things."

Jesus' Sonship and Heirship (along with His Kingship and Priesthood) are beautifully combined in the book of Hebrews. The author introduces this epistle by showing the superiority of Jesus over prophets, angels, Moses, and all other beings — earthly and heavenly — mystical and otherwise — past, present, and future. Everything that needs to be written on Jesus' Sonship is summed up in the first chapter of this epistle. All that God has done in the past and all that He will do in the future are briefly condensed in this one text — all of which has its beginning and ending in God's One Son, the Lord Jesus Christ. *Jesus' Sonship is the basis for all the claims made for Him by the writer of the Hebrews epistle.* The reader cannot afford to overlook this crucial passage of Scripture:

> God, who at sundry times and divers manners spake in time past unto the fathers by the prophets,
> Hath in these last days spoken unto us by *His Son, whom He hath appointed heir of all things, by whom also He made the worlds:*
> Who (Son) being the brightness of His glory, and the express image of His person, and upholding all things by the word of His power, when He had by Himself purged our sins, *sat down on the right hand of the majesty on high:*
> Being made so much better than the angels, as He *hath by inheritance obtained a more excellent name than they* (and that name is "Son").
> For unto which of the angels said He at any time *Thou art my son, this day have I begotten thee?* And again, *I will be to him a father, and he shall be to me a son?*

And again, when He bringeth in the *firstborn* (Son) into the world, He saith, And let all the angels of God worship Him.

And of the angels He saith, *Thy throne, O God is forever and ever: A scepter of righteousness is the scepter of Thy Kingdom* (Hebrews 1:1-8).

The book of Colossians uses language very similar to that of the epistle to the Hebrews. Paul begins his greetings in this letter by speaking of the relationship of all believers to God the Father and the Lord Jesus Christ:

"...Grace be unto you, and peace, from God *our Father* and the Lord Jesus Christ"(1:2).

God is the Father of all believers. In the next verse the generalities are dropped and God is specified as the "Father of our Lord Jesus Christ" (verse 3). In the eyes of the Jews, even this statement on the "Fatherhood" of God would not be unique — all devout Jews claimed God as their Father (John 8:41). The kinship of Christ to the Father is not left in limbo — Christ is "God's dear Son" to whom the Kingdom is given (verse 13). The Apostle does not stop with the affectionate title, "God's dear Son" — Christ is the very image of God, the firstborn of every creature, the *source,* and *sustainer* of *all things:*

Who (Christ) is the *image of the invisible God,* the *firstborn of every creature:*

For by Him were all things created, that are in Heaven, and that are in earth, visible and invisible, whether they be *thrones,* or *dominions,* or *principalities,* or *powers: All things were created by Him and for Him:*

And He is before all things, and by Him all things consist (Colossians 1:15-17).

The Apostle Paul wishes to impress upon the Colossians the truth that *all things* (including the Kingdom of God) belong to Christ because of His "Sonship" with the Father.

We learn from Paul's letter to the Romans that proper views on the *created order* are a prerequisite to spiritual insight and knowledge of God. Improper views on the creation lead to all kinds of sin and wickedness: a denial of the Godhead, vain imaginations, and glory, which belongs only to God, being given to man, birds, beasts, etc. The evil results are limitless. Study carefully Paul's remarks in Romans

1:20-32 and let him that readeth take heed. The natural descendants of Abraham are not entitled to anything — all things belong to Christ.

From the Colossian letter, we learn that Jesus is given the "rights of the *Firstborn*" which no other person or persons can claim. This, too, confirms Paul's statement concerning Abraham's "Seed" and "seeds." All the promises of God are made directly to Christ, God's *Firstborn,* and not to Abraham's carnal offspring. All of the Jewish people, past, present and future, if they are to share in the promises of God, must come by faith in God's "only begotten Son" — God's *Firstborn.*

The magnitude of Jesus' Sonship and Heirship can also be seen from His enemy's vantage point. In any kind of battle or conflict, the enemy strikes at his opponent's greatest stronghold. This fact is no less true in the spiritual realm. Jesus' Sonship was His greatest stronghold and it was contested by His adversaries more than any other aspect of His life and ministry.

Satan's first assault, according to the Gospels, centered around Jesus' Sonship. After Jesus' baptism and anointing of the Holy Spirit, He was led into the wilderness to be tempted by the Devil. "If thou be the Son of God, etc." was Satan's first statement to Jesus. The last statement made to Jesus by His enemies, as He hung on the cross, was of the same nature: "If thou be the Son of God, come down from the cross" (Matthew 27:40).

When Jesus healed a blind man, as recorded in the fifth chapter of John's Gospel, He was apprehended by certain Jews and accused of working on the Sabbath. Jesus replied: "My Father worketh hitherto, and I work" (John 5:17). Those who heard Jesus' statement fully understood what He meant. He was declaring His equality with the Father.

The Jews were already seeking His life because He had violated the Sabbath, but His claim of being God's Son intensified their thirst for His blood:

> Therefore the Jews *sought the more to kill Him* because He had not only broken the Sabbath, but said also that *God was His Father, making Himself equal with God* (John 5:18).

Jesus' Sonship was the central issue in His trial before Caiaphas, the high priest. Caiaphas used his office and authority as high priest to force Jesus into an open confession of His Sonship. This confession resulted in the death sentence:

...I adjure thee (command thee) by the living God, that thou *tell us whether thou be the Christ, the Son of God.*

Jesus saith unto him, Thou hast said: Nevertheless I say unto you, hereafter shall ye see the Son of man sitting on the right hand of power, and coming in the clouds of heaven.

The high priest rent his clothes, saying *He hath spoken blasphemy.* What think ye? They answered and said, *He is guilty of death* (Matthew 26:63-66).

From the beginning of Jesus' career to the end, man and Satan used His Sonship as a lever to intimidate Him, to sway public opinion, and eventually to secure His death. An attack upon His Sonship is an attack upon His Heirship.

In the parable of the "wicked husbandman," Jesus gives a cosmic view of the conflict between the powers of darkness and the kingdom of light. The power struggle centers around Jesus' Sonship and Heirship.

Jesus tells a story of a certain man who planted a vineyard. The owner of the vineyard goes into a far country and leaves the vineyard in the care of husbandmen. When the time came to reap the harvest the owner of the vineyard sent his servant to receive the fruit. But the husbandmen "beat him and sent him away empty." A third servant was sent and they "wounded him and cast him out." Finally, the owner of the vineyard said: "I will send my *beloved Son:* it may be they will reverence him when they see him." But the husbandmen collaborated together and said: *"This is the heir:* come, let us *kill him,* that the *inheritance may be ours.* So they cast him out of the vineyard, and *killed him"* (Luke 20:14b-15a).

The parable of the "wicked husbandmen" is quite simple: the owner of the vineyard is God; the servants sent to the husbandmen represent the prophets of the Old Testament period. Jesus is the "beloved Son" (Mark's Gospel says "one Son") and also the "Heir." The husbandmen, of course, represent the Jewish people of both the Old and New Testament eras who fulfilled the parable to the letter.

There is not a single clue in the above parable that would involve the natural descendants of Abraham in the inheritance. The entire conflict centers around One Heir and that Heir is Christ.

Heirship and Sonship go hand in hand. There is not a single descendant of Abraham who can claim a Sonship with God that parallels that of Jesus. Furthermore, no Jew would have the audacity to make such an assertion. Their own testimony confirms this fact. The Jews expected the Messiah to be the "Son of the Blessed" (Mark 14:61) or the Son of God, and a false claim to this unique role was blasphemy and punishable by death. They loved their lives too much. If a single Jew was able to claim a relationship to God, comparable to that of Christ, then all Jews would be able to make the same claim. Since the unbelieving Jew is not a son of God, he cannot be an heir of God. Jesus is the sole Heir and all others (Jew and Gentile) become heirs through faith in Him:

> But the scripture hath concluded *all under sin,* that the *promise by faith* of Jesus Christ might be given to them that *believe...*
> And if ye be Christ's, then are ye *Abraham's seed,* and *heirs* according to the *promise* (Galatians 3:22, 29).

How amazing it is to find so many words in the Scriptures that mean practically the same thing — such as promise, blessing, covenant, Gospel, inheritance, etc. But what's more amazing, in the New Testament, the "Land of Canaan" is never mentioned in conjunction with them. Every one of them are consummated in a *person,* namely, the *Lord Jesus Christ;* and why shouldn't they culminate in Him? He is the Eternal *Word* — all divine words begin and end with Him. He is the *Alpha* and *Omega.* The Apostle Paul writes: "...ye are *complete in Him*" (Colossians 2:10a). The person who is in Christ shares in all of the above concepts and more.

Chapter 5

Corruptible Seed Vs. Incorruptible Seed

The old adage "like begets like" is not only true of man and nature, it is also true of God. In the Old Testament, the Hebrew idiom, to be a "son of" (child of) meant to share the nature of one's father — this is an unchangeable truth. God's children should bear His image or likeness. In the Scriptures, God is portrayed as a "Father" and as "begetting children." John writes:

> But as many as received Him, to them gave He power to become the *sons of God,* even to them that believe on His name.
> Which were *born,* not of blood, nor of the will of the flesh, nor of the will of man, *but of God* (John 1:12-13).

The phrase "were born" in verse thirteen can also mean "begotten." The Greek word used for this phrase literally means: "to beget, *of the father;* to bring forth, *of the mother.*"[1] This Greek Word is used to distinguish between the procreation of the father and the birth process of the mother. In other words, God's children are begotten by Him and not by the "will of the flesh, nor the will of man."

If men are *born of God* and are *sons of God,* then they must bear His nature or likeness. Every Bible student should be familiar with most of the attributes or nature of God. God is described in such terms as love, light, life, holy, eternal, power, righteous, wisdom, grace, peace, etc. These are some of the more common terms that express the nature of God. Whatever else God's nature may consist of, there are two concepts in the Scripture that sum up all of His attributes in a nutshell. They are: (1) the *Word of God,* and (2) the *Spirit of God.*

In the prologue of John's Gospel, we are told that God is synonymous with His *Word.* John is very careful to link the two together: "In the beginning was the *Word,* and the *Word* was with *God,* and the *Word* was God. The *same* was in the beginning with *God*" (John 1:1-2).

Let us not tamper with John's unadorned statement on the "Word." There is no way of explaining all the mysteries in the first verse of John's

---

1. Bullinger, Ethelbert W., *A Critical Lexicon and Concordance to the English and Greek New Testament,* Zondervan Publishing House, 1975, 109.

Gospel. His thoughts are in perfect harmony with all that is said elsewhere in the Scriptures relative to the "Word." The profundity of the Scriptures are oftentimes found in their simplicity. John simply says "...and the *Word was God."*

Not only is God *Word,* He is also *Spirit.* In Jesus' conversation with the Samaritan woman, on the subject of worship, He declares that ... "God is *Spirit,* and they that worship Him must worship Him in *Spirit* and in *truth"* (John 4:24).

Jesus could just as well have said that "men must worship God in *Spirit* and in *Word."* In the Scriptures "truth" is always synonymous with "Word." In Jesus' intercessory prayer for His disciples, He uses the two terms interchangeably. Uppermost in His mind was the disciples' oneness with the Father and Himself; therefore He prayed, "Sanctify them through thy *truth:* thy *Word* is *truth"* (John 17:17). The New Testament epistles leave no doubt about the synonymity of these two terms. The following passages of Scripture will show conclusively that "truth" and "Word" are one and the same thing: Ephesians 1:13; Colossians 1:5; James 1:18; 1 Thessalonians 2:13; 2 Timothy 2:15; 2 Corinthians 6:7.

When the Apostle Paul stresses the importance of the "Word" and "Spirit" in the worship of the believer, it is a reverberation of the words of Jesus to the Samaritan woman:

> Let the *Word* of Christ dwell in you *richly* in all wisdom; teaching and admonishing one another in *Psalms* and *hymns* and *Spiritual songs, singing* with grace in your hearts to the Lord (Colossians 3:16).

Corresponding results will follow when the believer is "filled with the *Spirit* of God:"

> And be not drunk with wine, wherein is excess; but be *filled with the Spirit:*
> Speaking to yourselves in *Psalms* and *hymns* and *Spiritual songs, singing and making melody* in your hearts to the Lord (Ephesians 5:18-19).

A copiousness of the "Word" and "Spirit" produce a worshipful experience for the believer.

The essence of God's nature is *Word* and *Spirit.* This is further shown in the birth of Jesus. Jesus was God Incarnate. "The *Word* was *God* ... and the *Word became flesh* and dwelt among us, etc." (John 1:14). Jesus was conceived by the Holy Spirit and the Spirit of God was given to Him "without measure." The Word spoken to the serpent in Genesis 3:15, the *Word* (or Promise) spoken to Abraham, and the *Word* uttered by the prophets in the Old Testament crystallized in the birth of Jesus. Jesus was the "brightness of His (God's) glory, and the express *image of His person* (Hebrews 1:3). *Word* and *Spirit* are not airy notions or abstract ideas when seen in relationship to the Incarnation. Paul affirms that in Him "dwelleth all the fulness of the Godhead bodily" (Colossians 2:9).

If we look again at the aforementioned attributes of God, i.e., love, light, life, power, wisdom, grace, etc., we will find the same attributes used in conjunction with His Word and Spirit. Acts 20:32 speaks of the *Word of His grace*. Hebrews 5:13 the *Word of righteousness*. Hebrews 4:12 describes the *Word* as *quick* (alive) and *powerful* ... and a *discerner* of thoughts. Philippians 2:16 speaks of holding forth the *Word of life*. Psalm 119:105 says Thy *Word* is a *lamp* ... and a *light*. Hebrews 11:3 states that the worlds were *framed* by the *Word* of *God*. Psalm 19:8 describes the *Word* as *rejoicing the heart* and *enlightening the eyes*. Romans 1:16 says that the Gospel (Word) is the *power* of God unto salvation. In Ephesians 5:25-26 the *Word* is said to *sanctify*, *cleanse* and *wash*, etc.

The above attributes of God are equally seen in the ministry of the *Spirit*. Hebrews 10:29 speaks of the *Spirit of grace*. Hebrews 9:14 reveals that Jesus offered Himself through the *eternal Spirit*. Jesus stated in Acts 1:8 that *Power* would attend the gift of the *Holy Spirit*. Romans 14:17 describes the kingdom of God in terms of *righteousness*, *peace*, and *joy* in the *Holy Ghost*. According to 1 Corinthians 6:11, the Holy Spirit effects *washing*, *sanctification*, and *justification*. The fruit of the *Spirit* is *love, joy, peace, longsuffering, gentleness, goodness*, etc. In the words of Paul, the *love of God* is synonymous with the *Holy Spirit (Romans 5:5)*. The *Spirit of God* was active in the creation as it moved upon the face of the waters (Genesis 1:2), etc.

The Scripture passages just quoted are only a few which show that every attribute of God can be summed up in His Word and His Spirit. If the essence of God's nature is Word and Spirit, then His children must be partakers of the same — and they are.

In the natural order, children are conceived by seed — by sperm. Medical science says that the woman has no seed. Seeds come from the male only. The noun form of the Greek word for "seed" is *sporos* which conveys the idea of extending. Children (or seed) are an extension of their parents. God's children are an extension of Himself. Our English word "sperm" has its roots in the above Greek word. God's Word is a seed (sperm) by which He begets children. This truth is expressed very clearly in Peter's first epistle:

> Seeing ye have purified your souls in obeying the truth *(Word)* through the *Spirit* unto unfeigned love of the brethren, see that ye love one another with a pure heart fervently:
>
> Being *born again,* not of corruptible seed *(spora),* but of *incorruptible* (seed or spora implied), by the *Word of God* which liveth and abideth for ever.
>
> For all flesh is as grass, and all the glory of man as the flower of the grass. The grass withereth, and the flower thereof falleth away:
>
> But the *Word* of the Lord endureth forever. And this is the *Word* which by the Gospel is preached unto you (1 Peter 1:22-25).

According to Peter, God's children are born of an eternal, indestructible, incorruptible seed *(sporos)* which is the Word of God. In obedience to the "truth *(Word)* through the *Spirit* they were born again." There is no way that the natural seed of Abraham per se can be the children of God. The incorruptible seed comes from God the Father and it alone has everlasting significance.

Parallels in nature have always served as a means of communicating divine truth. The same terminology that is used for the birth of a child in nature is used for the birth of a child of God — but they are poles apart. In the natural order, "flesh begets flesh," but in the divine order, "Word begets Word." There are no hybrids in God's family. Notice the language used in James' epistle:

> Of His own (God's) will begat (conceived) He us with the Word of truth, that we should be a kind of firstfruits of His creatures ...
>
> *Wherefore lay apart all filthiness and superfluity of naughtiness, and receive with meekness the engrafted (implanted) Word, which is able to save your souls (James 1:18, 21).*

We find very similar language in John's first epistle:

> *Whosoever believeth that Jesus is the Christ is born of God (since God is Word then men are born of His Word); and every one that loveth Him that begat (conceived) loveth Him also that is begotten of Him (1 John 5:1).*

The classic Scripture that has echoed this truth across the centuries is to be found in Jesus' conversation with Nicodemus. Jesus seems to show an element of surprise that Nicodemus, a teacher in Israel, did not know about being born again. When Nicodemus came to Jesus at night asking certain questions about His person and ministry, Jesus replied:

> Verily, verily, I say unto thee, Except a man be *born again,* he cannot see the Kingdom of God.
>
> Nicodemus saith unto Him, How can a man be born when he is old? Can he enter the second time into his mother's womb, and be born? Jesus answered, Verily, verily, I say unto thee, except a man be born of water and of the *Spirit,* he cannot enter into the Kingdom of God.
>
> That which is *born of the flesh, is flesh,* and that which is *born of the Spirit is Spirit.*
>
> Marvel not that I said unto thee, *Ye must be born again* (John 3:3-7).

The word "again" as used in the King James Version can be translated "from above." Thus it would read, "Except a man be *born from above,* he cannot see the Kingdom of God."

One of the first (if not *the* first) parables that Jesus taught was that of the "sower and the seed." It is no coincidence that it was given in the early dawn of His ministry. Of course, the "seed" in the parable is the "Word of God." If men were to understand the other parables that He taught, or even other portions of Scripture, they must understand this one: "... know ye not this parable? and how then will ye know (or understand) all parables?" (Mark 4:13).

The lesson in the parable of the "sower and the seed" should not be missed by anyone. To receive God's Word and to be born of God's Word is a prerequisite to knowing and understanding God's Word. Flesh understands flesh — Word understands Word. If man is to be a part of God's family, he must become a partaker of His divine nature through His *Word* and *Spirit.* This is the *only* way he can know the things of God. The same lesson is taught again by Jesus in John 8:43. Some of the Jews were having difficulty in understanding His speech. His reply was: "Why do ye not understand my speech? even *because ye cannot hear My Word.*"

The parable of the "sower and the seed" also teaches that not everyone who hears the Word of God will receive it. Some of the seed fell on unproductive soil, but it was no fault of the seed — it was the unsuitable ground. Only those who *receive the Word* and are *born of the incorruptible seed* can be the children of God or the true Israel of God: "And these are they which are sown on good ground; such as *hear the Word, and receive it, and bring forth fruit,* some thirtyfold, some sixty, and some an hundred" (Mark 4:20).

God's nature, which is Word and Spirit, is reproduced in His children. The seed (or Word), which can come only from the Father, is the source of His image or likeness.

❊❊❊

The Word and Spirit come into prominence in the book of Acts. It has been suggested that the book of Acts be called "The Acts of the Holy Spirit." I would like to offer a better title than this: "The Acts of the Holy Spirit and the Word." There is a very conspicuous balance of Word and Spirit to be found in the book of Acts. Luke, who wrote the book of Acts, which is a sequel to his own Gospel, states that he, along with the other disciples, were "eyewitnesses and *ministers of the Word*" (Luke 1:2). Repentance and regeneration, which are the mutual work of the Word and Spirit and the cornerstone for those who are in Christ, can be seen throughout this remarkable book.

The book of Acts opens like a burst of volcanic lava. The "grain of wheat" that fell into the ground (John 12:24) began to grow in Jerusalem. The resurrection of Jesus and the coming of the Holy Spirit on the day of Pentecost disrupted the religious climate of that day. Judaism was being threatened by the Apostles — new and strange doctrines were being taught — signs and wonders were wrought at the hands of the Apostles — multitudes of sick people were healed — converts by the thousands were being added to the new faith — religious pandemonium was breaking out all over Jerusalem.

The high priest and his cohorts became very indignant and had the Apostles put in prison. The Word of the Lord must not become stagnant. An angel of the Lord opened the prison door and brought the Apostles forth with this admonition: "Go, stand and speak in the temple to the people all the *words of this life*" (Acts 5:20).

This they did, but the persecution intensified. Stephen was stoned to death and it was only a matter of time until many of the disciples ... "were scattered abroad (and) went every where preaching the *Word*" (Acts 8:4).

Alongside the persecution were new problems within the church. Dissension arose between the Hebrew and Grecian widows over the daily distribution of food. The Apostles agreed that their labors should not be jeopardized by such matters. New structures within the church must be made in order to correct the situation. The twelve called the multitude of believers together and said:

> ... It is not reason that we should leave the *Word* of God, and serve tables.
>
> Wherefore, brethren, look ye out among you seven men of honest report, full of the Holy Ghost and wisdom, whom we may appoint over this business.
>
> But we will give ourselves continually to prayer, and to the ministry of the *Word* (Acts 6:2b-4).

The Apostles knew that the church could never increase and grow apart from the Word of God. In the book of Acts, the "growth of the church" is equated with the "growth of the Word." Notice the following references:

> And the *Word* of God *increased:* and the number of the *disciples,* etc. (Acts 6:7).
>
> But the *Word* of God *grew* and *multiplied,* etc. (Acts 12:24).
>
> So mightily *grew* the *Word* of God and *prevailed* (Acts 19:20).

The Word did not operate in a vacuum. This combination of the Word and Spirit is to be seen throughout the book of Acts. In Peter's Pentecostal sermon (Acts 2), he promised the gift of the Holy Ghost to those who would repent and be baptized. The overwhelming response to this promise is found in verse forty-one: "Then they that gladly received his *Word* were baptized: and the same day there were added unto them about three thousand souls."

It is implied (Acts 2:38) that the Pentecostal converts received both the Word of God and the Spirit of God as a result of their repentance and faith.

A taste of the Pentecostal experience made a deep impression upon the Apostles. The tempest of persecution was set in motion. A holy boldness was needed to counteract the adversary. The Word alone was not enough for the task they faced. When they had prayed "... the place was shaken where they were assembled together; and they were all *filled with the Holy Ghost,* and they spake the *Word of God* with boldness" (Acts 4:31).

The Apostolic preaching was always characterized by the combined ministry of the Word and Spirit. When Philip preached the Gospel in Samaria, news came back to the Apostles in Jerusalem,

> ...that Samaria had received the *Word* of God, (and) they sent unto them Peter and John:
>
> Who when they were come down, prayed for them, that they might receive the *Holy Ghost:* (Acts 8:14-15).

The conversion of Cornelius, under the preaching of Peter, is a remarkable illustration of the Word and Spirit at work in man's redemption. After Peter arrived at the house of Cornelius, he immediately began to tell him what he must do to be saved:

> Then Peter opened his mouth, and said, Of a truth I perceive that God is no respecter of persons:
>
> But in every nation he that feareth Him, and worketh righteousness, is accepted with Him.
>
> The *Word* which God sent unto the children of Israel, preaching peace by Jesus Christ: (He is Lord of all):
>
> That *Word,* I say, ye know, which was published throughout all Judaea, and began from Galilee, after the baptism which John preached;
>
> How God anointed Jesus of Nazareth with the *Holy Ghost* and with *power,* who went about doing good, and healing all that were oppressed of the devil; for God was with him ...
>
> While Peter yet spake these words (about Jesus and His death), the *Holy Ghost* fell on all them which heard the *Word,* etc. (Acts 10:34-38; 44).

One of the most significant events in the book of Acts for the church, apart from the day of Pentecost, is the Jerusalem Council as recorded in chapter fifteen. This meeting of Apostles and elders settled forever the dispute about circumcision and other facets of the Mosaic law. In a few words Peter sets the record straight as to what is required of both Jew and Gentile in matters of redemption. After some disputation in the council, Peter stood up and said:

> ...Men and brethren, ye know how that a good while ago God made choice among us, that the Gentiles by my mouth should hear the *Word* of the Gospel, and believe.
>
> And God, which knoweth the hearts, bare them witness, giving them the *Holy Ghost,* even as He did unto us;
>
> And put no difference between us (Jews) and them (Gentiles), purifying their hearts by faith (Acts 15:7-9).

The book of Acts does not stand alone in this association of Word and Spirit effecting man's redemption. Even a casual study of Paul's church letters will reveal a very marked pattern of this combination. He begins his epistle to the Ephesian church by reminding them of the wonderful things that God has predestined for His elect in Christ. Their reception of the Gospel was only the beginning of a glorious, heavenly inheritance. In fact, the Holy Spirit, which they received upon conversion, was the "earnest" (or guarantee) of this inheritance:

> In whom (Christ) ye also trusted, after that ye heard the *Word* of truth, the Gospel of your salvation: in whom also after that ye believed, ye were sealed with that *Holy Spirit* of promise,
> Which is the earnest of our inheritance until the redemption of the purchased possession, unto the praise of His glory (Ephesians 1:13-14).

The above passage describes the groundwork of the Ephesian believers. They heard the Word of truth and were sealed with the Holy Spirit of promise. A similar pattern is to be found in Paul's letter to the Colossians. The Apostle could not claim responsibility for the believers at Colossae. His knowledge of these people came to him through Epaphras, a fellow laborer. One of the most glorious things that the Gospel brought to the Colossians was a "hope laid up in heaven." This "heavenly hope" came to them through hearing the Word of the Gospel. In the following passage we see both the Word and Spirit producing the fruits of the Gospel in the lives of the Colossians. Paul was thankful for their faith and,

> For the hope which is laid up for you in heaven, whereof ye heard before in the *Word* of the truth of the Gospel:
> Which is come unto you as it is in all the world; and bringeth forth fruit, as it doth also in you, since the day ye heard of it, and knew the grace of God in truth:
> As ye also learned of Epaphras our dear fellow servant, who is a faithful minister of Christ;
> Who also declared unto us your love in the *Spirit* (Colossians 1:5-8).

We cannot condone the sins of men but we can be thankful for some of the personal problems arising out of the labours of the Apostles. These problems have provided us with a good deal of insight into the role of the Word of God and the Spirit of God in the apostolic ministries. The Corinthian church was perhaps the most problematic of all the

New Testament churches. Some of the members of this church, more than any other body of believers, questioned the character and motives of the Apostle Paul. One of the false charges brought against him was the deceitfulness with which he handled the Word of God — or as the King James Version puts it "corrupted the Word of God" (2 Corinthians 2:17). But the Apostle, as proof of his sincerity in ministering the Word, appeals to the Corinthians themselves. If a "letter of commendation" was needed to vindicate his reputation as a minister of the Gospel, they were that "letter" — they were his credentials. The "change" that had come about in their lives was a witness to the authenticity of his apostleship. The preaching of the Word by the Apostle was translated into "living epistles" for the Corinthians:

> For as much as ye are manifestly declared to be the epistles (Words) of Christ ministered by us, written not in ink, but with the Spirit of the living God; not in tables of stone, but in the fleshly tables of the heart (2 Corinthians 3:3).

Paul's ministry among the Corinthians was quite different from that of his counterparts, i.e., the advocates of the Mosaic law. The law of Moses, which the Judaizers promulgated, was external — "written on tables of stone." The Corinthian church reflected the Gospel or Word of Christ "written in fleshly tables of the heart" by the Spirit of God. In the words of the Apostle, they became "living epistles" (Words) known and read of all men.

Perhaps the best illustration of the Word and Spirit working jointly to effect man's salvation is found in Paul's first epistle to the Thessalonians. In this letter Paul tells how the Gospel was delivered to these people and their response to it. The Gospel was *received* in the same manner it was *delivered*. Notice first how Paul proclaimed the Gospel to them:

> For our Gospel came not unto you in *word* only, but also in *power,* and in the *Holy Ghost,* and in much assurance; as ye know what manner of men we were among you for your sake (1 Thessalonians 1:5).

In the next verse, Paul says that the Thessalonians, "received the *Word* in much affliction, with *joy* of the *Holy Ghost.*"

It seems that Paul took great delight in rehearsing the reception of the Gospel among his converts. This is a pattern that is to be found in almost all of his epistles. We find him recounting the initial experience of the Thessalonians in his second epistle.

After Paul's departure from Thessalonica, there developed, among his converts, some misgivings concerning the Second Coming of Christ. There were some within the church who were expecting the parousia within their life time. Paul informed them that certain events must precede the return of Christ. In spite of their shortcomings, the Apostle had great confidence in them because of the Word and Spirit in their lives:

> But we are bound to give thanks always to God for you, brethren beloved of the Lord, because God hath from the beginning chosen you to salvation through sanctification of the *Spirit* and belief of the *truth* (or Word) (2 Thessalonians 2:13).

One of the most important roles of the Holy Spirit is to seal and confirm the Word of God to those who repent and believe in Christ. For this reason, Paul was very protective of the Word. In fact, his concern for its pristine purity had cost him a good deal of suffering. Paul's second letter to Timothy is written in this context. This young minister of the Gospel must imitate the Apostle and endure any hardship for the Word's sake:

> Hold fast the form of sound *words*, which thou hast heard of me, in faith and love which is in Christ Jesus.
> That good thing which was committed unto thee keep by the *Holy Ghost* which dwelleth in us (2 Timothy 1:13-14).

Timothy was instructed to "hold fast" the "sound words" (or Gospel) that was entrusted to him by the Lord. The Holy Spirit would assist him in "guarding" or "preserving" the Gospel (or Word). God, in His providence, has raised up men, born of His Spirit and filled with His Spirit, who have maintained its purity over the centuries. Had this not happened, the Word of God (or Gospel) would have been lost in the traditions of men.

We learn from Isaiah that it is the Word of God and the Spirit of God that confirms the New Covenant to the believer. The prophet foretold this well-grounded truth several hundred years before the covenant was ratified in Christ. The Apostle Paul makes reference to this covenant in Romans 11:25-27 and quotes Isaiah in part:

> For I would not, brethren, that ye should be ignorant of this mystery, lest ye should be wise in your own conceits; that blindness

> in part is happened to Israel, until the fulness of the Gentiles be come in.
>
> And so all Israel shall be saved: as it is written, There shall come out of Sion the Deliverer, and shall turn away ungodliness from Jacob:
>
> For this is *My covenant* unto them, when I shall *take away their sins* (Romans 11:25-27).

The premillennialists have a theological jubilation with the above passage. It has become a cure-all for their millennial views. They interpret Paul as saying that Christ will come to the earthly Zion — the Jews will turn from their sins — and "all Israel" will be saved. This is God's covenant with them.[2]

The covenant mentioned by Isaiah and quoted in part by Paul does not apply to national Israel in some future millennial age. Evidently the Apostle expected men to be discreet enough to read the remainder of Isaiah's prophecy on the covenant or to understand the Scriptures sufficiently to interpret his words aright. Both men are speaking of the New Covenant that was validated in Christ and is confirmed to all believers by the Word and Spirit of God. Let's notice the remainder of Isaiah's thoughts on the covenant:

> And the Redeemer shall come to Zion, and unto them that turn from transgression in Jacob, saith the Lord.
>
> As for me, this is *My covenant* with them, saith the Lord; My *Spirit* that is upon thee, and my *Word* which I have put in thy mouth, shall not depart out of thy mouth, nor out of the mouth of thy seed, nor out of the mouth of thy seed's seed, saith the Lord, from henceforth and for ever (Isaiah 59:20-21).

The above text speaks of a Redeemer, a covenant, the problem of sin, and the Word and Spirit of God. Isaiah's thoughts are a perfect condensation of this work. They are a mirror of Jesus' mission to deal with sin, to ratify the covenant spoken to Abraham, to manifest His person, His kingdom, His power, His glory, His mercy, and to reveal a "world to come" — all of which are accomplished by His Word and Spirit. The book of Romans and the remainder of the New Testament

---

2. See Scofield's comments, page 1204; note 2.

confirm this interpretation with undeniable force. When we have said "Word and Spirit," we have said *everything*.

The millenarians will look in vain to find a single passage of Scripture that associates the Word and Spirit of God with a "land-covenant" as found in conjunction with the doctrine of "sin" and all the other facets of Jesus' life and works. The Scriptures depict the Word and Spirit of God as producing many wonderful and glorious things, but they are never associated with an earthly, millennial kingdom as they are with "regeneration," "sanctification," "revelation," "eternal life," and many, many more magnificent works of God.

The "promise" that God gave to Abraham was first and foremost the Word. That Word would result in God giving Himself in the Person of His Son, Jesus Christ, for man's redemption (John 1:14; 3:16). There is a double warranty in God's promise to Abraham. The epistle to the Hebrews states that when God promised to bless Abraham, He confirmed it with an "oath." Because God could "swear by no greater, He sware by Himself" (Hebrews 6:13-14; Genesis 22:16). The oath that God gave to Abraham was no less than His Word. Literally, the "Word swore unto the Word."

All of God's acts, character, and eternity belong to or are in essence His Word. All that God has wrought in the past and all that He will effectuate in the future appertain to His Word. The Psalmist declares: "...for thou hast *magnified thy word* above all thy name" (138:2). The Psalmist also wrote: "...my heart standeth *in awe of thy word*" (119:161):

God is *Word* (John 1:1)
Christ is *Word* (John 1:14); Revelation 19:13)
The Promise is *Word* (Romans 9:9)
The Covenant is *Word* (Isaiah 59:21; Haggai 2:5)
The Inheritance is *Word* (Acts 20:32; 26:18)
The Gospel is *Word* (1 Peter 1:25)
The Seed is *Word* (1 Peter 1:23; Luke 8:11)
The Church is *Word* (Acts 6:7; 12:24; 19:20)
The Truth is *Word* (John 17:17)

All of the above concepts exist and co-act with the Holy Spirit of God. Apart from the Holy Spirit these ideas are only articles of religion — mere intellectual dogmas — with no substance whatsoever. But with the mind, energy, and power of the Holy Spirit they become more than a creedal system. There is nothing with more solidarity and reality than that which the Word and Spirit effect in fulfilling God's purpose. God, and the things of God, cannot be reduced to a non-entity. The creation is very real. The Word that became flesh is very real. The miracles of Scripture are very real. The new birth and sanctification are very real. The promises of God are very real. The church is very real. And heaven and hell are very real.

That which does not have its origin and being in the Word of God will perish. Jesus said: "Heaven and earth shall pass away, *but My Word shall not pass away*" (Matthew 24:35). With these thoughts in mind, it is understandable why Moses, the prophets, Jesus, and the New Testament writers had an indomitable commitment to the Word of God.

The role of the Holy Spirit is of equal importance. The consequences of the Holy Spirit for those who are in Christ stagger the imagination — the inherent powers in the Third Person of the Trinity are incomprehensible. The Promise (or Word) made to Abraham in Genesis 12:2-3, and its ensuing "blessings," have their beginning and fulfillment in the gift of God's Spirit. This truth is the crux of the Galatians epistle.

The Galatian church had an excellent beginning — to put it in the language of the King James Version: "Ye did run well ..." (Galatians 5:7). Their faith in the Gospel was rewarded by the gift of the Holy Spirit (Galatians 3:1-5). This fact was very, very important. According to Paul, their faith in Christ, which resulted in the gift of the Holy Spirit, was commensurate with the "blessing of Abraham" — the ultimate of God's promise. But some of the Galatians were on the verge of making shipwreck of their faith.

We can assume that the Galatians continued to have the "promise of Abraham" as their goal; but they had taken a detour in the process. They were diverted in their objective by substituting the "works of the law" for faith. Such a foolish move (3:1) would bring them under the "curse of the law" again. The faith that resulted in the gift of the Holy Spirit was to be sustained throughout their lifetime. The Apostle digresses from his first thoughts on the Holy Spirit to show that Abraham, himself, obtained the promise by faith.

Abraham was not exempt from believing the Gospel (Galatians 3:6-9). Faith was the sole means of Abraham's claim to the promise that is given in the Genesis story. The "unconditional promise" that the futurists write and speak about for the Jews in a millennial age is a hoax. The Scriptures extol Abraham as a "pattern of faith" and the "father of the faithful" for every age and generation. Will the so-called millennial

Jews be "better" and "greater" than the one to whom the promise was made and the one from which they sprang — even Abraham? Anything less than faith, as a means of justification, is to be under the "curse of the law," which is antithetical to the "blessing of Abraham" (Galatians 3:6-9).

I might add that Paul's thoughts on the "blessing of Abraham" disprove the breach that the millenarians have created between the Old and New Testament saints. The New Testament believer is blessed *with* "faithful Abraham" and *not apart from* "faithful Abraham" (Galatians 3:9). This truth was brought to my attention by some comments in the *Pulpit Commentary:*

> Some modern sects hold that the Church is a New Testament organization, and that the Old Testament saints have no part in it. How can this be, if we believers "are blessed with" — not apart from — "faithful Abraham" (ch. iii. 9)? The apostle shows how Abraham has the heirship, the sonship, the kingdom, the glory, on the ground of the promise. He did not, therefore, receive the promise only for his children. Take the promise of the Spirit from Abraham; we take it from ourselves. Is the father of the family to be excluded, and only the children gain admission to the kingdom?[3]

There is more written on Abraham, in the New Testament, as a "model" and one to be "imitated" than any other Biblical personage — except Jesus. There is not a single passage — not even the slightest hint — that Abraham expected the "Land of Canaan" to be the fulfillment of the promise. The premillennialists are putting words in Paul's mouth when they attempt to incorporate the "Land of Canaan" in the "promise" that is discussed in the third chapter of Galatians. The promise is no less than the Gospel that was fulfilled in the death and resurrection of Christ. The Gentile world is to "imitate" Abraham as well as the Jews. The Gentile is justified by faith in the *same* Gospel that Abraham believed:

> And the scripture, foreseeing that God would *justify the heathen* (Gentiles) *through faith, preached the Gospel unto Abraham,* saying In thee *shall all nations be blessed.*
> So then they *which be of faith,* are *blessed with faithful Abraham* (Galatians 3:8-9).

---

3. *Pulpit Commentary,* Vol. 20, 149.

The epistle to the Hebrews affirms that the Israelites who came out of Egypt under Moses had the *same* Gospel preached to them that was preached to the New Testament people — but the Word that was preached to the Israelites availed them nothing because it was not "mixed with faith" (Hebrews 4:2). Who are we to believe regarding the relationship of the Old and New Testament saints — the millenarians or the New Testament writers?

After Paul's comments on Abraham's faith, he returns to his thoughts on the Holy Spirit. His objective is to convince the Galatians that they were imitating Abraham in the early stages of their Christian walk. Their reception of the Holy Spirit and His activities in their midst, which occurred as a result of their faith, was confirmation of this fact. The following passage is actually a description of what the Galatians had already experienced; but its truth needed to be reemphasized. The apostle reminds these unstable Christians again that Christ became a "curse" in order that the

> ...*Blessing of Abraham* might come on the Gentiles through Jesus Christ; that we (Jew and Gentile) *might receive the promise of the Spirit through faith* (Galatians 3:14).

The "blessing of Abraham" is no less than Christ Himself (Galatians 3:22). The "blessing of Abraham" comes through faith in Christ, but it is confirmed and guaranteed by the gift of the Holy Spirit (Ephesians 1:13-14). The "blessing of Abraham" and the "promise of the Spirit" are correlative terms, and belong only to those who believe the Gospel (Jew and Gentile). The "blessing of Abraham," which began as the Word, and afterwards became the Word Incarnate, has its aggregate in the gift of the Holy Spirit and not in the literal "Land of Canaan." The Spirit of God, which is received by faith in the Word of God, results in the blessing of Abraham.

Many hymn writers of the past century understood the role of the Word of God and the Spirit of God in man's redemption and taught it in Gospel songs. Samuel J. Stone (1839-1900), in one of the classical hymns of the church, expresses it very clearly:

> The church's one foundation is Jesus Christ her Lord:
> She is His *new creation,* by *Spirit* and the *Word:*

From heaven He came and sought her, To be His holy bride,
  With His own blood He bought her, and for her life He died.[4]

The same lesson is conveyed in the words of Eliza E. Hewitt (1851-1920), but with a different style of language:

More about Jesus let me learn, More of His holy will discern;
  Spirit of God my teacher be, Showing the *Things of Christ* to me.
More about Jesus in His *Word,* Holding communion with my Lord;
  Hearing His voice in *every line,* Making each *faithful saying*
mine.[5] (emphasis mine.)

The cooperate work of the Word and Spirit is also seen in another evangelical hymn written by Daniel W. Whittle (1840-1901):

I know not how the *Spirit* moves, Convincing men of sin,
Revealing Jesus thro' the *Word,* Creating faith in Him.[6] (emphasis
mine.)

Over the centuries, true religion has suffered tremendously by an imbalance of the Word and Spirit. There is a strong tendency to emphasize one to the exclusion of the other. The Word of God apart from the Spirit of God becomes a "dead letter" — it "kills" — it ends in condemnation rather than eternal salvation. On the other hand, an excessive emphasis on the Spirit of God, without a knowledge of and obedience to the Word of God, will result in spiritual chaos.

True Jewishness belongs to those who have been "begotten" by the incorruptible Seed — by the Word of God in conjunction with the Spirit of God. God's children are those who bear His image and likeness and share in His nature, the essence of which is Word and Spirit. Natural Israel has never been, nor will ever be, the children of God. *For Abraham's natural descendants to be God's children would require Him to change His entire nature; and methinks He will never do this.*

---

4. "The Church's One Foundation"
5. "More About Jesus"
6. "I Know Whom I Have Believed"

Chapter 6

Individual Importance
vs.
National Importance in the Scripture

Man doth not live by bread only, but by *every word* that proceedeth out of the mouth of the Lord shall *man* live (Deuteronomy 8:3b; Matthew 4:4).

One of the most perplexing features of premillennial doctrine is their view on a future "national" state for the Jews. The confusion arises out of their ability to shuffle the terms "physical" seed of Abraham, "national" Israel, and "Israel" in a manner that deceives the very elect. The futurists believe that God will revive and restore the ancient Davidic kingdom of the Old Testament era to the Jews (as a "nation") at the beginning of the so-called millennial kingdom. Israel's restoration to the status of a "nation" in an earthly, millennial kingdom is the heart and soul of premillennialism. They lead us to believe that God is more interested in restoring "national" Israel than He is in saving the souls and bodies of men.

The futurists short-circuit the things that belong to eternity by their insistence upon an earthly, "national" state for the Jews. The New Testament deals with eternal verities and not a "national" Jewish state. Eternal, everlasting life for mankind is the crux of the New Testament and the entire Old Testament prepares the way for this all-important truth. If the premillennialists wish to structure their doctrine on the ministry and work of Christ, then they should take a second look at their beliefs.

It is "individuals," not nations, who have hearts, souls, and bodies. The ultimate objective in God's eternal plan of salvation is the "redemption" of the *body* (Philippians 3:21). This truth applies to the Old Testament saints as well as the New. God's interest in the human body does not begin at the return of Christ with the "resurrection" of the body — it begins *here* and *now*. All the crucial doctrines of the New Testament are cast in this direction. Men are justified to the end that they might glorify God in their *bodies* (1 Corinthians 6:20). The Holy Spirit quickens (infuses with life) the body of the believer (Romans 8:11). Men are sealed with the Holy Spirit until the redemption of the *body*

(Ephesians 1:14). Sanctification is meant to effect a clean, holy *body* (1 Thessalonians 5:23; 2 Corinthians 7:1; Hebrews 10:22). Jesus is saviour of the *body* (Ephesians 5:23). The *body* is for the Lord and the Lord for the *body* (1 Corinthians 6:13). The believer's body is a member of Christ's body, of His flesh, and of His bones (Ephesians 5:30; 1 Corinthians 12:27). The *body* is an "earthen vessel" in which a "treasure" (light and glory of Christ) is placed (2 Corinthians 4:6-7). The life of Jesus is to be made manifest in the *body* (2 Corinthians 4:10-11). The *body* is to be a living sacrifice unto God (Romans 12:1). The human *body* is God's dwelling place for time and eternity (1 Corinthians 6:19). The *body* of the believer will be fashioned like unto the glorious body of Christ (Philippians 3:21). Men will be rewarded according to the deeds done in the *body* (2 Corinthians 5:10). In summary, faith in the finished work of Christ makes it possible for man's mortal *body* to be quickened (Romans 8:11) and to *walk* in the "steps of Abraham."

By a "guestimate," I would say there is more written (directly and indirectly) on the use and destiny of the human *body* in the New Testament than any other single subject. The millenarians are asked to exhibit a series of coherent doctrines from the New Testament that will justify their theories on "national" Jewry comparable to that above. If the premillennialists wish to apply the above doctrines (faith, justification, regeneration, quickening, sanctification, resurrection, glorification, etc.) to "national" Israel, then they must wait until some future date. Unbelievingly, some of them do just that. Nowhere in the Word of God does it say that these doctrines have been "postponed" to some millennial kingdom. The case against "national" Israel should be closed both now and forever.

The importance of man's body can be seen in its relationship to Jesus' fleshly body. Jesus took on Himself the *seed* of Abraham for the purpose of redeeming man's body (Hebrews 2:16). *The employment of Jesus' body in God's eternal plan of redemption is the central feature in all of Scripture and not a Jewish, millennial kingdom.* According to Peter, it was the only means by which man could be *brought to God:* "For Christ also hath once suffered for sins (in a body), the just for the unjust, that He *might bring us to God,* being put to death in the flesh (body), but quickened by the "Spirit" (1 Peter 3:18). The same truth is stated in the book of Hebrews: "But we see Jesus, who was made a little lower than the angels for the *suffering of death* (in a body) crowned with glory and honor; that He by the grace of God *should taste death* (in a body) *for every man.* For it became Him (it was fit or proper) ... in *bringing many sons unto glory,* to make the captain of their salvation perfect through *sufferings* (in a body)" (Hebrews 2:9-10).

The importance of man's body can also be seen as it translates into the church or the body of Christ. Paul states that Christ loved the church and gave Himself for it (Ephesians 5:25). According to Paul, "... we *are* (here and now) members of His *body,* of His *flesh,* and of His *bones"* (Ephesians 5:30). In short, the church consists of men's *bodies* in which the Holy Spirit resides (1 Corinthians 6:19-20). Men's bodies or the church is the body of Christ in a similar way that a wife's body is the body of her husband (Ephesians 5:30). The true church is not a bodiless entity today, nor will it be in the eons of eternity. The church triumphant will consist of the bodies of men that have been transformed into an incorruptible, immortal, glorified, redeemed body. All that God has decreed for man in the future is contingent upon this truth. Even the redemption of the *created order* has nothing to offer man apart from a redeemed body (Romans 8:21-23).

It is interesting to note that the clearest, the most concise, and the most comprehensive definition of the "Gospel" in all of Scripture is given in conjunction with the resurrection of the *human body* (1 Corinthians 15:1-4). In this passage of Scripture the Gospel is confined to the death, burial, and resurrection of Christ; all of which is "according to the Scriptures" i.e., the Old Testament Scriptures. The Gospel of Christ has a stubborn tenacity that will not lend itself to a "national" Jewish state.

The culmination of God's plan of redemption with regard to this present age will be when the bodies of the elect are changed from a perishable, mortal state to an incorrupt, immortal existence (1 Corinthians 15:51-54). A "national" Jewish state of the past has contributed nothing to this truth; nor will it serve any useful purpose in the future. A "national" Jewish state in the past and a "national" Jewish state in the future is out of character with the central issues of Scripture — especially the New Testament. What a difficult undertaking it must be for the futurists to impregnate the New Testament with their millennial "doctrine!" The offspring of this crossbreed can be no less than a mongrel theology.

God's relationship to Israel as a "nation" is not as important as the futurists make it appear. This is demonstrated from their own works. Some premillennialists unwittingly expose their own error regarding "national" Israel. Dr. H. A. Ironside, a dispensational premillennialist, while writing about the people of the Old Testament dispensation, states very clearly that God did not recognize "all who were born of Israel's blood." Only the regenerate Jew could be called the "children of the promise." He says that God

> ... ever had in mind a regenerate people as the people of the promise. Not all who were born of Israel's blood belonged to Israel, as recognized by God. Neither because of the natural seed of Abraham were they necessarily the children of promise.[1]

The above quote is almost a carbon copy of what the Apostle Paul writes concerning Israel in the ninth chapter of Romans (verses 6-8). The subtlety of Dr. Ironside's views on "national" Israel does not come into full focus until we come to another statement in the same book where he implies that the Jews will be restored to a status they once enjoyed in former years, i.e., a "national" status. Dr. Ironsides writes:

> Israel forfeited all title to be called His people. During the present dispensation, when grace is going out to the Gentiles, they would be *set to one side nationally,* as by-and-by the same grace that is now being shown to the nations will be manifested *again to them,* and they shall *once more* be called the children of the living God.[2] (emphasis mine)

Knowingly or unknowingly, Dr. Ironside has presented us with a very tricky statement. He affirms that Israel has been *set to one side nationally,* but shall *once more* be called the "children of the living God." If the logic of Dr. Ironside's statement is followed, we must conclude that at some point in the history of mankind "national" Israel *was* called the "children of the living God." Otherwise how can Israel *once more* bear this title? Our dilemma arises when we try to figure out the period of history in which "national" Israel lived up to this name. Dr. Ironside, by his own admission, has ruled out the Old Testament dispensation when he says that God "... ever had in mind a *regenerate* people as the people of the promise." If regeneration is the only thing that God recognized in the Old Testament dispensation, then Jewish

---

1. H. A. Ironside, *Lectures on the Epistles to the Romans, 1928, p. 114-115, used by permission of Loizeaux Brothers, Inc., Neptune, New Jersey.*
2. Ironside, 123-124.

"nationalism" has never been a significant factor in God's eternal plan of redemption. Sound biblical exegesis will not allow us to lump *all* the Jewish people together (as a "nation" or otherwise) and call them the "children of the living God." Redemption has always been an *individual* matter and always will be. The above quote from Dr. Ironside is a classic example of how the millenarians are able to use their "tricks of the trade" and confound thousands of people.

Dr. John F. Walvoord, another dispensational premillennialist, reduces the "national" image of Israel in the Old Testament period by saying:

> The realization of most of the promises, however, depends upon *an individual Israelite* being *spiritual*. Only thus will he ever enter into the future millennial kingdom, either as a survivor of the tribulation or as a resurrected saint. The blessings of God to Israel in this life as recorded in the Old Testament have been largely *limited to spiritual Israel*. Upon *natural Israel* in *unbelief* God has heaped His judgment and divine discipline.[3] (emphasis mine.)

Dr. Walvoord implies very clearly that membership in the "nation" Israel did not automatically entitle all Israelites to be beneficiaries of the promise to Abraham. At best, "national" Israel was a secondary issue in the eternal plan and purpose of God. What advantage was there in belonging to the Israelite "nation" if there was no faith in and obedience to God's Word? Privileges do not guarantee eternal rewards. Israel's experience in the wilderness under Moses is proof of this fact (1 Corinthians 10:1-12).

It is true that God decreed a visible, tangible "nation" to represent Him on the earth during the old dispensation; but at the same time it was to be a people interfused with His righteous character and life. The only way this was possible was by faith in His Word. No man is born with the "nature" of God within him (Psalm 14:1-3); Romans 3:9-11). In the Scriptures, faith is always an "individual" matter and not a "national" one. When the New Testament writers wish to point out examples of faith and obedience from the Old Testament Scriptures, it is always "individuals" and never the "nation" Israel. The names of men and

---

3. Walvoord, 38.

women are always given — names like Abel, Enoch, Noah, Abraham, Sarah, Isaac, Jacob, Rachel, Rebecca, Joseph, Moses, Ruth, David and on and on. These "names" are representative of thousands of "individuals" in the old economy who *believed and obeyed*. Faith was meant to bring man (Jew and Gentile) into a relationship with God and into an eternal inheritance that a "national" status could never accomplish. "National" Israel is far from being the primary issue in the everlasting plan of God.

The Apostle Paul reveals that it was the "righteousness of God" that every Israelite should have pursued rather than a "national" image. Paul shows conclusively that Israel as a "nation" failed to attain unto the righteousness of God. It would be a great mistake to hold the "nation" Israel up as an example of faith and obedience (Romans 10:16). But there were thousands of "individuals" within the "nation" who *did not fail* in this quest. Therefore the "national" aspects of Israel's existence carried no weight whatsoever. There is overwhelming evidence that God was far more concerned with a "righteous" people than He was with a "nationalistic" people. The book of Romans stands as an everlasting monument to Israel's failure as a nation. But the premillennialists wish to continue a national image for the Jews that should have been abandoned two thousand years ago.

According to the Scriptures, it is "names" that are written in the Book of Life and not "nations" per se (Exodus 32:32; Daniel 12:1; Luke 10:20; Philippians 4:3; Hebrews 12:23; Revelation 3:5; 13:8; 17:8; 20:15; 21:27). It is this distinction between the Jews as a "nation" and as "individuals" that enables Paul to arrive at his thoughts on the "two Israels." This distinction is better known as the "remnant" within the "nation." The Apostle's emphasis upon "whosoever will" makes it abundantly clear that redemption is an individual matter and not a national one (Romans 10:13).

The central message in the Scriptures is not the formation and continuation of national Israel but God's eternal purpose *in Christ*. The millenarians, by their overdrawn picture of national Israel, have confused thousands of people by creating a rupture in the two Testaments. However, when our priorities are right, there is perfect unity between the two Testaments and the redeemed of both Testaments. God's eternal plan of redemption that was determined "before the foundation of the world" is the crux of both Testaments and not national Israel.

The overriding truth throughout the Old Testament is God and His

Word and everything else is subordinate to this fact. The Old Testament begins with God and ends with God — and the God of the Old Testament became the Christ of the New (John 1:1). The two Testaments blend together, making a complete revelation of God and His infinite purpose in Christ. It has already been shown that the cord that binds the two Testaments together is God's Word and Spirit — and all of this apart from national Israel. The God who spoke the worlds into being (by His Word) is the Christ of the Gospels and epistles. If this is not true, then the entire New Testament is a farce. Christ was as much with the Father in the days of creation and in the days of Moses as He was when He appeared in the flesh.

If their priorities were right, the millenarians could dispell the confusion they have created between the two Testaments and the redeemed of both Testaments. It was God's Word that was crucial for every Israelite and not membership in the nation. To *know God* should have been the ultimate concern of every descendant of Abraham. The Hebrew people were to have been a people of the Living Word, rather than slaves to the "dead letter of the law." The Word of God was more important than national Israel, the Land of Canaan, blood ties with Abraham, or anything else that can be dubbed into the millennial charade. When God's Word and Spirit are given their proper place in both dispensations, national Israel will fade into oblivion.

The term "Wordite," which may seem inappropriate to some Bible students, is a perfect synonym for the elect of God in both dispensations. It has already been proven that those who believe are an offspring of His Word. God has never dealt with man apart from His Word. In the very beginning Adam and Eve were confronted with the Word of God. It was disregard or violation of the Word that allowed sin to enter the human race, resulting in man's alienation from God. Man's restoration is by a converse manner — reconciliation to God comes by attention to and faith in His Word (Romans 10:8, 17).

"A man is no better than his word," is a truism that infers far more than appears on the surface. To put it another way, a man is synonymous with his word. Can we say any less for God? One of the most common traits of God is that He "speaks." If God were always silent, man would never know His mind, will, or purpose. The whole story of "God speaking" is compressed into a few sentences in the epistle of the Hebrews. God spoke in creation (Hebrews 11:3). God spoke at Mt. Sinai (Hebrews 12:18-27). God spoke through the prophets (Hebrews 1:1).

Finally, *God spoke through His Son* (Hebrews 1:2). The most important thing from the *creation* to the *conflagration* is the *voice* of God. Very serious warnings are given to those who refuse to "hear His Voice" (Hebrews 3:15). To believe in God is to believe His Word.

God's revelation of Himself is always in conjunction with His Word. It has pleased God, in the course of history, to reveal Himself piecemeal (Hebrews 1:1 Amplified Bible). The "dawn" of His Self-revelation came before the "midday sun." The "glow of dawn" and the "midday splendor" come from the same source.

Only a glimmer of the Gospel was given to man before Christ came in the flesh. It is the same God and the same Word in both the Old and New Testaments — it is a matter of degree. The full orb of God's Self-disclosure did not come until His appointed hour (Galatians 4:4). Behind the Word given to Abraham, Moses, and the prophets was the *Person* who would eventually become man. Those who *believed and obeyed* this partial revelation were heirs of eternal life as much so as those living during and after the first century A.D.

The only difference in the Old and New Testaments is that the Word had not become flesh in the former. Let's state it this way: The God who spoke to Abraham, Moses, and the prophets was clothed in garments of flesh when Jesus was conceived in the womb of the virgin Mary:

> In the beginning was the *Word,* and the *Word* was *with God,* and the *Word was God* ... and the *Word became flesh,* etc. (John 1:1, 14).

The unity between the Old and New Testaments and the oneness of God's nature, in both dispensations, are clearly seen in the first evangel to Abraham. This brief but glorious promise (or Word) to the Patriarch would have been sufficient for the Incarnation:

> And I will bless them that bless thee, and curse him that curseth thee: and in thee shall all families of the earth be blessed (Genesis 12:3).

This one passage would have been fulfilled had no further word been given relative to the coming of Christ in the flesh. All the other declarations or prophecies pertaining to the Incarnation are merely enlargements of the original pledge. They all *stem from and point to* the first message given to Abraham. Additional statements in the Old Testament linked to the coming of Christ (including Genesis 3:15) are only icing on the cake. Even the "types" and "shadows" of the first dispensation are addenda to the solemn vow made to Abraham.

Several books of theology could be written on Genesis 12:3. The two basic factors in God's nature, that would eventually be expressed in the Person of Christ, are wrapped up in this passage, i.e., His *love* and His *wrath*. Both the blessings and cursings in this verse are directly related to the phrase "in thee." From the loins of Abraham would come One in the combined figures of a Lamb and a Lion (Revelation 5:5-6) who would fulfill the "blessing" and "cursing." John the Baptist describes this twofold role of Christ in the figure of a winnower:

> Whose fan is in his hand, and he will thoroughly purge his floor, and gather his wheat into the garner; but he will burn up the chaff with unquenchable fire (Matthew 3:12).

There is no breach in the "righteousness of God" from the Old Testament to the New. The Apostle Paul assures us that the "righteousness of God" that came in Christ was attested by the "law and the prophets" long before the Incarnation:

> But now the *righteousness of God* has been manifested apart from the law, although the *law and the prophets bear witness to it* (Romans 3:21 RSV).

A good deal of Paul's theology is simply a confirmation and expansion of the Old Testament prophets. The "word of righteousness" was as important for the people of Isaiah's day as it was for Paul's, and "individual" responsibility is to be seen in the works of both men. The following quote from Isaiah should be considered in conjunction with Paul's words in Philippians 2:10-11:

> I have sworn by myself, the *word is gone out of my mouth in righteousness,* and shall not return, That unto me every knee shall bow, and every tongue shall swear.
>
> Surely shall one say, *In the Lord have I righteousness* and strength: even to him (Lord) shall men come; and all that are incensed (enraged) against him shall be ashamed.
>
> *In the Lord shall all the seed of Israel be justified, and shall glory* (Isaiah 45:23-25).

The Pulpit Commentary translates verse 24 in the above passage in this manner: "… only in the Lord, shall *each man* say to me, is their righteousness."[4] (emphasis mine) Verse 25 in the above quote reveals

---

4. *The Pulpit Commentary,* Vol. 2 of Vol. 10, Isaiah, 177.

clearly that "*all* the seed of Israel," if they were to be justified, must be justified by believing the "word of righteousness." Abraham's descendants were not justified on a national scale in Isaiah's day; neither will this happen in the future.

Moses informed the Hebrew people that the Word of God would become their "righteousness" if they feared God and obeyed His commandments. Such loyalty would be for their "good always:"

> And the Lord commanded us *to do all these statutes,* to fear the Lord our God, for our good always, that he might preserve us alive, as it is at this day.
> And *it shall be our righteousness, if we observe to do all these commandments* before the Lord our God, as he hath commanded us (Deuteronomy 6:24-25).

To this hour, it is possible for men to be justified and "counted righteous" by believing passages from the Old Testament Scriptures. When Charles H. Spurgeon, the great London preacher, heard a message from the book of Isaiah, he believed, obeyed and was gloriously converted. Upon speaking of his conversion, Mr. Spurgeon would always call attention to the following text as the beginning of his spiritual awakening:

> Look unto me, and be ye saved, all the ends of the earth, for I am God, and there is none else (Isaiah 45:22).

When Spurgeon died, a Bible was placed on his casket and opened at the above text. What a tribute to the Old Testament Scriptures!

Since God's nature does not change from one dispensation to the other, neither does His mode of redemption. Faith in God's Word is a prerequisite to man's salvation, regardless of the age in which one lives. If Abraham was "counted righteous" and made an heir of God through faith in His Word, so were millions of others who lived prior to the New Testament period.

God is not an innovationist — changing His plan of redemption from one age to another. Faith in God's Word has always been and always will be God's method of reconciling men unto Himself. It is admitted that the words *faith* and *belief* are not found in great abundance in the Old Testament Scriptures. However, their equivalent is found over and over again. Faith in God's Word is implied and anticipated in the old economy by such expressions as "hearken unto my voice," "take heed and hearken," "obey my commandments," "walk in my statutes," "keep my words," "remember ye the law of Moses," "walk ye in the light of the Lord," "observe and hear all these words," "cleave unto the Lord," "serve the Lord," "ye shall love the Lord," etc.

The negative side of the above terms is also found in the Old Testament code. "Faithlessness" and "unbelief" in God's Word are to be seen in such phrases as: "turned their backs," "hardened their hearts," "uncircumcised in heart," "walked contrary to me," "ye would not be obedient," "ye have rebelled against the Lord," "ye believed him not," "stiffnecked people," etc.

The Magna Carta for Israel was spelled out in very clear language at the beginning of her history. God did not wait until the days of Isaiah or Jeremiah to give them His Word. The cornerstone of Israel's faith and hope is to be seen primarily in the first five books of the Old Testament. I doubt seriously if there is any new truth, pertinent to Israel's salvation, beyond the Pentateuch. (See Psalm 78.)

Isaiah admonished the people of his day to look back as far as Abraham and Sarah for examples of faith and obedience to God's Word. If the blessings of God were to be enjoyed, they should imitate the couple from which they sprang:

> Hearken to me, ye that follow after righteousness, ye that seek the Lord: Look unto the rock whence ye are hewn, and to the hole of the pit whence ye are digged.
> *Look unto Abraham your father,* and unto *Sarah* that bare you: for I called him alone, and blessed him, and increased him, etc. (Isaiah 51:1-2).

No nation or people were privileged to experience such signs and wonders as the Israelites. Such consequential events were unheard of since the creation of man. A search of heaven and earth could not yield such demonstrations of God's love and power:

> For ask now of the days that are past, which were before thee, since the day that God created man upon the earth, and ask from the one side of heaven unto the other, whether there hath been *any such thing as this great thing is,* or *hath been heard like it?*
> Did ever people hear the voice of God speaking out of the fire, as thou hast heard, and live?
> Or hath God assayed to go and take him a nation from the midst of another nation by *temptations, by signs,* and *by wonders,* and *by war,* and *by a mighty hand,* and *by a stretched out arm,* and *by great terrors,*

according to all that the Lord your God did for you in Egypt *before your eyes?*

Unto thee it was shewed, that thou mightest know that the Lord He is God: there is none else beside Him, etc. (Deuteronomy 4:32-35).

The mighty acts of God, displayed at the inception of this nation, would be anterior to anything that would follow in the Old Testament dispensation. Deliverance from Egyptian bondage, the wilderness experience, the giving of the law, the conquest of Canaan, and God's wrath were never to be forgotten.

These miraculous events would in time be translated into the *Word of God.* Also the various laws, as given to Moses, were recorded and preserved, i.e., the Ten Commandments, the ceremonial, and civil laws. Certain prophetic utterances, pertaining to the coming of Christ in the flesh, became a part of the early Scriptures. This initial light, given at the dawn of Israel's history, was to be a beacon to succeeding generations. Israel was to draw faith, comfort, and hope from these early writings. Men like Isaiah, Jeremiah, Hosea, etc., were continually reminding the Hebrew people of their spiritual heritage — calling them back to these original truths.[5] The later prophets would only add light to light when they came on the scene.

The credibility of God's nature (i.e., His love, power, wisdom) was established in the natal period of Israel's history and was to be kept alive until the Incarnation. The religious festivals were given to this end — they were memorials of a former age. The later prophets did not introduce any new religious feasts or fasts — all of them had their origin in Moses.

The Passover Feast, in particular, was to be the most significant of all Hebrew feasts. The spotless lamb, the sprinkling of the blood, the eating of the flesh, the unleavened bread, the bitter herbs, and the powerlessness of the death angel were to be a perpetual reminder. This was to be an annual celebration that reminded the Israelites of the love, power, and wrath of God.

Although the Passover Feast was observed in retrospect, it was to be a means of making God contemporary with every age. The Hebrew

---

5. Isaiah 48:20-22; 58:13-14; 63:7-14; Jeremiah 2:1-8; 11:1-8; 32:16-33; Daniel 9:1-15; Hosea 13:4-6; Micah 6:3-5; and Malachi 4:4-6.

people would be reminded that they had access to and were to serve the same God as their forefathers under Moses. This would be the night of nights for generations to come:

> It is a night to be *much observed* unto the Lord for bringing them out from the land of Egypt: *This is that night of the Lord* to be observed for *all the children of Israel in their generations* (Exodus 12:42).

The unleavened bread and bitter herbs were given in prospect as well as retrospect. They were symbolic of the bitter conditions under which their forefathers lived in Egypt. They would also serve as a warning to future Israelites, lest they forget God and suffer a similar captivity.

The Feast of Tabernacles was another reminder of some very significant days before the Hebrew people were permanently settled in the Land of Canaan. A part of this religious feast consisted of living in "booths" which were simple constructions made from boughs of trees. These crude shelters were a reminder of the life style of their forefathers when they came through the wilderness. They were to represent living conditions of a people "on the move."

These less than shanty abodes were to convey a very meaningful lesson for all Israelites. Even in the Land of Canaan, they were to regard themselves as a people "on the move." Canaan must not be considered as their permanent dwelling place. They were to "desire a better country," and like Abraham, they were to anticipate a "city which hath foundation, whose builder and maker is God" (Hebrews 11:10).

The Feast of Tabernacles lost its significance shortly after the conquest of Canaan under Joshua. A spirit of permanency settled over the people when they came into the land, and the idea of living in booths for seven days as a religious rite evaporated into nothingness. It was not until the days of Ezra and Nehemiah that the Feast of Tabernacles was carefully considered and observed, as set forth in the law of Moses. When the exiles reflected their true status in the land by living in booths, by becoming strangers and pilgrims, they experienced a joy their homes and land could not provide:

> And all the congregation of them that were come again out of the captivity made *booths,* and *sat under the booths:* for since the days of Joshua the son of Nun unto that day had not the children of Israel done so. And there was *very great gladness* (Nehemia 8:17).

The Passover Feast, the Feast of Tabernacles, and all other religious celebrations would be only hollow ceremonies unless God was made relevant in every period of Hebrew history.

Most of the "heroes of faith" as given in the eleventh chapter of Hebrews are associated with the Pentateuch era. Their exploits were recorded and preserved as "patterns of faith" for future generations. This unique chapter is unfriendly to the millenarians in more ways than one. "Individuals" are highlighted in this chapter and not "nations" — especially the "nation" Israel. In matters of faith, Abel, Enoch, and Noah, who lived prior to Abraham's day, are placed in the same category as Abraham, Sarah, Isaac, Jacob, Moses, etc. According to the writer of this epistle, the names of the people (or "individuals") are too numerous to mention (verse 32). Heaven or the "unseen world" into which the believer is brought is the issue at stake in this chapter and not the Land of Canaan (Hebrews 10:34; 11:1; 10, 13, 27).

All of the Hebrew people who came out of Egypt served as a "model" or "guide," not only for the people of the Old Testament period, but for all mankind in every age. Their reaction to the providence of God, whether good or bad, would also become divine history. Future generations would not have to literally experience the Passover in Egypt, the crossing of the Red Sea, the pillar of fire, the cloud by day, the manna, etc., but they would have to believe in a God equal to these miraculous events. "Faith comes by hearing the Word of God," and not by seeing.

This principle is no less true for men living in the twentieth century, A.D. The apostles and other New Testament believers were to serve as a prototype for the ages to follow. It is not necessary for the existing generation to be eyewitnesses to the death and resurrection of Christ, but if men are to enter into eternal life, they must be believers of the testimony of those disciples who did. Jesus wrote not a word of Scripture, but to this hour the church is

> ... built upon the foundation of the *apostles and prophets,* Jesus
> Christ Himself being the chief corner stone (Ephesians 2:20).

The Hebrew nation was wrapped in the swaddling clothes of miracles. God demonstrated His power and gave them His Word without stint. Moses was perhaps the greatest single exponent of the Word of God of all the Old Testament writers:

> And there arose not a prophet since in Israel like unto Moses, whom

the Lord knew face to face,
In all the signs and the wonders, which the Lord sent him to do in
the land of Egypt to Pharaoh, and to all his servants, and to all his land,
And in all that mighty hand, and in all the great terror which Moses
shewed in the sight of all Israel (Deuteronomy 34:10-12).

But the Word of the Lord was largely ignored and forgotten. Many of the important commandments, such as the Passover Feast, the Sabbatical Year, the Year Jubilee, the treatment of strangers, and laws providing for the poor and needy, were never observed with any diligence. In process of time, some of these commandments would become almost extinct. False prophets and heathen worship caught the attention of many Israelites, and the Word of God was given only a semblance of recognition.

We see the same pattern in the early church. The fundamentals of the Christian faith were laid before and shortly after the resurrection of Christ. But very soon heresy and worldliness drew the church away from its original moorings. It was not until the 16th Century, the Reformation era, that men began to return to the Scriptures as the sole authority for faith and practice. Progress in the church will always be very minimal, unless there is a total commitment to the Scriptures.

This early precedence of God's love, power, and wrath would leave future Israelites without excuse. In other words, long before the days of the prophets, God proved Himself equal to any circumstance or condition. The Word of God is designed to stimulate and evoke faith and the Lord did not leave the Hebrew people lacking. They were given the opportunity to imitate Abraham's faith and believe in God,

...who quickeneth the dead, and calleth those things which be not
as though they were.
Who against hope believed in hope ... (Roans 4:17b-18a).

There is no portion of Scripture that calls attention to and emphasizes the importance of the Word of God for the Hebrew people as the book of Deuteronomy. One becomes almost weary with its repetitious mood: "If ye will obey my voice," "do all these statutes," "hearken diligently to my commandments," "observe and hear all these words," "keep therefore the words of this covenant," etc. There is a slight variation in the above words and phrases, but the message is always the same. This echo and re-echo on the Word of God in the book of Deuteronomy is conclusive enough that the Hebrew people were left with no option — the Word was to become their *life*.

"Individual" importance, as opposed to "national" importance, is clearly delineated in the book of Deuteronomy. When the Hebrew people were confronted with God's Word, every "individual" had to make a "choice." But no "option" was open to them relative to their "national" status. Their natural birth automatically qualified them to be members of the "nation." An Israelite could be the personification of "wickedness" and continue to be a part of the Hebrew "nation" — *nothing* could change this. But in matters of "life" and "death" and "blessing" and "cursing" from God, every "individual" was faced with a "choice:"

> I call heaven and earth to record this day against you, that I have set before you *life* and *death, blessing* and *cursing:* therefore *choose life,* that both you and thy seed may *live:*
> That thou mayest love the Lord thy God, and that thou mayest *obey his voice,* and that thou mayest *cleave unto him:* for *he is thy life,* and the length of thy days ... (Deuteronomy 30:19-20).

From the above passage, we conclude that God was not the "life" of "every" Israelite unless he believed and obeyed the Word. For "God to be their life" meant that the "Word must be their life." The two ideas cannot be separated. Their "national" status contributed nothing to this fact. Moses' final words to the congregation of Israel were "set your hearts unto *all these words* ... it is your life" (Deuteronomy 32:45-47).

This truth did not stop with Moses — it would be emphasized again by the later prophets. Several hundred years after Moses' day, we find a group of Hebrew exiles coming to inquire of Ezekiel. They were probably interested in what the future held for them. But they were never permitted to ask their question(s). Instead, Ezekiel began immediately to rehearse the history of their forefathers in the wilderness. Ezekiel affirms that God gave the Israelites under Moses His statutes, and they were expected to "live in them." The same truth was applicable to the Israelites prior to and during the captivity. Ezekiel quotes almost verbatim Leviticus 18:5:

> I gave (past tense) them my *statutes,* and shewed them my *judgments,* which *if a man do, he shall even live in them* (Ezekiel 20:11).

It should be noted in the above passage that Ezekiel's words are addressed to the Hebrew people en masse, but "individualism" is the key to the realization of God's promise. Ezekiel writes: "...if a *man* do, *he* shall live in them." When the nitty-gritty of redemption is brought to light, "national" Israel passes out of the picture.

Some of the most basic and universal lessons on the Word of God, in all of Scripture, are to be found in the Pentateuch. The wilderness journey of the Israelites was a hand-picked experience to teach them (and others) the importance of the Word of God for time and eternity. They were deliberately deprived of food, water, and other necessities that they might rely altogether on the Word of the Lord. Ere they left Egypt and before they arrived at Mt. Sinai, the Lord had given them His Word that He would bring them into the Land of Canaan. Throughout this adventure, they were to trust Him rather than their own wisdom and strength. Every need, however great or small, was to be cast upon the Lord. They must learn that God is synonymous with His Word. He was to be their life and sustainer from the beginning to the end. The entire wilderness experience centered around the Word of God:

> All the commandments (Words) which I command thee this day shall ye observe to do, that ye *may live,* and multiply, and go in and possess the land which the Lord sware unto your fathers.
>
> And thou shalt remember all the way which the Lord thy God led thee these forty years in the wilderness, to humble thee, and to prove thee, to know what was in thine heart, *whether thou wouldest keep His commands* (Words), or no.
>
> And He humbled thee, and suffered thee to hunger, and fed thee with manna, which thou knewest not, neither did thy fathers know; that He might make thee know that *man doth not live by bread only, but by every word that proceedeth out of the mouth of the Lord doth man live* (Deuteronomy 8:1-3).

If the lesson arising out of the wilderness experience was to be effectual for the Hebrew "nation," then it must be learned on an "individual" level. Every Israelite was to understand that *"Man* doth not live by bread alone, etc." Jesus taught the same lesson in the New Testament (Matthew 4:4).

The privations in the wilderness experience were preparatory for occupying the Land of Canaan. A precedence was established in this event that would resound across the centuries. When the Israelites came into the "land," they were not to trust in the "land," per se. Canaan would yield her abundance, but the "blessings of the land" must not overshadow the Word of the Lord. This warning was rehearsed before the people time and time again (Deuteronomy 4:1; 4:14; 5:31-33; 6:1-25;

8:1; 11:8ff; 15:4-5; 30:15-20; Ezekiel 5:5-17; Daniel 9:3-16). The Word
of the Lord was to be foremost in the "land" as well as in the desert.

A careful analysis of Deuteronomy 8:6-20 will show conclusively
that the "land" would afford the Israelites *no more comfort than the
wilderness, if they ignored the Word of God.* The productivity of the soil,
minerals, increase of herds, the blessing of children, and even their
remaining in the "land" was contingent upon their *faith in* and *obedience
to* the Word of the Lord. A drought of the Word meant a drought in the
land. The yield of the land was requisite to the Word of the Lord; but the
Word was not requisite to the land.

This is a note that needs to be sounded today, when so much
emphasis is being placed upon the land by the premillennialists. The Jew
can exist outside the land, as has been proven over the centuries, but he
cannot live "eternally" apart from the Word of God.

Moses' remarks on the Word of God in Deuteronomy 8:1-3 has to
do with more than physical sustenance for the Hebrew people within the
wilderness or within the land — it has to do with eternal life as well.
Without question, there are blessings and privileges that accrue to men
in the "natural" order because they believe and obey the Word of God.
In one sense, the natural order and the spiritual order cannot be separated
— but in another sense, they can be poles apart. The Apostle Paul says
that,

> ...godliness is profitable unto all things, having promise of the *life
> that now is* (present), and of *that which is to come* (future) (1 Timothy
> 4:8).

God intended that temporal blessings and spiritual blessings go
hand in hand. Eternal life cannot be divorced from this present life for
the believer, but it can be for the non-believer. Eternal life, which comes
through faith in God's Word, is designed to enhance and elevate
physical life. When Moses admonished the Israelites to obey God's
commandments (Word) and *live,* he was speaking of eternal life as well
as physical life.

Isn't it wonderful that redemption for the Jew does not depend upon
his being in the land or in a national setting? If this were necessary, then
very, very few would be saved. This is the lesson that was being taught
them in the wilderness experience. They were to *live by the Word of God
whether in the land or out of the land.* Salvation is in the Lord and not
in the hills and mountains, says the prophet Jeremiah:

> Truly in vain is salvation hoped for from the *hills* and from the multitude of *mountains; truly in the Lord our God is the salvation of Israel* (Jeremiah 3:23).

The "privations of the desert" and the "abundance in the land" were two extremes designed to teach two universal and eternal lessons: (1) The Word of God is to be first and foremost in times of distress as well as in periods of abundance; and (2) we are taught man's relationship to the world and the things of the world. This was to be an essential part of the New Testament Gospel, arranged many centuries before the "Word became flesh."

Jesus must also demonstrate this truth in His relationship to the Father and the world. If He is to be "tempted and tried in all points such as we" (including the Old Testament people), He must have His "wilderness experience." Immediately after His baptism He was driven by the Spirit into a barren area to be tempted by the Devil. After forty days and forty nights without food, Jesus was asked by Satan to change the stones of the desert into bread. Jesus did not respond to Satan with a new truth. The words of Moses were as applicable to Jesus' trial as they were to the Israelites in the wilderness and in the Land of Canaan:

> But He (Jesus) answered and said, It is written *Man shall not live by bread alone, but by every Word that proceedeth out of the mouth of God* (Matthew 4:4).

From both the great "lawgiver" (Moses), and the great "Lifegiver" (Jesus), come the words, "Man shall not live by bread alone, but by every Word that proceedeth out of the mouth of God." Jesus began His ministry with an emphasis upon the Word of God and ended it with an emphasis upon the Word of God (Luke 24:44-46). The crucial things that Jesus taught have their genesis in the Old Testament Scriptures.

When Satan offered Jesus "all the kingdoms of the world, and the glory of them," he replied: "Get thee hence, Satan; for it is *written,* Thou shalt worship the Lord thy God, and Him only shalt thou serve" (Matthew 4:10). Obedience to God's Word was more important to Jesus than possessing "all the kingdoms of the world."

What shall we eat? What shall we drink? Wherewithal shall we be clothed? — are questions raised by Jesus in the New Testament but answered several centuries earlier by Moses in the desert experience. The answer that Jesus gave to the above questions is of the quintessence that Moses gave in the book of Deuteronomy:

> But seek ye first the kingdom of God, and His righteousness: *and all these things* (temporal things) *shall be added unto you* (Matthew 6:33).

The lesson that the Israelites were to learn in the wilderness and in the Land of Canaan, relative to the Word of God, is also expressed in the life and ministry of the Apostle Paul:

> I have learned, in whatsoever state I am, therewith to be content.
>
> I know both how to be *abased,* and I know how to *abound: everywhere* and *in all things* I am instructed both to be *full* and to be *hungry,* both to *abound* and to *suffer need.*
>
> I can do all things through Christ which strengtheneth me (Philippians 4:11-13).

Whether in "plenty" or in "want," Christ, the Eternal Word, was sufficient for the apostle — it should have been so with the first generation of Israelites in the wilderness.

Every New Testament writer, along with the Old Testament prophets, confirms this truth on the Word of God as given at the outset of Israel's history. Love of the world and the things of the world, to the exclusion of the Father, is equivalent to idolatry — a violation of the first commandment. The creation reflects the attributes of God, but it is not God (Romans 1:19-20). God would have men know that He exists apart from His creation. The creation, which includes the Land of Canaan, is not to take priority over God and His Word.

The spiritual content and import of the Pentateuch would be felt at various stages of Israel's history. Revival and renewal would come as attention was drawn to its truths. When Josiah, the 16th king of Judah and contemporary with the prophet Jeremiah, came to the throne, he set about to purge his kingdom of the multiple evils that had beset the nation. Heathen idols and worship were rampant; the temple of God was in dire need of repair and cleansing. Josiah launched a major campaign to alter these conditions. But it was not until a "book of the law" was found in the temple that the heart of the problem was revealed and corrected. Most Bible scholars are unanimous in believing that the discovered "book of the law" was that of Deuteronomy.

When Shaphan, the scribe, read the book of the law to Josiah, he immediately rent his clothes. The king readily discerned why the wrath of the Lord was upon the nation:

> ... our fathers have *not kept the Word of the Lord,* to do after all that

is *written in this book* (2 Chronicles 34:21).

Josiah felt the need of more light and understanding from the Lord regarding this book of the law. So, Hilkiah, the priest, took the book of the law to Huldah, the prophetess, for confirmation and direction. Hilkiah was informed that the wrath of the Lord, as described in the book of the law, would be poured out on Judah unless there was obedience to the Word of the Lord:

> ... My wrath shall be poured out upon this place, and shall not be quenched (2 Chronicles 34:25b).

Josiah rallied to the occasion and gathered all the people together and "read in their ears all the words of the book of the covenant that was found in the house of the Lord" (verse 30b). As for the king, "he made a covenant before the Lord, to walk after the commandments, and his testimonies, and his statutes, with all his heart, and with all his soul, to perform the *words of the covenant* which are written in this book" (verse 31). Thus, this book of the law, believed to be Deuteronomy, had a profound effect upon Josiah and his subjects. It is implied that a turn of events took place in the nation for good. If the truths contained in the "book of the law" produced repentance and faith in Josiah and his people — to the point of pleasing and averting the wrath of God — the same truths should have been effectual at any given time during the Old Testament period.

The law of Moses was a key factor in uniting and encouraging the exiles that returned from the captivity. The people were few in number and the work of restoration was beset with many difficulties. They needed comfort and spiritual strength for the task that was before them. The law of Moses supplied that need:

> And all the people gathered themselves together *as one man* into the street that was before the water gate; and they spake unto Ezra the scribe to bring *the book of the law of Moses,* which the Lord had commanded to Israel (Nehemiah 8:1).

Ezra stood upon a platform made of wood and read the law of Moses to the people from early morning until midday. When the book of the law was opened, the people immediately stood up; "and Ezra blessed the Lord ... and the people answered, Amen, Amen, with lifting up their hands; and they bowed their heads, and worshipped the Lord with their faces to the ground" (Nehemiah 8:6).

This was a very emotional event. The people wept when they heard the law of Moses read (Nehemiah 8:9b). Their weeping turned into joy as they were dismissed with this benediction from Ezra:

> ... Go your way, eat the fat, and drink the sweet, and send portions unto them for whom nothing is prepared: for this day is *holy unto the Lord:* neither be ye sorry; *for the joy of the Lord is your strength* (Nehemiah 8:10).

Just a cursory reading of certain Pentateuchal books will show that the Hebrew people were to literally "live and move and have their being" in the Word of God. By day and night, in the home, and by the wayside, the Word of God was to occupy their minds and hearts. They were to have a three hundred and sixty degree exposure to the commandments of the Lord. In every place and in every direction they were to be confronted with God's truth. This confrontation was not to cease with a given generation. The Word of God was to be passed on to their children:

> And thou shalt teach them diligently unto thy children, and shalt talk of them when thou sittest in thine house, and when thou walkest by the way, and when thou liest down, and when thou risest up.
> And thou shalt bind them for a sign upon thine hand, and they shall be as frontlets between thine eyes.
> And thou shalt write them upon the posts of thy house, and on thy gates (Deuteronomy 6:7-9).

The Lord used some unusual methods to teach the Hebrew people His Word. The modern day billboards that we see along our highways today are not new. The Lord used a similar technique to teach His Word many centuries ago. Instructions for the material and erection of this signboard were given to Moses shortly before he died. The billboard was to be made of huge stones and covered over with plaster. Upon the plastered stones would be written "all the words of this law" (Deuteronomy 27:1-3).

This signboard was to be erected on Mt. Ebal, a short distance from the Jordan River. On the opposite side of Mt. Ebal was Mt. Gerizim and a valley between. The commandments of the Lord were placed in a conspicuous spot for all people passing to and from the Land of Palestine to see.

In connection with the above command, Moses was instructed to divide the twelve tribes into two groups. One group, composed of

Simeon, Levi, Judah, Issachar, Joseph, and Benjamin, was to stand on Mt. Gerizim and announce in unison with a loud voice the "blessings" of the law. The other six tribes, Reuben, Gad, Asher, Zebulum, Dan, and Naphtali, were to stand on Mt. Ebal and proclaim in unison the "curses" of the law. At the conclusion of the "curses" the tribes were to shout:

> Cursed be he that confirmeth not *all the words of this law to do them*. And all the people shall say, Amen (Deuteronomy 27:26).

This command was actually executed under the leadership of Joshua after the Israelites came into the "land" (Joshua 8:33-35). These "blessings" and "curses" were proclaimed upon the "land" as well as upon the people (See Deuteronomy 11:29-30).

In any given age man's response to God's Word can be summed up in the two concepts — "blessing" or "cursing." These two ideas were expressed in the covenant given to Abraham and they were to be kept before the Israelites at all times. The "blessings" of the Lord for the people were contingent upon *faith in* and *obedience to* the the Word of God. The Abrahamic covenant and Mt. Ebal/Mt. Gerizim bear witness to this fact.

The Hebrew people were given very meaningful object lessons that were designed to communicate God's power and might from one generation to the next. When Joshua crossed the Jordan River, the Lord instructed him to select twelve men — a man from each tribe. Every man was to choose a stone from the Jordan River and carry it to their campsite that night. These stones were to be placed in an orderly pile. These well-arranged stones were meant to arouse the curiosity of their children for years to come. Succeeding generations, upon seeing these stones, would ask, "What mean ye by these stones?" This question would open the door for their parents to tell them of the mighty act of God in crossing the Jordan River. This miraculous event would inspire fear and respect for God from one generation to the next. These stones from the Jordan River, designed to arouse the curiosity of unborn Israelites, would become both the verbal and written Word of God (Joshua 4:22-24).

Another important means of communicating God's Word to the people was the role of the priests. In addition to their temple ministry, they were to teach the law to the laity. Their ability to discern between the "holy" and "unholy" and between the "clean" and "unclean" made them suitable instruments for this purpose. This knowledge of the sacred and profane was to be shared with the people (Leviticus 10:11).

See also Deuteronomy 24:8; 33:10; Nehemiah 8:2, 8; Jeremiah 18:18; and Malachi 2:7.

The priests were expected to read the law to the people periodically. One such public reading of the law was the "year of release" that was to be observed in conjunction with the feast of tabernacles. Moses commanded the priests to read the law before all the people — from the least to the greatest. This solemn event was to occur every seven years (Deuteronomy 31:9-12).

The teaching of the law by the priests was a major factor in the spiritual renewal initiated by Jehoshaphat, the fourth king of Judah. Besides destroying the high places and groves within his kingdom, this goodly king sent the priests throughout the land teaching the law of God to his subjects. This wise act not only affected the people of Judah but also several nearby nations (2 Chronicles 17:9-10).

The oral teaching of the law by the priests carried a lot of clout for the Hebrew people. It seems to have been a powerful deterrent for evil whenever the priests fulfilled their duty. However, we find the opposite effects when the teaching of the law was neglected. Such was the case in Hosea's day. The Lord said through Hosea, "My people are destroyed for lack of knowledge." This "lack of knowledge" actually meant a drought of God's Word. Hosea placed this shortage of the Word of God directly upon the shoulders of the priests (Hosea 4:6, 9).

The importance and sanctity of the Word is also seen in the safeguards that Moses placed upon it. Its pristine purity was no doubt the responsibility of every Israelite. Its content and form must not be altered in any manner whatsoever. To keep the Word of God intact it must not be "added to" or "diminished" to any degree (Deuteronomy 12:32).

Neither were the Israelites to incorporate the laws of other nations into their code. Moses warned them against the ordinances and statutes of Egypt, from whence they came, and of the ordinances of the Canaanites of the future. The one would be diametrically opposed to the other (Leviticus 18:3-5).

Any kind of selectiveness in their attitude toward the Word of God was disallowed by Moses. They were to "set their *hearts* unto *all the words*" given by God. This was Moses' admonition to the Israelites in what is commonly called the "Song of Moses:"

> And he said unto them, *Set your hearts unto all the words* which I testify among you this day ...

> For it is not a vain thing for you; because *It* (Word) *is your life ...*
> (Deuteronomy 32:46-47a).

The seriousness of choosing and picking God's Word can be seen in connection with the many "curses" that would come upon those who quibbled with the commandments of the Lord. Very drastic consequences are pronounced upon the guilty. Moses' warning is directed to the "individual" Israelite but was to be confirmed by all the people.

> Cursed be *he* that *confirmeth not all the words of this law to do them.* And all the people shall say, Amen (Deuteronomy 27:26).

Moses used some very common, everyday language to impress upon his disciples the importance of keeping all the commandments of God. They must not "turn aside to the right hand or the left." Also, they were encouraged to "walk in *all* the ways of the Lord." This grass-roots language should have been understood by every Israelite (Deuteronomy 5:32-33).

So dramatic would be the life style of the Hebrews (if they obeyed the Word of the Lord) that other nations would be aware of it. By believing and obeying God's commandments, they would be wisdom and understanding personified (Deuteronomy 4:6).

Surely there can be no caviling as to the role and importance of the Word of God for the Hebrew people in the Old Testament economy. The revelation of God that was given through Moses was very great and left the people without excuse. Jesus seemed to value the words of Moses with His own. If the Jews of Jesus' day had believed Moses' writings, they would have believed His message:

> For had ye *believed Moses,* ye would have *believed Me:* for he *wrote of Me.*
> But if ye *believe not his writings,* how shall ye *believe My Words?*
> (John 5:46-47).

In the views of Jesus, the message of Moses and the prophets was greater than the testimony of a man returning from the dead. Jesus tells the familiar story of a "certain rich man who died and lifted his eyes in hell." So great was this man's anguish that he asked Abraham to permit Lazarus to return to life again that he might warn his five brothers lest they come to the same place of torture (Luke 16:27-28). His five brothers must have had ample light to escape such punishment. Abraham is reported as saying:

> If they hear not *Moses* and the *prophets,* neither will they be
> persuaded, though *one rose from the dead* (Luke 16:31).

The Word of the Lord would not leave the people in the Old
Testament period as it found them, and it contained only two alterna-
tives — "cursings" or "blessings" — there was no middle ground. Those
who would please God and know His "blessings" must conform to His
Word. There must be unanimity between Word and people. To express
it another way, the Word and people, like the modern day blending of
milk and cream, were to be homogeneous. This conformity of the people
to God's Word would undoubtedly reflect the name "Israel" — one
ruled by God. The ultimate of God's "blessing" for the faithful Israelites
was His personal, intimate *love.*

The last sentence in the above paragraph opens the door to another
important doctrine in the Old Testament that belongs to the "individual"
Israelite far more than it does to the Israelite "nation" — and that is the
work of the Holy Spirit. The "dead letter of the law" (or the Word alone)
is incapable of producing this personal, intimate *love* of God. Zechariah
speaks for *all* of God's handiwork when he says: "Not by might, nor by
power, but by my *Spirit,* saith the Lord of hosts" (4:6b). The interrela-
tionship of the Holy Spirit and the Word of God has been dealt with
throughout this work. Both the Old and New Testaments affirm that any
divine activity pertaining to creation, redemption, or any other manifes-
tation of God's power, is accomplished by the joint working of His *Word*
and *Spirit.* The Godhead cannot be divided. Though the persons of the
Trinity are separate entities, they cannot be segmented.

When reference is made in the Scripture to the Word *only,* or the
Spirit *only,* the presence and ministry of the other is assumed. For
example, when Jesus spoke to Nicodemus about being born of the *Spirit,*
nothing is said about being born of the *Word;* and yet man must be born
of both. This fact is clearly spelled out in Peter's first epistle as he writes:

> Being *born again,* not of corruptible seed, but of incorruptible, by
> the *Word of God,* which liveth and abideth for ever (1 Peter 1:23).

We have already shown how the Apostle Paul speaks of the *Word*
of God apart from the *Spirit* of God and vice versa. In Colossians 3:16,
he emphasizes the importance of the *Word* for the believer in the
worship of God, but does not mention the *Holy Spirit:*

> Let the *word* of Christ dwell in you richly in all wisdom; teaching

and admonishing one another in psalms and hymns and spiritual songs, singing with grace in your hearts to the Lord (Colossians 3:16).

The above experience is described again in the Ephesians letter by Paul, but in this epistle it is the fulness of the *Spirit* that makes such worship possible — the *Word* is omitted:

... be not drunk with wine wherein is excess; but be filled with the Spirit;
Speaking to yourselves in psalms and hymns and spiritual songs, singing and making melody in your heart to the Lord (Ephesians 5:18b-19).

A corresponding pattern is followed by Paul as he differentiates between the births of Ishmael and Isaac in the book of Romans and in his epistle to the Galatians. Ishmael was "born after the flesh" but Isaac's birth was of a different nature. In Romans 9:8-9, it is stated that Isaac was born as a result of the "Word of promise" that was given to Abraham. The Holy Spirit is not mentioned in the Romans passage in connection with Isaac's birth, but in Galatians 4:29 the Apostle implies that the Spirit of God was also active in the conception of Isaac:

But as then he (Ishmael) that was born after the flesh persecuted him that was *born after the Spirit* (Isaac), even so it is now (Galatians 4:29).

To separate the Word and Spirit would be to divide the Godhead — both are required in the activities of God.

When Jesus gave His discourse on the "Bread of Life," as recorded in the sixth chapter of John's Gospel, He spoke of "eating His flesh and drinking His blood." This statement was very repulsive to the Jews who heard Him. The law of Moses forbad the drinking of any kind of blood, but the idea of eating human flesh and drinking human blood was offensive to His own disciples. Jesus tried to relieve the tension by telling them there was a spiritual content to His statement. He said, "... the *Words* that I speak unto you they are *Spirit* and they are life" (John 6:63). Jesus is saying that His words have a spiritual capacity ... they are *Spirit* and they are life.

If Jesus' words *are* Spirit, then the rest of the words of Holy Scripture *are* Spirit. They have a spiritual accommodation as they fulfill their ministry. The prophecies of the Old Testament were not spoken or written by the prophet's own initiative — they were inspired by the

Spirit of God. This truth is confirmed in Peter's words as he writes:

> For the prophecy came not in olden time by the will of man: but
> holy men of God *spake as they were moved by the Holy Ghost* (2 Peter
> 1:21).

Paul affirms that "All Scripture is given by inspiration of God" (2 Timothy 3:16a); and the "Scripture" is the Old Testament writings. When the Word of God was believed and received in the old dispensation, it had a spiritual accommodation. And when the Spirit of God is not mentioned in conjunction with the Word, His presence and activity are assumed.

There is no way for man to understand the "things of God" except by the Spirit of God (1 Corinthians 2:11). One of the most misunderstood aspects of God's revelation of Himself was the cross of Jesus. Those who crucified our Lord did it in total ignorance. According to Paul, the "princes of this world" would not have "crucified the Lord of glory" had they known who He was (1 Corinthians 2:8). In conjunction with this truth, he declares that it is impossible for unregenerate man to understand the "things of God," apart from the Holy Spirit:

> But the *natural man receiveth not the things of the Spirit of God:*
> for they are foolishness unto him: *Neither can he know them,* because
> they are *spiritually discerned* (1 Corinthians 2:14).

If the "things of God" are "spiritually discerned" or understood, then we must conclude that it is only through the Holy Spirit that this is possible. The *Word of God* belongs to the "things of God" more than any other aspect of His revelation. If man is to know God, and the "things of God," then he must be acquainted with the Holy Spirit, regardless of the dispensation in which he lives.

Even the law of God is spiritual (Romans 7:14), but where there is no faith response to the Word of God, it kills — its bent is toward death (2 Corinthians 3:6). We must believe that the Spirit of God was operative with the Word of God in the Old Testament period, even though the word "Spirit" is not always mentioned in connection with it.

The work of the Holy Spirit is tempered with the age. The Old Testament period was the infantile stages of the Gospel. The ministry of the Holy Spirit was to equip men to this end. For this reason, the people in the Old Testament era were gifted in a way that is somewhat foreign to the New Testament dispensation. However, there are similarities in both. I might add, it is "individuals" who are gifted by the Holy Spirit in the old economy and not the "nation" of Israel.

In the Old Testament period we discover that men were endowed with special skills to work in metal, wood, stone, and other materials by the direction of the Spirit of God. Men were given unusual strength by the Spirit of God that is unheard of in the Christian era. There are a number of spiritual phenomena in the Old Jewish economy that are totally out of place in our day. It is our bounden duty to recognize this difference in the two dispensations and to interpret the Scriptures accordingly.

The forty-first chapter of Genesis informs us that Joseph, a very prominent figure in the old dispensation, was given special ability to interpret dreams and to possess unusual wisdom in matters of government. After Joseph interpreted Pharoah's dream regarding the seven years of plenty and seven years of famine, he suggested that the king find a "discreet and wise" man and set him over this matter. Pharoah did not have to look too far — he immediately made Joseph prime minister over Egypt. Pharoah said to his servant:

> ... can we find such a one as this, a man in whom the *Spirit of God* is? (Genesis 41:38).

The "Spirit of wisdom" seems to characterize the leadership of Israel more than any other gift of the Spirit. Moses was anointed with the Spirit of God, and when the burden of judging the people became too heavy Jethro, Moses' father-in-law, advised him to select elders to assist him:

> And Moses went out, and told the people the words of the Lord and gathered the seventy men of the elders of the people, and set them round about the tabernacle.
> And the Lord came down in a cloud, and spake unto him, and took of the *Spirit* that was upon him, and gave it unto the seventy elders: and it came to pass, that, when the *Spirit* rested upon them, they prophesied, and did not cease (Numbers 11:24-25).

When Moses died and the need of another leader arose, we find that Joshua was endowed with the same "spirit of wisdom:"

> And Joshua the son of Nun was full of the *Spirit of wisdom;* for Moses had laid his hands upon him: and the children of Israel harkened unto him, and did as the Lord commanded Moses (Deuter-

onomy 34:9).

The intricate construction of the tabernacle was not left to human wisdom or skill. The Lord gave certain men the Spirit of wisdom in cutting stones, carving wood, and designing metal work that exceeded natural abilities. Bezaleel and Aholiab were key men whom God called for this purpose. Also, the Lord put it in their hearts to teach others the same skills:

> And Moses said unto the children of Israel, See, the Lord hath called by name Bezaleel the son of Uri, the son of Hur, of the tribe of Judah;
> And he hath filled him with the *Spirit of God,* in wisdom, understanding, and in knowledge, and in all manner of workmanship;
> And to devise curious works, to work in gold, and in silver, and in brass,
> And the cutting of stones, to set them, and in carving of wood, to make any manner of cunning work.
> And he hath put it in his heart that he may *teach* both he, and Aholiab, the son of Ahisamach of the tribe of Dan.
> Them hath He *filled with wisdom* of heart to work all manner of work, etc. (Exodus 35:30-35).

The priestly garments of Aaron and his sons were not left to chance. For the purpose of making these, the Lord selected special men and provided them with supernatural wisdom:

> And thou shalt make holy garments for Aaron thy brother for glory and for beauty.
> And thou shalt speak unto all that are wise hearted, whom *I have filled with the Spirit of wisdom,* that they may make Aaron's garments to consecrate him, that he minister unto Me in the priest's office (Exodus 28:2-3).

The Spirit of the Lord came upon some of the judges of Israel who ruled immediately before the days of the kings. The Spirit of the Lord came upon Othniel (Judges 3:10), upon Gideon (Judges 6:34), upon Jephthah (Judges 11:29), and upon Samson (Judges 13:25). Under the influence of the Spirit of God, several of the judges became great leaders and accomplished unusual feats. The anointing of the Lord may have been upon all the judges of Israel, but only the above are mentioned in the Scriptures.

The construction of the temple, like the tabernacle, was given by divine illumination. David desired to build the house of the Lord himself, but was not granted this privilege — Solomon, David's son, was given the honor and responsibility. However, the Spirit of God directed David in drafting the blueprint for the temple:

> Then David gave to Solomon his son the pattern of the porch, and of the houses thereof, and of the treasuries thereof, and of the upper chambers thereof, and of the inner parlours thereof, and of the place of the mercy seat,
>
> And the pattern of all that he had *by the Spirit,* of the courts of the house of the Lord, and of all the chambers round about, of the treasuries of the house of God, and of the treasuries of the dedicated things (1 Chronicles 28:11-12).

Some of the most phenomenal experiences of the Holy Spirit are to be found in the book of Ezekiel. We find miraculous events attending Ezekiel's ministry that are unparalled in Biblical revelation. It seems that Ezekiel was transported from one locality to another by a supernatural power that defies our understanding.

Ezekiel was among the exilic populace in Babylon when he encountered some unusual manifestations of the Holy Spirit. While in his own house, sitting amid the elders of Judah, the Lord appeared to him in an unprecedented manner:

> ... He (Lord) put forth the form of an hand, and took me by a lock of mine head; and the *Spirit lifted me up between the earth and heaven,* and brought me in visions of God to Jerusalem, to the door of the inner gate that looketh toward the north; where was the seat of the image of jealousy, which provoketh to jealousy (Ezekiel 8:3).

It is not the purpose of this work to interpret the enigmas that are connected with the above event. Our primary purpose is to point out that the prophet, in some inexplicable, mystical manner, was lifted up by the Spirit of God and transported to Jerusalem. Whether he was actually transported bodily, or in his spirit only, remains a mystery.

There are two important lessons that can be learned from Ezekiel's experience: (1) God is not static; and (2) the ministry of the Spirit of God is very diverse. We must not limit the activities of the Spirit in either dispensation; but at the same time, we would do well to give heed to John's warning in the New Testament:

Beloved, believe not every spirit, but *try the spirits whether they are of God:* because many false prophets are gone out into the world (1 John 4:1).

The nearest parallel to Ezekiel's experience in the New Testament would be that of Philip, the evangelist, which is reported in the book of Acts. After Philip baptized the Ethiopian eunuch, it is written that "the Spirit of the Lord *caught away Philip,* that the eunuch saw him no more" (Acts 8:39). A similar experience is described by Paul when he (or some acquaintance of his) was "caught up into paradise and heard unspeakable words, which it is not lawful for a man to utter" (2 Corinthians 12:1-5).

The diversity of the Holy Spirit's work in the two dispensations does not mean that they have nothing in common. There are certain functions that the Holy Spirit performs in both. For example, the conviction of sin is the work of the Holy Spirit in both the Old and New Testaments.

When the wickedness of man had reached a certain peak in Noah's day, we find the Lord saying: "My *Spirit* shall not always *strive* with man" (Genesis 6:3). A broader definition of the Hebrew word for "strive" will reveal that the Holy Spirit performs the same office in the Old Testament that He does in the New. "Strive" comes from a Hebrew word which means to judge (as an umpire) ... to contend, to execute, (as in judgment), to minister judgment, and to plead (the cause).[6]

This expanded definition of the word "strive" accords with Jesus' statement on the Holy Spirit in John's Gospel:

When He (Holy Spirit) is come, He will convince the world of sin and of righteousness and of judgment (John 16:8).

Also, in John's Gospel, the Holy Spirit is referred to as the "Comforter." The Greek word for Comforter is *paraclete,* an advocate, one who pleads for the believer. The work of the Holy Spirit in Noah's day was the same as that of John's day and ours.

Denouncing and exposing the sins of the Hebrew people was one of the chief ministries of the prophets in the Old Testament. Proper judgment into the nature of sin (as well as righteousness) and the courage to expose it was needed by every servant of God. The Holy

---

6. James Strong, *Dictionary of the Words of the Hebrew Bible, 30.*

Spirit provided this knowledge and power. Micah distinguished himself from the princes, priests, and false prophets by this rule of thumb:

> ... truly I am *full of power* by the *Spirit of God,* and of *Judgment,* and of *might,* to declare unto Jacob his *transgression,* and to Israel his sin (3:8).

A comparison of Micah's words with the book of Acts will reveal a similar pattern among the New Testament apostles. When courage was needed to confront the adversaries of the Gospel, the disciples prayed, and,

> ... the place was shaken where they were assembled together; and they were all *filled with the Holy Ghost,* and they spake the *Word of God with boldness* (Acts 4:31).

It is common knowledge that the prophets who wrote the Old Testament Scriptures, as well as the writers of the New Testament Scriptures, were inspired by the Holy Spirit. There should be no question about David's unusual anointing by the Spirit of God in writing the Psalms. The Holy Spirit enabled him to write with an inspiration that no mortal man can begin to duplicate:

> Now these be the last words of David. David the son of Jesse said, and the man who was raised up on high, the *anointed* of the God of Jacob, and the *sweet psalmist* of Israel said,
>   The *Spirit of the Lord* spake by me, and His *Word* was in my tongue (2 Samuel 23:1-2).

Peter says that all the Old Testament prophets spoke under the inspiration of the Spirit of God:

> For the *prophecy* came not in old time (Old Testament period) by the will of man: but holy men of God *spake* as they were *moved by the Holy Ghost* (2 Peter 1:21).

There are few problems with the Holy Spirit's relationship to the leaders of Israel in the old economy. We know that many of the kings, all true prophets, judges, etc., were anointed by the Spirit of God. Our main difficulty is the Holy Spirit's relationship to the laity. Did the nominal believer enjoy the work and presence of the Holy Spirit in his life? If so, to what extent did he experience the Holy Spirit? This is difficult to answer. In the light of some New Testament passages, I am constrained to believe that the nominal believer experienced "something" of the Spirit of God — but "how" and to "what degree" we may never fully understand.

The days of Moses and Joshua produced more information on the Holy Spirit than any other period of Jewish history. A study on the Holy Spirit's activities during these formative years will enable us to understand His work in the years that followed. More theological lessons are associated with this period of history than any other period. The works of the Old Testament prophets and the New Testament apostles confirm that the people under Moses and Joshua established several spiritual precedents that would affect succeeding generations. In other words, the light and knowledge on the Holy Spirit, coming from this brief era, would be applicable to all individuals living beyond this period — including both the Old and the New Testament dispensations.

Paul, who was the brainchild of the Gospel, was given a pre-Gospel and a post-Gospel revelation that no other New Testament apostle received. He was given extra knowledge regarding the wilderness experience that cannot be found in the writings of Moses. Paul says that the "manna" and "water," given to the Israelites under Moses, had a spiritual content that is not mentioned in the Pentateuch:

> Moreover, brethren, I would not that ye should be ignorant, how that all our fathers were under the cloud, and all passed through the sea;
> And were all baptized unto Moses in the cloud and in the sea;
> And did all eat the same *spiritual meat;*
> And did all drink the same *spiritual drink:* for they drank of that *spiritual rock* that followed them: and that *rock was Christ* (1 Corinthians 10:1-4).

The Exodus account of the "cloud" and "sea" does not say that this was a "baptism" for the Israelites, but Paul declares it was. In like manner, we are not told that the "meat" and "drink" in the wilderness had a spiritual accommodation — but it did. Exactly "how" and to "what degree" the people ate and drank, remains a mystery. But they ate and drank in "some measure" of the Spirit of Christ. The Apostle is careful to point out that "all" were baptized and "all" ate and drank of the spiritual sustenance. No one was excluded. All of this was experienced *before* the Israelites came into the Land of Promise.

Isaiah gives some very pertinent information on the Holy Spirit that arises out of the wilderness experience. We learn from Isaiah that the first generation of Israelites "rebelled and *grieved God's Holy Spirit.* So

He turned and became their enemy and He Himself fought against them" (Isaiah 63:10 NIV). Isaiah uses the consequences of this rebellious act to warn the Babylonian exiles, lest they repeat the mistake of their forefathers.

The Holy Spirit is a very sensitive Person and can be easily hurt or wounded by the actions of men. This offense against the Holy Spirit in Moses' day, and in the days of Isaiah, seems to be no different from the New Testament dispensation. Paul deals with the same truth and warns the Ephesian church, lest they commit the same sin. In all probability, Paul derived his inspiration from the words of Isaiah:

> And *grieve* not the *Holy Spirit* of God, whereby ye are sealed unto the day of redemption (Ephesians 4:30).

But this offense against the Holy Spirit by the first generation of Israelites did not abort God's love and mercy for them. This fact was a source of faith and comfort for the exiles in Babylon. If the Lord had shown mercy and patience toward the people under Moses and Joshua — in spite of their rebellion — He would no doubt do the same for the Israelites in captivity. Isaiah, in very dramatic literary style, speaks on behalf of the exiles:

> ... Where is he that brought them up out of the sea with the shepherd of his flock? Where is he that put his *Holy Spirit within him?*
> That led them by the right hand of Moses with his glorious arm, dividing the water before them, to make himself an everlasting name?
> That led them through the deep, as an horse in the wilderness, that they should not stumble?
> As beast (cattle) goeth down into the valley, the *Spirit of the Lord caused him to rest:* so didst thou lead thy people, to make thyself a glorious name (Isaiah 63:11b-14).

The Pulpit Commentary lists several Bible scholars who interpret the last pronoun in verse 11b ("him") as meaning "the people:"

> The "him" of this passage undoubtedly refers to "the people" (Rosenmuller, Knobel, Delitzsch, Kay, Cheyne). God gave to the people in the wilderness "His good Spirit to instruct them" (Nehemiah ix. 20), and guide them (Habbakuk ii. 4-5), and govern them (Numbers xi. 17).[7]

7. *The Pulpit Commentary,* Vol. 2 of Vol. 10, 443.

The above passage from Isaiah teaches another important lesson on the Holy Spirit that is associated with the early history of the Hebrew people. Isaiah says that "the *Spirit* of the Lord caused him to rest" (Isaiah 63:14). In the light of what is written on the "rest of God" in the epistle to the Hebrews, we *must* interpret the "him" in this passage as meaning "the people."

The Israelites should have experienced more than a "physical rest" when they came into the Land of Promise. If they had believed God's Word, they would have shared in the "rest" that God enjoyed after He created all things. This "rest for the people of God" is discussed in great detail in the third and forth chapters of the book of Hebrews. According to this epistle, both Joshua and David, who were separated by several hundred years, speak of a "rest" for the Hebrew people in their particular age. The author of the Hebrews epistle argues that it would have been unnecessary for David to promise the people of his day a "rest" if the Land of Canaan (under the leadership of Joshua) had been the ultimate "rest of God" (Hebrews 4:7-10). The Hebrews of David's day were already in the land, and yet David writes of a "rest for the people of God" (Psalm 95:8-11). The only feasible way for the Israelites of Joshua's day and of David's day to experience the "rest of God" was through the *Word* and *Spirit* of God.

The book of Hebrews shows conclusively that Canaan was not the primary blessing for the Israelites at any time during their history. The settlement of Canaan, which is described as a "rest" for the Jewish people (Joshua 1:13), would become a "curse" if they missed the "rest of God." The Land of Canaan is not so much as mentioned in the Hebrews letter — it is only implied. The "rest of God," which He enjoyed after He created all things, is the outstanding feature in this remarkable epistle. The Priesthood of Christ, which follows the comments on the "rest of God" in the Hebrews epistle and takes up a good deal of time and space, is given to explain how this "rest" may be acquired. The "rest of God" was not obtained by their occupancy of the land — it was experienced by *hearing His voice* or by believing His *Word:*

> Wherefore as the *Holy Ghost* saith, *Today* if ye will *hear His voice,*
> Harden not your hearts, as in the *provocation,* in the day of temptation in the wilderness:
> When your fathers tempted me, proved me, and saw my works forty years.

> Wherefore *I was grieved* with that generation, and said, They do
> always err in their heart; and they *have not known my ways.*
> So I sware in my wrath, *They shall not enter into my rest* (Hebrews
> 3:7-11).

In the Hebrews epistle, and throughout the Scripture, the *voice of
God,* or His *Word,* is the foremost thing for the Jewish people. The
author of this epistle emphasized the word "today" as the *time* for every
generation (Jew and Gentile) to hear His *voice* and enter into His "rest."
Dare we encourage the Jews (or anyone else) to anticipate the land of
Palestine as an inheritance, when the eternal "rest of God" is available
to them *today?* It is difficult to believe that Christian men would
capitalize on a future millennial kingdom for the Jews rather than the
voice of God for them *here* and *now.* The above passage contains a
severe warning to those who refuse His *voice* at any given period of
history.

The "rest of God" in the New Testament era is the same as that of
the Old Testament period. God has not changed His position — He is
still "resting." According to the Hebrews epistle, the "rest of God" is
experienced in the same manner in both dispensations — i.e., by *faith
in His Word.* The Israelites, under Moses, had the Gospel preached unto
them, but it was not "mixed with faith:"

> For unto us (New Testament generation) was the *Gospel preached,*
> as well as them (Old Testament generation): but the *Word preached*
> did not profit them, *not being mixed with faith* in them that heard it
> (Hebrews 4:2).

The "Gospel" is the source of "God's rest" in every age of history.
If the "Gospel" was more important for the Israelites in Moses' day than
the Land of Canaan — it should be so today. The "Gospel" brings men
into a dimension and realm where even the thoughts of Canaan cannot
enter. *To believe the "Gospel" is the most important thing in all of
Scripture.* To hear the *voice* of God and to be born of His *Word* and *Spirit*
is to be a partaker of His divine nature and an heir of eternal life. This
is the crux of the "blessing of Abraham" (Galatians 3:14). This is what
God planned for mankind from the beginning.

Isaiah's emphasis on the "rest of God" does not stand alone among
the prophets. It was a vital part of Jeremiah's message to the Judean Jews
who were being threatened by the Babylonian captivity. The people of
Jeremiah's day were still "in the land," but more was needed for their

well-being than the land per se. Jeremiah's promise to these fearful
Israelites was not a new idea — it belonged to the Patriarchal age. It
should be noted that the promise made by Jeremiah pertains to the "soul"
and not the "body:"

> Thus saith the Lord, Stand ye in the ways, and see, and ask for the
> *old paths,* where is the good way, and walk therein, and *ye shall find
> rest for your souls.* But they said, We will not walk therein (Jeremiah
> 6:16).

When the religious leaders of Nehemiah's day wanted to encourage
their fellow Jews to seek the Lord's help, they did so by giving them a
flashback of their religious heritage, beginning with the call of Abraham. But the most detailed aspect of this historical review centered
around the wilderness experience under Moses. According to Nehemiah, one of the outstanding favors that God bestowed upon the
Israelites in the wilderness was His "good Spirit to instruct them." It
should be noted that the Holy Spirit is mentioned in connection with the
"manna" and "water:"

> Thou gavest also thy *good Spirit* to instruct them, and withheldest
> not thy *manna* from their mouth, and gave them *water* for their thirst
> (Nehemiah 9:20).

A parallel to the above truth can be found in the book of Haggai.
When the second temple was about to be built, under the leadership of
Zerubbabel, governor of Judah, and Joshua, the high priest, there was a
degree of trepidation in their hearts. They were afraid the temple project
would fall far short of the first temple that was built by Solomon. The
Lord sent Haggai to encourage Zerubbabel, Joshua, and the people in
this endeavor. Haggai assured them that the "same Spirit" that was with
their forefathers, who came up out of Egypt, would be with them:

> Yet now be strong, O Zerubbabel, saith the Lord; and be strong, O
> Joshua, son of Josedech, the high priest; and be strong all ye people
> of the land, saith the Lord, and work: for I am with you saith the Lord
> of Hosts:
> According to the *Word* that I *covenanted* with you when ye came
> out of Egypt, so *my Spirit remaineth among you:* fear ye not (Haggai
> 2:4-5).

We must not overlook an opportunity to call attention to Haggai's
association of the "Word" and "Spirit" in the above passage, which is

central to this work. Evidently, the Word and Spirit that worked jointly for the Israelites who "came up out of Egypt" would do the same for the exiles who returned from captivity.

Let us say parenthetically that the same combination of "Word" and "Spirit" is expressed in the book of Proverbs. As Solomon attempts to personify "wisdom" and turn the people of his day from their sins, he writes:

> Turn you at my reproof: behold, I will pour out *my Spirit* unto you,
> I will make known *my words* unto you (Proverbs 1:23).

The "pouring out of the Spirit" in the above passage does not seem to be limited to any special leadership within the nation — it implies that all who conform to God's commandments can share in the Spirit and Word of God. It also insinuates that it is impossible to *know* and *understand* the Word of God apart from the Spirit of God.

A summary of the Holy Spirit's relationship to the first and second generation of Israelites, who came out of Egypt, will be very helpful. More information is given on the subject than is generally assumed. Paul said that the Israelites under Moses "ate and drank" of the spiritual Rock, which was Christ; Isaiah affirms that God "put His Holy Spirit within him" (people), and that God caused the people to "rest by the Spirit of God;" Jeremiah promised a "rest for the soul" if the Israelites of his day would return and walk in the "old paths" as did their believing forefathers; Nehemiah states that God gave the people under Moses His "good Spirit to instruct them;" Haggai vowed that God's Spirit would "remain among them" (exiles). The capstone on the Spirit's role in the Old Testament, which produced a "rest for the people of God," provided they believed, is to be found in the third and fourth chapters of the epistle to the Hebrews. The author of the epistle of Hebrews is writing in retrospect as well as for his day and ours. The prophets and apostles, who wrote on the work of the Holy Spirit during the Pentateuchal years, implied that succeeding generations, as well as the first and second generations of Israelites, should be acquainted with the Holy Spirit.

There are other similarities between the two Testaments, regarding the work and ministry of the Holy Spirit, that need to be considered. To resist the inspired Word of God, whether in the old dispensation or the new, was to "resist" the Holy Spirit. The reaction that Stephen received from his Jewish colleagues (as recorded in the seventh chapter of the book of Acts) was no different from that received by the Old Testament prophets from their unbelieving contemporaries. Stephen, who was full of faith and the Holy Ghost, charged his Jewish kin with the same sin and crime that many of the Old Testament Jews were guilty of:

> Ye stiffnecked and uncircumcised in the heart and ears, *Ye do always resist the Holy Ghost:* as *your fathers did,* so do ye.
> Which of the *prophets* have not your *fathers* persecuted? And they have slain them, etc. (Acts 7:51-52b).

The response of the unbelieving Jews in both dispensations (to the inspired Word) stands out very clearly. Both "resisted" the Holy Ghost and both "killed" God's spokesmen. The accountability of the Jews in one period was as great as the other.

The ministry of the Holy Spirit in both dispensations is a matter of *tense.* In the Old Testament, the Holy Spirit spoke of the coming of Christ in the flesh (Acts 7:52); but in the New Testament the Holy Spirit confirms the fact that He *has come* in the flesh. *This change in tense is very important to sound theology.* It is by this truth that the "Spirit of Christ" and the "spirit of Antichrist" are distinguished.

A few years after Jesus' resurrection, there arose false teachers who taught that Christ had "not come in the flesh." To combat this heresy, John writes:

> Hereby know ye the *Spirit* of God: Every *Spirit* that confesseth that Jesus Christ *is come in the flesh is of God:*
> And every spirit that *confesseth not* that Christ *is come in the flesh* is *not of God:* and this is that *spirit of Antichrist* (1 John 4:2-3a).

John's statement could not have been written prior to Jesus' Incarnation. The above passage affirms that God is not static; He is working in *time* and *history.* At this point *in time,* the coming of Christ in the flesh is the *apex* of all history. This is why history is divided into B.C. and A.D. Regardless of the dispensation, it is the same Spirit.

The above truth suggests a transition period in the revelation and ministry of the Holy Spirit from the Old Testament period to the New. This transition from one dispensation to the other is seldom recognized, and it is rarely dealt with by those who interpret the Scriptures. Jesus implies this transition period in one of His notable metaphors on the Holy Spirit. In the Gospel of John, the Holy Spirit is compared to "rivers of living water" that would flow from within the believer (John 7:38). These "rivers of living water," which the Holy Spirit would provide, would be a consequence of Jesus' glorification or resurrection:

> He that believeth on me, as the Scripture hath said, out of his belly shall flow rivers of living water.
> But this spake he of the *Spirit,* which they that believed on him should receive; for the *Holy Ghost was not yet given;* because that Jesus was not yet glorified (John 7:38-39).

Jesus is not inferring that the Holy Spirit was unknown or inactive before His resurrection and the day of Pentecost. The Holy Spirit was "alive and well" long before these eventful days. Jesus is implying a change from the "shadow" of the Gospel to the "substance" of the Gospel. Pentecost marked the beginning of the "substance" of the Gospel and the end of the "shadow." The *promise* of the Old Testament was fulfilled in the death and resurrection of Christ. The Holy Spirit must confirm and reveal this truth to the Apostles and those who would believe their witness (John 16:7-15; Galatians 1:11-12). The ultimate transition of the Holy Spirit's revelation and ministry did not occur until Jesus returned to the Father (John 16:7).

However, the final change from the old dispensation to the new is preceded by some wonderful manifestations of the Spirit of God. We are confronted with some activities of the Holy Spirit in the New Testament that, in a sense, belong to the Old Testament era. The birth narratives of Jesus are surrounded with the activities of the Holy Spirit. The Spirit of God touched the lives of several ordinary people in the birth of our Lord. Zacharias, Simeon, Mary, and Elisabeth cannot be classified as "special leaders" (such as prophets, priests, kings, etc.) in the Jewish nation; yet we find that the Holy Spirit worked in and through them to accomplish God's purpose. Except for Zacharias, who was perhaps a common priest (as over against the high priest), these people were only unpretending people. Simeon, although a very devout man, seems to have been only a layman in his day. However, it is written that the

> ... *Holy Ghost was upon him,* And it was revealed unto him by the *Holy Ghost,* that he should not see death, before he had seen the Lord's Christ (Luke 2:25b-26).

Zacharias, Simeon, Mary, and Elisabeth are singled out in the birth narratives for two special reasons: (1) to verify the Holy Spirit's activities before Pentecost, and (2) to show that the faithful Israelite in the Old Testament dispensation, though not a prophet, priest, or king, could have been acquainted with and used by the Spirit of God.

God has called and anointed special leaders throughout the history of the world, but this does not mean that the laity did not have access to the Holy Spirit. Paul calls attention to special leaders within the church, but they are not an entity within themselves. They are listed according to their importance, but they are not exclusive:

> And God hath set some in the church, *first apostles, secondarily prophets, thirdly teachers,* after that miracles, then gifts of healing, etc. (1 Corinthians 12:28).

The Holy Spirit is responsible for the members and offices of those whom we consider "less honorable," as well as those on whom we may "bestow more abundant honor" — all are a part of the whole body (1 Corinthians 12:22-27).

Are we to censure Jesus who implied that Nicodemus should have known about being born of the Spirit (John 3:1-8)? Jesus' implication on the new birth was given to Nicodemus several months before Pentecost and the coming of the Holy Spirit. Nicodemus was most likely a teacher in Israel several years before our Lord's public ministry. In all probability he was expected to know this truth long before his meeting with Jesus that night. What inferences are we to draw from Jesus' implications? Was this lengthy discourse on the Holy Spirit for naught? Was Jesus imposing a doctrine upon Nicodemus that did not belong to his age?

We are faced with a similar dilemma in Jesus' encounter with the Sadducees. When the Sadducees confronted our Lord with their anti-quated question on the resurrection of the dead, He implied that they should have known a "power" that is associated with the Scriptures:

> "... Do ye not therefore err, because ye know not the scriptures, neither the *power* of *God* (Mark 12:24)?

Isn't Jesus saying that the Sadducees should have known the Holy Spirit? What other "power" could He have in mind? The above state-ment antedates the day of Pentecost and the coming of the Holy Spirit. Jesus insinuates that the "power" (Holy Spirit) would have led the Sadducees to know (from the Scriptures) that God was not a God of the *dead* but of the *living.* Abraham, Isaac, and Jacob, though dead many years before Moses' day, were still "living" (Mark 12:26-27).

It is not my intention to impose the New Testament upon the Old unduly, but at the same time, we must not sell the people of the old dispensation short of the light they were expected to follow. The accountability of the people to God that is taught throughout the Old Testament Scriptures would suggest that the Israelites were expected to know more about the God of Abraham, Isaac, and Jacob than the "dead letter" of the law (Deuteronomy 10:12).

Some vagueness on the role of the Holy Spirit in the Old Testament period has been admitted. It is impossible to know all that we would like to know about His ministry during this period. However, if the Word of the Lord was to be effectual, creating the results that God desired in His people, it seems that the saints of the Old Testament era would have to be familiar with the Holy Spirit. If this is not true, then every Israelite would have to live under condemnation that the "dead letter," of itself, would produce. According to Paul, "the letter killeth, but the *Spirit giveth life*" (2 Corinthians 3:6).

The First Commandment or Man's Love for God

"And thou shalt *love* the Lord thy God with all thine heart, and with all thy soul, and with all thy might" (Deuteronomy 6:5; Matthew 22:37).

The Scriptures address themselves to three primary areas of revelation. They are: (1) God, (2) man, and (3) Satan. The central feature in this threefold revelation is the power struggle between "good" and "evil" — between God and Satan. Man is in an intermediate position between the two — he casts his lot with one or the other. God is forever and always "on the side" of man. His love for His creature is unwavering. This fact dictates that man is expected to love both God and his fellow man.

Most of the Bible is written with the above truth in mind. The two testaments can be summed up in a single word — love. The Old Testament carries its own weight in revealing this well-grounded axiom. The most repeated commandment in the Pentateuch is the commandment to "love God," which also implies obedience to God. The tandem truth to "love of God" is "love of neighbor." This twofold love takes priority over any and all "national" relationships.

Since the Word of God is so important to man's salvation, the first and second commandments should have been the "Word of Words" for the Israelites. They should have given attention to "love of God" and "love of neighbor" more than any other portion of Biblical truth. Israel's disregard of the first two commandments epitomizes their lack of faith more than any other aspect of their religious activities. It is not necessary to examine the entire Old Testament to prove this truth. Wherever there is an absence of *love,* there is an absence of faith. Faith and love go hand in hand. Paul says "Faith ... worketh by love" (Galatians 5:6). Faith and love interact with each other. Love is the expression of faith — the arms and legs of faith. Love inspires faith, and faith in turn inspires love. Faith and love will increase or diminish together.[8] Faith and love is an "individual" matter, not a "national" one.

"Love of God" is always the first in order, but "love of God" was not native to the Hebrew heart. In matters of sin and wickedness, their hearts were no different from any other race of people (Romans 3:9-18). This truth was proven to them in the very outset of their history. The wilderness experience under Moses served a multiple purpose, one of which was to show them exactly what was in their hearts:

> And thou shalt remember all the way which the Lord thy God led thee forty years in the wilderness, to *humble thee,* and to *prove thee, to know what was in thine heart,* whether thou wouldest keep his commandments, or no (Deuteronomy 8:2).

We find many sins surfacing under the pressures of the wilderness — complaining, murmuring, doubt, fear, idolatry, conspiracy, anarchy, nakedness, murder, sexual immorality, exaggeration, rebellion, hate, evil imaginations, frivolity, stiffneckedness, sedition, etc. These are only a token of the many evils that would emerge in the centuries ahead.

If the Hebrew people were to "love God," as taught by Moses and the prophets, their sinful nature must be supplanted by the Word of God. "Love of God" is contingent upon *faith* in the "Word of God." There is an inseparable relationship between the two concepts. Love is greater than faith, but they do not work independently of each other. The necessity of faith for the Hebrew people in the Old Testament era is incontestable. The author of the Hebrews epistle states that the Israelites, under Moses, had the Gospel preached unto them, "but the *Word* preached did not profit them, not being mixed with *faith* in them that heard it" (Hebrews 4:2).

It is inconceivable that the natural descendants of Abraham could

---

8. Excerpts from *The Pulpit Commentary,* Vol. 20, Galatians, 268...290.

"love God" without the gift of His love and grace within — which is given as a result of faith. The New Testament truth, "We love Him because He first loved us," must be applied to the Old Testament saints. God is man's source of love for Himself and others, regardless of the dispensation in which one lives. Man *receives* the capacity to love God and his fellow man — it is not innate in him (Jew or Gentile). God would bestow His love to the degree the Hebrew people believed and obeyed His Word.

If the above statement is not true, then how are we to interpret God's love for the saints in the Old Testament era? Are we to define His love as impersonal, stoic, and passive? Was His love objective only? Were the material and physical needs of the people the sole factor in their relationship to Him? Or was God's love subjective — was it personal and intimate? — was it passionate and emotional?

The Hebrew people were commanded to "love God with all their heart, mind, and soul." Was their relationship to Him a one-sided love affair? Was God's love reciprocal? Was there an interchange of love between God and His people? Or was God to be inert and unresponsive? Just how are we to evaluate God's total relationship to His people?

It is my conviction that the Lord's relationship to the Old Testament saints was more than just a "meal ticket" for them. Over and over again we are informed by Moses and the prophets that obedience to God's Word would result in temporal blessings; but we are also taught that His presence would be with them, i.e., His Personhood or Godhood:

> And I will set my *tabernacle among you:* and my soul shall not abhor you.
> And I will *walk among you,* and will be *your God,* and ye shall be my *people* (Leviticus 26:11-12).

Paul quotes the above passage in the sixth chapter of Second Corinthians and interprets it to mean that God's presence among the Israelites would be more than His abode in the tabernacle:

> ... as God hath said, I will *dwell in them,* and *walk in them;* and I will be *their God,* and they shall be *my people* (2 Corinthians 6:16).

Paul declares that the people were more truly the "tabernacle of God" than the frail structure in which He "lived." The same truth, regarding Christ's relationship to His church, is expressed in the New Testament. Jesus is the "temple of God" and so are His people. The two "temples" are actually one. This seems to be the way that Paul interprets Moses' remarks in Leviticus 26:11-12.

The same truth is expressed in the Old Testament by the concept of an "inheritance." Not only were the people "God's inheritance" (Deuteronomy 9:29), God was the "inheritance of His people" (Psalm 16:5). It was a two-way street.

In the Scripture God is revealed as being very high and exalted in character — seemingly, above and beyond an intimate and personal relationship with man. But when this aspect of God's nature is described in the Scripture, it is generally given in a polarity context. There is also a condescending spirit in God's character. These two particularities in God's nature, so well established in the New Testament, were beautifully portrayed by Isaiah several hundred years before Christ was born. In the words of Isaiah, God dwells with those who are of a "contrite heart and humble spirit." The prophet implies an *inner dwelling* of God that would result in an "inner healing" of man's heart and spirit that God alone can accomplish:

> For thus saith the high and lofty One that inhabiteth eternity, whose name is Holy; I dwell in the high and holy place, with *him also that is of a contrite and humble spirit,* to revive the *spirit of the humble, and to revive the heart of the contrite* (Isaiah 57:15). Consider also verses 18-19 in the same chapter.

According to Paul, the heathen world was able to discern and understand some of the predominant attributes of God through His creation, such as His power, wisdom, intelligence, and love (Romans 1:19-21). This revelation of God in nature was so outstanding that a rejection of it made the heathen world accountable. Surely the Jewish people had a greater revelation of God than empirical knowledge — and even greater than the law that was written on tables of stone. The Apostle Paul, while writing on the advantages of the Jewish people in the old dispensation, says:

> ... to whom (Jews) pertaineth the *adoption,* and the *glory,* and the *covenants,* and the *giving of the law,* and the *service of God,* and the *promises,* etc. (Romans 9:4).

I am in agreement with those Bible students who believe that the covenant of grace that was fulfilled in the death and resurrection of Christ was retrospective for the sins of the saints in the Old Testament era. Therefore, it is my opinion that the "man of faith" in the old economy had a foretaste of God's covenant love. The law of Moses, or the covenant of works, was cold, legalistic, and written on tables of stone; but the covenant of grace was just the opposite. It was inward, personal, and very endearing.

The difference in God's people and the other nations of the world centered around the covenant made with Abraham, Isaac, and Jacob. God's promise to the Patriarchs (which was to be fulfilled in Christ) was the principal reason for their being set aside as a "holy," "special," and "chosen" people. It was for this reason they were forbidden to inter-marry with the inhabitants of the land in which they were to dwell:

> For thou art an *holy people* unto the Lord thy God: the Lord thy God hath *chosen thee* to be a *special people unto Himself, above all people* that are upon the face of the earth.
>
> The Lord did not *set His love* upon you nor *choose* you, because ye were more in number than any people; for ye were the fewest of all people:
>
> But because the Lord *loved you,* and because He *would keep the oath* (promise) which He had *sworn unto your fathers* ...
>
> *Know* therefore that the Lord thy God, He is God, the faithful God, which *keepeth covenant* and *mercy* with them that *love* and keep His commandments to a thousand generations (Deuteronomy 7:6-9).

In the above passage Moses writes, *"Know* therefore that the Lord thy God, He is God." The word "know" is oftentimes used in both the Old and New Testaments to speak of the sexual relationship of man and wife (Genesis 4:1; Matthew 1:25). The word "know" is a very appropriate term to describe this God-ordained union. The sexual relationship between husband and wife is more than a carnal experience — it is a revelation. It results in the most intimate knowledge of the opposite sex that one can experience on the human level. Paul speaks of the oneness of husband and wife as a "great mystery" that defies explanation (Ephesians 5:32). Anthropomorphic language is the only means we have in understanding certain things about God. Although there are no sexual connotations in God's love for mankind, there is to be an intimacy and knowledge of God's love, similar to that of husband and wife.

Many of the Old Testament prophets used the metaphor of marriage to typify God's love for His people. According to Amos, God's fidelity to Israel was like that of a faithful husband to his wife. Israel may prove unfaithful and play the harlot, but God can never be untrue to His

178   ISRAEL VS. ISRAEL

covenant. The relationship between God and His people was in jeopardy
in Amos' day, but God's role as a "faithful husband" did not change. His
intimacy, which is expressed by Amos in the word "know," cannot be
shared with any people outside His covenant relationship:

> You only have I *known* of all the families of the earth; therefore I
> will punish you for all your iniquities.
> Can *two walk together, except they be agreed?* (Amos 3:2-3).

Dr. Norman H. Snaith, a renowned Old Testament scholar, states
that the Hebrew word for "know" is used to denote a personal knowledge of God more often than an intellectual knowledge. In commenting
on verse 2 of the above passage, Dr. Snaith says:

> The normal Hebrew word translated "know" (see *"know,"* 3:2) can
> be used of any type of knowledge, but *its characteristic use is
> personal rather than intellectual.* This is important when we are
> thinking either of God's knowledge of us or of our knowledge of God.
> The word can be used for the *most intimate of personal relations,* e.
> g. Genesis 4:1 and frequently. It is important that we should know
> facts about God, though we cannot know Him fully in the sense of
> knowing all about Him and understanding His thoughts and ways. But
> it is essential that we *know Him personally,* and there is a degree of
> fullness possible in personal knowledge such as is not possible in
> intellectual knowledge.[9] (emphasis mine.)

Jeremiah also used the analogy of husband and wife to symbolize
God's relationship to His people. The phrase, "I am married unto you,"
(Jeremiah 3:14) is very convincing language that cannot be taken
lightly. Some of the most forceful words to describe God's love are to
be found in Jeremiah's work:

> ... Yea, I have *loved* thee with an *everlasting love:* therefore with
> lovingkindness (*chesed*) have I drawn thee (Jeremiah 31:3).

The "everlasting love" in the above passage coincides with God's
"everlasting covenant" made with the Patriarchs and fulfilled in Christ.
Both the Old and New Testaments use the metaphor of husband and wife
to evince God's love for His people (Ephesians 5:22-33).

---

9. Norman H. Snaith, *Amos, Hosea, and Micah,* London: The Epworth Press, 1956, 21.

A good deal of Hosea's prophecy is written in the same context. God had espoused Himself to the Hebrew people and He anticipated a response similar to that of a faithful wife to her husband. The whorish heart of Gomer and her restoration was meant to reveal the infidelity of Israel and God's forgiving love.

The essence of God's nature is *love,* and if men are to know God personally, they must know His love. God's covenant love was to produce a oneness and union between Himself and His people that the law of Moses and temporal benefits could never create. His love was to be "known" through faith in His Word.

God did not intend the Hebrew people to "keep the law" in their own strength — it was not given for this purpose. God only asks of man what His grace is able to supply. "Without me ye can do nothing" are the words of Jesus, but the principle contained in this statement was expected of the Hebrew people (in their relationship to God) throughout their history (Deuteronomy 8:3).

According to Moses, the Israelites were to "serve God with *joyfulness* and *gladness* of heart" (Deuteronomy 28:47). Even their religious fasts and feasts were to be filled with godly exhilaration. Zechariah admonished the exiles with these thoughts:

> Thus saith the Lord of hosts; The fast of the fourth month, and the fast of the fifth, and the fast of the seventh, and the fast of the tenth, shall be to the house of Judah *joy* and *gladness,* and *cheerful feasts;* therefore *love the truth and peace* (Zechariah 8:19).

It should be noted that *joy, gladness,* and *cheerfulness* in the above passage are associated with *love of the truth* (or Word) and *peace.* These terms (joy, gladness, cheerfulness, love of the truth, and peace) are like a page out of the New Testament (compare Colossians 3:16). These ideas are conclusive enough that God does not change His intimacy with man from one dispensation to the other.

Surely a personal and intimate knowledge of God was expected when the Old Testament prophets admonished the Israelites to "seek" the Lord or "search" for Him with all their hearts. The commandment to "seek" the Lord is found numerous times in the Old Testament. It was announced so frequently that it may have become commonplace with most of the people. The following passages are only a sampling of its usage: Deuteronomy 4:29, 1 Chronicles 16:10-11, 2 Chronicles 7:14, Ezra 8:22, Job 5:8, Psalm 69:32, Proverbs 8:17, Isaiah 55:6, Jeremiah

29:13, Hosea 10:12, and Zechariah 8:21. It would be incompatible with
God's righteous character to ask the people to "seek" Him if He could
not be "found" or known. Would a loving God play a con game with
mankind? When the whole of Scripture is considered, the only logical
way that God could be "known" would be through His Word and Spirit.

The relationship of the Hebrew people to the law of God (or His
Word) was not to be one of servitude, but love. They were not to "serve
the law" (Galatians 3:19) but "fulfill the law" (Romans 8:4). There is a
vast difference in the two ideas. "Serving the law" is done in one's own
strength — "fulfilling the law" is accomplished through God's grace
and love. Faith in God and a knowledge of God does not result in a
doleful creed but a vibrant and exciting fellowship.

The above truth can be illustrated by the biblical laws on marriage.
According to the Scriptures, a wife is commanded to remain with her
husband as long as he lives (Romans 7:2). Incompatibility between the
husband and wife, regardless of its nature, cannot dissolve the relationship. The husband may be unkind and maltreat the wife in many ways
but she is bound to her mate by the law. The abused wife may smart and
pine for her freedom from the law but this is impossible as long as her
husband is alive. In a situation of this nature, the wife is "serving the
law" — she remains with her husband because the law demands this of
her. A "love" relationship does not exist between the two.

But suppose the husband dies — the wife is free from the law. She
is at liberty to marry another man. Her second marriage is entirely
different from the first. This time she marries a husband that is compatible with her. He treats her kindly and affectionately. It is a joy to remain
with this husband because there is a "love" relationship. She does not
smart and gall "under the law" as before. She is not even aware of the
law that binds her to her husband. In this case she is "fulfilling the law"
rather than "serving the law."

The above analogy is the very lesson that Paul is teaching in
Romans 7:1-6. The unregenerate man (Jew and Gentile) is not compatible with the law of God — his sinful nature will not allow him to delight
in the law — and because of this the law is a source of vexation. The law
is not at fault, but the sin principle which is in man is the culprit (Romans
7:12-13).

When the "old man" dies the man of faith can be married to another
— who is Christ (7:4). The sinner is given a new nature (2 Peter 1:4) —
one that is compatible with the law of God — a nature that delights in

the law of God. Rather than "serve the law," as in his unregenerate state, the man of faith "fulfills the law" (Romans 8:4).

The religion of the Hebrews was not to be one of passivity or of apathy. Their faith in God's Word was to have a profound effect upon their *heart* and *soul*. It would affect their innermost being. In both the Old and New Testaments, the "heart" is the center of man's life. It stands for the whole of his nature — of thought, will, and emotions. It is from the "heart" that man's moral and immoral actions arise. Jesus said:

> For from *within, out of the heart of man,* proceed *evil thoughts, adulteries, fornications, murders, thefts, covetousness, wickedness, deceit, lasciviousness, an evil eye, blasphemy, pride, foolishness:*
>
> All these *evil things come from within,* and *defile* the man (Mark 7:21-23).

The proverbalist of the Old Testament, knowing that man's actions for good and evil are cradled in the heart, sums the whole matter up in a word — including a note of warning:

> Keep thy *heart* with all diligence; *for out of it are the issues of life* (Proverbs 4:23).

Since the "heart" is the seat of man's being — the fountainhead of good and evil — it seems logical that the Old Testament Scriptures would have a good deal to say about this all important aspect of man's being.

The word "heart" is used approximately 580 times in the Old Testament Scriptures and, with a few exceptions, it is a reference to the Hebrew people in one form or another. There are both positive and negative words to describe the innermost being of Abraham's descendants. On the positive side there is the "perfect heart," "tender heart," "new heart," "pure heart," "heart as the heart of God," "clean heart," "whole heart," "joy of heart," "sound heart," "all the heart," "pureness of heart," "soft heart," "willing heart," "uprightness of heart," "joyfulness and gladness of heart," "an understanding heart," "integrity of heart," "wise of heart," "free heart," "one heart," "faithful heart," "broken and contrite heart," "heart of flesh," and a "merry heart."

On the negative side, there is the "wicked heart," "stubborn heart," "deceitful heart," "obstinate heart," "hard heart," "double heart," "heart of stone," "evil heart," "fearful heart," "naughtiness of heart," "plague of heart," "pride of heart," "hypocrite in heart," "froward heart," "sorrow of heart," "revolting and rebellious heart," "exalted heart," "trembling heart," "stoutness of heart," "whorish heart," "without heart," "heart as fat as grease," "subtile of heart," "heart of fools," "backsliders in heart," "no heart," "madness of heart," and a "fool's heart."

These positive and negative terms on the "heart" reveal two "kinds" of people within the Hebrew nation. They are reminiscent of a "carnal Israel" and a "faithful Israel" that are traceable to Abraham. Faith (in the Word), which worketh by love (Galatians 5:6), is the distinguishing factor in the two Israels.

Many of the positive terms above are used to describe "God's people" in the New Testament and some of the negative terms are used to describe the "children of the Devil" in the New Testament. Once more, the gap that the futurists have created in the Old and New Testament saints is closed. Also, the above terms cannot apply to "national" Israel but to "individuals."

The relationship between "love of God" and the "Word of God" is to be seen in the *Shema*. The *Shema* is a portion of Scripture found in the sixth chapter of Deuteronomy and to this day it is the one passage that summarizes the belief of the Jewish people:

> Hear, O Israel: The Lord our God is one Lord:
> And thou shalt *love the Lord thy God* with *all thine heart,* and with *all thy soul,* and with *all thy might.*
> And these *words,* which I command thee this day *shall be in thine heart,* etc. (Deuteronomy 6:4-6).

Over the centuries the Jewish people have clung tenaciously to the "oneness of God" concept as taught in the *Shema* but at the same time it has turned to mock them. In every generation they have disregarded two of its most basic contingencies: (1) For many, the Word was never allowed to penetrate and thrive in the heart, and (2) They ignored many other significant passages of Scripture. It is possible to believe in monotheism and still turn a deaf ear to some very important commandments. When Moses used the plural "words" in the above passage, he meant all the *Word* of God. "And these *words* (plural) ... *shall be in thine heart.*"

The link between the "love of God" and the "Word of God" is also recognizable by the wearing of phylacteries (or frontlets),as taught by Moses. Phylacteries were small leather pouches, worn on the left arm and forehead, in which portions of Scripture were deposited. They were symbolic of the Word "laid up" in the heart and mind of every faithful Israelite:

> Therefore shall ye *lay up these my words* in your *heart* and in your *soul,* and bind them for a sign upon your hand, that they be as frontlets between your eyes (Deuteronomy 11:18).

When the left arm and hand were bent, the phylacteries containing the Scriptures would be directly over the heart. This was symbolic of a close relationship between the arm and hand, and the heart. The arm and hand were to reflect the content of the heart. In other words, the "Word of God" and the "love of God" were to be seen in the use of the arm and hand. The same principle would apply to the head and mind on which the frontlets were worn.

The bond between the "Word of God" and the "love of God" comes into full focus in the covenant of circumcision as given to Abraham. "Circumcision in the flesh" was only a foreshadowing of "circumcision of the heart." "Circumcision of the heart" is not peculiar to the Christian era. Long before the New Testament was written, the book of Deuteronomy makes reference to this unique operation. It should not be necessary to point out that circumcision of the heart was an "individual" matter and not a "national" one. Is it possible to circumcise a "nation" in the heart? Circumcision of the heart is a very critical doctrine in both Testaments.

Moses' statement on "circumcision of the heart" is given in connection with a prophetic utterance. This great leader of Israel was more than a lawgiver — the Lord endowed him with special insight into Israel's religious future. He foresaw that the sins of the people would result in their being taken captive and scattered among the other nations of the world. However, such judgments or chastisements of the Lord could be overcome if they would remember and return to the Word of God with all their *heart* and *soul.* This would result in their being "circumcised in the heart" by the Lord. All Israelites were circumcised in the flesh, but Moses states that God will circumcise them in the heart — and there is a tremendous difference:

> ... return unto the Lord thy God, and shall *obey His voice* (or Word) according to *all that I command thee this day,* thou and thy children, *with all thine heart* and *with all thy soul,* etc. ...
>
> And the *Lord thy God will circumcise thine heart,* and the *heart of thy seed,* (and for what purpose?) *to love the Lord thy God with all*

thine heart, and *with all thy soul, that thou mayest live* (Deuteronomy 30:2...6).

Jeremiah declares that circumcision of the heart for the Hebrew people will have far-reaching effects upon them and upon the other nations about them. For themselves, their knowledge of God will be enhanced with much assurance. They will acclaim with great confidence that the "Lord liveth, in truth, in judgment, and in righteousness." And other "nations shall bless themselves in him, and in him shall they glory:"

> If thou wilt return, O Israel, saith the Lord, return unto me: and if thou wilt put away thine abominations (idols) out of my sight, then shalt thou not remove.
>
> And thou shalt swear, *the Lord liveth, in truth, in judgment,* and *in righteousness;* and the nations shall bless themselves in him, and in him shall they glory.
>
> *Circumcise yourselves to the Lord,* and take away the *foreskins of your heart,* ye men of Judah and inhabitants of Jerusalem: lest my fury come forth like fire, and burn that none can quench it, because of the evil of your doings (Jeremiah 4:1-4).

Jeremiah makes no distinction in the "circumcised Israelite" and the "uncircumcised Gentile" where there is no "circumcision of the heart." God's judgment will be upon the "circumcised Israelite" as well as the "uncircumcised Gentile." Jeremiah announces God's judgment upon Judah as well as Egypt, Edom, Ammon, and Moab. It is implied by the prophet that "circumcision of the heart" is necessary for a "knowledge of God" (Jeremiah 9:24-26).

The Apostle Paul must have relied very heavily upon the works of Jeremiah for his theology. He assured the Roman Church, as well as others, that Jewish "circumcision in the flesh" would become "uncircumcision" if the Word of the Gospel was rejected (Romans 2:25-29). The similarities between Paul's mind and that of Jeremiah on "circumcision of the heart" should put "national" Jewry in the deepfreeze forever.

According to David and Isaiah, the "law in the heart" (or Word) would produce the very thing that God desired in His people, namely, the "righteousness of God" — a concept which also implies the "love of God:"

> The mouth of the *righteous* speaketh wisdom, and his tongue

talketh of judgment.
The *law of God is in his heart;* none of his steps shall slide (Psalm 37:30-31). See also Isaiah 51:7.

The Hebrew Alphabet Psalm (119) is one of the most comprehensive and exhaustive treatments of the Word of God to be found anywhere in Scripture. There are 176 verses in this Psalm and almost every passage makes reference to God's Word in one form or another. The consequences of God's Word, as it ministers to man's multiple needs, are limitless. Some of the ideas expressed in this Psalm on the Word of God parallel the New Testament and in some instances surpass it. If the Word of God had such a profound effect upon the Psalmist's *heart* and *soul,* surely it could have done the same for multitudes of others had it been believed and received. (See verses 11, 34, 80, 97, 111, and 112)

According to Joel, inner "changes" of heart and mind were necessary if the Hebrew people were to know God's love and grace. A "rending of the heart" and a "turning of the heart" were to be simultaneous acts whereby God's blessings may be received. These two ideas are used by Joel as a warning of God's final judgment or "the great and terrible day of the Lord." Joel's message is as relevant today as the day it was written (Joel 2:12-13, 31).

The relationship between the "Word of God" and the "love of God" is to be seen throughout the Old Testament. The commandments of the Lord were not to be some kind of external ritual or ceremony that left the heart and soul of the Israelite untouched. A faith response to God's Word would result in "love of God" and "love of one's fellow man." The faithful Israelite was to be an expression of God's love and Word.

As the years came and went, religious form began to replace the "inner life" in every generation. The utmost concern of Moses and the prophets was a genuine "heart and soul" relationship to God. As we have already shown, men like Isaiah, Jeremiah, Amos, and Hosea were forever decrying the heartless worship that characterized their particular generation. In fact, it would require a sizeable book to record all their denunciations. If membership in the Hebrew "nation" was as important as the premillennialists make it appear, then the prophets in the old dispensation labored, suffered, and died in vain.

For many of the Hebrew people the law of God, as given to Moses, remained on tables of stone — the Word was never allowed access into the heart (2 Corinthians 3:3). The first and second commandments were given to counteract all forms of idolatry but they were ignored in every period of Hebrew history. Idol worship, which started with the golden calf in the wilderness, was like an infectious disease that broke out in every generation (unless it was discontinued after the exiles returned to their homeland). Solomon was the first in a long series of kings that were given to this heathen practice. Almost all the kings of the northern kingdom followed Jeroboam in worshipping the golden calves erected at Dan and Bethel — which in turn, had a devastating influence upon the Hebrew populace. Idol worship, which replaced the first commandment, is well documented by the prophets.

The Word of God was to have had a profound effect upon the people in the Old Testament days — its inward results stagger the imagination. It was able to penetrate the innermost part of a man's soul, spirit, and body. There is no power equal to it:

> For the *Word of God* is *quick* (alive), and *powerful,* and *sharper than any twoedged sword,* piercing even to the dividing asunder of soul and spirit, and of the joints and marrow, and is a discerner of the thoughts and intents of the heart (Hebrews 4:12).

The above passage is describing the effects of God's Word in the Old Testament era. The New Testament had not been compiled at this time. If all the Old Testament passages that are quoted in the New Testament were assembled and studied carefully, along with their proper interpretation, we would see immediately that the Old Testament Scriptures were endowed with life-changing qualities for the Hebrew people. We would be constrained to agree with Moses when he admonished the people: "...Set your hearts unto all the *words* which I testify among you this day ... *It is your life* (Deuteronomy 32:46-47a).

Can we ignore the insight and remarks of Jesus regarding the Pharisees of His day without impunity to His reputation as the Son of God? The Pharisees were characterized by an "outer" and "inner" religious life style that did not harmonize with each other. The whitewashed sepulchres of that era reminded Jesus of this dualistic nature in them. The "outside" of the sepulchres was indeed beautiful; but the "inside" was "full of dead men's bones, and all uncleanness" (Matthew 23:27). Evidently Jesus expected an "inner life" in the Pharisees that corresponded with the things taught by Moses and the prophets in the Old Testament.

When the Sadducees confronted Jesus with questions on the resurrection of the dead, He informed them that more was needed for a knowledge and understanding of the Scriptures. In a very tactful manner He exposed their spiritual deficiency with these words:

> Ye do err, not knowing the Scriptures, nor the *power of God* (Matthew 22:29).

Had the Sadducees known the "power" *(dunamis)* associated with the Scriptures, they would have understood the Scriptures. Their knowledge must go beyond the letter of the Word — they must know God Himself. The Scriptures were not to have been an end within themselves but a means of bringing the faithful Israelite into a joyous and knowledgeable relationship with the One who gave the Scriptures.

The squabbles of the Pharisees and Sadducees over the law of Moses in New Testament days bring to mind the wrangling of the premillennialists among themselves over events in the so-called millennial age. The multiple interpretations on the law of Moses by the Pharisees and Sadducees sidetracked them from dealing with the critical issues of Scripture. We are seeing a similar pattern in this age in the literature of the millenarians. There is constant bickering within their own ranks over minute details in the millennial kingdom. This "family quarrel" has become a "stumblingblock" to the futurists, just as the law of Moses did to the Pharisees and Sadducees. This millennial dialogue between themselves contributes little if anything to the issues at stake, namely, the love of God and love of one's fellow man.

The Second Commandment or Love of Neighbor

"Am I my brother's keeper?" (Genesis 4:9b).

Any emphasis on the "Word of God" and the "love of God" in the Old Testament Scriptures would not be complete without a special consideration of the second commandment or "love of neighbor." *Faith in* and *obedience to* the second commandment was as important as the first. From the tone of Scripture, it seems that the Israelite was to love his neighbor to the same degree that God loved him. Instructions (or the Word) on "love of neighbor" were also given in great abundance.

The essence of God's nature is love and man is the chief object of His love. Moses describes God as,

... merciful and gracious, longsuffering, and abundant in goodness
and truth,

Keeping mercy for thousands, forgiving iniquity and transgression
and sin, etc. (Exodus 34:6-7).

Since God is love, we should see a corresponding nature in His
children. "Love of neighbor" should have been par excellence for the
Hebrew people. Man's supreme duty is to God and one's fellow man,
and faith is meaningless unless it leads us to these.

The bottom line for both the Old and New Testament is "love." But
this has been a blind spot in man's religious beliefs since the first murder
(Genesis 4:8). A good deal of the New Testament is devoted to prove
that love of God and love of one's neighbor are the heart of the Old
Testament Scriptures. What greater authority can we look to for confirmation of this fact than Jesus Himself? Jesus put the entire Old
Testament Scriptures in their proper perspective when a certain lawyer
asked him, "...which is the great commandment in the law?" This
thread-worn question, so common among the Jews, was meant to
intimidate Jesus, but His answer was never contested. Jesus said:

Thou shalt love the Lord thy God with all thy heart, and with all thy
soul, and with all thy mind.

This is the first and great commandment.

And the second is like unto it, Thou shalt *love thy neighbor as
thyself*.

On these two commandments hang all the law and the prophets
(Matthew 22:37-40).

All the commandments that God has given to man in every age are
summed up in the last verse of the above passage. All the other
commandments, of whatever nature, are only clarifications of the first
two. Additional commandments are merely "aids" in understanding the
negative and positive factors in love.

Moses and the Apostle Paul are in perfect agreement as to man's
first and foremost duty to man. Moses wrote:

Thou shalt not avenge, nor bear any grudge against the children of
thy people, but *thou shalt love thy neighbor as thyself:* I am the Lord
(Leviticus 19:18).

The Apostle confirms the words of Moses and condenses the entire
Old Testament code into one word — love:

For all the law is fulfilled in *one word,* even in this: Thou shalt *love thy neighbor as thyself* (Galatians 5:14).

The law of Moses, when conjoined with God's grace, was not without love, mercy, and compassion. This truth is to be seen in almost every line of both Moses and the prophets. Human relationships were not left to chance. Moses gave the Israelites a moral and ethical code which Jesus affirmed and on which most of the New Testament rests. God's Word was designed to create a fellowship of love and oneness that would magnify Him before the other nations of the world.

The Hebrew people were not to discriminate between each other because of social or economic differences. Whether rich or poor, they were to judge one another in righteousness. They were not to seek vengeance or hold grudges against one another. Talebearers and opinionated hate for a fellow Hebrew were forbidden by the law of Moses. Love was to be the predominant feature in all of their relationships (Leviticus 19:15-18 Living Bible).

Buying and selling has been a vital part of human intercourse since the dawn of history. Although commerce between individuals and nations has made a wonderful contribution to humankind, it has also been beset by many evils. Moses gave the Hebrew people some principles in weights, measurements, and balances that should be practiced as long as the world stands:

> Do not use dishonest standards when measuring length, weight or quantity. Use honest scales and honest weights, an honest ephah and an honest hin. I am the Lord your God, who brought you out of Egypt (Leviticus 19:35-36 NIV).

Human labor was also a form of buying and selling. This area of human relationships has been exploited in every age and generation. But the labouring class of people was not overlooked by Moses. The hired man, whether Hebrew or non-Hebrew, was to be given proper consideration with regard to his wages (Deuteronomy 24:14-15 NIV).

Manservants and maidservants were to enjoy the Sabbath rest along with those for whom they laboured. Even the domestic animals were included in the Sabbath rest (Deuteronomy 5:14).

The judgeship that was begun under Moses was to be a perpetual office throughout Hebrew history. This was a very precarious position and would be open to bribes, partiality, and unfair judgments. This office, so necessary in almost every society, must be administered with the utmost candor (Deuteronomy 16:18-20).

Skinflints were not to be found in the Hebrew community. Generous giving to the "poor brother" was symbolized by the "open hand." Their giving was not to be "strained" in any sense of the word. There was to be no regret or "withdrawal symptoms" in their giving — they were to give out of a cheerful heart (Deuteronomy 15:7-11).

The law of Moses covers practically every facet of human behavior. Sometimes very broad terms are used in dealing with certain sins, but the principles in the commandments are easily understood and applied. In the following passage Moses does not spell out a single item that one might steal; neither does he mention a particular fraudulent act; nor does he specify a situation wherein a falsehood may be told. But he gives some general terms that can be applied to any and all kinds of stealing, deceit, and lying:

> Ye shall *not steal,* neither *deal falsely,* neither *lie one to another*
> (Leviticus 19:11).

The Hebrew people were taught to respect old age; they were to be kind to the deaf and blind; they were to honor parenthood; two or more witnesses were required to convict a guilty party; the sanctity and privacy of a man's home were provided for in the law of Moses; raiment, a stray animal, or anything that was lost was to be returned to its rightful owner; refuge cities were provided for those who accidentally killed another; assistance was to be given to a neighbor whose animal had fallen; railings were placed around rooftops to prevent injury; a stray ox, belonging to one's enemy, was to be returned to its owner; humane laws provided for domesticated animals and certain wild life; interest was not to be charged to a fellow Hebrew; and the man who found himself in debt through some misfortune was assisted by the "year of release" law.

These are only a few of the laws governing human relationships within the Hebrew community. From the king upon the throne to the lowest peasant in the field, love, mercy, and justice were to be the prevailing virtues among the descendants of Abraham (Micah 6:8).

It seems almost superfluous to point out that the Hebrew was to love the Hebrew. But racial ties alone are not sufficient to create harmony and oneness within a community or nation — not even between members of a family. Man's sinful tendencies must be restrained by faith and love — love of God and love of one's fellow man — which includes the Hebrew people.

Underprivileged people have always been subjected to neglect, abuse, and lovelessness even within races. Knowing this in advance, the Lord called special attention to certain classes of people within the Hebrew nation, namely, the poor, the fatherless, the widow, and the stranger. Such people were precious in God's sight and became a testing ground of faith and love for others.

Several penalties were prescribed for the offenders. One of the most graphic terms used by Moses to describe God's anger is "wax hot," which literally means "blaze up" with anger. A distress cry from the widow or fatherless child would mean death by the sword:

> Ye shall not afflict any *widow*, or *fatherless child*.
> If thou afflict them in any wise, and they cry at all unto me, I will surely hear their cry;
> And my *wrath shall wax hot*, and *I will kill you with the sword:* and your wives shall be widows, and your children fatherless (Exodus 22:22-24).

The Mosaic law made special provisions for the poor, the widow, the fatherless, and the hired servant. When the more fortunate people harvested their crops, they were not to glean their fields and vineyards with a miserly spirit; a certain portion of their yield was to be left for the poor and needy (Deuteronomy 24:19-22, Leviticus 19:9-10). This commandment, along with many others, fell into disrepute. We find most of the later prophets decrying this sin and pronouncing God's judgment upon the abusers. For Isaiah, it was equal to "beating God's people to pieces" and "grinding the faces of the poor" (Isaiah 3:13-15).

The poor and needy were not always neglected for lack of wealth on the part of the Hebrew populace. The "have nots" were overlooked in seasons of prosperity more than any other time. Jeremiah describes the wealthy in his day as those who have "become great, and waxen fat (rich)." Their prosperity had caused them to ignore the deeds of the wicked and at the same time they refused to "judge the rights of the needy." Wealth, unbridled wickedness, and oppression of the poor are oftentimes partners in crime (Jeremiah 5:28-29; 22:16).

The above truth can be seen in Amos' prophecy. The worship of mammon was very prevalent and the wealthy had heaped treasures upon themselves without any consideration of the poor and needy. It seems that the well-to-do people had built their stone houses at the expense of the poor. However, Amos predicts that God will eventually relieve them of their elaborate homes and pleasant vineyards (Amos 5:11-12; 4:1; 2:6-7; 8:4ff).

Abuses and neglect of the poor and needy within the Hebrew community arise in almost every period of Old Testament history. Hosea depicts the Lord as having a "controversy," not with those outside the Israelite nation, but with the "inhabitants of the land," namely the Hebrew people. Why?

> ... because there is *no truth, nor mercy, nor knowledge* of God in the land.
>
> By *swearing,* and *lying,* and *killing* and *stealing,* and *committing adultery, they break out,* and *blood toucheth blood.*
>
> Therefore shall the land mourn, and every one that dwelleth therein shall languish, etc. (Hosea 4:1-3a).

Human relationships were at a very low pitch in Ezekiel's day. These bad relationships are described in analogous form by the prophet. They were like "gaps" in a "hedge" (fence) that had been broken by "robbery," "vexation of the poor," and "oppression of strangers." According to Ezekiel, the Lord sought a man who would "make up the hedge and stand in the gap," but found none. Many sermons have been delivered on the quality of man that was needed to fulfill this mission, but the gut issue of the man's task is oftentimes overlooked in most homilies. A man was needed who could lead the people away from these inhumane activities in order that they might be spared the judgment of God (Ezekiel 22:29-30).

"Love of neighbor" — the second commandment — was, in the words of Jesus, "like unto the first." This one area of God's Word, if neglected, would negate all the other commandments. The sacrificial system of the temple, the priesthood, and all the religious fasts and festivals were only a stench in God's nostrils when "love of neighbor" was absent. Isaiah called the religious trappings of his day "iniquitous" and "evil." The sacrifices, prayers and religious assemblies would only widen the gap between God and the so-called worshipper if there was no "love of neighbor." The "evil" and "iniquity" that Isaiah decries is improper behavior toward the oppressed, the fatherless, and the widow (Isiah 1:11-17).

Amos was confronted with the same problem. He, too, describes God's distaste for the hollow ritual that excluded "love of neighbor:"

> *I hate, I despise your feast days,* and *I will not smell in your solemn assemblies.*
>
> Though ye offer me burnt offerings and your meat offerings, *I will not accept them:* neither will I regard the peace offerings of your fat beasts.
>
> Take thou away from me the *noise of thy songs; for I will not hear the melody of thy viols.*
>
> But let *judgment run down as waters;* and *righteousness as a mighty stream* (Amos 5:21-24).

Concern for the oppressed is a major theme throughout Amos' prophecy. Righteous judgments in human relationships were far more important to this prophet than pompous ceremonies and religious zeal. (See also Amos 2:6-8; 5:8-15; and 8:4-10.)

Jeremiah gives one of the most striking revelations in all of Scriptures relative to the poor and needy. This prophet implies that a "knowledge of God" is commensurate with proper attitudes toward underprivileged people. Jeremiah rebuked Shallum, king of Judah, by the example of his father-king, Josiah. Shallum had built an elaborate house by men who received no wages for their labor. But King Shallum's costly house would not guarantee his continued rulership. He should have imitated his father, Josiah, who gave special consideration to the poor and needy. To care for such people was to "know God:"

> Shalt thou (Shallum) reign, because thou closest thyself in cedar? did not thy father (Josiah) eat and drink, and *do judgment* and *justice,* and then *it was well with him?*
>
> He (Josiah) *judged the cause of the poor* and *needy; then it was well with him: was this not to know me?* saith the Lord.
>
> But thine (Shallum) eyes and thine heart are *not but for covetousness,* and *for violence,* to do it (Jeremiah 22:15-17. See also 1 John 5:1-3).

Hosea, like Jeremiah, links "mercy" and a "knowledge of God" together. He says that "mercy" and a "knowledge of God" are more important than all sacrifices and burnt offerings:

> For I desire *mercy,* and *not sacrifice,* and the *knowledge of God* more than *burnt offerings* (Hosea 6:6).

The Apostle James' familiarity with the Old Testament Scriptures may have been the source of his inspiration as he deals with the same truth in the New Testament:

Pure religion and *undefiled* before God and the Father is this, *to visit the fatherless* and *widows in their affliction,* and to keep himself unspotted from the world (James 1:27).

Micah, perhaps, reaches the pinnacle of God's disgust for religious ritual when "love of neighbor" is lacking. According to Micah, there is no sacrifice pleasing to God, not even the sacrifice of a *firstborn child,* where there is no justice, love, and mercy among the people (Micah 6:6-8; 7:1-6).

Daniel declares that a Gentile king (Nebuchadnezzar) would be spared God's judgment if he would begin to live righteously and show mercy to the poor. "Righteous living" and "showing mercy to the poor" seem to be components of each other:

Wherefore, O king, let my counsel be acceptable unto thee, and *break off thy sins by righteousness,* and *thine iniquities by showing mercy to the poor:* if it may be a lengthening of thy tranquility (Daniel 4:27).

The capstone for our thoughts on the poor and needy within the Hebrew community is to be found in the words of the Psalmist. The tactics that wicked men use in oppressing the underprivileged are Satanic in nature. The poor seem to be a special target for the forces of evil. An attack upon the poor is a strike at the heart of God. Even the security that wicked men feel as they oppress the poor corresponds to that of Satan:

He (wicked) hath said in his heart, *I shall not be moved:* for *I shall never be in adversity* (Psalm 10:6).

The cunning nature of the Devil emerges in full strength through the evil devices of men as they afflict the poor and needy:

His (wicked) mouth is *full of cursing* and *deceit* and *fraud:* Under his *tongue is mischief* and *vanity.*

He sitteth in the *lurking places* of the villages: in the *secret places doth he murder the innocent: His eyes are privily set against the poor* (Psalm 10:7-8).

The stealth of a lion, another figure of Satan, is seen in the actions of the wicked as they prey upon the poor:

He (wicked) *lieth in wait secretly as a lion* in his den: he *lieth in wait to catch the poor:* he *doth catch the poor,* when he *draweth him into his net.*

He *croucheth,* and *humbleth* himself, that the poor may fall by his strong ones.

He hath said in his heart, *God hath forgotten:* he hideth his face; he will never see it (Psalm 10:9-11).

But God did not forget! God did not hide His face! The cry of the oppressed poor caught the attention of God more than any other voice. The tables would be turned — the "oppressors" would become the "oppressed." The "afflicters" would become widows, fatherless, and childless; they would perish by the sword (Exodus 22:24). Similar consequences are expressed by the Proverbialist who wrote: "Whoso stoppeth his ears at the cry of the poor, he also shall cry himself, but shall not be heard" (Proverbs 21:13). What greater catastrophe can befall men than to pray to an inattentive God?

The prophets of the Old Testament era did not abrogate the temple and its ministry per se. The sacrificial system became a minus only when "love of God" and "love of neighbor" were forgotten. The tabernacle, with all of its regalia, was glorious and divine in its origin and purpose. The earthly tabernacle was a replica of the "true tabernacle, which the Lord pitched, and not man" (Hebrews 8:2). David was so enamored by the tabernacle in Jerusalem that he envied the sparrows and swallows that built their nests in its precincts (Psalm 84:1-3).

The tabernacle ministry was eventually replaced by the temple ministry. Both ministries were emblematic of God's redeeming love for all mankind. They were to have their larger fulfillment in the sacrifice of Christ. To abuse and oppress those for whom Christ died was to make the tabernacle and temple ministries without effect — the one was diametrically opposed to the other. The actions of the Israelites against the poor and needy were a contradiction of what the tabernacle and temple represented.

The above truth stands out very clearly in Jeremiah's famous "temple sermon." This faithful prophet had grown weary of the religious jargon of his day. His ears were filled with the pious chatter: "The temple of the Lord, the temple of the Lord, the temple of the Lord, are these" (Jeremiah 7:4). Such vexatious clamor was like "sounding brass or a tinkling cymbal." The temple ritual had become an end within itself — it had become a substitute for Jehovah God. Jeremiah describes such religiosity as "lying words." In short, the people were living a lie. Their life style was at cross-purposes with the tenor of the temple ministry.

The temple worshipper was supposed to meet God in love, mercy, and forgiveness. But the majority of people in Jeremiah's day were bereft of these graces because of improper attitudes toward their fellow man. Temple worship was meaningful only when there was a God-like character reflected in the participant. The relationship between the temple worshipper and his neighbor is fully developed in the seventh chapter of Jeremiah:

> Trust ye not in lying words, saying, The temple of the Lord, The temple of the Lord, The temple of the Lord, are these:
> For if ye throughly amend your ways and your doings; if ye throughly *execute judgment between a man and his neighbour;*
> If ye *oppress not the stranger,* the *fatherless,* and the *widow,* and *shed not innocent blood in this place,* neither walk after other gods to your heart:
> Then will I cause you to dwell in this place, etc. (Jeremiah 7:4-6).

Love for God and one's neighbor has never been received with open arms. Religious pomp and ceremony have always taken precedence over a right relationship to God and one's fellow man. The response that Jeremiah received is repeated in almost every generation. It was within the temple walls that the priests and false prophets accosted Jeremiah and said: "Thou shalt surely die" (Jeremiah 26:8).

Premillennial views on "national" Israel fall into the same category as religious pomp and ceremony. For the most part, a "nation" is a vague, impersonal, faceless, soulless, bodiless, non-entity in comparison to "individuals." Men are very skilled at substituting some unimportant religious issue for "individual" responsibility. Men delight in "hiding" themselves in the masses. It is much easier to become "obscure" in a conglomerate of people than it is to face one's sins and contribute to the moral and ethical values that are essential to a godly society in every age and generation. A "national" Jewish kingdom of the past and a "national" Jewish kingdom of the future is just another loophole for the Jews to avoid "individual" responsibility. God did not say, "Thou shalt love thy *nation* as thyself." But He did say, "Thou shalt love thy *neighbor* as thyself." Truly, we are our *brother's* keeper. A disruption of the premillennial euphoria on "national" Israel could mean a fate similar to that of Jeremiah.

God's Word is emblazoned with simplicity. There is no other work of literature that can be limited to a single word, and that one word is *love*. But the central message of the Bible has been missed in every age by the masses of people. Over the centuries men have only complicated the Word of God with their intellectual shenanigans. Thank God for honest, sound Biblical translations and exegesis — the church's ministry would have been greatly jeopardized without them. But on the other hand, some exponents of the Scriptures are guilty of worshipping at the shrine of Athena far more than the throne of Christ. Many hours have been wasted in the study of elaborate and detailed prophecies that will end up on the prophetic garbage heap. Hairsplitting over certain Greek and Hebrew words have contributed very little to the real import of God's written revelation to man. Squabbles over pet doctrines and ideologies have inflicted incalculable wounds in the body of Christ. What atrocities men have committed against God and their fellow man! *Agape* love has been and always will be the hallmark of God's people.

When our priorities are right, we will find perfect agreement between the Old and New Testament Scriptures, the saints of both Testaments, and the eschatology of both Testaments. To love God and one's fellow man is the most crucial thing in both Testaments and the goal of God's elect in both dispensations is a "heavenly country" and not the Land of Canaan (Hebrews 11:16). When the three issues above are put together as they should be, they spark. To force "national" Israel into this triad, as the millenarians attempt to do, is like trying to put a square peg in a round hole.

Love of Strangers or Non-Hebrews

The inclusion of the Gentiles into the household of faith has been one of the most neglected and misunderstood areas of biblical truths in the Old Testament. Among the first instructions given to the Israelites before they left Egypt was the treatment of "strangers" within the Hebrew community or nation. There was to be both an *exclusive* and *inclusive* attitude toward the Gentile world. It is perhaps no coincidence that the first commandments dealing with "strangers" was given at the initial Passover Feast which was to become the central feature in Hebrew worship. Before the law was formally given on Mt. Sinai, God made provisions for the "stranger" or non-Israelite.

The Gentile was to be admitted or rejected by the community of faith on the basis of his conformity or non-conformity to the ordinances of God:

> And the Lord said unto Moses and Aaron, This is the ordinance of
> the passover: There shall *no stranger eat thereof:*
> But every man's servant that is bought for money, when thou hast
> circumcised him, then *shall he eat thereof.*
> A foreigner and an hired servant shall not eat thereof ...
> And when a *stranger* shall sojourn with thee, and *will keep the
> passover to the Lord,* let all his males be circumcised, and then let him
> come near and keep it; and *he shall be as one that is born in the land:*
> for no uncircumcised person shall eat thereof.
> *One law* shall be to him that is *homeborn* (Hebrew) and unto the
> *stranger* (non-Hebrew) that sojourneth among you (Exodus 12:43-
> 49).

Within the community of faith, there was to be *"one law"* for both
the Hebrew and the Gentile. This was to be an inviolable commandment
that was to be kept with all diligence. This "one law" concept is
mentioned at least four times in the Old Testament (Exodus 12:49,
Leviticus 24:22, Numbers 9:14, 15:15-16).

The above truth is expressed again in the book of Deuteronomy but
with different terminology. In the Deuteronomic passage Moses states
that "God regardeth not persons" and that God loves and provides for
the "stranger" (non-Hebrew) as well as others:

> For the Lord your God is God of gods, and Lord of lords, a great
> God, a mighty, and a terrible, which *regardeth not persons,* nor taketh
> reward:
> He doth execute the judgment of the fatherless, and widow, and
> *loveth the stranger,* in giving him food and raiment.
> *Love ye therefore the stranger:* for ye were strangers in the land of
> Egypt (Deuteronomy 10:17-19).

The Apostle Paul's theology coincides perfectly with that of
Moses. One of the outstanding themes in the Romans epistle is found in
chapter two, verse eleven: "For there is *no respect of persons with God."*
A good deal of the epistle is written to prove this truth.

The "one law" for Hebrew and Gentile covers the whole gamut of
the religious life in the Old Testament period. The covenant or promise
made to Abraham would be fulfilled to the "stranger" or Gentile on the
same basis as that of the Hebrew. When the Israelites came into the land
of Moab, the Sinaitic covenant was renewed and additional instructions
were given in conjunction with it (Deuteronomy 29:1). Coupled with
the precepts at Moab was the oath made with Abraham, Isaac, and Jacob.

No distinction is made between the "stranger" and the Hebrew people. Obedience to God's Word was the sole condition for both:

> Keep therefore the *words of this covenant*, and *do them*, that ye may prosper in all that ye do.
> Ye stand this day all of you before the Lord your God; your captains of your tribes, your elders, and your officers, with all the men of Israel,
> Your little ones, your wives, and thy *stranger* that is in thy camp, from the hewer of wood unto the drawer of water.
> That thou shouldest enter *into covenant with the Lord thy God*, and into his *oath*, which the Lord thy God maketh with thee this day:
> That he may establish thee to day for a *people unto himself*, and that he may be unto thee a God, as he hath said unto thee, and *as he hath sworn unto thy fathers*, to *Abraham*, to *Isaac*, and to *Jacob* (Deuteronomy 29:9-13).

It should be noted that the "little ones," "wives," and "stranger" are mentioned conjointly in the above passage (verse 11). In addition to this, the covenant made with Abraham, Isaac, and Jacob would extend to the same class of people far into the future. Notice the next two verses from the same chapter:

> Neither with *you only* do I make this *covenant* and *oath*.
> But with him that standeth here with us this day before the Lord our God, and *also with him that is not here with us this day* (Deuteronomy 29:14-15).

Isaiah's remarks on the "stranger" and his relationship to the covenant of God in the Old Testament era cannot be called in question:

> Let no foreigner (stranger) who has *joined himself to the Lord* say, The Lord will surely exclude me from his people; neither let the eunuch say, Behold I am a dry tree.
> For thus saith the Lord unto the eunuchs that keep my Sabbaths, and choose the things that please me, and *take hold of my covenant;*
> Even unto them *will I give mine house and within my walls a place and a name better than of sons and of daughters:* I will give them an *everlasting name, that shall not be cut off.*
> Also the *sons of the stranger, that join themselves to the Lord, to serve him, and to love the name of the Lord, to be his servants, every one that keepeth the Sabbath from polluting it, and taketh hold of my covenant;*
> Even them (eunuchs and strangers) will I bring to my holy mountain, and make them joyful in *my house of prayer:* their burnt offerings

and their sacrifices *shall be accepted upon mine altar:* for *mine house shall be called an house of prayer for all people* (Isaiah 56:3-7, NIV).

The "one law" for Hebrew and non-Hebrew (stranger) can be seen throughout the Old Testament Scriptures. The "Sabbath rest" was a very important commandment for God's people. It was a paragon of the eternal rest that belonged to God's elect. The "stranger" was to be included in this Sabbath rest:

> "... the seventh day is the Sabbath of the Lord thy God: in it thou shalt not do any work, thou, nor thy son, nor thy daughter, nor thy manservant, nor thy maidservant, nor thine ox, nor thine ass, nor any of thy cattle, nor thy *stranger* that is within thy gates; that thy manservant and thy maidservant may *rest* as well as thou (Deuteronomy 5:14).

The "stranger" was to share in the three great religious feasts along with the Hebrew people. He was to "rejoice" during the feast of Passover, the feast of Pentecost, and the feast of Tabernacles as much so as the Hebrews:

> And thou shalt *rejoice before the Lord* thy God, thou and thy son, and thy daughter, and thy manservant, and thy maidservant, and the Levite that is within thy gates, and the *stranger,* and the fatherless, and the widow, that are among you, etc. (Deuteronomy 16:11).

The judges appointed under Moses were to be impartial in their office. They were commanded to hear both sides of a dispute between brethren and "judge righteously." The stranger was to receive the same consideration as the Hebrew when a controversy arose:

> And I (Moses) charged your judges at that time saying, Hear the causes between your brethren, and judge righteously between every man and his brother, and the *stranger that is with him.*
>
> Ye shall *not respect persons in judgment:* but ye shall hear the *small* as well as the great; ye shall not be afraid of the face of man; for the *judgment is God's:* and the cause that is too hard for you, bring it unto me, and I will hear it (Deuteronomy 1:16-17. See also Deuteronomy 24:17; 27:19.)

For an Israelite to mistreat a "stranger" in any shape or form was a violation of God's commandment. The Israelite, who knew the heart of the stranger, was to love the Gentile as himself. He, too, was once a stranger in the land of Egypt:

> And if a *stranger* sojourn with thee in your land, ye shall not *vex* (mistreat) him.

> But the *stranger* that dwelleth with you *shall be unto you as one born among you,* and *thou shalt love him as thyself;* for ye were strangers in the land of Egypt; I am the Lord your God (Leviticus 19:33-34. See also Exodus 22:21).

There was to be no difference in the Hebrew people and the non-Hebrew in matters of civil and religious punishment. The law of God demanded severe penalties for certain sins. Blaspheming the name of the Lord was an offense punishable by death. The "stranger" born in the land was subject to this law and others as well as the Hebrews:

> And he that *blasphemeth the name of the Lord,* he shall surely be put to death, and all the congregation shall certainly stone him: as well as the *stranger,* as he that is *born in the land,* when he *blasphemeth* the name of the Lord ...
> Ye shall have *one manner of law,* as well for the *stranger,* as for *one of your own country:* for I am the Lord your God (Leviticus 24:16...22).

Very often Moses spoke of the "place that God would choose" when the Israelites came into the Land of Canaan. This "place," of course, came to be the temple site in Jerusalem. The Hebrew people would gather at this "place" periodically and the law of God was to be read in their hearing. The "stranger" was to hear the law read along with the Israelites:

> When all Israel is come to appear before the Lord thy God in the place which he shall choose, thou shalt *read this law before all Israel in their hearing.*
> Gather the people together, men, and women, and children and thy *stranger* that is *within thy gate, that they may hear and that they may learn, and fear the Lord your God, and observe to do all the things of this law:* (Deuteronomy 31:11-12).

God's love and concern for the stranger (non-Israelite) is reflected in one of the most significant events in Jewish history. Approximately 450 years after Moses' death, king David wanted to build a temple for the Lord. God sanctioned David's good intentions but he was not permitted to build the Lord's house. Solomon, David's son, was given that honor. After the temple was completed, Solomon was elated and

inspired — an elaborate ceremony was held to dedicate the building.
This wise king wanted all the people of the earth to know that the house
which he had built was called by the name of the Lord. Solomon's
dedicatory prayer was a vital part of the celebration. In this special
prayer, Solomon asked the Lord to hear the prayers of the stranger
(Gentile) from far and wide and grant his request:

> Moreover concerning a *stranger* that is *not of thy people Israel,* but
> cometh out of a *far country* for thy name's sake;
>
> (For they shall hear of thy great name, and of thy strong hand, and
> of thy stretched out arm:) when he shall *come and pray toward this
> house;*
>
> Hear thou in heaven thy dwelling place, and do according to *all that
> the stranger calleth to thee for:* That *all people of the earth* may know
> thy name, to fear thee, as do thy people Israel; and that this house,
> which I have builded, is called by thy name (1 Kings 8:41-43. See also
> 2 Chronicles 6:32-33).

How much of Solomon's prayer on behalf of the stranger was
prophetic, we are not told; but we do know that it was fulfilled in part
during his lifetime by a visit from the Queen of Sheba to his kingdom.
Solomon's concern for "all the people of the earth" is an indication of
God's love for the non-Hebrew world.

Moses gave the Hebrew people many instructions regarding the
"stranger" before they came into the Land of Canaan. But these
commandments were disregarded in every generation. Very early in the
nation's history we find David, Israel's second king, crying out against
the abuse of the non-Hebrew. The "wicked who triumphed" in David's
day were not foreign oppressors, but those within the Hebrew community:

> Lord, how long shall the wicked, how long shall the wicked
> triumph?
>
> How long shall they utter and speak hard things? and all the
> workers of iniquity boast themselves?
>
> They break in pieces thy people, O Lord and *afflict thine heritage.*
> (And who are the Lord's heritage?)
>
> They slay the widow and the *stranger,* and murder the fatherless,
> etc. (Psalm 94:3-6).

It seems tenable that Jerusalem, of all the Hebrew cities, would be
a righteous city — a divine sanctuary for the Lord. Jerusalem was meant

to be the symbol of all that is good and holy — the religious capital of the world. But in the words of Ezekiel it had become a "bloody city" — one rife with sin. Amid the evils that Ezekiel denounces is the treatment of "strangers" by the princes:

> Behold, the princes of Israel, every one were in thee to their power to shed blood.
>
> In thee have they set light by father and mother: in the midst of thee have they *dealt oppression* (or deceit) *with the stranger:* in thee have they vexed the fatherless and widow (Ezekiel 22:6-7).

In the twenty-ninth verse of the above chapter, Ezekiel includes more than the princes of Jerusalem in his denunciation — the populace in general were guilty of the same sin:

> The people of the land have used oppression, and exercise robbery, and have *vexed* the poor and needy: yea, they have *oppressed the stranger* without right (Ezekiel 22:29).

Malachi, the last of the Old Testament prophets, writes of a day in which the Lord will come in the person of the Messiah whose mission will be to purge and purify His people as a "refiner's fire." Another aspect of the Messiah's role will be to judge and bear witness against evil doers. Malachi enumerates a number of serious sins that will be dealt with, one of which is that of "depriving the *stranger* of his *rights:*"

> And I will come near to you to judgment; and I will be a swift witness against the sorcerers, against false swearers, and against the adulterers, and against those that oppress the hireling in his wages, the widow, and the fatherless, and that *turn aside the stranger from his right,* and fear not me, saith the Lord of host (Malachi 3:5).

According to Jeremiah, true repentance for the Hebrew people was impossible without a proper attitude and relationship to one's neighbor — including the "stranger" or Gentile:

> For if ye thoroughly amend your ways and your doings; if ye thoroughly execute judgment between *a man and his neighbour;*
>
> If ye *oppress not the stranger,* the fatherless, and the widow, and shed not innocent blood in this place, neither walk after other gods to your hurt:
>
> Then will I cause you to dwell in this place, in the land that I gave to your fathers, for ever and ever (Jeremiah 7:5-7. See also Jeremiah 22:3).

From the institution of the Passover feast to the closing of the Old Testament Scriptures, the "stranger" (non-Hebrew) was a central figure in God's Word. The stranger was admitted into the Abrahamic covenant on the same grounds as the Israelite. The "cursings" and "blessings" of the law were as applicable to the Gentile as they were to the Hebrew — depending upon the faithfulness or unfaithfulness of both groups. The stranger was subject to the same religious regulations that governed the Israelite — no more and no less (Leviticus 24:22). Therefore the "strangers," as well as the natural descendants of Abraham, would come under the umbrella of "love of neighbor."

There are Bible students who practically close the "book of life" to the Gentiles of the Old Testament period — the Israelites are the sole actors in the drama of redemption. But the Scriptures give us an entirely different view from this. The Gentiles, as well as the physical seed of Abraham, had access into God's covenant and grace. The "inclusion of the Gentiles" was not as "well known" in the old dispensation as in the new, but it was, nevertheless, a part of God's program. The names of several Gentile people who believed in God are given in the Old Testament . In fact, an entire city, the city of Ninevah, is reported to have repented and believed at the preaching of Jonah. The Gentile nations did not go unnoticed in the days of Moses and the prophets. God dealt with them as well as with the nation of Israel.

The above truth is clearly seen in the call and ministry of Jeremiah. Jeremiah was destined to be a prophet to both Judah and the "nations" (Gentiles) before he was born (Jeremiah 1:5). This twofold ministry is briefly condensed in Jeremiah 12:14-17. In this short passage we discover that God's judgment and salvation are universal in nature — Judah is no better than her "neighbours" (Gentiles). The pagan nations who had spoiled God's heritage and taught Israel to worship Baal would be removed from their land — but so would Judah. And the restoration of Judah and her "neighbours" to their respective land is also without partiality. In addition to this, if the Gentile nations who seduced God's people to idolatry will learn the "ways of my people" they will be "built in the midst of my people." In other words, if the Gentile nations will reverse their life style and show the same diligence toward God that they did in teaching Israel to worship Baal, they will be God's people as much so as the obedient Hebrews:

Thus saith the Lord against all mine evil neighbours, (Gentiles) that

> touch the inheritance which I have caused my people Israel to inherit;
> Behold, I will pluck them (Gentiles) out of their land, and pluck out
> the house of Judah from among them.
>
> And it shall come to pass after that I have plucked them (Judah and
> her neighbours) out I will *return* and *have compassion on them,* and
> will *bring them again,* every man his heritage, and every man his land.
>
> And it shall come to pass, if they will diligently *learn the ways of
> my people,* to *swear by my name, the Lord liveth;* as they taught my
> people to swear by Baal; then shall they (Gentiles) be *built in the midst
> of my people* (Jeremiah 12:14-16).

As pointed out earlier, the premillennialists believe that the "inclusion of the Gentiles" was a "mystery" that did not come to light until New Testament days. However, it has been shown that Christ is the "mystery" in Ephesians three and not the "inclusion of the Gentiles" per se. The "inclusion of the Gentiles" that is discussed in Ephesians three is the enhanced "knowledge" or "revelation" that was given to Paul regarding the Gentiles and other Gospel truths (Galatians 1:11-12). How could the "inclusion of the Gentiles" be a "mystery" and unknown when so many passages of Scripture in the Old Testament say otherwise? A special revelation was necessary to convince *any* Jew that the Gentiles were as dear to God as the Jews (Acts 10:9-18). There were many other truths in the Old Testament that were ignored and glossed over by the Hebrews. The doctrine of "faith," the "righteousness of God," the true "nature of sin," and many other crucial doctrines needed to be brought to the forefront. The "inclusion of the Gentiles" was only one among many.

Paul was given more knowledge and insight into the Gentile situation than any other New Testament writer. The Apostle derives most of his information on the Gentiles from the Old Testament Scriptures. He quotes passage after passage from the Old Testament as proof of their inclusion. In Romans 15:9-12 he cites four Old Testament references (Psalm 18:49, Deuteronomy 32:43, Psalm 117:1, and Isaiah 11:1, 10) to convince the Roman Church that the Gentiles were embodied in God's eternal program. It is perhaps no coincidence that he quotes from the "law," the "prophets," and the "Psalms." The following New and Old Testament references should be compared also: Romans 10:13 and Joel 2:32, Romans 15:21 and Isaiah 52:15, Romans 4:17, Galatians 3:8-9, 14 and Genesis 12:3. Paul's consistent reference to Genesis 12:3 should be sufficient to convince an unbiased person that the Gentiles were in the framework of God's covenant with Abraham — and that covenant was in effect the day it was made. The admission of the Gentiles into the household of faith was very evident in the Old Testament Scriptures but it was ignored by the majority of the Hebrew people. A given truth can be well documented in the Scriptures and still be disregarded.

Regardless of the religious note that was sounded in the Old Testament period, if "love of neighbor" was omitted (including the non-Hebrew), it resulted in the wrath of God. Any prophecy, no matter how optimistic and blissful it might appear, would only rise to haunt the Hebrew people if this momentous truth on "love of neighbor" was neglected.

Many of the Jewish people knew more about the law of Moses than they were willing to practice. For some it was a deliberate rejection of the Scriptures, under the pretense of ignorance. When a certain lawyer came to Jesus asking what he must do to "inherit eternal life," Jesus allowed him to answer his own question. Jesus replied: "What is written in the law? how readest thou?" The lawyer responded with a good deal of insight into the law of Moses:

> Thou shalt *love the Lord thy God* with all thy heart, and with all thy soul, and with all thy strength, and with all thy mind; and *thy neighbor as thyself* (Luke 10:27).

Jesus readily accepted the lawyer's abridgment of Moses' law and admonished him with these words:

> ... Thou hast answered right: *this do and thou shalt live* ("eternally" is implied, Luke 10:28).

The response of this lawyer is proof that many of the Jewish people knew what was necessary to please God but they refused to walk in the light they possessed. We find the lawyer, who answered his own question so admirably, hedging and feigning ignorance of the law by asking, "And who is my neighbor?" This pretentious question inspired Jesus to give the well-known parable of the "Good Samaritan."

From the very beginning to the present hour, men have willfully ignored the first two commandments, and like their first parents, have gathered their own variety of fig leaves to mask their disobedience. In every period of history religious zealots have clothed themselves in their own special brand of doctrine without a shred of love showing. Pious groups are distinguished, not by love of God and man, but by certain man-made labels sown in their religious garbs. All religious beliefs, ancient or modern, biblical or otherwise, need to be examined in the light of First Corinthians thirteen. The Apostle Paul says it best — without love, "I am nothing." The absence of love for God and one's fellow man annuls all religious beliefs of whatever hue or form.

Hillel, a highly revered Jewish teacher of the first century, B. C., and whose insight into the Torah is respected to this day, is quoted as saying: "What is hateful to thee, do not unto thy fellow man; *this is the whole law;* the rest is mere commentary."[10] (emphasis mine) Whether or not Hillel knew the "grace of God in truth" may never be known, but he is setting forth a divine axiom that all men (Jews and Gentiles) should know and practice. It does not require a man of letters to cipher this truth from the Scriptures. It is not codified; nor is it eclipsed by ornate words and ambiguous phrases. Also, it is not put "under a bushel, but on a candlestick; and it giveth light unto all that are in the house" (Matthew 5:15).

To love God and one's fellow man are the very nectar of Scripture. These two commandments have nothing to do with a "national" Jewish state in the past or a millennial kingdom of the future, but they have everything to do with the *present* and with *eternity.* If my faith in God does not include the so-called millennial reign, then I have not missed very much. After all, what is one thousand years compared to eternity? John Newton, in his immortal song, "Amazing Grace," tries to describe eternity with these familiar words:

When we've been there ten thousand years,
Bright shining as the sun,
We've no less days to sing God's praise
Than when we first begun.

"We've no less days ... than when we first begun" means that ten thousand years cannot begin to exhaust eternity — it is dayless and endless. If more time, thought, and energy were given to the first two commandments, instead of so many scruples about the future, we would have a better society in every age. Men must love God and their fellow man *here* and *now* if they are going to live with Him eternally.

The man of whom it is written, "foxes have holes and the birds of the air have nests, but the Son of man hath not where to lay His head,"

---

10. *The World Book Encyclopedia,* Vol. 9, 220.

willingly and lovingly identified Himself with the "unfortunates" of His day. It was He who said, "inasmuch as ye did it *not unto the least of these my brethren, ye did it not unto Me.*" "Love of neighbor," which spotlights the underprivileged in Scripture, is synonymous with *faith in* and *love of God.*

Attention has been drawn to "love of God" and "love of neighbor" (including the non-Hebrew) for two special reasons. The first reason is to show that these two concepts were given to the Israelites in great abundance and with much simplicity. The bulk of God's commandments pertain to Himself and humankind. Sufficient light was given to them on both commandments. If the Hebrew people had given heed to these two precepts, they would have pleased God to the fullest (1 John 3:23). "Love of God" and "love of neighbor" would have distinguished the Israelites as "God's people" more than all the other religious activities combined.

Secondly, the two ideas are expanded to show that "individual" relationships (love of neighbor) take precedence over "national" relationships in every period of Hebrew history. The widow, fatherless, stranger, poor, etc., were "individuals" within the "nation" but they were not the "nation" per se. Men do not stand or fall by their relationship to a particular "nation" but they do stand or fall by their relationship to "individuals" within a family, community, province, or nation. God was far more concerned with a faithful, loving, and holy people (including the non-Hebrew) in the old economy than He was with an earthly, visible Hebrew "nation" (Exodus 19:5-6). And God's concern did not change with the coming of the New Testament era (1 Peter 2:9); nor will He subscribe to a "national" Jewish, earthly kingdom in the future, as taught by the premillennialists. The New Testament closes on an "individual" emphasis. John writes: "And the Spirit and the bride say, Come. And let *him* that heareth say, Come. And let *him* that is athirst come. And *whosoever will,* let *him* take the water of life freely" (Revelation 22:17).

Chapter 7

The Land of Canaan
vs.
A Better Country

> For they that say such things declare plainly that they *seek a country.*
>
> And truly, if they had been mindful of that country from whence they came out, they might have had opportunity to have returned.
>
> But now they desire a *better country,* that is, an *heavenly:* wherefore God is not ashamed to be called their God: for *he hath prepared for them a city* (Hebrews 11:14-16).

The "Land of Canaan" has certainly left its mark upon the world. It has been the source of more controversy than any other piece of real estate on the face of the globe. More wars have been fought, more blood has been shed, more hate and bitterness have arisen, more misunderstanding has been associated with this small territory than any other country in the world. The caldron of controversy is still seething, just waiting to boil over on those who stoke its fires.

This little strip of land has also left its theological scars on the world. The verbal artillery that has divided and created so many wounds in the body of Christ is still being heard in many lands. Some interpreters of the Scriptures have used all kinds of tactics to build up the ramparts of Canaan in defense of the so-called Jewish millennium. Reason is oftentimes laid aside in this mad struggle to be the "conqueror" in this theological battle. But the man-made bulwarks, built of straw, hay, and stubble, cannot withstand the power and might of the Gospel. The Gospel of Christ brings men to a "better country" — a "heavenly country" that obliterates the literal "Land of Canaan" (Hebrews 11:8-16). If the Jewish people and the Christian church had imitated the faith of Abraham, we would not have this trail of blood that has dripped and flowed from the Land of Canaan. The struggle over Canaan is a classic example of men interpreting the Scriptures to their own destruction (2 Peter 3:16).

The controversy on the "Land of Canaan" for the futurists centers around the covenant that God made with Abraham in the book of Genesis. For them, the covenant consists of two important things: (1) It was to be an *unconditional covenant* (or promise) to Abraham's natural descendant, and (2) It was to be an *everlasting covenant* (or promise) to Abraham's natural descendants. These two concepts are vital to pre-millennial doctrine.

The promise made to Abraham must be pressed into the premillennial mold before it can emerge as an "unconditional" promise. Dr. John F. Walvoord, a strong defender of the "unconditional" theory, tells us what God *really* had in mind when He gave the promise to Abraham. But the promise must undergo some premillennial word-mongering before it can be understood as an unconditional promise:

> By using the word unconditional, it is not intended to imply that there were no human contingencies, but rather that God took all these contingencies into consideration when He made the promise. Further it should be understood that the promise is not necessarily in all of its aspects fulfilled to every individual Israelite, but that some aspects of the promise are reserved for particular Israelites in a particular generation and limited to a large extent to those in Israel who are qualified as the spiritual seed of Abraham. The promise is not necessarily fulfilled therefore by *all* the seed of Abraham, but by *some* of the seed of Abraham.[1] (Italics his)

The above quote from Dr. Walvoord is a good example of how the millenarians confound the Word of God. If we can eliminate certain "human contingencies" in the seed of Abraham, and if we are able to separate the "particular" Israelite from the non-particular, and if we can determine the "particular" age in which certain aspects of the promise is to be fulfilled, and if we limit the promise to those who "qualify" as the spiritual seed of Abraham, then we can arrive at an "unconditional" promise as taught by Dr. Walvoord. Can we believe that a simple promise made to Abraham and fulfilled in Jesus Christ could be made so complicated and complex?

It is very obvious from the above quote that Dr. Walvoord has no problem with "spiritualizing" the seed of Abraham. But he objects very

---

1. Walvoord, 42-43.

strongly to those who "spiritualize" the Land of Canaan. "Spiritual-izing" for most millenarians is a matter of convenience or expediency.

It is an unpleasant task to question the rationale of so many well-intended men in the premillennial camp, but they leave us no option. M. R. DeHaan, who follows the usual premillennial bent of mind, believes that God is punishing the Jews of today and centuries past because of their sin. However, their disobedience does not altar God's promise to them. God will fulfill His covenant regarding the Land of Palestine in spite of their defiance of His Word. According to Dr. DeHaan, the Land of Canaan was given to the seed of Abraham as an everlasting posses-sion before they were "born."[2]

If the covenant (or promise) was "unconditional" and soley of God's grace, i.e., without human involvement, and given to the seed of Abraham before they were born, then every "natural" son of Abraham is entitled to share in the Land of Canaan — there must be no exceptions.

If God fulfills His "unconditional," "everlasting" covenant to one segment of Abraham's seed (which was made before they were born) and not *all* of Abraham's children, then those who are deprived of its fulfillment will have a real controversy with God because of His double-dealing. Either the premillennialists write one thing and mean another, or they come from an alien school of thought.

If the covenant made to Abraham's "unborn" seed was "uncondi-tional" and "everlasting," why did God allow Canaan to be overrun by foreign countries, the Jews taken captive and dispersed among the nations? If it was an "unconditional," "everlasting" promise, then God should have fulfilled it to every Jew in every age. There should have never been any kind of interruption in the Jews' possession of the land. From the day that Abraham entered the Land of Canaan to this present hour, his natural seed should be occupying the Land of Palestine. Abraham's descendants should have never gone into Egypt to remain there for 430 years; they should have never been taken into captivity by the Babylonians; they should have never been scattered over the world. And every present day Jew should be living in the state of Israel rather than in so many other countries. Do the words "unconditional" and "everlasting" have a double meaning for the premillennialists — are

---

2. Ideas expressed in M. R. DeHaan's book: *The Jews and Palestine in Prophecy,* p. 50.

they talking out of both sides of their mouths?

If all the natural seed of Abraham are to return to the Land of Canaan in spite of their sin, what will be their fate *after* the thousand year reign? Will the Jews be ushered into eternity (in spite of their sin) to be included in the eternal inheritance that Christ purchased with His blood? Is the "inheritance of Canaan" synonymous with "eternal, everlasting life" as set forth in the New Testament? Will the Jews share in the "better country," regardless of their sin and unbelief? The futurists leave us in a real quandary.

If the promise made to Abraham is "unconditional" and "everlasting" as the premillennialists claim — and since it has not been fulfilled to the Jews as yet — then the only recourse for the fulfillment of this promise would be to resurrect every son of Abraham at the beginning of the millennial period. This seems to be the only feasible way that the "unconditional" and "everlasting" promise can be fulfilled. Although such a feat would be contrary to the Scriptures, it would not be out of harmony with many other things the millenarians teach.

According to Dr. DeHaan's interpretation, today is the "punishing age" for the Jews — tomorrow will be the "fulfillment age" for them. These two ideas seem to permeate a good deal of his theology concerning the Jews and the millennium. Is it consistent with God's righteous character to "punish" present and past generations of Jews and "spare" the Jews of the millennial age a similar "punishment?" Is there a double standard for the Jews? How are we to reconcile the Jews who have been "punished" for their sins and the Jews who will share in the millennium "in spite of their sins?" Is God such a respecter of persons? (Romans 2:11).

The "unconditional" promise that the millenarians propound is not new. It was initiated by the Jews themselves long before premillennialism was ever known (John 8:33). It has been the Jews' Achilles' heel in every age and generation. It has been responsible for more anxieties and woes for them than any other aspect of their religious scenario. It was their belief in an "unconditional" promise that elevated them to a point where they could criticize, condemn, and crucify the Son of God. The New Testament rebukes them, shames them, and condemns them on every hand for clinging to this "unconditional" promise. The millenarians are asked to produce a single shred of evidence that an "unconditional" promise has ever been favorable to the Jews. Whether consciously or unconsciously, the premillennialists contribute to this "superior," "self-righteous" and "irresponsible" attitude among the Jewish people. The "unconditional" promise in the Land of Canaan is all theater with no substance or reality.

The premillennialists are pleased to emphasize the word "everlasting" in their claim of Palestine for the natural descendents of Abraham. The word "everlasting" is used many times in the Old Testament but it does not always mean infinity. In many places it is used to describe a long period of time but not timelessness. Several examples can be cited from the Old Testament. According to Genesis 17:12-13, circumcision in the flesh was to be an "everlasting" covenant:

> And he that is eight days old shall be circumcised among you, every man child in your generation...
> ... and my covenant shall be in your *flesh for an everlasting covenant.*

We know from both the Old Testament and the New that "circumcision in the flesh" had its ultimate fulfillment in "circumcision of the heart" and was considered as naught (in matters of redemption) without the latter. The *first* was to be supplanted by the *second*. This same principle is to be seen in many areas of Biblical revelation:

The *old covenant* is supplanted by the *new covenant*

The *first tabernacle* is supplanted by the *True Tabernacle*

The *old man* (man's sinful nature) is supplanted by the *new man* (Christ)

The *first Adam* is supplanted by the *Second Adam*

The *old heart* is supplanted by the *new heart*

The *old body* will be supplanted by the *new body*

The *old Jerusalem* will be supplanted by the *new Jerusalem*

The *old Zion* will be supplanted by the *new Zion*

The *old heaven* and *earth* will be supplanted by the *new heaven* and *earth*

The *old Land* of *Canaan* is supplanted by a *better country*

Need we more proof of this principle? "Circumcision in the flesh" was not an "everlasting" covenant. And we should not regard the "Land of Canaan" as an "everlasting" covenant.

Also, the book of Exodus speaks of the Levitical priesthood as an "everlasting" priesthood. Moses wrote concerning Aaron's sons:

> And thou shalt anoint them (Aaron's sons), as thou didst anoint their father, that they may minister unto me in the priest's office: for

their anointing shall surely be an *everlasting priesthood* throughout their generations (Exodus 40:15).

Every student of the New Testament should know that the Levitical priesthood had its fulfillment in the finished work of Christ and was not meant to be an "everlasting" priesthood.

The phrase "for ever" is sometimes used in the King James Version in connection with the promise made to Abraham (Genesis 13:14-15). It, too, can represent a long period of time but not uninterrupted existence. This phrase is frequently used in the same way that the word "everlasting" is used in the Old Testament. From the book of Exodus we learn that it is used to describe the duration of a man's life. If a Hebrew man became a bondsman for another, and wished to remain with his master after the prescribed six years of service, he was allowed to do so according to the following instructions:

> Then his master shall bring him (bondsman) unto the judges; he shall also bring him to the door, or unto the door post; and his master shall bore his ear through with an aul; and he shall serve him *for ever* (Exodus 21:6).

When Moses gave instructions to be followed by Aaron and his sons regarding the lamp in the tabernacle, it was to be a statue "for ever:"

> And thou shalt ... cause the lamp to burn always.
> In the tabernacle of the congregation without the vail, which is before the testimony, Aaron and his sons shall order it from evening to morning before the Lord; it shall be a statute *for ever* unto their generations on the behalf of the children of Israel (Exodus 27:20-21).

Must a "literal" interpretation be given to the above quote? The lamp that burned perpetually in the tabernacle had its fulfillment in the One who was the "Light of the world." The word "forever" is used many, many times in the Old Testament, but it does not always mean an endless duration.

According to 2 Chronicles 7:16, God's name was to be in the temple that Solomon built "forever" (Living Bible). Also, His eyes and heart were to be there "perpetually." But this temple was destroyed by the Babylonians around 588-586 B. C. The tabernacle and temple in the old dispensation were only types and shadows of the True Temple who is Christ (John 2:19; Hebrews 8:5).

When will the "everlasting" promise begin for Abraham's descendants? Evidently it will begin at the discretion of the premillennialists. It seems logical that it would have begun the day it was given to Abraham. But according to the futurists, this did not happen. Furthermore, the word "everlasting" can never be restricted to a "thousand years." There is a vast difference between the terms "everlasting" and a "thousand years." But this difference creates no problem for the millenarians.

Dr. John F. Walvoord believes that Israel's title to the land is "unending." But the word "unending" must be given the usual premillennial treatment before it can be fully understood. Dr. Walvoord says:

> ... the title of the land is declared to be *unending* in its character. By this we should understand that the *land belongs to Israel as long as the present earth endures.* Fourth, not only is the title to be given *forever,* but the land is actually to be possessed as *long as the earth endures,* once it is given to Israel at the beginning of the millennial kingdom.[3] (Italics mine.)

For Dr. Walvoord, the words "unending," "forever," and "everlasting" mean as long as the present earth stands. The premillennialists have a unique way of making words say what *they* want them to say. When you write the script, you can say whatever you please. From a Scriptural point of view, it is impossible to connect the "duration of the earth" with the "everlasting" promise made to Abraham. Perhaps William E. Cox has the best explanation of how the words "eternal" and "everlasting" are used in the Old Testament Scriptures. He writes: "A promise was 'eternal' or 'everlasting' for the duration of time God decreed to use a given method of dealing with His people."[4]

In the light of biblical and secular history, we know that the words "everlasting" and "forever" should not be interpreted as the futurists interpret them. Canaan, like many other Old Testament concepts, was to be a schoolmaster directing the Israelites to a "better country, that is, an heavenly" (Hebrews 11:16a). A good deal of the Old Testament revelation was to serve this purpose.

Egypt was also a part of the Old Testament curriculum. Egypt represented the nature and character of sin and Satan, which is cruel,

---

3. Walvoord, 72.
4. William E. Cox, *Biblical Studies in Final Things,* Presbyterian and Reformed Publishing Co. Nutley, New Jersey, 1977, 96.

oppressive, and slavish. Egypt was not to remain the archenemy of God and the Jews throughout their history. Joseph and Mary found more protection and security for the infant Jesus in Egypt during the reign of Herod the Great than they did in the land of Israel (Matthew 2:14-15). Today, this nation is no more the adversary of God and the Jews than any other nation of the world.

The role of Egypt in the old economy was to be a part of the educational program for the Jews of that era and for centuries to follow. We still benefit from the lessons stemming from the Egyptian bondage.

In like manner, the "Land of Canaan" was to be the classroom for the Israelites of that day and of the future. It was not to be an "everlasting" possession as advocated by the futurists. In recent years it has become a political asylum for many Jews, but it cannot be regarded as a "Mecca" for the majority of them. There are more Jews in New York City than in the state of Israel.

The books of Joshua and Nehemiah cast an even darker cloud over the futurists' interpretation of the promise made to Abraham and his natural descendants. According to these books, the promise was fulfilled in its entirety when the Israelites came into the land under the leadership of Joshua:

> And the Lord gave unto Israel *all the land* which he *sware to give unto their fathers;* and *they possessed it,* and dwelt therein.
>
> And the Lord gave them rest round about, according to *all that he sware unto their fathers:* and there stood not a man of *all their enemies* before them; the Lord delivered *all their enemies* into their hand.
>
> There *failed not ought of any good thing which the Lord had spoken unto the house of Israel; all came to pass* (Joshua 21:43-45). See Nehemiah 9:23-24.

The same truth is repeated again in the book of Joshua along with a note of warning. Their remaining in the land was contingent upon their obedience to the Word of the Lord — it was not "unconditional." Joshua, on the day of his death, affirmed that God's promise had not failed:

> And, behold, this day I am going the way of all the earth: and ye know in all your hearts and in all your souls, that *not one thing hath failed of all the good things* which the Lord your God spake concerning you: *all are come to pass unto you,* and *not one thing hath failed thereof.*

> Therefore it shall come to pass, that *as all good things are come upon you,* which the Lord your God promised you; so shall the Lord *bring upon you all evil things,* until he have *destroyed you from off this good land* which the Lord your God hath given you (Joshua 23:14-15). See also 1 Kings 8:56.

In addition to this, the Israelites were instructed by Moses never to sell the land in which they dwelled. Why? Because it was *not theirs* — ultimately, it belonged to God:

> The land *shall not be sold* for ever: *for the land is mine;* for ye are *strangers and sojourners with me* (Leviticus 25:23). See also Deuteronomy 32:43; Joel 2:18; Jeremiah 27:5.

The above passage teaches more than one lesson. We are informed that Jehovah God condescended to dwell in a frail tent (tabernacle) among His people. But the Land of Canaan was *not* to be His permanent dwelling place; nor was it to be for the Israelites. The tabernacle (and later the temple) in which God dwelled was only temporary in His eternal plan (See 2 Chronicles 2:6; Acts 7:48). God's role in the Land of Canaan was that of a "stranger" and "sojourner," and the Israelites were to imitate Him when they occupied the land. In fulfilling this role they would be following in the steps of Abraham, who considered himself a "stranger" in the Land of Canaan (Hebrews 11:9). God's presence in the tabernacle foreshadowed the One who would dwell (tabernacle) among men in a fragile human body (John 1:14).

There is no period in all of Jewish history that would approach the dream of the futurists concerning the Land of Canaan as an everlasting inheritance for the descendants of Abraham. Even the reign of David, Israel's most glorious era, would not come close to an age of Jewish nationalism and dominance that epitomizes premillennialism. David did not regard the Land of Canaan as the fulfillment of God's promise to Abraham. In fact, the king, himself, speaks of an alienation and estrangement from the land that upholds the words of Moses. This great monarch, along with his believing forefathers, saw himself as a *stranger* and *sojourner with the Lord* in the land:

> Hear my prayer, O Lord, and give ear unto my cry; hold not thy peace at my tears: for I am a *stranger with thee,* and a *sojourner,* as *all my fathers were* (Psalm 39:12). See also 1 Chronicles 29:14-16.

The example of Abraham as a "stranger" in the Land of Canaan, the words of Moses on the same subject, the testimony of David, and the role of God Himself refute any and all claims of Palestine as an everlasting possession for the Jewish people.

The Old Testament does not stand alone in this confutable issue. One of the most comprehensive books on the state of affairs in the Old Testament period is the book of Hebrews. Almost every important aspect of God's revelation to Moses and the prophets is dealt with in this portion of inspired Scripture. The advocates of premillennialism can find no support or comfort for their "doctrine" in this epistle. The book of Hebrews contradicts practically everything the futurists teach. The word "better" is used to show the superiority of Christ over every outstanding feature in the old dispensation — including the Land of Canaan.

Jesus is "better" than the angels because of His unique Sonship with the Father (Hebrews 1:4); Abraham, who is inferior to Melchizedek (a type of Christ), is blessed by the "better" (Hebrews 7:7); Christ brought a "better" hope than the law of Moses (Hebrews 7:19); Jesus was a guarantee of a "better" covenant (Hebrews 7:22); the new covenant is established upon "better" promises (Hebrews 8:6); Christ was a "better" sacrifice than the sacrifices under the old dispensation (Hebrews 9:23); heaven consists of a "better" and more "enduring substance" than the things of this world (Hebrews 10:34); the promise to Abraham pertained to a "better" country rather than the Land of Canaan (Hebrews 11:16); the Old Testament saints were willing to suffer in order that they might share in a "better" life than this world had to offer (Hebrews 11:35).

Why would Abraham, Isaac, Jacob, and all other Old Testament saints, who either sojourned in the Land of Canaan or lived in the Land of Canaan, want to return to an earthly, millennial habitat when they are brought to a "better" country, a "better" life, a "better" world, etc? If Christ's death has brought a "better" sacrifice and a "better" covenant, why would God's elect want to revive animal sacrifices for one thousand years? It is always sane and logical to prefer the "better." Millennial teaching is a deviation from the "things that God hath prepared for them that love him" (1 Corinthians 2:9).

Also, the breach which the premillennialists have created between the Old and New Testament saints is not tolerated in the Hebrews epistle. The Old Testament saints "saw" and "embraced" the promise of Christ "afar off" but were denied its ultimate realization in their day — they must wait for the "better" things which belong to the New

Testament saints (Hebrews 11:13-16). The finality of the promise is shared by both. This truth is proven by the example of some outstanding Old Testament saints who suffered and died without realizing the promise:

> All these won a glowing testimony to their faith, but they *did not then and there receive the fulfillment of the promise.* God had something *better* planned for our day (New Testament saints), and it was *not His plan that they should reach perfection without us* (Hebrews 11:39-40 - Phillips Translation).

The fracture that the futurists have created between the Old Testament saints and the church has been decried and ridiculed by some time-honored men of the past. Charles H. Spurgeon (1834-1892) found the idea very loathsome. He chides the proponents of the "fracture theory" in these words:

> Distinctions have been drawn by certain exceedingly wise men (measured by their own estimate of themselves), between the people of God who lived before the coming of Christ, and those who lived afterwards. We have even heard it asserted that those who lived before the coming of Christ do not belong to the church of God! We never know what we shall hear next, and perhaps it is a mercy that these absurdities are revealed one at a time, in order that we may be able to endure their stupidity without dying of amazement. Why, *every child of God in every place stands on the same footing ... Those living before Christ were not saved with a different salvation to that which shall come to us.*[5] (Italics mine.)

As stated earlier, the Hebrews epistle deals with most of the important things that were associated with the old dispensation. The writer's objective is to show that the Mosaic law has been replaced by something that is far "better." The climax and solution to all that has been discussed throughout this epistle is found in the following passage:

> Wherefore Jesus also, that he might sanctify the people with his own blood, *suffered without the gate. Let us go forth therefore unto him without the camp, bearing his reproach.* For here we have *no continuing city, but we seek one to come* (Hebrews 13:12-14).

---

5. *The Treasury of the New Testament,* Zondervan Publishing House, Grand Rapids, Michigan, Vol. IV, 247.

Jesus' sufferings "without the gate" are very suggestive. In biblical days the "gate of the city" was representative of the entire city. Public assemblies were oftentimes held at the gate of the city. Judges and courts convened there to mete out justice. Public markets were conducted within the precincts of the city gate, i.e., merchandise was bought and sold. Outside news was received and circulated in this area of the city. The gate of the city was the "Grand Central Station" of Jerusalem and other ancient cities.

Jesus suffered outside the walls of Jerusalem. Jerusalem represented the religious and secular spirit of the Jewish nation. The real attitude of the false religionists and the secular world is to be seen "outside the gate" of Jerusalem. It was "outside the gate" that Jesus completed His earthly mission by His death on the cross. Those to whom the book of Hebrews was written were asked to "go forth" unto Him without the gate "bearing His reproach." In other words, they were to identify themselves with Christ and His cross and sever themselves from *all* that Jerusalem connotes — both religious and secular. Why? Because *"here* we have *no continuing city, but we seek one to come"* (verse 14). Even the earthly Jerusalem, which the premillennialists prize so highly, had no primacy in that day; nor will it have in the future. The epistle of Hebrews is anti-premillennial through and through.

The above passage (Hebrews 13:12-14) is a very appropriate conclusion for the book of Hebrews. It depicts the very heart of the Gospel. The recipients of this epistle were asked to exit "one gate" and "enter another" — the gateway to heaven. The shame of one was the glory of the other. Jessie Brown Pounds (1861-1921) expresses this truth in a heaven-born hymn entitled "The Way of the Cross Leads Home:"

> I must needs go home by the way of the cross,
> There's no other way but this;
> I shall ne're get sight of the gates of light,
> If the way of the cross I miss.
>
> I must needs go on in the blood-sprinkled way,
> The path that the Saviour trod,
> If I ever climb to the heights sublime,
> Where the soul is at home with God.

> Then I bid farewell to the way of the world,
> To walk in it nevermore;
> For my Lord says "Come," and I seek my home,
> Where He waits at the open door.

According to the epistle of Hebrews, there is no permanency whatsoever regarding the present creation. The writer of this epistle uses the Sinai experience to show the transitoriness of the world and its ultimate removal. When God gave the law on Mt. Sinai, it is recorded that His voice "shook the earth" (Hebrews 12:26). The shaking of the earth on this occasion is only a springboard for this author to say that God will one day "shake both heaven and earth." The conclusion of the matter is that the present heaven and earth, which can be shaken, will one day be replaced by a "kingdom that cannot be shaken" (Hebrews 12:28).

The destruction of the heavens and earth is taught in both the Old and New Testaments. The epistle of Hebrews is in perfect accord with what the prophets and the apostles have to say on this subject. Peter gives one of the most graphic descriptions of this truth to be found in Scripture:

> But the day of the Lord will come as a thief in the night; in the which the *heavens shall pass away* with a great noise, and the *elements shall melt with fervent heat,* the *earth also* and the works that are therein *shall be burned up...*
> Nevertheless we, according to *His promise,* look for *new heavens* and a *new earth,* wherein dwelleth righteousness (2 Peter 3:10, 13).

According to the above passage, the "promise" of God does not pertain to a Jewish millennium in the land of Palestine, but a "new heaven and a new earth wherein dwelleth righteousness." Peter's comments on a "new heaven and a new earth" are in perfect agreement with the Old Testament prophets (see Isaiah 13:13, 34:4, 66:22, Psalm 102:25-27, Joel 3:16). The "promise" made to Abraham and fulfilled in the Gospel will eventually give birth to a new creation (Romans 8:19-20). The death and resurrection of Jesus warrant this fact (Colossians 1:20). As A. W. Tozer writes: "The blood of Jesus has covered not only the human race but all creation as well."[7]

---

7. A. W. Tozer, *The Pursuit of God,* Christian Publications, inc., Harrisburg, Pennsylvania, 80.

Many of the first century Jews were blind to the central message of both the Old Testament prophets and the New Testament Apostles. They were certain that the "promise," as taught by Moses and the prophets, was being undermined by the disciples of Christ (Acts 6:11). It was for this very reason that Paul was arrested and his freedom (and life) was threatened. According to Paul, there was no contradiction between what he taught and the teachings of Moses and the prophets. This fact is brought to light in his defense before King Agrippa. Agrippa was of Jewish descent and well versed in the Scriptures. Paul stood before a man who would have no problem in understanding that the New Testament saints share in the same "hope of promise" that the Old Testament saints anticipated:

> And now I stand and am judged for the *hope of the promise made of God unto our fathers:*
> Unto which *promise* our twelve tribes, instantly serving God day and night, *hope to come.* For which *hope's sake,* king Agrippa, I am accused of the Jews.
> Why should it be thought a thing incredible with you, that *God should raise the dead?* (Acts 26:6-8).

The "resurrection of the dead" to which Paul alludes in the above text is the resurrection of Christ. The "hope of the promise" that Moses and the prophets looked forward to was that Christ "should suffer and be raised from the dead." This was the central message of the Old Testament writers as well as the New. From the beginning of Paul's career to the end, the death and resurrection of Christ was the crux of his message:

> Having therefore obtained hope of God, *I continued unto this day,* witnessing both to small and great *saying none other things than those which the prophets and Moses did say should come:*
> *That Christ should suffer,* and that *He should be the first that should rise from the dead,* and should show light unto the people (Jews), and to the Gentiles (Acts 26:22-23). See also Luke 24:25-26; Acts 3:18-26 and Acts 28:23.

The "hope of the resurrection" in conjunction with a "new heaven and a new earth" is the ultimate of the "promise" made to Abraham and not an earthly, millennial kingdom. The emphasis that the futurists have placed upon the Land of Canaan in recent years has only brought chaos and confusion to the Christian church. Every time some bizarre event occurs in the state of Israel or the Middle East, the canon of Scripture is reopened by the premillennialists and a new chapter is added to the Bible. The Six-day War in 1967, the prospects of oil in the Land of Palestine, or minerals from the Dead Sea are occasions to update the prophecies of Scripture. Such prophetic gymnastics serve only to distract men's minds from the real heart of the Gospel — resulting in disillusionment for multitudes of people.

Secular history (past and present) is not the source of our understanding and interpretation of the Scriptures. Biblical history, yes, but not the textbooks of men. Any student of church history knows that the church, both evangelical and institutional, has been plagued with some of the most absurd prophecies that men and Satan can conceive. It is not necessary to look outside the Bible for its interpretation — the Scriptures interpret themselves. Secular events, both past and present, can be anybody's game — one man's views can be as good as another's. All the truth that men need for their knowledge of God and the things that shall be hereafter are found in the canon of Scripture.

The counterpart (Canaan) of the "better country" has many lessons to offer. When Moses sent the twelve spies into the promised land, two of them returned with a favorable report and with clusters of grapes as a token and surety of the land's wealth. There is a parallel to this incident in the New Testament. When Jesus returned to the Father, the Holy Spirit accompanied Him as a witness to His redemptive work and all that it encompasses (Hebrews 9:11-15). The Holy Spirit espied the glories of heaven and returned to the disciples (and others) with a favorable report — and with the "grapes of heaven." The Holy Spirit is a token and surety of heaven and its wealth (Ephesians 1:13). Those who are in Christ have already tasted the "grapes of heaven" and they can scarcely be compared with the old grapes of Canaan (1 Corinthians 2:9-10; Hebrews 6:4-5).

The facts presented in the above paragraph should make the millenarians somewhat envious. They are cramped to find such a warranty in Scripture relative to their millennial kingdom. No spies or witnesses have entered the millennial kingdom and returned with "grapes" from that region — no token or foretaste is available. Such a kingdom does not exist. When Moses commissioned the twelve spies, the Land of Canaan *existed* — it was *for real*. Our analogy is enhanced by this fact. Heaven *exists* — heaven is *for real*. The Holy Spirit confirms the believer's inheritance both now and forever (Ephesians 1).

The premillennialists would rebuttle to the above statements by saying that the Word of God assures the Jews of a millennial kingdom in the future. If the Land of Canaan belongs to the Jews in the *future*, they should have a token and surety of it *today*. The future cannot be certain unless the *present* is certain. The religion of Jesus Christ is a *now* religion — a *today* religion (2 Corinthians 6:2; Hebrews 3:7, 15). The kingdom of God belongs to those who are in Christ *today* as much so as it will in the eons of eternity (Colossians 1:13). God does not give men a bone without some meat on it.

The Word of God by and of itself does not offer the Jews in this age an ounce of assurance. Every Jew on this planet could have a Bible in both hands and still have no assurance of a millennial kingdom in the future. No "grapes" or "spies" can be found, because it does not exist. As proven earlier, the Word of God, apart from the Holy Spirit, condemns, kills, and is a dead letter — the Spirit giveth life.

The Jews have had a theological romance with the Land of Canaan for centuries and it can be compared to a courtship that never ends in marriage. They are tantalized by its bright prospects — excitement builds at every favorable episode in the Zionist movement — their Shangri-La is just around the corner. However, generations come and go and no engagement ring is given — no wedding bells are heard. Old age creeps upon them and the marriage altar becomes smoke. The honeymoon is never enjoyed. Neither time nor history has liberated them from this enchantment. The jilted Jews of today and ages past must stand by and watch their "unborn" relatives come to the marriage altar, enjoy the honeymoon, and live happily ever after. Israel's courtship with the Land of Canaan has been a one-sided love affair for centuries. The millenarians "play cupid" for the Jews and add to their illusion. While "heaven" and the "marriage supper of the Lamb" can be both sure and steadfast for any Jew today, most of them prefer to be "married to calamity" (to use one of William Shakespear's famous lines).

The "hope" that the evangelical church has cherished over the centuries has always been a "heavenly" one rather than an "earthly." The hymns of the church never speak of a "millennial age" in which the saints of God will reign a thousand years on earth. In the years that I have been associated with Gospel music, I know of only one song written about the millennium. Others may exist, but I am not aware of them.

I have listened very intently to funeral messages by evangelical ministers (some of them premillennialists) and not one time have I ever heard a message on the "thousand years reign" for those who die in Christ — it is always a "heavenly hope."

The prospects of "heaven" are almost nil in this age because the present generation knows very little about afflictions and persecutions as a result of their faith. We are living in a day of compromise, easy-living and a "love of the world and the things of the world" (1 John 2:15). This affluent life style has made a tremendous impact on most of the Christian church.

Paul's day, the Reformation era, and the Puritan age were quite different. It was Paul's sufferings and persecutions as a minister of the Gospel that enhanced his hopes of a "better world." His sufferings and persecutions were paradoxical in nature — they served a twofold purpose. While they served as a counteragent to self-trust, human wisdom, and self-righteousness, they opened the door to a new dynamic with Christ (2 Corinthians 4:8-12; 12:9-10; 13:4). This is why Paul could say: "For our *light affliction,* which is but for a moment, *worketh for us* a far more exceeding and eternal weight of glory; While we look not at the things which are *seen,* but at the things which are *not seen;* for the things which are seen are *temporal;* but the things which are not seen are *eternal"* (2 Corinthians 4:17-18). Note the contrasts in the passage just quoted:

Light affliction for a moment	Eternal weight of glory
Things which are seen	Things that are not seen
Things temporal	Things eternal

Those who are in Christ should never "court" persecutions and sufferings. However, if some of the theology of the futurists was written from a dungeon cell or after being stoned and left for dead, they might be willing to by-pass some of their theories on the Land of Canaan and dwell upon the glories of heaven. It is very unlikely that anyone in this age will suffer as did the Apostle Paul. Notwithstanding this fact, it is plain to see that his sufferings and persecutions did not "work" (or produce) a Land of Canaan mentality, but an "eternal weight of glory." Whose theology are we required to emulate — those who write from the school of experience or those who theorize?

The same principle worked in the lives of the Old Testament saints. The *promises* of God had a different relevance for those who underwent

severe trials and testings than they did for those who were "at ease in
Zion." The Old Testament saints found the world very hostile to their
godly lives. However, the fiery ordeals such as the lions mouths, death,
torture, scourgings, imprisonment, stoning, living in caves, dens, deserts, mountains, etc., refined their faith until it was as pure as gold
(Hebrews 11:33-40). Their hope in God inspired them to endure all
manner of hardships in order that they might "obtain a *better
resurrection*" (Hebrews 11:35).

According to the Apostle Paul, the "faith" that sustained him in the
hour of trial was no different from that of the Psalmist. This truth strikes
the eye like a meteor passing through a star-studded sky that is already
filled with beauty. It seems to come from nowhere. Paul reaches back
into the Old Testament Scriptures just for a moment and produces a
golden spike to nail down what he has written relative to his sufferings.
Paul felt a close companionship with the man who wrote the 116th
Psalm:

> We have the *same spirit of faith*, according as *it is written*, I believe,
> and therefore have I spoken; *we also believe*, and therefore speak (2
> Corinthians 4:13).

The above quote from Psalm 116 was written in the same mode that
Paul's thoughts are written. The Psalmist knew the power of God that
was able to sustain him in the hour of adversity. Notice the last phrase
in Psalm 116:10: "I believed, therefore have I spoken: *I was greatly
afflicted*." When the larger context of 2 Corinthians 4:13 and Psalm
116:10 is considered, it will be found that both men were looking
forward to a "life" beyond death. (See Psalm 116:9, 15). There is a direct
relationship between Paul's sufferings in 2 Corinthians 4:8-12 and the
"heavenly" hope that he cherished in 2 Corinthians 4:16—5:1-4).

Human sufferings and pain do not give rise to a speculative and
visionary theology. The faith of the Old Testament saints was not a shot
in the dark. It is affirmed that they *saw* the "promises afar off" and were
"*persuaded* of them," and "*embraced them*" (Hebrews 11:13). The
"promises" that the Old Testament saints "saw," and by which they were
"persuaded," and which they "embraced" was a "*better country*, that is
an *heavenly*" (Hebrews 11:14-16). Those who suffered for their faith in
the Old Testament era were a different breed of people — and this fact
has not changed (2 Timothy 3:12).

Circumstances and conditions, both good and bad, affect man's theology. Religious men have a unique way of adapting the Scriptures to the times in which they live. In days of prosperity, leisure, and materialism men search for passages that will justify their self-indulgence. Beds of ivory, soft couches, lamb chops, T-bones, lively music, and choice wines usually translate into religious pomp and hypocrisy (Amos 6:1-6). As someone has said: "If adversity has slain its thousands, then prosperity has slain its ten thousands."

When times are good the present world becomes a veritable paradise — it is attractive to the carnal mind. But faith, hope, and *agape* love conduct men into a dimension as large as God Himself. Premillennial views on the Land of Canaan play fast and loose with the doctrine of faith. While the futurists attract our attention to the visible and tangible (Palestine), the Apostle Paul would insist that we "fix" our eyes upon the *unseen world,* i.e., heaven (2 Corinthians 4:18 N.E.B.). *Faith* is the media by which we look beyond the *temporal* (Hebrews 11:1). The idea of "heaven" screams in our ears from almost every page of the New Testament. The Christian's *hope* is laid up in heaven (Colossians 1:5); his *affections* are to be in heaven (Colossians 3:2); his *name* is written in heaven (Luke 10:20); all of his *spiritual blessings* are from heaven (Ephesians 1:3); his *citizenship* is in heaven (Philippians 3:20, N.E.B.); he has a *building of God,* an *house not made with hands* eternal in the heavens (2 Corinthians 5:1); there is an *earnest longing* to be clothed upon with his house from heaven (2 Corinthians 5:2); he has an *incorruptible inheritance* that will *never fade* reserved in heaven (1 Peter 1:4); and it is from heaven that he *looks for the Saviour* who will change his physical body and make it compatible with the heavenly realm (Philippians 3:20-21). Can such a list of important ideas be found in the Scripture with regard to the Land of Canaan?

Even "natural religion" conveys the idea of a "better" world. The most primitive people in history have had some apprehension of a "better" existence than the present life. The American Indian's "happy hunting grounds" are only one among many. The "human situation" is enough to motivate people to anticipate a superior place than they now know. Man's confrontation with sin, death, disappointments, disease, pain, poverty, sorrow, oppressions, etc., prompts him to hope for a "better" country.

The message of heaven is a "fool's paradise" if there is not something "better" for those who are in Christ than this present world order. While trying to correct some false views in the Corinthian church on the resurrection of Christ, and at the same time comfort those whose loved ones had already died, Paul wrote: "Truly, if our hope in Christ were *limited to this life only* we should, of all mankind, *be the most pitied!*" (1 Corinthians 15:19, Phillips Translation).

The above passage (1 Corinthians 15:19) must be understood in its proper context. It is given with the hypothesis that Christ may not have been raised from the dead. If Christ is not risen, Paul reasons, then his preaching is vain (verse 14). Along with this, he would be a false witness (verse 15). As for the Corinthians, their faith would be worthless and they would still be in their sins (verse 17). The climax of Paul's logic is that those who die in Christ are *perished* (verse 18). This is why Paul could say, "if our hope in Christ is limited to a few years in this world, then we are the most deluded people on the face of the earth." We are to be "pitied" more than all mankind. *But this is not the way it is.* Paul goes on to write that Christ is the firstfruits of the resurrection and those who die in Christ will be resurrected at His coming (verse 23). When this happens, "Then *comes the end,* when He delivers the kingdom of God the Father after destroying every rule and every authority and power" (verse 24, R.S.V.). According to Paul, there is no interlude of one thousand years after the resurrection of the saints. When Christ returns for His elect, "then *cometh the end.*"

The ultimate purpose of God, as He works in and through His people, is to direct their attention toward a "heavenly inheritance." In the views of Paul, this accomplishment is a sign of Christian maturity. *Christian growth is to be equated with a perfected heavenly hope.* It was this "heavenly hope" that moved the Apostle to forsake his Jewish heritage and press on toward the "mark of the prize of the high calling of God in Christ Jesus" (Philippians 3:4-9). He appeals to the Philippians to imitate his example in pursuing this "heavenly" goal:

> All of us who are *spiritually adult should set ourselves this sort of ambition,* and if at present you cannot see this, yet you *will find that this is the attitude which God is leading you to adopt.* It is *important that we go forward in the light of such truth as we ourselves attained to.*
>
> Let me be your example here, my brothers: Let my example be the standard by which you *can tell who are the genuine Christians among those about you.* For there are many, of whom I have told you before and tell you again now, even with tears, that they are the enemies of

> the cross of Christ. These men are heading for utter destruction —
> their god is their own appetite; their pride is in what they should be
> ashamed of; and *this world is the limit of their horizon.* But *we are
> citizens of heaven;* our *outlook goes beyond this world to the hopeful
> expectation of the Savior who will come from heaven,* the *Lord Jesus*
> (Philippians 3:15-20, Phillips Translation).

The above truth is expressed also in Paul's farewell address to the
elders at Ephesus. As in the Philippian passage, the Apostle's final
words are given in the context of a warning (Acts 20:29-30). Ground
swells of heresy were already apparent in the church at Ephesus and
Paul's departure would only increase the potential threat. The solution
to the problem would be a more mature body of believers that could
counteract the false teachers. For this reason, the Apostle commends
them to God and to the "word of his grace." The "word of his grace"
would serve a twofold purpose: (1) It would build them up (mature
them) in the faith; and (2) It would enhance their "inheritance" in Christ:

> And now, brethren, I commend you to God, and to the *Word of His
> grace,* which is *able to build you up,* and to *give you an inheritance*
> among all them which are sanctified (Acts 20:32). See also Acts
> 26:18.

"Christian growth" always brings the believer into a greater awareness and appreciation of the "heavenly inheritance"— the two concepts
go hand in hand. Paul uses the same Greek word for "inheritance"
(kleronomia) that Peter uses when he writes of an "incorruptible
inheritance" in his first epistle. According to Paul, this "inheritance"
belongs to those who are "sanctified"— a concept which Peter uses in
conjunction with his comments on the believer's inheritance (1 Peter
1:2-4) — and sanctification is always the work of God's Word and
Spirit.

It is time (and past time) for the church to "grow up" and shake the
dust of Canaan from its feet— the "school age" is past— the chalkboard
is put away — the yardstick (or pointer) has been replaced by the very
things to which it pointed. May the true Israel of God imitate their
"father of faith," even Abraham, and look for a "better country, that is
an heavenly"— and to an "inheritance incorruptible, and undefiled, and
that fadeth not away, reserved *in heaven* for you" (1 Peter 1:4).

This chapter, "The Land of Canaan Vs. A Better Country," has been
written with a good deal of reluctance. That one should have to defend

the glorious inheritance in Christ is, within itself, somewhat degrading. It is an insult to the writers of the New Testament. The New Testament knows nothing of the "Land of Canaan" as an inheritance for either Jew or Gentile. The saints are always admonished to anticipate a "better country" or a "heavenly inheritance." And the New Testament should always take priority over the Old in Biblical interpretation.

Chapter 8

The Kingdom of God Here and Now
vs.
The Kingdom of God Postponed

The Scofield Reference Bible has been a harbinger of the "postponement theory" on the Kingdom of God for the futurists. Mr. Scofield does not use the word "postponement" in his notes but it is implied. He believes that the "Davidic Kingdom" should have been established at Christ's first coming but the Jews' rejection of the "King" and "Kingdom" resulted in the cross and consequently the beginning of the church age.[1]

The "postponement theory" on the Kingdom of God is one of the cornerstones of premillennialism. Although Mr. Scofield does not use the word "postponement" in his notes, his disciples use it very freely. Dr. M. R. DeHaan, a dispensationalist, and a protégé of Mr. Scofield, believes that Jesus offered the "kingdom" to Israel, but the "kingdom" along with the "King," was rejected. According to Dr. DeHaan's views, the angelic message of "peace" that was announced to the shepherds at Christ's birth (Luke 2:14) was postponed until Christ returns the second time.[2]

Dr. DeHaan's thoughts on the "peace" that was announced at Christ's birth are just the opposite of what the Scriptures teach. Are we to ignore the words of Jesus when He said: "My *peace* I leave with you, *My peace I give unto you;* not as the world giveth, give I unto you" (John 14:27a). Must we disregard Paul's words when he writes: "And the *peace of God,* which *passeth understanding,* shall keep your hearts and minds through Christ Jesus" (Philippians 4:7)? Neither the "Kingdom of God" nor the "peace of God" were postponed because the Jews rejected Jesus. The relationship between the "Kingdom of God" and the "peace of God" is clearly established in Paul's letter to the Romans:

> For the Kingdom of God is not meat and drink; but righteousness, and peace, and joy in the Holy Ghost (Romans 14:17)

---

1. *The Scofield Reference Bible,* 998.
2. M. R. DeHaan, *The Second Coming of Jesus,* 168.

Dr. DeHaan is not a soloist in the premillennial pageantry. Two of the most prominent men in the premillennial camp teach the "postpone-ment" theory relative to the Kingdom of God. J. Dwight Pentecost, a very prolific writer in the dispensational school, says concerning the establishment of an earthly kingdom at Christ's first coming: "This kingdom was proclaimed as being 'at hand' at Christ's first advent (Matthew 3:2; 4:17; 10:5-7); but was rejected by Israel and therefore *postponed* (Matthew 23:37-39). It will *again be announced to Israel* and *set up* at the second advent of Christ (Isaiah 24:23; Revelation 19:11-16; 20:1-6."[3] (Emphasis mine.)

John F. Walvoord, who is also widely acclaimed in the dispensa-tional school, strongly supports the same theory. While cunningly interfusing Jesus' statement in Acts 1:8 with his millennial views, Dr. Walvoord *forces* Jesus to say that before an earthly kingdom could be established for the Jews "there had to be a fulfillment of God's purpose in the church. The consummation of the prophecies regarding the (millennial) kingdom therefore was postponed, but not cancelled."[4] (Parenthesis and emphasis mine.)

Any means of biblical interpretation seems to justify the end for the premillennialists. This fact is readily discerned in their attempt to make a distinction in the terms "Kingdom of God" and the "Kingdom of Heaven." Mr. Scofield is probably the architect of this endeavor (see Scofield's notes, p. 1003). Matthew's Gospel, with a few exceptions, uses the term "Kingdom of Heaven," while the other Gospels (Mark, Luke, and John) employ the term "Kingdom of God." The strained relationship that the futurists have created in the two concepts is just another epitaph etched in the tombstone of premillennialism. Mr. Scofield, himself, asserts that "the two have almost all things in common."[5] Mr. Scofield would have been correct had he omitted the word "almost" in his statement. The "Kingdom of Heaven" and the "Kingdom of God" have *everything* in common. Even a novice should be able to see the fallacy of this trumped-up distinction between the "Kingdom of Heaven" and the "Kingdom of God."

If the English language has any intelligibility, then one should be able to see that the terms "Kingdom of God" and "Kingdom of Heaven"

3. Pentecost, 142.
4. Walvoord, 91.
5. Scofield, 1003.

are used interchangeably in the New Testament. Please compare the contrapositioned passages:

Mark 1:14-15	Matthew 4:17
Mark 4:30-31a	Matthew 13:31
Luke 6:20	Matthew 5:3
Luke 7:28	Matthew 11:11
Luke 9:2	Matthew 10-7-8a
Luke 16:16	Matthew 11:12
Luke 18:24b-25	Matthew 19:23-24
Mark 10:14a	Matthew 19:14

The above passages show conclusively that the millenarians and the Scriptures are not singing from the same sheet music relative to the "Kingdom of God" and the "Kingdom of Heaven." This subtle distinction in the two concepts should immediately raise the eyebrows of those who are unfamiliar with premillennial tactics.

Dr. Fred W. Walvoord, in his book *Israel in Prophecy*, tries to justify the "postponement" theory and the "literal" fulfillment of the Kingdom of God by imposing the "natural" or "normal" mind of the Hebrew people upon the Word of God. Dr. Walvoord says that it was perfectly "normal" and "natural" for the Old Testament people to expect a "literal" kingdom to be established when Christ made His first appearance. When the people of that era were confronted with the covenant made with David in 2 Samuel 7, 1 Chronicles 17, and related passages, it would be right and proper (according to Dr. Walvoord) to expect a literal fulfillment of these texts. While Jesus rebuked the religious people of His day for failing to perceive His mission in the world, Dr. Walvoord condones their expectation of a "literal" kingdom. He writes: "…the people of Israel were *acting in good faith* when they expected God to revive their kingdom, deliver them from their enemies, and restore them to their ancient land. Such as was their expectation when Christ came the first time, and such can be their expectation at His second coming."[6] (Emphasis mine.)

Dr. Walvoord says that the people of Israel "acted in *good faith*" when they expected a "literal" kingdom to appear at Christ's first coming. If the Jews acted in "good faith" at Christ's first appearance, they are *still* "acting in good faith." But the "good faith" that is described

---

6. Walvoord, 88.

in the above quote is actually "bad faith." The Jews' "expectation" of a "literal" kingdom at Christ's first appearance is no guarantee of a literal kingdom at His second appearance. Dr. Walvoord gives the Jews one chance in two of being right. If the Jews were wrong one time, they can be wrong a second time. The record confirms that they have been wrong many times over. After almost two thousand years, the majority of them are still wrong. Their utopian "expectations" have failed them in every age and generation.

"Acting in good faith" and "true faith" can be, and oftentimes are, two different things. Religious people have been "acting in good faith" for centuries but this does not mean they hold to and practice sound doctrine. The Protestant Reformation was a reaction to a very large and old religious body that was "acting in good faith." If Martin Luther was correct on his doctrine of "justification by faith alone," then the "good faith" of the Roman Catholic Church was in error. This is just one among many illustrations of religious groups "acting in good faith," while still in conflict with sound doctrine.

Dr. Walvoord's "normal" and "natural" approach to the Scriptures has never been God's method of understanding His Word. He has taken a Spirit-inspired Book and imposed a "normal" or "natural" understanding upon it. The Apostle Paul writes for the Old Testament dispensation as well as the New when he says: "But the *natural man receiveth not the things of the spirit of God:* for they are *foolishness* unto him: *neither can he know them,* because they are *spiritually discerned*" (1 Corinthians 2:14). Paul has presented us with two areas of understanding — that which is perceived by the "spiritual mind" and that which is understood by the "natural mind." Only the spiritual-enlightened mind is capable of understanding the "things of God." The need of spiritual insight into the "things of God" is stressed throughout the New Testament.

Dr. Walvoord also applies his "normal" and "natural" understanding of the Scriptures to Mary, the mother of Jesus. He simulates a knowledge of prophecy for Mary that cannot be found in the text. Dr. Walvoord creates a hypothetical case that would make Mary a "literalist" and a key figure in the premillennial drama. He says concerning the announcement of the angel to Mary:

> According to Luke 1:30-33 the angel said:"Fear not, Mary: for thou hast found favor with God. And behold, thou shalt conceive in thy womb, and bring forth a son, and shalt call his name *Jesus.* He shall be great, and shall be called the Son of the Most High: and the Lord

shall give unto Him the throne of His father David: and He shall reign
over the house of Jacob for ever; and of His kingdom there shall be
no end."In the light of the prominence given to the same subject in the
Old Testament, the question may be fairly raised: What would such
a prophecy mean to Mary? *For any Jewish maiden who accepted and
entertained the hope of a coming Messiah, would hardly question the
prophecy given by the angel would be interpreted literally,* that is, she
would understand by the throne of David an earthly throne such as
David enjoyed in his lifetime.[7] (Emphasis mine).

Just a casual consideration of Luke 1:30-33 will reveal that Mary
did not raise a single question relative to a *literal fulfillment* of the
angel's words. Mary's only concern at this point was how she could bear
a child without a husband. Dr. Walvoord is actually imposing "millennial doctrine" upon Mary. We have no way of knowing *how much* Mary
knew about Old Testament prophecy. To say that she would have
understood it "literally" is to inject ideas into her mind that cannot be
proven. These are Dr. Walvoord's personal ideas about Mary's knowledge of prophecy and nothing more. If premillennial views are so
widespread in the New Testament, one should not have to resort to such
backdoor tactics as this to prove his theological position.

Dr. Walvoord expands Mary's mind somewhat more when he
writes:

Further, it is declared that Mary's Son would reign over the house
of Jacob forever. Mary certainly would not understand by the phrase
"the house of Jacob" a reference to saints in general regardless of
racial background. To her it would mean only one thing and that is the
descendants of Jacob, namely, the twelve tribes of Israel. Inasmuch
as this would be the *normal* and *natural understanding* on the part of
Mary in such a prophecy, it is *almost unthinkable that God would
have used this terminology* if as a matter of fact the hope of Israel was
a mistake and the prophecies given in the Old Testament were not
intended to be understood literally.[8] (Emphasis mine.)

Again, Dr. Walvoord is imposing the premillennial mind upon the
mother of Jesus. He has no idea how the phrase "the house of Jacob"
came across to Mary. Dr. Walvoord is telling us how the millenarians
would "understand" the angel's message and not how Mary actually

7. Walvoord, 89.
8. Walvoord, 89-90.

perceived it. Such a method of interpretation would not begin to pass the litmus test of sound biblical exegesis.

Dr. Walvoord brings a bold charge against God for using "terminology" that would be misleading to Mary if a "literal" kingdom was not intended. The same principle would apply to others who lived prior to Christ's first appearance. It goes without saying that Christ did *not* establish a "literal" kingdom at His first coming. Therefore, God can be blamed for sending a wrong signal to thousands of people.

If Dr. Walvoord had read a few verses beyond the angel's message to Mary, he would know how she came to perceive her Son's mission in the world. It was only a matter of days until Mary went to visit Elizabeth, the mother of John the Baptist (verse 39). While at Elizabeth's house she was given more light into the role of her Son and that of herself in the years that would follow. In what is commonly called the "Hymn of Mary," Mary perceives God, not as a king reigning over "the house of Jacob" per se, but as a "merciful Saviour" (verse 47). Mary came to understand that God, through her Son, would establish a covenant of "mercy" and not a "literal" kingdom.

Mary portrays God as a "mighty" power and the essence of His power is to be seen in an "act of mercy" upon them that fear him from generation to generation (verse 50). The strength of God's arm will be manifest as He scatters the proud and puts down the mighty from their seats. The reverse of such power can be seen as He exalts the lowly. His mighty arm is also displayed when He fills the hungry with good things and the rich are sent away empty handed (Luke 1:49-53). All of this sounds like a preview of the Sermon on the Mount. But the crowning act of God's "mercy" is to be revealed in the death and resurrection of His Son. Mary came to understand that God's "mercy" in Christ was the fulfillment of His promise to Abraham and his seed (verse 55). The promise made to Abraham was to be in the form of a covenant (oath) that dealt with *sin* and *death,* and not a "literal" kingdom.

Mary may have received additional information regarding her Son from Zacharias, the father of John the Baptist. Zacharias, under the inspiration of the Holy Ghost, declares that the "oath" and "covenant" made with Abraham was first and foremost a "covenant of *mercy*" (verse 72). The concluding remarks of Zacharias' revelation were sufficient to show that Christ's mission in this world was to "redeem" His people from *sin* and *death* rather than to establish an earthly kingdom. According to Zacharias, God was in the process of fulfilling that which

He promised through His holy prophets since the world began (verse 70). John the Baptist (Zacharias' son) would play an important role in the fulfillment of this tremendous event (Luke 1:76-79).

Zacharias' prophecy could serve as a prelude to Paul's letter to the Romans. The first eight chapters of the Romans epistle (half the book) are written to establish the doctrine of *sin* and its consequence which is *death*. The term "covenant" is used twice in the book of Romans. The only comment that Paul gives in conjunction with the term "covenant" is coupled with the problem of *sin* and God's *mercy* in Christ to deal with it. The Romans letter can be summarized in a word: "For this is my *covenant* with them, when I shall *take away their sins* ... For God hath concluded them all (Jews) in unbelief (or sinners) that He might have *mercy upon all*" (Romans 11:27-32).

It has already been shown that the *summum bonum* of God's covenant with Abraham was the *mercy* that was *to be revealed* and *was revealed* in the death and resurrection of Christ. It is far more likely that Mary would understand her Son's role as that of a Saviour rather than One who would establish a "literal" kingdom. All the New Testament writers are completely silent on the Land of Palestine as a vital part of the Abrahamic covenant.

The "normal" and "natural" understanding of the Scriptures that Dr. Walvoord delights in using can be very dangerous. A good many of the Old Testament prophecies have a secondary meaning and should be interpreted and understood in the light of the New Testament revelation. We need to be reminded of the words of Isaiah when he wrote: "For my thoughts are not your thoughts, neither are your ways my ways, saith the Lord. For as the heavens are higher than the earth, so are my ways higher than your ways, and my thoughts than your thoughts" (Isaiah 55:8-9). The "natural" or carnal mind is at a complete loss to understand the true facts concerning the Kingdom of God.

The Greek word for "kingdom" *(basileia)* is derived from another Greek word, *basileus*, which means a foundation of power, a sovereign, a king. According to *Strong's Greek Lexicon*, neither term has to do with a specific period of time or a geographical location. The Kingdom of God pertains to God's sovereign rule, authority, and power, regardless of *time* and *place*. The Kingdom of God is represented as an invisible force or power inherent in the Trinity, capable of magnifying either the Father, or the Son, or the Holy Spirit, or all three. It is this intrinsic energy or power exerted upon man, demons, and the physical universe that constitutes the sovereignty of the Godhead and thereby makes known the absolute power, authority, and rule of God that transcends time, space, and matter.

The above statement on the Kingdom of God finds support throughout the New Testament. Immediately after Jesus' baptism and temptation in the wilderness, He began His public ministry by "preaching the Gospel of the *Kingdom of God*, and saying, The time is fulfilled, and the *Kingdom of God is at hand:* repent ye, and *believe the Gospel*" (Mark 1:14b-15). It should be noted that Matthew's Gospel uses the term "Kingdom of Heaven" in expressing the same truth (Matthew 4:17). Jesus continued to emphasize the Kingdom of God during His public ministry and to commission His disciples with the same message: "And this *Gospel of the Kingdom* shall be preached in all the world for a witness unto all nations; and then shall the end come" (Matthew 24:14).

Throughout the New Testament, the Kingdom of God is associated with the preaching of the Gospel. It goes without saying that the Gospel was not "postponed" to some distant millennial age. When Jesus spoke of the "Kingdom of God being at hand," He meant the power, authority, and rule that was in Himself and would soon be manifest in His body — the church.

It has already been shown that the Hebrew word "Isra EL" means "ruled by God" and this rule is through His *Word* and *Spirit*. God does not change His nature or plan of redemption from one era to the next — neither does He change His mode of rule. The *Word* and *Spirit* are invisible forces that fulfill God's purpose in both the Old and New Testaments.

By the Word and Spirit of God, the "mysteries" of the Kingdom of God are unveiled and understood (Matthew 13:11; Mark 4:11; Luke 8:10). Jesus' comments on the "mysteries" of the Kingdom are followed immediately by the parable of the "sower and seed." This introductory parable is the "parable of parables." The things of God cannot be known and understood apart from the Word and Spirit of God and this includes the Kingdom of God (John 8:43; 1 Corinthians 2:14).

It is no coincidence that the parable of the "sower and seed" (as found in Matthew thirteenth) was given *in advance* of all the other parables in this chapter. *The remaining parables are a consequence of this one parable.* The beginning, importance, growth, and ultimate end of the Kingdom of God (on earth) are couched in language that is easily understood. While some of the parables teach only one facet of the Kingdom, others teach several.

In the parable of the "wheat and tares," the "wheat" represents those individuals of the Gospel age who have received the "good seed" or the Word of God. The "tares" are false professors sown among the "wheat" by the enemy — or Satan. The "wheat" and "tares" are allowed to grow together until the end of the harvest. When the harvest is reaped there will be a separation of the wheat and tares according to their own design.

The parable of the "mustard seed" is just another way of describing the "corn of wheat" that would fall into the ground and its ensuing consequences (John 12:24). The full potential of the tree that accommodated the birds of the air was in the tiny mustard seed. The full potential of the Kingdom of God was in Christ and men find a shelter and divine rest in Him.

The remainder of the parables in Matthew 13 will adapt to the interpretation given on the Kingdom of God through the Word and Spirit of God. It is by the same Word and Spirit that Christ is revealed and glorified. Jesus is the "treasure hid in a field" (verse 44) and the "pearl of great price" (verses 45-46) and men should be willing to part with any and all things in order to gain this priceless possession (Matthew 16:25). Every parable in Matthew 13 can be summed up in the brief phrase: "the Word of the Kingdom" (verse 19).

Jesus performed all of His miracles by the Word and Spirit of God and these mighty works were proof of the Kingdom's presence. The people of Jesus' day readily recognized the power of the spoken Word. On Jesus' first visit to Capernaum, a city of Galilee, He entered into the synagogue and taught the people. Luke records the response of the people with these word:

> And they were astonished at His doctrine: for His *Word was with power* (Luke 4:32).

On the same occasion there was a man in the synagogue who had a "spirit of an unclean devil" who openly objected to Jesus' presence among them. Jesus rebuked the man for disturbing the assembly and commanded the unclean spirit to come out of him. Again, the people were awestricken at the supernatural power that was demonstrated before their very eyes:

> And they were all amazed and spake among themselves, saying What a *word* is this! for with *authority* and *power* He commandeth the

unclean spirits and they come out (Luke 4:36).

Not only were evil spirits cast out by Christ's *Word* — individuals were healed by the same means. After the healing of Peter's mother-in-law, we are informed that multitudes were brought to Jesus to be healed:

> When the even was come, they brought unto Him many that were possessed with devils: and He *cast out the evil spirits* with *His Word,* and *healed all that were sick* (Matthew 8:16).

Let us say parenthetically that the Psalmist declared the same truth several hundred years before Christ came in the flesh. When an earnest cry was heard from a distressed or troubled Israelite, God "sent His *Word* and *healed them*" (Psalm 107:20).

There are several illustrations on the power of the spoken Word in the Gospels. The Roman centurion's request for Jesus to heal his sick servant is a classic one. When Jesus agreed to go to the centurion's house to heal his servant, the centurion declined the visit because of his unworthiness. However, he responded with these very familiar words: "Speak the *Word* only, and my servant shall be healed" (Matthew 8:8). The Roman centurion understood the power of the spoken Word. He, himself, was accustomed to giving commands. He did not personally perform the commands he gave; he simply issued them — he spoke the word. This Roman centurion, though perhaps unawares, was expressing an important principle in the Kingdom of God as well as an earthly kingdom.

When the above principle is applied to an earthly kingdom and the Kingdom of God, the results are astounding. A secular king does not accomplish the objectives of his kingdom by and of himself — they are wrought by his decrees — by his *word*. His commands (word) are performed by subordinates, by governors, by captains, by soldiers, by appointed citizens, etc. It is not necessary for him to lift a finger. The king's *words* are expressions of his mind and will. The king's *words* are equivalent to his "power" and "authority." Ideally, the activities of a secular kingdom should be within the "bounds" of the king's *words* (laws, decrees, commands, etc.). A secular king is not compelled to reside *in* a particular country or city over which he has jurisdiction for his rule to be effectual — he can live miles away. All of this being true, a king's *words* are synonymous with his "reign" or "rule." In short, the king's *words* reflect the essence and nature of his kingdom. A closer look at the true nature and essence of an earthly kingdom will enhance our understanding of the Kingdom of God.

The terra firma of an earthly kingdom is not its primary component — nor is it brick, concrete, steel, marble, or other materials out of which cities and villages are built. A secular kingdom is first and foremost people — everything else is secondary. Material resources and location of an earthly kingdom play an important role in its strength or weakness, but the conduct of the people take priority over everything else. Wealthy nations (kingdoms) have fallen as well as impoverished nations. Ancient Babylon and Rome are two cases in point. The constituents of an earthly kingdom can submit to the "powers that be" within that kingdom (in biblical days it was ultimately the king) or they can create anarchy. Generally speaking, the *rule* of the king, whether good or bad, and the conduct of the people decide the fate of a secular kingdom. At this point our analogy between a secular kingdom and the Kingdom of God breaks down. God's rule is always a righteous one — it can never be otherwise (Hebrews 1:8-9).

God's Kingdom, like that of an earthly kingdom, is composed of people. To be in the Kingdom of God is to be under God's *rule* (Word, commands, precepts, etc.). God's Words are expressions of His mind and will. God's Words are equivalent to His "power" and "authority." The citizens of God's Kingdom are expected to live within the "bounds" of His Word (decrees, rules, commands). God's Words reveal the essence and nature of His Kingdom which is a holy, righteous Kingdom (Romans 14:17; 1 Peter 2:9). It is very apparent that *God's Word, God's rule,* and *God's Kingdom* are correlative terms. These three concepts are not confined to a geographical location; nor are they limited to a timetable that men may impose upon them. When the power and authority of God were displayed by the spoken Word of our Lord, He could rightly say, "The Kingdom of God is at hand." And the Kingdom of God is still "at hand" by the power of His Word (Gospel) — it was not postponed.

The elements of nature were subject to Christ's Word. The horrendous experience of the disciples in a stormy sea confirms this fact. Jesus was with His disciples on this occasion but He had fallen asleep. The terrified disciples immediately woke Jesus up and He "rebuked the wind and the raging of the water; and they ceased and there was a calm" (Luke 8:24b). The disciples were overwhelmed at such a demonstration of power and began to say one to another, "What manner of man is this! for

He *commandeth* even the *winds* and *water,* and they *obey* Him" (Luke 8:25).

The association of the Word of God and the Spirit of God has been dealt with throughout this work. The same pattern is to be found in conjunction with the "Kingdom of God." The Spirit of God always operates concurrently with the Word of God. When the Pharisees accused Jesus of casting out devils by the power of Beelzebub, the prince of devils, He replied:

> But if I cast out devils by the *Spirit of God,* then the *Kingdom of God* is come unto you (Matthew 12:28).

Jesus' discourse with Nicodemus in the third chapter of John's Gospel confirms the spiritual aspects of the Kingdom of God. Verse three says: "unless one is born anew, he cannot see the Kingdom of God," and verse five reads, "unless one is born of water and the *Spirit,* he cannot enter the Kingdom of God." The spiritual birth qualifies one to *see* the Kingdom of God, and by the same means he *enters into* and actively participates in the Kingdom of God which has been from eternity.

We know that the Kingdom of God was not postponed, as the premillennialists teach, because Jesus spent forty days, after His resurrection, instructing His disciples in "things pertaining to the *Kingdom of God*" (Acts 1:3b). Jesus' emphasis upon the subject revived the age-old question among the disciples as to when the kingdom would be restored to Israel. Jesus answered their question in connection with the promise of the Holy Spirit. Again, Jesus associates the Holy Spirit with the Kingdom of God:

> It is not for you to know the times or the seasons, which the Father hath put in His *own power.*
> But ye shall *receive power,* after that the *Holy Ghost* is come upon you, etc. (Acts 1:7-8a).

Jesus' statement was meant to settle forever the kingdom controversy. As promised, the Holy Spirit would guide the disciples into all truth; He would glorify Jesus; and He would show them *things to come* (John 16:12-15). The disciples' curiosity on the "restoration of the kingdom of Israel" was to be satisfied with the coming of the Holy Ghost on the day of Pentecost. Why? Because the Holy Spirit would show them a *world* that was far superior to an earthly kingdom (1 Corinthians

2:9-10; Hebrews 6:4-5). According to the remainder of the New Testament, the disciples never raised the question again; nor did the Holy Spirit inspire them to write about a "restored kingdom to Israel."

Jesus' views on the Kingdom of God were always antithetical to the expectations of the Jewish people in the New Testament era. His teachings ran counter to all of the current beliefs regarding a Messiah for Israel. The establishment of a political, earthly kingdom that would replace the ruthless Roman rule was a concern of every devout Jew. The time and appearance of such a kingdom became a stock question for every new seer or religious zealot to deal with when they came on the scene. Jesus was no exception. When the Pharisees confronted Jesus with the appearance of the Kingdom of God, He answered:

> The Kingdom of God *cometh not with observation:* Neither shall they say, Lo here! lo there! for behold, the *Kingdom of God is within you* (Luke 17:20b-21).

The Kingdom of God "within you" would be the power, authority, and rule of God by the Word and Spirit.

Some individuals would object to the above interpretation by saying that Jesus was addressing the Pharisees who could not have had the Kingdom of God "within" them. I would remind my objector that Jesus made a statement to Satan that could not possibly apply to him. Jesus said to the Devil: "It is written, thou shalt worship the Lord thy God, and Him only shalt thou serve" (Matthew 4:10). For whose benefit did Jesus make this statement? Did Jesus really expect Satan to fall down and worship God and serve Him? Of course not! Jesus was actually speaking for *Himself* and *all mankind* who would face similar temptations. Likewise, Jesus was not saying that the Kingdom of God was literally "within" the Pharisees. This statement was not made exclusively for them. Jesus was setting forth a divine truth that would be applicable to all men if they are to enter the Kingdom of God. The Kingdom of God would be experienced "within" and not in the form of a materialistic kingdom as advocated by the futurists.

One of the most controversial passages on the Kingdom of God in the Scripture is to be found in the ninth chapter of Mark's Gospel. While discussing the cost of discipleship, Jesus said to His audience:

> Verily I say unto you, That there be some of them that stand here, which shall not taste of death, till they *see the Kingdom of God come*

244 ISRAEL VS. ISRAEL

with power (Mark 9:1).

The controversy on the above passage disappears if we follow the basic supposition of this chapter on the Kingdom of God. When Jesus spoke of "some who would be living when the Kingdom of God came with power," He was speaking of Pentecost and the coming of the Holy Spirit.

All of the Synoptic Gospels record Jesus' statement as found in Mark 9:1, but each one gives a different version. The language that is used in the other two Gospels is somewhat different from Mark's account but it poses no serious problem. Luke quotes Jesus as saying:

> … there be some standing here, which shall not taste death, till they *see the Kingdom of God* (Luke 9:27).

Again, the Holy Spirit is the solution to our problem. The Holy Spirit is the *revealer* of the Kingdom of God. Jesus' words to Nicodemus is proof of this fact: "Except a man be born again (of the Spirit), he cannot *see the Kingdom of God*" (John 3:3). The Greek word for "see" *(eido)* is used by both Luke and John. According to James Strong, *eido* can be used in a very broad sense. It can mean *to know, be aware, have knowledge, perceive, be sure, understand,* etc. It is very obvious that the Greek word *eido* does not always mean to "see literally" or to perceive with the senses.

The passage in Matthew's Gospel can be resolved in a similar manner. Matthew's version reads as follows:

> There be some standing here, which shall not taste of death, till they *see the Son of man coming in His Kingdom* (16:28).

Jesus did *not* absent Himself from the disciples by His Ascension to the Father. He promised to be *with them* in the person and ministry of the Holy Spirit. Jesus said to His disciples: "I will not leave you comfortless: *I will come to you.* Yet a little while and the world seeth me no more; but *ye see me:* Because I live, ye shall live also" (John 14:18-19). The same Greek word for "see" *(eido)* that is used by Mark, Luke, and John is used by Matthew.

The three phrases, *"See* the Kingdom of God come with power," *"See* the Kingdom of God," and *"See* the Son of man coming in His Kingdom," are three different versions of the same thing. But there is no contradiction when the Holy Spirit's role is recognized for what it is worth. If the old adage "familiarity breeds contempt" is true, then "unfamiliarity" breeds fear and denseness. Man's "unfamiliarity" with the Spirit's knowledge, revelations, and power forces him to rely upon the carnal mind and consequently "literalism." "Literalism" for the carnal mind is one thing, but "literalism" in the spiritual realm is another thing (Romans 8:5-9; 1 Corinthians 2:9-16; 2 Timothy 3:16; 2 Peter 1:20-21; 3:16).

Jesus' refusal to "eat or drink until the Kingdom of God shall come" (Luke 22:15-18) should be understood in a similar manner. This statement was made in connection with the final Passover Feast that Jesus shared with His disciples. The bread and wine ended Jesus' intake of food until after His death and resurrection. It is recorded that Jesus ate with His disciples after His passion (John 21:4-14). Therefore, Luke 22:18 cannot be speaking of a distant future kingdom. It is a reference to the New Testament age and the coming of the Holy Spirit that would rule or reign in the hearts of men (Romans 14:17).

It is also worthy of note that Jesus speaks of "receiving" the Kingdom of God rather than "setting up" or "establishing" the Kingdom of God. When some small children were brought to Jesus to be touched by His loving hands, the disciples rebuked those who brought them. But Jesus was displeased at His disciples' behavior. Our Lord used this occasion to teach an important truth regarding the Kingdom of God. Mark's Gospel records Him as saying: "Whosoever shall not *receive* the Kingdom of God as a little child, he shall not enter therein" (10:15). Matthew records the same incident but uses the term "Kingdom of Heaven." "Receiving" the Kingdom of God is synonymous with "receiving" the Word and Spirit of God. The need of "receiving" the Word and Spirit of God is expressed throughout the New Testament (John 20:22, Acts 1:8, 2:38, 2:41, 8:15, 17, 19, 10:47;,19:2, Galatians 3:2, 14; 1 Thessalonians 1:6, 2:13, 1 John 2:27). Once more the major premise of this chapter is set forth with unmistakable clarity.

Evidently Paul did not believe in the "postponement theory" relative to the Kingdom of God. Someone has sarcastically but aptly said that Paul should have been informed that the Kingdom of God was postponed. On his last missionary journey he encountered twelve men in the city of Ephesus who knew only the "baptism of John the Baptist." After explaining to them the need of the Holy Ghost for the Christian experience, Paul laid hands on them and they received the gift of the Holy Spirit. The Apostle remained at Ephesus for three months — visiting the synagogue — "disputing and persuading the things *con-*

cerning the Kingdom of God" (Acts 19:8).

Some weeks later, as he was returning to Jerusalem, Paul had further contact with the church at Ephesus. He called the elders of the church aside and admonished them to adhere to the things he had taught. He had taught them publicly and from house to house — both Jews and Gentiles. Repentance toward God and faith toward Jesus Christ are singled out as crucial aspects of his message. Paul kept back nothing that was profitable unto them. His entire ministry, while in the city of Ephesus, is summed up in a single phrase — "among whom I have gone *preaching the Kingdom of God"* (Acts 20:25).

Paul did not cease to preach the Kingdom of God. At the close of the book of Acts we find him under Roman guards in his own hired house in the city of Rome. While he was in this semi-confinement, many outsiders were permitted to visit him:

> And Paul dwelt two whole years in his own hired house, and received all that came unto him.
>
> Preaching the *Kingdom of God,* and *teaching* those things which concern the Lord Jesus Christ, with all confidence, no man forbidding him (Acts 28:31).

Emphases upon the Kingdom of God are not lacking in Paul's epistles. He, too, associates the Kingdom of God with the gift of the Holy Spirit. One such passage is found in his letter to the Romans:

> For the *Kingdom of God* is not meat and drink (satisfying the carnal appetite); but righteousness, peace, and joy in the Holy Ghost (Romans 14:17).

Philip Mauro's thoughts on the above verse are superb. Mr. Mauro shows conclusively that the Kingdom of God has no relationship to the historical kingdom of David; neither can it consist of a carnal kingdom in the future. It would be a serious mistake to deprive the conscientious Bible student of his comments on Romans 14:17:

> The Kingdom is here defined both negatively and positively. We are told first what it is *not,* and then what it *is;* and hence the text is the more enlightening for our present purpose. For a contrast is here presented between the Kingdom of God and the historical Kingdom of David, which the rabbinist supposed (as the dispensationalists do now) were one and the same. Concerning the kingdom of David it is recorded that they who came to make him king "were with David three days, *eating and drinking"*; and that those who lived in the

territory of the other Tribes, even unto Issachar, and Zebulon and Naphthali, brought bread on asses, and on camels, and on mules, and on oxen; also meat, meal, cakes of figs, and bunches of raisins, and wine, and oil, and oxen and sheep abundantly; for there was *joy in Israel"* (1 Chronicles 12:39-40). Also it is written that David in those days "dealt to every one of Israel, both man and woman, to every one a loaf of bread, and a good piece of flesh, and a flagon of wine." (Id. 16:3).

But the Kingdom of God is *not like that*. Everyone in that Kingdom has (1) the *righteousness* of God, has (2) *peace* with God, and has (3) *joy in the Holy Ghost*. And it is worthy of note that Paul is here summarizing the blessings of the Gospel, as he had already stated them in chapter 5. For there is declared the fundamental doctrine that (1) being justified (made *righteous*) by faith, we have (2) *peace* with God through our Lord Jesus Christ" ... and not only so, but (3) "We also *joy* in God" (Romans 5:1, 11). The blessings of the Kingdom of God are not the fruits of the land of Canaan, but the fruits of the Holy Spirit; and the "joy" that was in Israel because of the good things to eat and drink, is replaced by "joy in the Holy Ghost." This is "the Gospel of the Kingdom," as preached and taught by Paul.[9] (Emphasis mine.)

The term "Kingdom of God" is also used by Paul in his letter to the Corinthians. The Apostle had some serious doubts about the spiritual status of certain members within this church. Their speech, behavior, and attitudes gave little, if any, evidence that they were citizens of the heavenly kingdom. Some of the Corinthians were given to worldly wisdom — they were, in the words of the King James Version, "puffed up." This fact was reflected in their speech. Paul informed them that heirs of the Heavenly Kingdom are known, not by their worldly verbiage, but by the "power" of a changed life. And this "power" is associated with the Kingdom of God. Paul assures these fledgling Christians that he will deal with the problem on his second visit (1 Corinthians 4:19-20).

If the Kingdom of God was revealed through the mighty power of the Word and Spirit of God in the days of Jesus' flesh and in the ministry of the Apostles, then the Kingdom of God was not postponed. Men continue to enter the Kingdom of God through the Word and Spirit of

---

9. Philip Mauro, *The Gospel of the Kingdom*, Reiner Publications, Swengel, Pennyslvania, 1987, 95-96.

God. This truth alone should strike a death blow to the "postponement" theory.

Those who are in Christ do not wait for a coming kingdom — they are already in the Kingdom of God. It has been truly stated that "heaven comes to men before men are brought to heaven." The writer of the book of Hebrews assures us that the "powers of the world to come" are within those who believe by the Word and Spirit of God. This truth is written in conjunction with a warning regarding apostasy:

> For it is impossible for those who were once enlightened, and have *tasted of the heavenly gift,* and were made partakers of the *Holy Ghost,*
>   And have tasted the *good Word of God,* and the *powers of the world to come,* etc. (Hebrews 6:4-5).

The same truth is expressed by Paul in his first letter to the Corinthians. When writing upon the wisdom of the cross and the blindness of those who crucified Jesus, he says:

> But as it is written, Eye hath not seen, nor ear heard, neither have entered into the heart of man, *the things which God hath prepared for them that love Him.*
>   But *God hath revealed them unto us by His Spirit:* for the *Spirit* searcheth *all things,* yea, the *deep things of God* (1 Corinthians 2:9-10).

Jesus taught His disciples that the Holy Spirit would "show them things to come" (John 16:13). In the light of many other passages of Scripture we can be confident that He was speaking of the "world to come." We are constrained to agree with A. W. Tozer who writes: "We must avoid the common fault of pushing the *other world* into the future. It is not future but present."[10]

The believer's position in the Kingdom of God *here* and *now* and a knowledge of the "world to come" can be confirmed apart from the Scriptures. The reality of heaven is not to be regarded as "pie in the sky" for those who are in Christ — men of all ages attest this fact. Those who are born of God's Word and Spirit have a miniature heaven in their hearts. Fanny J. Crosby (1820-1915), one of the great hymn writers of the past, assures us of this truth in one of her very familiar songs:

---

10. A. W. Tozer, *The Pursuit of God,* Christian Publications, Inc., Harrisburg, Pennyslva-
    nia, 58.

Blessed Assurance, Jesus is mine,
Oh, what a *foretaste of glory divine!*
Heir of salvation, purchase of God,
Born of His Spirit, wash'd in His blood.[11] (Emphasis mine.)

According to Isaac Watts (1674-1748), another great hymnologist, the savoriness of heaven is enjoyed in this *present life* as well as in the ages to come:

The hill of Zion yields a thousand sacred sweets, *before we reach the heavenly fields, before we reach the heavenly fields,*
Or *walk the golden streets,* or *walk the golden streets.*[12] (Emphasis mine.)

It is very obvious that many hymns of the church are no less than a book of theology set to music. The bliss of heaven and the rule of God in the human heart have been articulated in many ways since New Testament days. Charles H. Spurgeon, though not a hymn writer per se, was inspired to write on the rule of the Holy Spirit in very salient language:

He dwells within our soul, an ever welcome guest;
He *reigns* with *absolute control, as monarch in the breast.*[13]
(Emphasis mine.)

Every New Testament believer should feel a sense of shame at second thoughts on a carnal kingdom as taught by the premillennialists. An earthly Zion and an earthly Jerusalem should be beneath our notice and interest. We have something to occupy our hearts and minds that is far superior to anything in this world. We have already come to Mt. Zion, the city of the living God, the heavenly Jerusalem. There is no delay or waiting period for the believer's position in the Kingdom of God:

But ye are come unto *Mount Sion,* and unto the *city of the living God,* the *heavenly Jerusalem,* and to an innumerable company of angels,
To the general assembly and church of the firstborn, which are

11. From the hymn: *Blessed Assurance*
12. From the hymn: *We're Marching to Zion*
13. From the hymn: *The Holy Ghost is Here*

written in heaven, and to God, the Judge of all, and to the spirits of just men made perfect (Hebrews 12:22-23).

It is in this same context that Paul writes: "... our commonwealth is in *heaven,* and from it we wait a Savior, the Lord Jesus Christ" (Philippians 3:20). The believer in Christ has already been "delivered from the power of darkness, and *translated into the Kingdom of His dear Son"* (Colossians 1:13). Whether or not all men, or even the majority of men, can affirm the truths under consideration is not the ultimate test in things pertaining to God. Truth is determined, not by human experience, but by the Word of God. Men must not sit in judgment upon the Word — the Word sits in judgment upon men.

C. I. Scofield and those who write and speak on the possibility of an earthly kingdom at Christ's first appearance are overlooking the Jews' greatest enemy. The first and foremost enemy of the Jewish people was not the Roman Empire, but *sin* and *death* — the source of all their problems — past and present. Many centuries before the coming of Christ in the flesh, Isaiah wrote: "But your *iniquities* have separated between you and your God, and your *sins* have made him hide his face from you, that he will not hear" (Isaiah 59:2). To theorize on a political kingdom that would solve the Jews' problems without an answer to *sin* and *death* would be like cursing the dark rather than turning on the light.

Paul portrays sin as a tyrant that *reigns* over unregenerate men — men are held in sin's bondage — they are "dead in trespasses and in sins" (Ephesians 2:1). But Christ has broken the power of sin and conquered death by His own death and resurrection. Where sin once *reigned* unto death, Jesus makes it possible for "grace to *reign* through righteousness unto *eternal life"* (Romans 5:21). This could not be possible if Jesus had established a political kingdom rather than die on the cross.

Jesus' rule or reign is to be associated with "life" which is antithetical to "sin and death." This fact emerges very clearly in Peter's temple sermon as recorded in the book of Acts. Peter's message is directed to the "men of Israel" who killed the "Prince of life" and chose a murderer (Barabbas) instead (Acts 3:14-15). The title "Prince of *life"* is set in contrast to the "Prince of death and darkness" who is Satan. Jesus reigns over "life" which has its source in God. Eternal, everlasting "life" is one of the predominant themes in the New Testament.

Jesus' kingship and lordship are also given in connection with "immortality" and "light." The Apostle Paul describes Jesus as the "blessed and *only* Potentate, the King of kings, and Lord of lords; who *only* hath *immortality,* dwelling in the *light,* etc. " (1 Timothy 6:15b-16a). "Life" and "light" are primary for any type of existence. Immortal "life" and "light" belong *only* to Jesus and it is in this realm that He rules without contest. Jesus is Lord over a kingdom of life and light — and both are to be known and experienced in another dimension and not in an earthly kingdom.

Christian heirship is associated with life and light. When Peter gives instructions on the husband/wife relationship in his first epistle, he speaks of them as "being *heirs* together of the *grace* of *life"* (1 Peter 3:7). The Apostle Paul describes the Colossian believers as "partakers of the *inheritance* of the *saints* in *light"* (Colossians 1:12). The same truth is expressed again in Paul's letter to Titus: "That being justified by his grace, we should be made *heirs* according to the hope of *eternal life"* (Titus 3:7). There is a kingdom of *light and life* and there is a kingdom of *death and darkness.* The two concepts are discussed in great detail in John's first epistle. According to John, the two kingdoms never mix — light has no fellowship with darkness (1 John 1:6).

Paul's direct commission from the risen Christ summarizes the mission of our Lord and verifies the major premise of this chapter. The Apostle was instructed to preach the Gospel to both Jews and Gentiles (Acts 9:15) in order that he might "open their eyes, and turn them from *darkness* to *light,* and from the *power* of *Satan* unto *God,* that they might receive *forgiveness of sins,* and an *inheritance* among them which are *sanctified* by *faith* that is in me (Christ)" (Acts 26:18). The "inheritance" for both Jews and Gentiles is associated with the "opening of eyes," "light," "turning unto God," "forgiveness of sins," and "sanctification by faith" — all of which is realized by the Word and Spirit of God. The aforementioned words and phrases describe an "inheritance" that only Christ's death and resurrection could accomplish and they are completely foreign to an earthly kingdom.

Jesus' manhood and priesthood that are conjoined in the epistle of the Hebrews explodes the view of an earthly kingdom at Christ's first coming. If Jesus was to be "touched with the feelings of our infirmities," as the book of Hebrews affirms, then His first and foremost role on this earth could not be that of a high and exalted "king." This epistle declares that Jesus took on Him the "seed of Abraham" — and for what purpose? To reign as a king over the Jewish people as the futurist teach? By no means! He was made "like unto his brethren, that he might be a merciful and faithful *high priest* in things pertaining to God, to make *reconciliation for the sins of his people*" (Hebrews 2:16-17). The ultimate display of His mercifulness and faithfulness is to be seen when He "tasted death" for every man (Hebrews 2:9).

A king's role is not that of dealing with sacrifices and sins — this belongs to the priesthood. Severe penalties were meted out to the kings in the Old Testament period who assumed the authority of the priest (see 1 Samuel 13:9-14; 2 Chronicles 26:16-21). Sacrifices and sins bring to mind the need of a "mediator" in man's relationship to God — this, too, belongs to the priesthood. It is impossible for sinful man to approach God without an intercessor. Jesus' first appearance had to be that of a "priest" rather than a "king." It is only *after* He has "washed us from our sins in his own blood" that we can be made kings and priests unto God (Revelation 1:5-6). The reverse of this is not possible.

The law of Moses, which in the main consisted of the Levitical priesthood, the tabernacle and temple, the sacrificial system, etc., did not foreshadow a coming king for Israel, but a Deliverer from *sin* and *death*. These types and shadows of "good things to come" were given to direct the Jewish people to a Saviour rather than a king upon an earthly throne. It is Jesus' priesthood that is central in the book of Hebrews and not His kingship. Man's confrontation with Jesus as a king would result in eternal death and damnation. Man must acknowledge Jesus as his sin bearer and Great High Priest before he can share in His role as king.

It can be stated also that the Ten Commandments were not given to regulate man's conduct in an earthly kingdom. Their primary purpose was to reveal *sin* (Romans 3:20; 7:7). If the Hebrew people of the old dispensation had permitted the law of Moses (with all of its ramifications) to accomplish its God-given purpose, they would have known that the Messiah would deal with *sin* and *death* rather than establish a worldly kingdom (John 5:46) — so would the futurists.

Another determinant in favor of a Saviour for Israel (rather than an earthly king) was the message of the prophets. One of the primary roles of the prophets was to expose the *sin* and *unbelief* of the people and call them to a life style of faith and godliness. The Jews' "own righteousness" rather than the "righteousness of God" was their *besetting sin* (Romans 10:3). If the Israelites failed to recognize and honor their prophets who called them to repentance and faith, it is very unlikely they would recognize and honor their Messiah who declared the same message.

The premillennialists of today would have been received with open arms by most of the Hebrew people in the old economy. Their insistence upon a Messiah who would establish an earthly kingdom, rather than One who would deal with *sin* and *death*, would have brought many "hallelujahs" from the majority of people. Premillennial views on the "physical" seed of Abraham would have endeared them to these ancient people beyond measure. The "chosen people" reverie would have contributed to the Jews' "self-image" (self-righteousness) in every period of Hebrew history. The "unconditional" promise of a utopian land of one thousand years would bring the Jewish people bowing at the feet of the futurists. Although the millenarians would have created many problems for the prophets in the old dispensation, they would have been welcomed by a people without number. When the religious agreement between ancient Israel and the premillennialists is brought to light, it seems that the premillennialists are a people "born out of due time."

Jesus' primary mission at His first appearance was to save men from *sin* and *death* rather than the establishment of an earthly kingdom. In Peter's views, the "promise" made to Abraham deals exclusively with the *sins* of the Jews and the prospect of eternal, everlasting life. The central message of both Moses and the Old Testament prophets was of the same nature (Acts 3:18-24). The foremost role of Jesus was to "turn the Jews from their iniquities" in order that they might realize the "promise" made to Abraham. According to Peter, the covenant made with Abraham was meant to turn *every Jew* in *every age* from his *iniquities:*

> Ye (Jews) are the children of the prophets, and of the *covenant* which *God made with our fathers,* saying unto Abraham, And *in thy seed shall all the kindreds of the earth be blessed.*
>
> Unto you (Jews) first God, having raised up his Son Jesus, sent him to *bless you* (Jews), in *turning every one of you* (Jews) *from his iniquities* (Acts 3:25-26).

The above truth is repeated again by Peter in his witness before the Jewish Sanhedrin. Peter reminds his fellow Jews of their crime against Jesus and tells them of Jesus' exaltation to the "right hand of God to be a *prince* and a *Savior,* for to give *repentance* to *Israel,* and *forgiveness of sins"* (Acts 5:30-31). Jesus' exaltation to the "right hand of God" suggests His position as a "ruler" as well as Savior. Both titles (Prince and Savior) are mentioned in conjunction with the "forgiveness of *sins*."

If *every* Jew was expected to *turn from his sin* as stated in Acts 3:26 — and if the Lord made *repentance* and *forgiveness of sins* possible through the death and resurrection of Christ as taught in Acts 5:31 — then it is impossible to claim an "unconditional" promise for the Jews in an earthly millennial kingdom as taught by the premillennialists. The "establishment of an earthly kingdom at Christ's first appearance" and the "unconditional promise" of the futurists are theological fiascoes that will not fly.

Jesus' objective in this world was not to overthrow the Roman Empire and set up an earthly kingdom. He did not come to destroy the lives of men — He came to save men's lives (Luke 9:56). Jesus' conflict was with the kingdom of Satan — the "powers of darkness" (Luke 22:53). Jesus' victory was won, not by carnal tactics, but by *love*. The Christian's warfare is of the same nature. Those who are in Christ lay down their arms at the cross and begin a crusade of love and peace. These peacemakers have already "beat their swords into plowshares, and their spears into pruninghooks" (Isaiah 2:4). Peter must put up his sword never to be unsheathed again. The Gospel of Jesus Christ brings men into a kingdom of *life, light,* and *love* — and that by the Word of God and the Spirit of God.

The premillennialists literally exploit what God decreed in His Son before the foundation of the world. They have devised a dual role for Christ that has no Scriptural basis. They advocate that God changed His mind *after* Jesus inaugurated His public ministry. At some point between Christ's baptism and His condemnation by the Jewish Sanhedrin, God was pressed to use "Plan B." This double role for Christ is necessary for premillennial doctrine.

By the above dualistic scheme, the premillennialists are able to create a unique role for the Jews in their fancy-woven millennial age and another role for the rest of mankind in the church age. In short, it results in two redemptive programs. Their theology is characterized by "twos" — this is why they attempt to make a difference in the terms "Kingdom of God" and the "Kingdom of Heaven."

A careful analysis of premillennialism will show that practically every doctrine that belongs to the church age is superimposed upon the millennial age. The "heavenly" atmosphere of the New Testament is traded for an "earthly" one. Christ, who now reigns on a heavenly throne must, during the millennial period, rule on an earthly throne in Jerusalem. The "heavenly tabernacle" which belongs to the church age is eclipsed by an "earthly temple" that is to be built in Palestine during the millennial age. "Spiritual sacrifices" which are offered by the church (Hebrews 13:15) are replaced by "animal sacrifices" during the millennium.

Premillennial doctrine creates *two programs* for the Jews — *one* for the Jews living during the church age and *another* for the Jews of the millennial age. Many futurists advocate *two* "promises" for the Jews — *one* for the church age, which is "conditional" — the *other* for the millennial age which, according to them, is "unconditional." The *one* "new covenant" which belongs to the church age (as well as the Old Testament era) must be given a *secondary* interpretation for the millennial age. The futurists are faced with *two* "inheritances" — one is "earthly" and pertains to the Land of Canaan — the other is a "heavenly inheritance" that belongs to the redeemed of all ages. "Earth tones" seem to be their favorite colors.

Premillennial doctrine results in two appearances of Christ — His first appearance is to rapture the church — His second appearance is to set up an earthly kingdom. These two appearances of Christ are falsely called the "rapture" and the "revelation." There must be two resurrections for the saints — one at the rapture of the church and the second at the end of the millennial period. Premillennialists teach two very deceptive and dramatic appearances of Satan — one is after the church is raptured and the second is at the end of the millennial age. What a potpouri of doctrine!

Isn't it strange that God would have two programs so much alike? Isn't it unusual that one program would follow immediately upon the heels of the other? Isn't it odd that God would switch His activities from a glorious heavenly scene to a mundane one? Can it be that God will give us a replay of Old Testament shadows? Are we not justified in decrying premillennialism?

A perfect example of this superimposition of church doctrine upon the millennial age is found in the words of Dr. J. Dwight Pentecost. In the following quote, Dr. Pentecost is *not* writing about the covenant that Christ established with the church — he is writing about a *second* covenant that is yet to be established with the Jews. Most futurists interpret Jeremiah 31:31 as a covenant made exclusively with Israel and not the church. Christ died *one time*. But according to the millenarians,

He initiated *two covenants* — one for the present dispensation and one for the millennial age. The covenant of Jeremiah 31:31 is held in abeyance until Christ's second advent. Notice the similarities between the doctrines of the so-called millennial age and that of the church:

> The new covenant (Jeremiah 31:31) guarantees to all who enter the millennium and to all who are born in the millennium and who thus need salvation (1) a *new heart* (Jeremiah 31:33), (2) the *forgiveness of sins* (Jeremiah 31:34), and (3) the *fulness of the Spirit* (Joel 2:28-29). The New Testament makes it very clear that the new covenant is based on the blood of the Lord Jesus Christ (Hebrews 8:6; 10:1-18; Matthew 26:28). It may, therefore, be affirmed that salvation in the millennium will be based on the *value* of the *death of Christ* and will be appropriated *by faith* (Hebrews 11:6) even as *Abraham appropriated God's promise* and was *justified* (Romans 4:3). The expressing of that *saving faith* will *differ* from the expressions that are required in this present day, but the sacrifices must be viewed *as mere expressions of faith* and not the means of salvation.[14] (Emphasis mine.)

There you have it! The "new heart," the "forgiveness of sins," the "fulness of the Spirit," and "justification by faith" all belong to the church age. Within a seven-year period (tribulation period) God shifts from one program to a second program whose fundamental doctrines are practically the same. The two programs, according to the above quote, originate from the same source, i.e., Christ's death. It seems that Dr. Pentecost has killed the goose that laid the golden egg. He has given away the candy store when he says that the millennial Jews will be "justified" in the same manner that Abraham was justified. His views on the covenant in Jeremiah 31:31 are a perfect description of the covenant that belongs to the church. However, there is one exception and it is discussed below.

Dr. Pentecost affirms that "saving faith" for the millennial Jews will be expressed differently from saving faith of today. We are told in the above quote that "animal sacrifices" will be the means of "expressing faith" during that period. The premillennialists are renowned for their emphasis upon a "literal temple" and "animal sacrifices" in the millennial kingdom.

---

14. Pentecost, 530-531.

The "sacrifices" that are offered in the millennium, and are called "expressions of faith" by Dr. Pentecost, are in reality "expressions of *another gospel.*" Dr. Pentecost and his premillennial brethren are repeating the same sin that Peter and the Galatian church were guilty of. Both Peter and the Galatian church were seduced into "another gospel" (Galatians 1:6-12). The "other gospel" that Paul describes and renounces in his letter to the Galatians is clearly the "works of the law." It is the "gospel" that the legalistic Jews believed and preached.

Paul's rebuke of Peter at the church in Antioch (Galatians 2:11) is used to warn the Galatian church against returning to the "works of the law." While Paul was at Antioch he realized that Peter, Barnabas and certain other Jews did not "walk uprightly according to the *truth of the Gospel*" (Galatians 2:14; see also 2:5). This history-making episode between Paul and Peter was translated into church doctrine. For Paul, it served as a springboard to differentiate between the "Gospel of Christ" and the "other gospel" that is discussed at some length in Galatians 1:6-12. Another contrast is made between the "two gospels" in Galatians 3:1. In this passage of Scripture, the Apostle rebukes the Galatians because they have "not obeyed the truth." It is very apparent that Paul is renouncing the "works of the law" throughout the Galatians epistle.

There is a clear-cut distinction between the "Gospel of Christ" and the "other gospel" or the "works of the law." A merger of the "two gospels" is an offense of great proportion, and in the words of the Apostle Paul, it should not be tolerated for a "single hour" (Galatians 2:5). But the premillennialists wish to revive "animal sacrifices" and continue them for one thousand years. Those who return to the "works of the law" are building again the very things that should be destroyed. The Apostle writes: "For if I build again the things which I destroy, I make myself a *transgressor*" (Galatians 2:18).

Peter's withdrawal from the Gentile believers at Antioch was sinful in more ways than one. It was wrong because he feared man more than God (Galatians 2:12). It was an evil act because he was responsible for causing Barnabas and other Jews to commit the same sin. Also, Peter's behavior can be classified as sin because it would jeopardize Paul's ministry to the Gentiles. Dr. Pentecost and those who advocate "animal sacrifices" in the millennial age are "building again" the very things that should be "destroyed." The Scriptures admonish those who are in Christ to "abstain from all appearance of evil" (1 Thessalonians 5:22), but Dr. Pentecost wants to restore "animal sacrifices" in the so-called millennial period as "expressions of faith."

Man's religious inclinations make him very gullible for the "works of the law" and he is easily "bewitched" thereby (Galatians 3:1). This bewitchment can have many evil ramifications. Legalism is capable of turning men into beasts. The bitterest enemies of the doctrine of "justification by faith" were the Judaizers who were obsessed with the "works of the law." Paul addressed them as the "enemies of the cross of Christ" (Philippians 3:18). Paul knew firsthand the bitter dregs of legalism. Paul's zeal for the "works of the law" prior to his conversion is described by Luke as "breathing out threatenings and slaughter against the disciples" (Acts 9:1). Should we encourage a practice that has been responsible for so much misery (including thousands of deaths) to the human race?

The works of the law are so attractive to men that they would rather submit to a complex system of rules and regulations than the "simplicity" that is in Christ (2 Corinthians 11:3). As a matter of fact, the magnetism of the law is so powerful that men will "gladly" suffer abuses at the hands of false teachers. Paul describes some in the Corinthian church who *indicated delight* in being deceived and led back into bondage. They "gladly" allowed men to "devour" them and hoodwink them — even to the extent of being slapped in the face (2 Corinthians 11:19-20 NIV). The false teachers who deceived and abused the Corinthians are described as "false apostles, deceitful workers, transforming themselves into the apostles of Christ (verse 13). This quirk in human nature has not disappeared. There are zealots today who would "gladly" suffer abuse in order to promote carnal sacrifices in a carnal kingdom instead of bringing to perfection the "simplicity" that is in Christ. They refuse to burn these bridges behind them.

We must not conclude that the Mosaic law was evil — it was not. The ceremonial law of the Old Testament dispensation was ordained by God, but it was to be a temporary institution until Christ should come. The role of the law was that of a schoolmaster—it was designed to teach and never to "justify." It is impossible for the "works of the law" to result in the *love* of *God* that comes through "justification by faith." This is why the Apostle Paul is careful to point out that Abraham was "justified by faith" several hundred years before the law was given. The real problem does not lie in the law per se, but in the deceitfulness of the human heart. The "works of the law" allow men to have a "measure of faith" in God, but at the same time they are their own lord and master.

The "works of the law" cater to man's religious nature in a way that becomes a subtle substitute for faith. This is why every shade of the ceremonial law — including Dr. Pentecost's "expressions of faith" — should be removed from the body of Christ.

The Apostle Paul affirms very clearly that the "law is *not of faith*" (Galatians 3:12). Animal sacrifices are diametrically *opposed* to faith. *"Expressions of faith" at any given age are to be seen first and foremost in man's love for God and his fellow man and not in "works of the law."* The whole law, according to our Lord, is summed up in a single word and that word is *love*. The premillennialists use the Old Testament Scriptures as their primary source for their millennial theories, but generally speaking, they overlook the central message of the prophets, which is the same as that of the New Testament — and that message is *love*. Hosea speaks for every period of Jewish history when he says: "For I (God) desire *mercy*, and *not sacrifice* and *the knowledge of God* more than *burnt offerings*" (Hosea 6:6). *Faith* and *love* are like hand and glove and "animal sacrifices" cannot enhance their image one iota (1 Corinthians 13).

Jesus endorsed the words of Hosea and used the example of David and his men (who ate the shewbread in the tabernacle, 1 Samuel 21:6) to teach the Pharisees that human life and needs (love) are far more important than "law-keeping." Jesus said to the Pharisees: "But I say unto you, that in this place is one *greater than the temple*. But if ye had known what this meaneth, I will have *mercy*, and *not sacrifice*, ye would not have condemned the guiltless" (Matthew 12:6-7). The condemnation brought against Jesus' disciples by the Pharisees reveals that they did not understand the essence of the Old Testament Scriptures. If they had understood the Scriptures, especially the words of Hosea, they would have known that God is far more concerned with *love* and *mercy* than He is with *sacrifice*. *Love* supercedes the "works of the law" at every juncture of human history, and since *love* and *faith* are so intricately woven together, "animal sacrifices" are altogether unnecessary — they benefit neither God nor man — they only distort.

The "works of the law" fuel man's ego in a way that is repugnant to the nature of God. They are a source of "boasting" and self-confidence that are contrary to the Gospel of Christ (Ephesians 2:8-9). The sacrifice of Jesus is a *gift* of God's *love* to which nothing can be added. The very essence of love is to give, and man insults the most High God by trying to please Him by his "good works." In a real sense, the only sacrifice that man should attempt to offer unto God is the "sacrifice of praise" (Hebrews 13:15; 1 Peter 2:5).

There are other negative aspects of the law that should be common knowledge to most Bible students. The "works of the law" are described as a *yoke of bondage* (Galatians 5:1), a *burden* (Acts 15:28), a *shadow* (Hebrews 10:1), *weak and beggarly elements* (Galatians 4:9), *leaven* (Galatians 5:9), et cetera. These terms alone should discourage any revival of the "works of law." The futurists would do well to follow Paul's advice to Titus when he stated that all "strivings" about the law were *"unprofitable and vain"* (Titus 3:9).

The last, but by no means the least, negative feature of the "works of the law" is the "curse" that is associated with them. If men are to gain God's favor by "law-keeping," then they must keep the *whole law*. To offend in *one part* of the law is to be "cursed" by the law (Galatians 3:10). The cards are stacked in favor of "faith" as the means of pleasing God and not by the "works of the law" (Hebrews 11:6). The odds of man being justified by the "works of the law" are zero. The penalty for *one offense* results in the "curse" of God. Every precaution that the church is able to muster should be used to discourage the "works of the law." Even the idea of "sacrifices" as a means of "expressing faith" should be renounced, lest they send the wrong signal to this present age.

If "animal sacrifices" will be beneficial in "expressing faith" in the millennial age, why were they discontinued with the death of Jesus? It seems that they should be as *useful* in one age as another. Of course, those who are familiar with premillennial doctrine know *why* the futurists are forced to resort to "animal sacrifices" in the millennium. This is the only way they can explain Ezekiel, chapters 40 through 47, and related passages.

Another attempt to explain the use of animal sacrifices in the millennial kingdom is the idea of "memorials." Animal sacrifices will be used as memorials of Christ's death. Animal sacrifices as "expressions of faith" and "memorials" of Christ's death are only theological apparitions that will haunt the millenarians until they are abandoned.

It is oftentimes said that history repeats itself and that men seldom profit from the past. This is true of sacred history as well as secular history. The evil propensities associated with the "works of the law" know no end. But the millenarians are willing to close their eyes to the evils of the past, along with the clear teaching of Scripture, and reinstate animal sacrifices as expressions of faith and memorials in a quasi-millennial age. Saving faith should be the death of all legal activities of whatever nature they may be (Galatians 2:19). It seems that Dr. Pentecost, along with all other futurists, would make every effort possible to protect men from the potential evils of the law, but they encourage the "works of the law." Men should avoid the "works of the law" as a plague.

It is very apparent that the millenarians attempt to create *two programs* from the death of Christ that will adapt to their "postponement" theory on the Kingdom of God. One program is for the church age and the second program is for the Jews in the so-called millennial age. It is impossible to develop "two doctrinal" positions from the death of Christ — but the premillennialists try it. This is why they *must* impose "church doctrine" on their millennial kingdom — they are left with no other choice.

It is also very obvious that Dr. Pentecost, along with many other futurists, try to blend the "works of the law" with the "doctrines of grace" in the millennial kingdom. But the two will no more mix than oil and water. The entire New Testament, especially the epistles, are written to distinguish between the two concepts so that men might cling to one and abhor the other. The premillennialists can call animal sacrifices "expressions of faith" or "memorials" of Christ's death if they please, but Paul would call them "expressions" and "memorials" of "another gospel" — and that is precisely what they are. Animal sacrifices are carnal ordinances (Hebrews 9:10) that please men rather than God. Paul plainly declares: "... do I seek to please men? for if I yet please men, I should not be the servant of Christ" (Galatians 1:10). He further warns: "If any man preach any *other gospel* unto you than that which we have preached unto you, let him be accursed" (Galatians 1:8). Paul's Gospel in a nutshell is the death, burial, and resurrection of Christ (1 Corinthians 15:1-4) and not a Jewish millennium. Jesus did not come to establish an earthly kingdom; neither did His death result in *two separate programs* as advocated by the millenarians.

The futurists are able to look back with hindsight and see very clearly that Jesus' death and resurrection were the focal point of His mission in the world; and yet they want to change God's arrangement to suit their theological whims. Peter, under the anointing of the Holy Ghost, declared that Jesus was "delivered by the *determinate counsel* and *foreknowledge of God*" to be crucified and slain (Acts 2:23); but according to the premillennialists, this was an *afterthought* in God's eternal purpose. Some futurists will admit that the cross of Jesus was in the predetermined counsels of God; but they insist that Christ would have established an earthly kingdom had the Jews received Him. *The millenarians can have one role of Christ or the other, but they cannot have both.*

Nowhere in the Scriptures do we find that God decreed an earthly, Jewish kingdom before the foundation of the world — but the cross of Jesus was so ordained. The reader can decide for himself whether or not God must "ponder over" what He should do — establish an earthly kingdom for the Jews or allow Jesus to go to the cross. The idea of God wavering between the two concepts creates a flaw in His character that is inconsistent with His divine nature.

It is a sad commentary on Christian theology when the futurists force us to consider the possibility of an earthly, Jewish kingdom in the place of the death of Christ. Jesus said: "Greater love hath no man than this, that a man lay down his life for his friends" (John 15:13). To lay one's life down in death is the *ultimate* of *love* — there can be *no greater*. The establishment of an earthly, Jewish kingdom would *not* have been the *ultimate act* of God's *love*. A thousand earthly kingdoms could *not* compare with God giving Himself in the person of the Lord Jesus Christ (Romans 5:6-10). When Jesus died on Calvary, the book on *love* was closed forever — no more can be written.

Over the centuries men have tried to express God's love with some very thought-inspiring lyrics and analogies. Our minds are stretched to the limit as we ponder their faculty of words. But those who attempt to describe God's love feel that they have fallen far short of their goal. Nothing in this world can begin to express God's love as the cross of Calvary. Fredrick M. Lehman, in his song "The Love of God," uses some very impressive analogies, but he readily admits their limitations. The third stanza reads:

> Could we with ink the ocean fill
> And were the sky of parchment made,
> Were ev'ry stalk on earth a quill
> And ev'ry man a scribe by trade,
> To write the love of God above
> Would drain the ocean dry,
> Nor could the scroll contain the whole
> Tho stretched from sky to sky.

The New Testament, from the beginning to the end, is concerned with God *revealing* Himself to mankind in the life, death, and resurrection of Jesus. God's passionate objective was to make His love, glory, nature, wisdom, and power known to fallen men. The "fulness of the Godhead" was embodied in Christ (Colossians 2:9). All the attributes of God converge at Calvary and the tomb. The futurists are challenged to say as much for the establishment of an earthly kingdom at Christ's first coming.

We are constrained to wonder how John 3:16 would read if Jesus had established an earthly kingdom two thousand years ago. In the light of premillennial views, it would probably read like this:

> For God so loved the world, that he sent his only begotten Son to establish an earthly kingdom for the Jews, and whoever receives that kingdom will enjoy it throughout his allotted days which are three-score years and ten.

The above version of John 3:16 is the *best* that the millenarians could say in favor of an earthly kingdom at Christ's first appearance. There is no solution to sin and death in the above version and it contains no promise of everlasting life.

A theological potter's field would be necessary to bury all the orphan doctrines of the New Testament in if Jesus had established an earthly kingdom at His first coming. The glorious Gospel that has inspired, motivated, and created hope for mankind over the centuries would turn to dust. Paul clearly states that men are justified by His *blood* (Romans 5:9; Ephesians 1:7). But if Jesus' *blood* had not been shed, there could be no justification for mankind; consequently, there could be no regeneration, no new creature, no sanctification, etc. Jesus would be forced to reign over a world of rebels — including the Jews.

A careful analysis of the first chapter of 1 Corinthians will show that God has reduced everything in the human theater to *nothing* by the cross of Jesus. According to Paul, the "wisdom of this world," the "understanding of the prudent," the "studious scribe," the "sophists," the "mighty things of the world," "all flesh" (Jew and Gentile), and the "things that are" are foolish pursuits of men that confound them on every hand. It is the "foolish things of the world," the "weak things of the world," the "base things of the world," the "things that are despised," and the "things that are not" that God has chosen to "bring to *nought* the things that are." The "things that are" in verse 28 is the "visible" world and its concomitancy. The "things that are not" is the "invisible" world that is known only to the Spirit of God and the man of faith (1 Corinthians 2:9-10). The "foolish things," the "weak things," the "base things," the "things that are despised," and the "things that are not" are concepts that pertain to Christ and His cross. This fact is established in Paul's second letter to the Corinthians as he writes: "For though he (Christ) was crucified through *weakness*, yet he liveth by the *power of God*. For we also are *weak in him*, but we shall live with him by the *power of God* toward you" (13:4; see also 1 Corinthians 2:3-5).

This "world," with all of its wisdom, prudence, knowledge, materialism, sophistication, might, and fleshly claims, ends at Calvary. It does not end at some future period of time. For the man of faith, it ends *here* and *now*. It is as though the "world" and the "things of the world" cease to be. Those who are in Christ identify themselves with the "foolish," the "weak," the "base," the "despised," and the "things that are not" when they take up the cross and follow the Master. However, foolishness becomes wisdom — weakness becomes might — baseness results in exaltation — despised turns into honor — and the "things that are not" translate into realism. Paul is unveiling a paradoxical situation that is at cross-purposes with everything that the natural man holds dear. It can be candidly stated that "Jewish flesh" and the "Land of Canaan" were brought to "nought" by the cross of Jesus as well as everything else that is associated with this world order. The elect of God would have to forego the glorious transformation that Paul has described if Christ had established an earthly kingdom at His first advent. God must surely be grieved — Christ offended — the Holy Spirit insulted — the prophets disappointed — and the angels perplexed when men speak and write of an earthly kingdom as an alternative for the cross of Calvary.

It would be *impossible* for God to redeem man and remain a righteous, holy, and *just* God without the cross of Jesus. This conclusion is drawn because God *must* punish sin. He must punish man's sin directly or through a substitute. God's word to Adam was: "...for in the day that thou eatest thereof thou *shalt surely die*" (Genesis 2:17). Sin and death came as a result of Adam's transgression. This was God's punishment — man's doom was sealed indefinitely. The only way that God could be *just* and save man from his plight was for Him to take the form of a man and bear man's punishment. He did this in the sufferings and death of Jesus. The Apostle Paul puts it this way: "For he (God) hath made him (Christ) to be *sin for us*, who knew no sin; that we might be made the righteousness of God in him" (2 Corinthians 5:21). The Judge who passed the sentence of *sin* and *death* bore the consequences Himself. Paul vindicates God's *just* and righteous character in the following passage:

> To declare, I say, at this time his righteousness: that *he might be just,* and the *justifier* of him which believeth in Jesus (Romans 3:26).

The death of Jesus can be compared to a two-way street. God not only displayed His *justice* in the *punishment of sin,* He also made it possible to *punish sinners* who reject His mercy in Christ. God could never be *just* and punish sinners without first of all providing a salvation for them. It is for this reason that God can *justly* punish men if they consistently refuse the light that is given them (Romans 1:18ff; 2:2-9). When the futurists lead us to believe that an earthly Jewish kingdom could be an alternative for the death of Jesus, they are compelled to take Adam's transgression and God's integrity very lightly.

The above passage (Romans 3:26) is another jewel from Paul's treasure house of theology. God's entire "system of justice" (if we may call it such) is related to the cross of Jesus. All of God's relationships to man are based on "law" except His *mercy* and *grace* that came in Christ, i.e., the Ten Commandments, the law of sin and death, etc. The "curse" that was pronounced upon the woman in the Garden of Eden and the "curse" that was pronounced upon the ground entail certain "laws." It goes without saying that the whole universe is based on specific metaphysical "laws." The laws of the natural order control everything from germination and growth to death and decay. All of these laws are potentially suspended in the death and resurrection of Christ. The "law of the Spirit" is a power that transcends the "law of sin and death" *here* and *now* (Romans 8:2). "Behold, I make all things new" (Revelation 21:5) means that all metaphysical laws *will be* suspended in the future because Jesus died and rose again. Jesus' atonement has provided a "new heaven and a new earth" in another dimension (Colossians 1:20; Romans 8:21). God's *just* and holy character was displayed at Calvary in more ways than one.

Another important truth to be found in Romans 3:26 is the *time factor* in Jesus' coming in the flesh. This passage affirms that God chose the *hour* to disclose His just and righteous character to the world. God's *timetable* is clearly seen in the words of Paul when he writes: "To declare, I say, *at this time* his righteousness; that he might be just, and the justifier of him which believeth in Jesus." The phrase "at this time" means that the stage was set for one special episode in history and not two. The idea of changing the script, actors, and props is absurd. The concept of two possible programs for our Lord at His first appearance is a theological basket case.

The Apostle Paul became very emotional when he dealt with the cross of Jesus. It was more than a rhetorical discourse that men could play fast and loose with. He found the content of its message so majestic, powerful, and overwhelming that he was moved to fear and trembling (1 Corinthians 2:2-5). When certain "enemies of the cross" threatened the progress of the Philippian church, he was constrained to weep (Philippians 3:18). Paul did not soft soap those whom he called "enemies of the cross." In his high-spirited boldness he calls them dogs, evil workers, and mutilators of the flesh (Philippians 3:2). The cross had a greater effect on the Apostle than any other facet of Jesus' life and works. His life was so impacted by the cross that he was willing to suffer and die for it (Philippians 1:20; Acts 20:24; 21:13). For some, Paul's zeal for the Gospel seemed almost "madness" (Acts 26:24-25). As the King James Version might say, his "bowels" were stirred within him when he proclaimed and defended the cross. But the millenarians can write and speak about the prospects of an earthly kingdom as a substitute for the cross without a single emotion being kindled. This cavalier spirit is reflected throughout their works.

The mission of Jesus is not a harp from which we can pluck any theological tune we wish to play — it has only one song: "For God so *loved* the world that he *gave* his only begotten Son." All divine history and nature are in harmony with this one melody. John Bowring (1792-1872) discovered this truth many decades ago when he wrote:

> In the cross of Christ I glory, Tow'r-ing o'er the wrecks of time,
> *All the light of sacred story* Gather round its head sublime.[15](Emphasis mine.)

John Bowring's words, "all the light of sacred story gather round its head sublime," bring to mind a very important biblical principle. The Scriptures are capable of bringing men additional *light* or pressing them into further darkness (2 Peter 3:16). If the "pilgrim" interprets the Scriptures in the *light* that streams from Calvary, he will never lose his way. The eons of eternity will never erase the imagery of Jesus as a "slain *lamb*." If the *Lamb* is the *Light* of the New Jerusalem (Revelation

---

15. From the hymn *In the Cross of Christ I Glory*

21:23), then the *Lamb* should be the *Light* in the present age.

As implied above, even the *natural order*, with its "sowing and reaping," which translates into "dying and living" (John 12:24), "first-fruits and harvest," the seasons of "winter and summer," "darkness and light," and many other aspects of the *creation*, reflects the cross of Christ (along with His resurrection). There would have to be a complete reorientation of nature before an earthly kingdom could supersede the cross of Calvary. To contend that Jesus' death was a secondary matter in the mind of God when Jesus made His first advent, and that the church age is a *temporary interruption* of a divine program for the Jews in an earthly kingdom, is both ludicrous and unthinkable.

The establishment of an earthly kingdom, instead of the sacrifice of Jesus, would have struck a death blow to the Old Testament Scriptures (Matthew 26:54; Mark 14:49). The rejection of Christ by the Jews (which resulted in His death) was a fulfillment of prophecy. The unbelief of the Jews was the umbilical cord that gave birth to the New Testament. Remove this (blindness of the Jews) and the New Testament would be nonexistent. The rejection of Christ by the Jews was a brief period of time in the history of the world wherein God would accomplish that which He decreed from the beginning. Therefore, God was not caught off guard when the Jews rejected His Son. Jewish unbelief was one of God's primary agencies in fulfilling His divine purpose.

Jewish unbelief gave credence to two important features in man's relationship to God. First, it revealed the depravity of the human heart in one of the most religious hours in Jewish history. Religion was at an all time high when Christ made His first appearance. The synagogues, which were started during the captivity (or shortly thereafter) were in full force during New Testament days. Synagogues were to be found in most major cities of the known world and were attended regularly by the Jews. There was an interest in the law of Moses that was unparalleled in Jewish history. Temple worship was never greater — people traveled far and wide to observe its ceremonies (Acts 2:9-11). It was during the celebration of the Passover Feast that our Lord was crucified. The rejection of Jesus at such a religious crescendo in Jewish history only magnifies man's sinful nature — it was the ultimate of sin (John 15:22-25).

Jewish religiosity in the first century A. D. represents man's greatest effort to please God without *faith* (Romans 10:2). Jesus came to a people who were supposed to know every jot and tittle of the

Scriptures — but they didn't. Jewish zeal for law-serving, circumcision in the flesh, and blood ties with Abraham became their stumblingblock. The example of the Pharisees and Saduccees has been preserved as a lesson and warning to future generations (Matthew 16:6-12). Such blind zeal was to be disdained forever. But the futurists would return the Jews to the very thing that caused them to stumble.

Secondly, Jewish unbelief magnifies the unsearchable riches of God's grace more than any other Jewish activity. The same people that were "used" to bring the Messiah into the world were "used" to crucify Him — the very blood for which they cried was the blood by which they were to be saved. While sin found its lowest level in the crucifixion of Christ, God's grace found its ultimate height in the same act. What a paradoxical arrangement! Where is boasting? There is none! The wisdom and grace of God stand out supremely. Those who were once the enemies of God could now be reconciled by the blood of His cross. This is the Lord's doing and it is marvelous in our sight (Matthew 21:42).

The *unbelief* of the Jews would actually contribute to their salvation. The unbelief of the Jews revived the ancient truth that all men are sinners (Psalm 14:3; Isaiah 53:3) and established a precedent for all mankind in the future, i.e., all men must see themselves in "unbelief" and as "sinners" before they can know the grace of God (Romans 11:32). Albeit, the premillennialists want to relieve the Jews of any and all guilt and offer them an "unconditional" promise in the so-called millennial age.

Both Peter and Paul, two key leaders in the Christian church, declared that the Jews crucified Jesus (Acts 3:15; 1 Thessalonians 2:15), but many people want to play this fact down. The very thing that God wanted the Jew to know (his sinful state) is toned down by those who want to exploit the carnal descendants of Abraham.

If Christ had come to the Gentiles "first" and had been rejected, the magnitude of man's sin and blindness would not have been nearly so great. But He came to a people in whose hands the truth had been deposited for centuries (Romans 9:4), but they "knew Him not."

The millenarians write and speak as though God cast a "spell" upon the Jewish people when Christ came in the flesh and that this mesmerization continues to this day. Such an idea arises out of Paul's comments on the remnant in both the Old and New Testaments:

What then? Israel hath not obtained that which he (God) seeketh for; but the election hath obtained it, and the rest *were blinded*

(According as it is written, God hath given them the *spirit of slumber, eyes that they should not see,* and *ears that they should not hear;*) unto this day (Romans 11:7-8).

The above passage is a composite quote from both Moses and Isaiah. A careful examination of Moses' original statement will reveal that God did *not* arbitrarily close the eyes and ears of the Jewish people in the days of Moses. Rather, *God refused to open their eyes and ears.* Their eyes and ears were *already* closed. The Lord performed many "great miracles" through Moses, but the people refused to "believe" in the One who was the source of the miracles. The people saw the mighty acts of God with their physical eyes, but they did not believe in God per se. Moses said of them:

The great temptations which thine eyes have seen, the signs, and those great miracles:
Yet the Lord hath not given you an ear to perceive, and eyes to see, and *ears to hear, unto this day* (Deuteronomy 29:3-4).

God did not anesthetize the Jews during Moses' day or at any other period of their history. God does not have to lull people to sleep (Jew or Gentile) to veil His Person and activities. Men without a redemptive faith are already beyond the stage of sleep — they are "dead in trespasses and in sins" (Ephesians 2:1). Spiritual perception comes *only* from God (Luke 10:21).

When Paul states that "God hath given them (Jews) the spirit of slumber, eyes that they should not see, and ears that they should not hear," it is an echo of Moses' statement in Deuteronomy 29:3-4. According to James Strong, the Greek word for "given" (*didomi*) has a very wide application. It can also mean: *deliver (up); grant;* and *commit.* In other words, Paul could be saying that God "committed them to this state of stupor without opening their eyes and ears." To put it another way, God allowed them to remain in this condition. The veil that was over the Jews' hearts in Paul's day and in this age will never be lifted until they believe in Christ (2 Corinthians 3:14-16; Matthew 11:27).

Jesus interprets one of Isaiah's prophecies in the same manner. He placed the dullness and blindness of the Jewish people squarely upon their own shoulders. Their inability to "see" and "hear" was a fulfillment of Scripture:

> And in them (Jews) is *fulfilled the prophecy* of Isaiah, which saith, By hearing ye shall hear, and *shall not understand;* and seeing ye shall see, and *shall not perceive:*
>
> For this *people's heart is waxed gross,* and their *ears are dull of hearing,* and their *eyes they have closed:* lest at any time they should see with their eyes, and hear with their ears, and should understand with their hearts, and should be converted, and I should heal them (Matthew 13:14-15).

If men are capable of a *negative* response to the Word of God, they are also capable of a *positive* response. We see a negative response to the Word of God throughout the Jews' history. A classic illustration of this fact is to be found in the words of Zechariah. When Zechariah called upon the Jewish people to show mercy and compassion toward their fellow man, he received a very negative response:

> But they refused to hearken, and pulled away the shoulder, and stopped their ears, that they should hear.
>
> Yea, *they made their hearts as an adamant stone,* lest they should hear the law, and the words which the Lord of hosts hath sent in his spirit by the former prophets, etc. (Zechariah 7:11-12).

Zechariah does not make God accountable for the Jews' reaction to his message. He says: "*They* made their hearts as an adamant stone." The Jews sent a negative signal to both God and His prophet. It is impossible for men to take a neutral position when confronted with God's Word.

The New Testament dispensation is no different from the Old. Paul and Barnabas received a similar response from the Jews at Antioch of Pisidia. It is very apparent that God did not close the eyes of these Antiochian Jews. They made their own decision — they "judged themselves:"

> But when the Jews saw the multitudes, they were filled with *envy,* and *spake against* those things which were spoken by Paul, *contradicting* and *blaspheming.*
>
> Then Paul and Barnabas waxed bold, and said, It was necessary that the word of God should first have been spoken to you: but seeing *ye put it from you,* and *judge yourselves unworthy of everlasting life,* lo, we turn to the Gentiles (Acts 13:45-46).

Paul's bold message was not an indictment against the entire Jewish nation, but only the Jews at Antioch. A few days later, we find

Paul and Barnabas speaking in the synagogue of Iconium, and a "great multitude both of the Jews and also of the Greeks believed" (Acts 14:1).

All men have a certain accountability to God when confronted with His Word and works. Christ's ministry was filled with signs and wonders (John 21:25, Matthew 11:20ff), but many of the Jewish people refused to believe on Him. The mighty works of Christ not only revealed the nature and power of God, they also revealed the "blindness" of the most religious people of that hour.

It is a law of nature that the farther one travels from an area of light, the darker the pathway becomes. The same principle is true in the divine order. The farther men travel from the light of the Gospel, the darker their pathway grows. The multiple "works of the law" had led the Jews farther and farther away from the One who was the Light of the world. That which was given to reveal the sinful nature of mankind (the law) had become their religion. The law which produces death (Romans 7:10) had become their "life." Their religious zeal literally became sin (Romans 10:2-3).

The "blindness" of the Jews and the "postponement" theory on the Kingdom of God go hand in hand for the land-covenant advocates. Both ideas create a theological gap, between the first century Jews and the so-called millennial Jews, that is hostile to God's love for Abraham's natural descendants. This distinction in the New Testament Jews and the millennial Jews has resulted in many erroneous interpretations of Scripture. A perfect illustration of this fact can be seen in their views on Zechariah 12:10.

The millenarians affirm that the first century Jews looked upon Jesus, mocked, ridiculed, and put Him to death. But in the same breath, they contend that another generation of Jews, 2000 years later (or whenever the so-called millennial age occurs), will "look upon him whom they pierced, mourn for him," believe in Him, and enter joyfully into the Land of Canaan, etc.

The above paragraph sounds innocent enough because it is based on Scripture (Zechariah 12:10). For the millenarians, the principle of "looking upon him, mourning," and believing upon Him went underground (at least to a very large degree) and does not emerge again until the beginning of the millennial kingdom. In other words, the real impact of Zechariah 12:10 will not be felt until the millennial age dawns. This is a consequence of the Jews' "blindness."

Contrary to the above views, Zechariah's prophecy (12:10) was set in motion on the day of Pentecost and continues to this day. Many of the Jews, who mocked and derided Jesus in the hour of His death, repented and believed upon Him a few days afterwards. Peter addressed his Pentecostal audience with these words: "Ye *men of Israel,* hear these words; Jesus of Nazareth ... ye have taken, and by *wicked hands* have *crucified* and *slain"* (Acts 2:22-23). Peter concludes his remarks on the same note: "Therefore let *all the house of Israel* know assuredly, that God hath made that same Jesus, whom *ye have crucified,* both Lord and Christ" (Acts 2:36). And the next verse reads: "Now when they (house of Israel) heard this, they were pricked in their hearts (convicted) and said unto Peter and the rest of the apostles, Men and brethren, what shall we do?" (verse 37). After the "house of Israel" was told what to do (verses 38-40), it is said that "the *same day* there were added unto them about *three thousand souls"* (verse 41). Peter admonished "all the house of Israel" to repent and believe upon Christ — even those who had a close encounter with His death — and a great number of them were converted. There can be no doubt that many of the Jews who scorned, spit upon, and shamefully reproached Christ fulfilled Zechariah's prophecy.

Zechariah's prophecy did not go into an eclipse after Pentecost to remain there (in part or whole) for 2000 years. Thousands of Jews have "looked upon him whom they pierced, mourned," and believed upon Him since New Testament days. In the Scriptures "looking" is often-times synonymous with "faith" (Numbers 21:8; Isaiah 45:22; Hebrews 12:1, etc.). Word pictures of Christ crucified make it possible for men to "look upon Him" in every age and generation. Paul writes as though the Galatians stood within sight of the cross the day Jesus died — but they were not there. Paul describes the Galatians' first encounter with Christ in these words: "... *before whose eyes* Jesus Christ hath been evidently *set forth, crucified* among you" (Galatians 3:1). It was by the "eye of faith" that the Galatians "looked upon" the crucified Christ and were made heirs of eternal life. The Galatians, along with millions of others (Jews and Gentiles), fulfilled Zechariah's prophecy.

Peter's Pentecostal sermon involves "all the men of Israel" and "all the house of Israel" in Jesus' death. There were many Jews in Jerusalem on the day of Pentecost (and elsewhere throughout the known world) who could not have had a *direct* hand in the death of Jesus. However, Peter addresses the whole "nation" or "all the house of Israel" as having a part in His crucifixion. At the same time he involves "all" Jews in the matter of repenting and believing. How can this be?

The above paragraph can be true because no man is an island unto himself — neither is a given generation. We cannot escape the fact that man is an accountable creature. He is answerable to God and he is answerable to his fellow man (Jew and Gentile). This is why the first two commandments are so important. The moral behavior of one generation (whether good or bad) affects another. All men are sinners and have the potential of remaining in that state. By remaining in that condition, they contribute to the untowardness of their generation — there is no neutral ground (Matthew 12:30). On the other hand, all men have the potential of repenting and believing on Christ — bringing light and hope to their generation.

The "house of Israel," the Jewish Sanhedrin, Pilate, and the Roman soldiers did to Jesus what all unregenerate men would have done if they had been present at the hour of His death — some more and some less. Those who participated in Jesus' death did it in varying degrees. A wide range of sin(s) can be seen in the death of Jesus — from the sin of unbelief to the shedding of His blood. The Adamic nature in man reached its peak in the conglomerate of people who crucified Christ. When they condemned and crucified Christ, those who were involved *represented* and *acted for* the entire human race. The sin principle, that rejected and crucified Christ, is inherent in all men.

Unbelief is enough to keep one out of the Kingdom of God (John 3:18). Every generation of Jews (and Gentiles) is accountable for the light it receives regarding the Word of God. Zechariah's prophecy (12:10) did not go underground after Pentecost (in part or whole) to appear again at the beginning of the so-called millennial kingdom. The "gap" theology, that the millenarians have created between the first century Jews and the so-called millennial Jews, is a two-legged stool.

If the millenarians wish to get technical regarding Zechariah 12:10, it can be pointed out that it was the Roman soldiers who "pierced" Jesus' brow with a crown of thorns, slashed His back with a whip, drove the spikes into His hands and feet, and opened His side with a sword, and *not the Jews*. (See *The Scofield Reference Bible*, p. 976, Note 1.)

There is another aspect of Jesus' death that is not favorable to the futurists' interpretation of Zechariah 12:10. No man or group of men (Jews or Gentiles) had the power to take Jesus' life from Him — He laid it down voluntarily — which translates into *Infinite love* (Matthew 26:53, John 3:16, 10:11, 18, 1 Corinthians 2:8). In one sense God's permissive role in the death of His Son removes it from the hands of *all* men — leaving them face to face with nothing except His love and mercy. That love and mercy did not go into latency (in part or whole) to be "kicked back in" two thousand years later for the land-covenant Jews. Neither can God's love be segmented in a way that would separate the first century Jews, present-day Jews, and the so-called millennial Jews from each other. The millenarians are playing with "holy fire" when they attempt to dole out the sacrifice of Jesus at their own discretion.

The premillennialists treat Zechariah 13:1, (as well as many other Old Testament passages) in a similar manner. The "fountain" that Zechariah describes in this verse was opened to the "house of David," and all mankind, the day Jesus died. This "fountain" did not "dry up" for the Jews (in part or whole) after New Testament days to be "opened again" at the onset of the so-called millennial age. Neither did the "house of David" go into remission after Pentecost to appear again 2000 years later. That "fountain" was opened for *all* mankind in every age and generation.

Jesus' application of the parable of the "Wicked Husbandmen" in Matthew's Gospel is another plus for the position I have taken on the Kingdom of God — that Kingdom was not postponed. It also affirms that the "death of Jesus" was not a substitute for the establishment of an earthly kingdom. When Jesus finished His discourse on the parables of the "Wicked Husbandmen," He said to the Jewish priests and elders:

> Did ye never read in the scriptures, The stone which the builders *rejected,* the same is become the head of the corner; *This is the Lord's doing, and it is marvellous in our eyes?*
>
> Therefore say I unto you, the *Kingdom of God* shall be *taken from you,* and *given to a nation* bringing forth the fruits thereof (Matthew 21:42-43).

A certain degree of latitude must be given in the interpretation of the above passage. First of all, it is common knowledge that the Jews did not "possess" the Kingdom of God. How could it be "taken from them" if it was not theirs? When Jesus speaks of the "Kingdom of God being taken from the Jews," He is speaking from a Jewish perspective. Jesus' statement is an overlay of the Jewish mind from the beginning. The Jews always felt that they had a monopoly on God and the things of God. Even in their blindness, they claimed a relationship to God that was entirely false (John 8:39-42).

Secondly, the "nation" mentioned in the above text cannot be the Gentiles per se. The Gentiles can never be spoken of as a single nation — it is always "nations" (plural). As given in 1 Peter 2:9, and elsewhere throughout the Scriptures, the "nation in verse 43 is a "holy nation." And that "holy nation" is the elect of God involving both Jews and Gentiles.

Lastly, the nation, to whom the Kingdom of God is given, is to "bring forth the fruits thereof." The "fruits" of the Kingdom of God are not the fruit of the vine or stalk, but the fruit of the Holy Spirit, i.e., love, joy, peace, longsuffering, gentleness, goodness, faith, etc., (Galatians 5:22). The Apostle Paul affirms, "the kingdom of God is not meat and drink; but righteousness, and peace, and joy in the Holy Ghost" (Romans 14:17).

Perhaps we should raise the question: "was Christ a 'king' when He made His first appearance?" Let us permit the Scriptures and the testimonies of some illustrious saints to answer this question. According to the Scriptures, Jesus' lineage is traceable to two royal lines — the Son of David and the Son of God. Jesus was begotten by God the Father and in His veins flowed the royal blood of heaven. Jesus was a "king" from His birth, but He was not perceived as such by the Jews; nor was He the "type" of king that the premillennialists wish to impose upon Him. When the wise men came from the East to Jerusalem, they are reported by Matthew as inquiring, "where is he that is born *king of the Jews?*" (Matthew 2:2). It is ironic that the first people to recognize and worship Jesus as "king" were most likely Gentiles.

Jesus was not only a "king" in His *birth,* He was also a "king" in His *death.* When Pilate wrote the famous title, "JESUS OF NAZARETH THE KING OF THE JEWS" in Hebrew, Greek, and Latin (John 19:19-20), and attached it to Jesus' cross, he was absolutely right. Although Pilate did it in total ignorance, it was as if the hand of God had written it. In the lowest hour of Jesus' humility, He was a "king" (John 18:37). It might be added, Pilate was also a Gentile. From the cradle to the cross, Jesus was a "king."

Jesus was the greatest Conqueror and Deliverer that the world will ever know. Contrary to human standards, Jesus proved His *strength* in His *weakness* (2 Corinthians 13:4). That strength is not to be seen in the clashing of swords nor the falling of men and mounts on the battlefield; nor was His strength displayed in the overpowering of cities and nations. Jesus' strength was revealed in His *love* for all mankind. Jesus' body was not red with the blood of His enemies that He had defeated in battle, but with His own blood by which He satisfied the justice of God and conquered death and hell.

Most millenarians want to restrict Jesus' "kingship" to the future, and at the same time revive the Old Testament era of nations against nations with swords, spears, and chariots, rather than a God of infinite *love* that was displayed at Calvary. They foresee some major nations of the world coming against Israel before the so-called millennial age occurs — and according to them, every present day war in the Middle East is leading up to that hour. They endeavor to portray Christ as riding upon a white horse and in shining armour leading Israel to victory. There have been "wars and rumors of wars" since New Testament days, but the only significant wars for the futurists (in which God is involved) are the wars in the Middle East — especially of recent years.

We need to be reminded over and over again that the Old Testament years were the "school days" of God's revelation of Himself and His plan of redemption. The superiority of God's power does not lie simply in physical power, but moral character and authority. While the Old Testament is interspersed with both His physical and moral power, the New Testament is primarily a revelation of God's *love* and *mercy*. The culmination of God's revelation for the present age is to be seen in the death of Jesus. This is not to minimize God's role in punishing men and nations, including Israel, in the Old Testament dispensation. This is not to say that God is not running the affairs of the world today. Nor does it imply that God will not pour out His wrath upon the world in the future. It is saying that the most significant battle that God ever fought for Israel (and all mankind) occurred the day Christ died on the cross. *God has already fought Israel's battle and won her victory.* What greater thing can God do for the Jews?

Jesus is first and foremost a *Moral Monarch* — His scepter is one of righteousness (Hebrews 1:8; Revelation 19:11). He is called "King of righteousness" and "King of peace" (Hebrews 7:2). The ultimate of Jesus' "kingship" is to be seen in the unfathomable dimension of *love* (Ephesians 3:18-19) *Love* is the most powerful force in heaven and in earth. This fact is well documented in Paul's great love chapter (1 Corinthians 13). In this unique chapter Paul escorts the reader through some glorious concepts and lofty realms. But the peak is not reached — man's vision is not clear — his knowledge is fragmented until he arrives at the plateau of *love*. This is the highest and most rewarding realm that one can experience. It is here that man meets God, his fellow man, and all the powers of the enemy in an inexplicable manner. It is here that we become *"More than conquerors through Him that loved us"* (Romans 8:37). There is no display of God's power in the past or a description of His power in the future that will commend itself to man as the one outlined in Romans 8:31-39. Why would the millenarians tantalize the Jews with an elusive millennial kingdom in the future when Romans 8:31-39 can be theirs today? — and that by the death and resurrection of Christ (verses 32, 34). Let the Armageddons come — let the Antichrist appear — let plagues and death stalk the earth — there is a refuge in the cross of Jesus that transcends all ages and embraces eternity.

It is unreal and vain to speak and write of Jesus' "kingship" apart from His death and resurrection. It was because of His "humility and obedience unto death" that God exalted Him and gave Him a name which is above every name (Philippians 2:6-11) — including the title "King of kings and Lord of lords." When Jesus' passion is seen through the eyes of the Holy Ghost, a remarkable image appears. The crown of thorns is transformed into a royal diadem. The mock reed that was placed in Jesus' hand by the Roman soldiers becomes a golden scepter. The blood that stained His garments and body is changed into regal purple. Such knowledge does not belong to the neophyte, but to those of whom Spurgeon would say have "built their house on Calvary."

The ideas expressed in the above paragraph are heard in many of the evangelical churches in this nation from Sunday to Sunday. But for the most part, they do not come from the pulpits of these churches — they are expressed in the songs that are sung. One of the most popular songs in Christian circles today (as well as ages past) is Isaac Watts' (1674-1748) song, "When I Survey the Wondrous Cross." The third stanza reads:

> See, from His head, His hands, His feet
> Sorrow and love flow mingled down;
> Did e'er such love and sorrow meet,
> Or *thorns compose so rich a crown.* (Emphasis mine.)

Most people vocalize the above words without an experiential knowledge of what they are singing. Thomas Kelly (1769-1855) expresses similar ideas in his song, "The Head That Once Was Crowned:"

278 ISRAEL VS. ISRAEL

The head that once was crowned with *thorns*
Is crowned with glory now;
A royal diadem adorns the mighty *Victor's brow*. (Emphasis mine.)

The above songs (along with many others that could be mentioned) were written several decades *before* the heyday of dispensational premillennialism. They reflect a strain of theology that belongs to another era. Charles H. Spurgeon, whom I have quoted several times and to whom I am tremendously indebted for my knowledge and experiences of Christ's glory, belongs to the same school of theology. In his sermon, "The Exaltation of Christ," Mr. Spurgeon says:

> A God is groaning on a cross! What! Does not this dishonor Christ? No; it honors Him! Each of the *thorns become a brilliant in His diadem of glory;* the *nails forged into His scepter,* and *His wounds do clothe Him with purple of empire.* The treading of the winepress hath *stained His garments,* but *not with stains of scorn and dishonor. The stains are embroideries upon His royal robes for ever.* The treading of that wine-press hath made His *garments purple* with the empire of a world; and He is the Master of a universe for ever.[16] (Emphasis mine.)

Do the Jews long for a "king?" Do the Gentiles desire a "king?" Then let both Jew and Gentile gaze upon the One who was "clothed with a *vesture dipped in blood* and His name is called the Word of God" (Revelation 19:13) ... and "he hath on his *vesture* and on his thigh a name written *King of kings, and Lord of lords"* (Revelation 19:16). While living in this present world, men will discover more of Christ's regality in His death and resurrection than any other place.

There is a divine principle throughout the Scriptures that every saint of God should learn and that is, "*glory* always follows *suffering.*" This is true in the life of Christ as well as the individual believer (1 Peter 4:13-14). The necessity of Christ's sufferings before He entered into His glory is repeated over and over again in the New Testament (Matthew 16:21; 17:12; Mark 8:31; 9:12; Luke 9:22; 17:25; 22:15; 24:46; Acts 3:18; 17:3; 26:23; Hebrews 2:9; 13:12; 1 Peter 1:11; 1:21). I realize that the following remarks may sound unbecoming and cruel, but sometimes

---

16. C. H. Spurgeon, *The Treasury of the New Testament,* Zondervan Publishing House, Grand Rapids, Michigan, Vol. III, 447.

provocative words prove to be a better tool than savory words. I cannot resist the temptation to say to the futurists what Jesus said to the Emmaus disciples: "O fools, and slow of heart to believe *all that the prophets have spoken;* Ought not *Christ to have suffered these things,* and to *enter into His glory?"* (Luke 24:25-26). If the millenarians would take the above words of Jesus seriously, the bedrock of premillennialism would be destroyed.

The establishment of an earthly kingdom at Christ's first appearance casts a pall over the New Testament that is repugnant to those who glory in nothing but the cross of Christ (Galatians 6:14). It makes the cross of Jesus a second-rate act of God that plays havoc with His unchangeable nature and infinite knowledge. It allows the acts of men (Jews) to determine the course of history and the destinies of men. It concedes to a carnal, worldly kingdom that blights a glorious heavenly inheritance made possible by the death and resurrection of Christ.

It is reasonable to say that the millenarians are within a hairsbreath of making an earthly kingdom as important as the death and resurrection of Christ. This can only weaken and minimize the most celebrated and conspicuous truth in all of Scripture. By their "postponement" theory, the futurists are sending bad vibes to the church at large and the rest of mankind.

How wonderful it is that men can enter the Kingdom of God HERE and NOW. This is one of the most glorious truths that ever fell on mortal ears. And yet, the premillennialists want us to believe that the Kingdom of God was "postponed" to some vague, indefinite period in the future. We are forced to accept the clear teachings of Scripture rather than the opinions of men.

Chapter 9

Christ vs. the Antichrist

"For unto you is born this day in the city of David a Saviour, which is Christ the Lord" (Luke 2:11). The New Testament opens with special emphasis on the Incarnation of Christ and continues this theme throughout. The paramount truth in the New Testament is that Christ *has come in the flesh*. The foremost ministry of the Holy Spirit is to bear witness to this fact (John 16:13-15). The testimonies of men (or the church) have confirmed and perpetuated this truth over the centuries. In other words, the world has been given three of the greatest witnesses that men can have relative to the Incarnation: (1) the Word, (2) the Spirit, and (3) the Church.

The "spirit of Antichrist" is just the opposite of the above truth — it is a denial that *Christ has come in the flesh*. The Apostle John, in both his Gospel and his first epistle, deals extensively with the fleshly nature of Christ. The *grand lie* that has its origin in Satan is a rejection of Christ's having *come in the flesh:*

> Who is a *liar* but he that *denieth* that Jesus is the Christ? He is *Antichrist,* that *denieth* the Father and the Son (1 John 2:22).

John warns against "any spirit" that refuses to confess the humanity of Jesus or that *Christ has come in the flesh*. There are two well-defined "spirits" that confront men in every age. One emanates from Satan and the other emanates from God. One confesses that *Christ has come in the flesh*, the other does not:

> Hereby know ye the *Spirit of God:* Every spirit that *confesseth that Jesus Christ is come in the flesh is of God:*
> And *every spirit* that *confesseth not* that Jesus Christ is *come in the flesh is not of God:* and this is that *spirit of Antichrist,* whereof ye have heard that it should come; and even *now already is it in the world* (1 John 4:2-3).

The "spirit" of Antichrist has been in the world for centuries, but the Antichrist himself is yet to appear. The Antichrist will appear in a body — in the form of a man *before* Christ returns for His Church. In short, the *Devil* will appear incarnate — all the forces of evil will be embodied in one man — the Antichrist. A number of names are attributed to the

Antichrist in the New Testament. He is called "the man of sin," the "son of perdition," the "wicked one," and others.

Since New Testament days the church has been confronted with the Antichrist "spirit" rather than the "person" of the Antichrist. This Antichrist "spirit" will prevail until the "person" of the Antichrist appears. The outstanding characteristic of both the spirit and person of the Antichrist is a deceptive temper which denies that *Christ has come in the flesh.* According to John's first epistle, this is the ultimate of the Antichrist "spirit" of his day and ours.

The decisive emphasis upon the humanity of Jesus in John's epistle is not the manger scene in Bethlehem, but a place called Calvary, outside of Jerusalem. The *flesh* and *blood* of Jesus are the only counter agents of the Antichrist "spirit." John says that the Antichrist "spirit" is associated with the "world" (1 John 4:3-5) and the only way to overcome the Antichrist "spirit" and the "world" is by faith in the atoning work of Christ (1 John 5:4-5). The Spirit of God who "confesses (and confirms to men) that *Christ has come in the flesh"* focuses attention on the death of Jesus:

> Who is he that *overcometh the world,* but he that believeth that Jesus is the Son of God?
> This is he that came by *water* and *blood,* even *Jesus Christ;* not by *water* only, but by *water* and *blood* (see John 19:34). And it is the *spirit that beareth witness,* because the *spirit is truth* (1 John 5:5-6). See also 2 John 7.

Paul also affirms that the "world," which is associated with the Antichrist "spirit," is overcome by faith in the cross of Jesus. The man who was given more insight into the death of Jesus than any other New Testament apostle refused to "glory" in anything except the cross of Christ. The Apostle Paul discovered something in the sacrifice of Jesus that severed him from the "world" in a twofold manner:

> God forbid that *I should glory,* save in the *cross of our Lord Jesus Christ,* by whom the *world is crucified unto me,* and *I unto the world* (Galatians 6:14).

To "glory" in some future earthly kingdom that dilutes or denies the *flesh* and *blood* of Christ for man's *present need* (especially the Jews) is part and parcel to the spirit of Antichrist. Any doctrine that encourages "hope" for the Jewish people apart from the present Gospel of Christ is Antichrist through and through. It is a denial that *Christ has come in the flesh* and that His *flesh* and *blood* are adequate for man's redemption *here* and *now* rather than in some uncertain millennial kingdom. Premillennialism, with its own brand of end-time doctrines, condones and encourages this Antichrist "spirit" among the Jewish people. The stage is being set by both the Jewish people and the premillennialists to play into the hands of the Antichrist.

The cross of Jesus is the watershed of all history and the primary role of the Holy Spirit is to establish and eternalize this truth. The coming of Christ in the flesh, which resulted in His death and resurrection, is the most important message of both the Old and New Testaments. The Lord used extraordinary measures to prevent any and all distractions from this glorious doctrine arising out of the Old Testament canon. *The Antichrist "spirit" can be imposed upon the Old Testament Scriptures as well as the New.* It is possible to take a monocled view of the Old Testament Scriptures and see nothing more than a "literal" Jewish kingdom from the beginning to the end. The spirit and concern of the Old Testament prophets, which in the main were Christ's sufferings and glory, can be replaced by a spirit of "literalism." It was the "sufferings of Christ and the glory that should follow" that every prophet of the old dispensation longed to see and not a national Jewish state. According to Peter, the prophets "enquired and searched diligently" of the salvation that was to come through Christ. This "enquiry" and "diligent searching" was prompted by the Holy Spirit:

> Of which salvation the *prophets* have *enquired* and *searched diligently,* who prophesied of the grace that should come to you:
> *Searching* what, or what manner of time the *spirit of Christ* which was *in them* did *signify* (make plain) when it *testified beforehand* the *suffering of Christ, and the glory* (resurrection) that should follow.
> Unto whom it was revealed, that not unto themselves (prophets), but unto us they did minister the things, which are now reported unto you by them that have preached the gospel unto you with the *Holy Ghost* sent down from heaven: which things the angels desire to look into (1 Peter 1:10-12).

The Holy Ghost that was in the Old Testament prophets is the *same* Holy Ghost that was "sent down from heaven" to instruct the New Testament Apostles and others concerning the "sufferings of Christ and the glory that should follow." It is difficult to believe that the same Holy Ghost would allow an emphasis on the "Land of Canaan" to overshadow the death and resurrection of Christ — even from the Old Testament

Scriptures. It goes without saying that the Holy Ghost did not allow such an emphasis to come from the pens of the New Testament writers. Andrew Murray is absolutely right when he says: "The highest work of the Spirit is to reveal the cross — because the cross is the wisdom and power of God."[1] From the same article Dr. Murray is quoted as saying, "The cross is the greatest of all mysteries ... the Spirit of God alone can reveal it."

As the Apostle Paul essayed to convince King Agrippa of the harmony between his message and that of the Old Testament prophets, he appealed to Christ's death and resurrection. The foremost message of Moses and the prophets was "That Christ should *suffer*, and that he should be the *first that should rise from the dead*, and should show light unto the people (Jews) and to the Gentiles" (Acts 26:23).

Jesus constricted "all that the *prophets wrote* concerning Him" to His sufferings, death, and resurrection and not a millennial kingdom. As Jesus approached His final hours in Jerusalem, He said to His disciples: "Behold, we go up to Jerusalem, and *all things* that are *written by the prophets* concerning the Son of man shall be accomplished. For he shall be delivered unto the Gentiles, and shall be mocked, and spitefully entreated, and spitted on: And they shall scourge him, and put him to death: and the third day he shall rise again" (Luke 18:31-33).

The above statement by our Lord is a hall of mirrors in the New Testament, i.e., it is repeated several times. The same words can be found in Jesus' remarks to the Emmaus disciples (Luke 24:25-26; 44-46). Peter echoes the same truth in his second sermon as recorded in the book of Acts (3:18). Similar language is used by Peter in his message to Cornelius (Acts 10:39-43). Paul goes over the same ground when he addresses the Jews in the synagogue at Antioch (Acts 13:26-29). In each of these passages "all that the prophets have written" is confined to Jesus' sufferings, death, and resurrection. How can this be? Because Jesus' sufferings, death, and resurrection is the axis on which *all* other Scriptures turn — it is the pulse of both Testaments.

The prophets of the Old Testament dispensation wrote about "many other things" apart from Jesus' passion and resurrection, but they are not worth the paper they are written on if they are isolated from

---

1. *Union Life* magazine, Glen Ellyn, Illinois, March/April, 1989, 8-10.

Calvary and the tomb. Whatever revelation the prophets received in their day pales in the light of Jesus' sufferings, death, and resurrection. The same principle would apply to the church. The church would fade into oblivion without the death and resurrection of Jesus. The death and resurrection of Christ was to be the most dominant feature for the prophets and not the so-called "millennial reign," the "church age," or any other doctrine. All doctrines, including the church, are subordinate to this one biblical fact.

According to Dr. Alexander Maclaren (1825-1910), a well-known English minister of Glascow, the sufferings and death of Jesus stand forth in the Old Testament and the New alike as the center of all. In conjunction with this statement he affirms: "And the same august Figure (Christ crucified) which loomed before the vision of prophets and shines through many a weary age, stands before us of this generation; ay! and will stand till the end of the world, as the centre, the pivot of human history, the Christ who has died for men. If your gospel is not that, you have yet to learn the deepest secret of His power." Dr. Maclaren concludes his thoughts on the sufferings and death of Jesus with this never to be forgotten statement: "Christ and His Cross are the substance of prophecy, the theme of the Gospel, the study of the angels."[2]

There is not the slightest hint in the New Testament that the Old Testament prophets were obsessed with an earthly kingdom as taught by the premillennialists. The New Testament writers show conclusively that the death and resurrection of Christ was far more important than any other message that came from the mouth of the prophets. According to Peter, the promise to Abraham was fulfilled in the death and resurrection of Christ and all the prophets of the old dispensation testified to this fact:

> But those things, which God before *had showed by the mouth of all his prophets,* that Christ should suffer, he hath *fulfilled* (Acts 3:18).

When Moses and Elijah, two renowned prophets of the Old Testament era, appeared with Jesus and the three disciples on the Mount of Transfiguration, they showed no interest in an earthly kingdom. The only thing they discussed was the *death* of Jesus (Luke 9:31). Moses, like the Apostle Paul, had discovered something in the sufferings of Jesus that exceeded any and all earthly glory. It is written of Moses that

---

2. Alexander Maclaren, *Exposition of Holy Scripture,* Epistle of St. Peter, George H. Doran Company, New York, pp. 48 and 51.

he "esteemed the *reproach of Christ* greater riches than the *treasures in Egypt*" (Hebrews 11:26).

Elijah was one of the most colorful prophets in the Old Testament Scriptures. No doubt his miracle-working power and his spectacular experiences with the Lord surpassed all other prophets. When this unique prophet appeared on the Mount of Transfiguration, along with Moses, the *death* of Jesus took precedence over every other topic that might have been discussed. If these two prophets considered any other subject matter while in the Mount, the Holy Spirit was not disposed to record it.

The Holy Spirit inspired the writers of the four Gospels (Matthew, Mark, Luke, and John) to give more attention to the crucifixion and resurrection of Jesus than any other single fact of His life. The last three or four chapters in each Gospel are devoted to the death and resurrection of Christ.

When the Holy Spirit was fresh upon the early disciples, the theme of their preaching was the death and resurrection of Jesus — the book of Acts demonstrates this truth throughout. The Apostle Paul vowed to know nothing among the Corinthian Church except "Jesus Christ and him crucified" (1 Corinthians 2:2). Many outstanding preachers of the past have followed the example of this great exponent of the Gospel. Charles H. Spurgeon declares that the "choicest saints in different ages of the world have studied most the passion of our Lord"[3]

Mr. Spurgeon's eminence as a preacher himself is traceable to his constant emphasis upon the cross of Christ. Mr. Spurgeon was never able to escape the revelation of Christ that was given him by the Holy Spirit at the time of his conversion — and that revelation consisted of Christ upon the cross. He describes his first encounter with Christ in these words:

> But I will tell you how I came to believe. Once upon a time, I was trying to make myself believe, and a voice whispered, "Vain man, vain man, if thou wouldst believe, come and see!" Then the Holy Spirit led me by the hand to a solitary place. And while I stood there, suddenly there appeared before me One upon His cross. I looked up, I then had no faith. I saw His eyes suffused with tears, and the blood still flowing; I saw His enemies about Him hunting Him to His grave; I marked His miseries unutterable; I heard the groaning which cannot

---

3. *The Treasury of the New Testament,* Zondervan, Grand Rapids, Michigan, Vol. II, 747.

be described; and as I looked up, He opened His eyes and said to me,
"The Son of man is come into the world to seek and to save that which
was lost." I clapped my hands, and said, "Jesus, I do believe, I must
believe what Thou hast said ..."[4]

Mr. Spurgeon's encounter with Christ and His cross did not end
with his conversion. The cross became his only glory throughout his
lifetime and ministry. Charles Spurgeon and some of the post-Reform-
ers saw a beauty and glory in the cross of Jesus that is practically
unknown in this age. Note carefully Mr. Spurgeon's language from his
sermon, "The Best Bread:"

> ... I find that I am never so comforted, strengthened, and sustained,
> as by deliberately considering Jesus Christ's precious death and
> atoning sacrifice. His sacrifice is the center of the circle, the focus of
> the light. There is a charm, a divine fascination, about His wounds.
>   O Sacred head, once wounded! O dear eyes, so red with weeping!
> O cheeks, with spittle all bestained! I could for ever gaze, admire and
> adore! There is no beauty in all the world like that which is seen in the
> countenance "more marred than that of any man." This one vision is
> enough for all eyes for all time. There is no sustenance to the heart like
> the sustenance that comes from His flesh and blood, given up in
> anguish and in death to work out our redemption.[5]

The language that is used in the above quote and elsewhere in Mr.
Spurgeon's messages to describe the cross of Jesus would be an offense
to most church-goers of this decade. Such language is almost unknown
and unheard of in the Christianity of America. I believe it would be safe
to say that it would not be welcomed in many seminary classrooms nor
among many ministers of the Gospel today.

In my opinion, the present generation is witnessing the most
shallow and immature Christian life style that has occurred since the
days of the Reformation. The theology of modern day Christianity has
only a faint resemblance to the theology of the Reforming fathers. I am
persuaded to believe that millennial teaching, which was popularized in
America by the Scofield Bible after the turn of the 19th century, has
made a significant contribution to this deteriorating process. An empha-

---

4. *The Treasury of the Old Testament,* Zondervan, Grand Rapids, Michigan, Vol. II, 225
5. 364

sis upon an earthly, Jewish millennium has by and large overshadowed
the cross of Jesus.

Satan always entrenches himself in the church when the flesh and
blood of Christ are not in the forefront of its theology. Dr. Andrew
Murray, in his book, *The Power of the Blood of Jesus,* concludes that it
was a rediscovery of the power of Jesus' blood by the Reformers that
broke Satan's hold on the Church of the 16th century. Dr. Murray writes:

> This (blood) was no less the secret power by which through the
> blessed Reformation, the mighty authority which Satan had gained in
> the church was broken down. "They overcame him by the blood of the
> Lamb." It was the discovery, and experience, and preaching of the
> glorious truth that we are "justified freely by his grace, through the
> redemption that is in Christ Jesus, whom God hath set forth to be a
> propitiation through *faith in His blood,"* that gave the Reformers such
> wonderful power, and such a glorious victory.[6] (Parenthesis and
> emphasis mine.)

From the same book and on the same page, Dr. Murray states that
the progress and effectiveness of the church will be in proportion to her
emphasis upon the cross of Christ:

> Since the days of the Reformation it is still apparent that in
> proportion as the blood of the Lamb is glorified in, the church is
> constantly inspired by a new life to obtain victory over deadness or
> error. Yes, even in the midst of the wildest heathen, where the throne
> of Satan has been undisturbed for thousands of years, this is still the
> weapon by which its power must be destroyed. The preaching of "the
> blood of the cross" as the reconciliation for the sin of the world, and
> the ground of God's free, forgiving love, is the power by which the
> most darkened heart is opened and softened, and from being a
> dwelling place of Satan is changed into a temple of the Most High.

The community of faith will never know the "deep things of God"
(1 Corinthians 2:10) until there is a renewed interest in the death and
resurrection of Christ. Paul's statement on the "deep things of God" is
given in conjunction with the Spirit of God and the cross of Christ (1
Corinthians 1 and 2). It is in the same context that the Apostle writes: "…
Eye hath not seen, nor ear heard, neither have entered into the heart of
man, the things which God hath prepared for them that love him. But

---

6. Andrew Murray, *The Power of the Blood of Jesus,* Hunt Barnard & Co., Ltd., London
    and Aylesbury, 1936, 111

God hath revealed them unto us by his Spirit; for the Spirit searcheth all things, yea, the deep things of God" (1 Corinthians 2:9-10). A rediscovery of "Christ crucified" will become an obsession that will dispel a carnal, worldly kingdom (1 Corinthians 2:2; Galatians 6:14).

There is a relationship between the cross of Jesus and the Holy Spirit in the book of Galatians that should be of deep concern to every New Testament believer. The Galatian Church had been given a very graphic picture of "Christ crucified" at its inception (Galatians 3;1). It was in conjunction with "Christ crucified" that the Galatians had received the Holy Spirit (Galatians 3:2-5). But this vivid presentation of Christ crucified had become distorted or totally eclipsed by the Judaizers of that day. The Judaizers insisted upon the rite of circumcision and other aspects of the Mosaic law as a means of sharing in the promise to Abraham. For this reason, many of the Galatians were "glorying" in the shadows of the Old Testament era, rather than in the One who fulfilled those shadows. Paul seems to imply that a return to "Christ crucified" would be the answer to all of their foolish behavior (Galatians 3:1). We are justified in drawing such a conclusion as this because the Apostle said of himself: "God forbid that I should glory, save in the cross of our Lord Jesus Christ, etc." (Galatians 6:14). It is important to understand that Paul's statement was made several years *after* his Damascus road conversion. This affirmation by the Apostle shows conclusively that the cross or blood of Jesus is to be the believer's triumph and glory throughout his lifetime (Revelation 12:11).

The "priesthood" of Jesus, which is highlighted in the book of Hebrews, was made possible by the sacrifice of Jesus. The "blood of Jesus" and the "veil of his flesh" continue to be man's only access into the "holy place" in the heavenly tabernacle (Hebrews 10:19-20). Man's participation in the "more perfect tabernacle" is synonymous with God's "rest" that is discussed in great detail in the third and fourth chapters of Hebrews. The Holy Ghost is still inviting men to share in that eternal "rest" (Hebrews 3:7).

The Lord purposed that the flesh and blood of Jesus be the central feature in the church until He returns — the Lord's Supper was given to this end (1 Corinthians 11:26). The hymns of the church have made a great contribution toward this goal. Most of the evangelical songs of the church, either directly or indirectly, magnify the cross of Calvary. Dare we deny the Holy Spirit's role in the inspiration and preservation of so many wonderful hymns? The witness of the church is always more effective when the cross of Jesus is the centerpiece of its message and worship. Any deflection from the flesh and blood of Jesus is no less than the "spirit" of Antichrist.

If the flesh and blood of Jesus can be translated into the "Lamb of God," then His humanity covers the whole spectrum of eternity — and the Holy Spirit is coupled with this truth at every turn in the life of our Lord — His pre-Incarnation as well as His Incarnation. The link between the blood of Jesus and the Holy Spirit was in the foreknowledge of God from the beginning. Peter describes the first century believers with these words: "Elect according to the fore-knowledge of God the Father, through sanctification of the Spirit, unto obedience and sprinkling of the blood of Jesus Christ" (1 Peter 1:2). The millenarians are invited to find an earthly kingdom in association with the "foreknowledge of God" as described by Peter (or anywhere else in Scripture). The "elect," "obedience," "sanctification of the Spirit," and the "sprinkling of the blood of Christ" are in perfect agreement with this entire work.

The Holy Spirit's relationship to Jesus as the "Lamb of God" can be seen throughout the New Testament. The foreknowledge of God became a tangible reality in the conception of Jesus by the Holy Spirit (Matthew 1:20) — this resulted in His *humanity* or His *flesh* and *blood*. After John the Baptist announced Jesus as the "Lamb of God," the Holy Spirit descended upon Him in the form of a dove and remained upon Him (John 1:29-33). The Holy Spirit could not be given to the first disciples until the flesh and blood of Jesus became an atonement for man's sin (John 7:37-39). In the book of Revelation, the "slain Lamb" is associated with the *"seven Spirits of God* that are sent forth into all the earth" (Revelation 5:6).

The name "Lamb" is used twenty-eight times in the book of Revelation to speak of Christ. As John unfurls the curtains of eternity, we are shown an infinite number of people proclaiming with a loud voice: "Worthy is the *Lamb that was slain* to receive power, and riches, and wisdom, and strength, and honor, and glory, and blessing" (Revelation 5:12). The "song of Moses and the *song of the Lamb"* will be the theme song of heaven forever. Neither time nor eternity can change Christ's role as the "Slain Lamb."

Any discussion on the relationship of the Holy Spirit and the flesh and blood of Jesus would be remiss without calling attention to the warnings that are found in the ninth and tenth chapters of the book of Hebrews on the subject. This portion of Scripture confronts mankind with an awesome responsibility regarding the two concepts. It was through the Eternal Spirit that Christ offered Himself and His blood for the sins of the world (Hebrews 9:14). Therefore a contemptuous act or word against the blood of the covenant is a contemptuous act or word against the Holy Spirit. The warning of the writer runs like this: If the people living under Moses and the prophets were severely punished for their disrespect of the old covenant, "Of how much sorer punishment, suppose ye, shall he be thought worthy, who hath trodden under foot the Son of God, and hath counted the blood of the covenant, wherewith he was sanctified, an unholy thing, and hath done despite unto the Spirit of Grace" (Hebrews 10:29). To despise the blood of Jesus is to despise the Holy Spirit.

The book of Hebrews is filled with dreadful warnings — and most of them are associated with the sacrifice of Jesus. In the light of Jesus' sacrifice, the "end of the world" has already come (Hebrews 9:26); See also 1 Corinthians 10:11; 1 Peter 4:7). Jesus' atoning death will never be repeated (Hebrews 9:25) and men will search in vain for another offering for their sins (Hebrews 10:26). From God's perspective, the clock that ticked before and during the hours of Jesus' death has stopped — the provision for man's salvation is accomplished — the next move belongs to man. When Jesus appears the second time, He will appear "without sin unto salvation" (Hebrews 9:28). In every age and generation, the powers of darkness insist upon "another Christ," "another Gospel," and "another spirit," (2 Corinthians 11:4) — this is the "spirit of Antichrist."

The evidence is overwhelmingly clear. The coming of Christ in the flesh, the shedding of His blood for the sins of the world, and His glorious resurrection are the nucleuses of both the Old and New Testaments. While the Holy Spirit of God is trying to call men's attention to the flesh and blood of Jesus, the Antichrist "spirit" is counteracting and opposing His efforts on every hand.

The Jewish people are among the greatest perpetrators of the Antichrist "spirit" since New Testament days. Their adamant denial of Christ means that they do not believe that Christ has come in the flesh. Those who have any kind of religious inclinations are looking for "another messiah" to appear. The Wailing Wall in Jerusalem is only one witness to this fact. Since the Jews are looking for "another messiah" to appear, they will be very gullible for the Antichrist of the future (John 5:43-44). They will be a prime target for the "signs and wonders" of the "man of sin" (2 Thessalonians 2:9-10). In fact, this false messiah, the Antichrist, may well be one of their own — he may be of Jewish descent.

Men have always been infatuated with "another Jesus," "another spirit," and "another gospel" (2 Corinthians 11:4). Paul uses some very strong language to counteract this evil in the Galatian Church. The Galatian Christians were being seduced by a Jewish faction within and without their ranks. The Apostle pronounced a "curse" upon anyone who dared preach "any other gospel" than he had preached — including an "angel from heaven:"

> But though we, or an *angel from heaven,* preach *any other gospel* unto you than that which *we have preached* unto you, *let him be accursed* (Galatians 1:8).

This anathema is repeated a second time in verse nine by the Apostle and the Phillips translation spares no words to describe the seriousness of replacing the New Testament Gospel for "another:"

> You have heard me say it before, and now I put it down in *black* and *white* — may any body who preaches *any other gospel* than the one you have *already heard be a damned soul!* (Galatians 1:9).

Any "gospel" of the *past* or any "gospel" of the *future* that distracts from the *present* Gospel is "another gospel." The present Gospel is the *only* Gospel that God has provided for the redemption of mankind. The "gospel" or "good news" that men are to believe and proclaim is the death and resurrection of Christ (1 Corinthians 15:1-4) and not a millennial reign in the Land of Canaan.

Substitutes for Christ's flesh and blood can be seen in every age and generation — including twentieth century America. The Antichrist "spirit" has become more prevalent in the past two decades in this country than ever before. Materialism and humanism, which have weakened the testimony and influence of the church, have allowed Satanic activities to flourish in America in a way that is unique. Human and animal sacrifices, which have their origin in Satan worship, are only tokens of man's attempt to replace the flesh and blood of Jesus. The Antichrist "spirit" is literally having a masquerade ball in this country. Phantoms of the "Dark Ages" are already on the horizon. The moral and ethical conditions that once characterized this nation are rapidly being replaced by an era of decadence. Darkened minds can only bring more chaos and corruption — no option is left. Intellectual paganism is just as devastating to society as any other type of paganism — and perhaps more so.

Paul's description of the heathen world (Romans 1:22-23) is readily discerned in many of the movies, animated cartoons, and books that come from a people who have no fear of God. All kinds of grotesque creatures can be seen in the entertainment world of today. The human body that came from the hands of a wise Creator is being distorted in a thousand and one ways — huge, bulged eyes, exaggerated noses, overdrawn mouths, gruesome ears, bizarre limbs and torsos, etc. A composite of man, beasts, and birds is characteristic of heathenism and arises out of a depraved mind. The human anatomy is being disgraced in a manner that brings to mind the caricatures and idols of Egypt, India, Greece, Rome, and many other unenlightened nations of the past. The weird musical beats of this age and the barbarian sensual dances are an echo of the tribal dances of Africa, Borneo, and other primitive countries of the past and present. Paul describes heathenism in every age when he writes: "Professing themselves to be wise, they became fools, and changed the *glory of the uncorruptible God* into an *image made like to corruptible man*, and to *birds*, and *fourfooted beasts*, and *creeping things*" (Romans 1:22-23). The only guarantee of a civilized society is the Gospel (flesh and blood) of Jesus Christ.

The flesh and blood of Christ that was offered up for the sins of the world (Jew and Gentile) must continue to be the principle message of the church. The cross of Jesus that spans time and eternity was the most striking and conclusive revelation of God that man *has ever* received or *ever will* receive in this present world order. The redemption and restoration of *all things* depends upon this one act of God (Colossians 1:20). A denial of this stupendous, historical event is the ultimate of the "Antichrist spirit."

From the beginning, Satan has sought to imitate the works and person of God. The incarnation of Satan will be his final scheme to be "like God." This is why Satan wishes to *deny that Christ has come in the flesh* — he wants to reserve this climactic mimicry for himself. This grand finale will be characterized by many signs and wonders and thousands of people will be deceived. The Apostle Paul gives a very vivid description of the Antichrist, his works and overthrow, in his second epistle to the Thessalonians:

> Let no man deceive you by any means: for *that day* (second coming

of Christ) *shall not come,* except there come a *falling away first,* and *that man of sin be revealed,* the *son of perdition;*

Who opposeth and exalteth himself above all that is called God, or that is worshipped; so that he *as God* sitteth in the temple of God, showing himself that *he is God.*

Remember ye not, that, when I was yet with you, I told you these things?

And now ye know what withholdeth that he might be *revealed in his time* (the Antichrist).

For the mystery of iniquity doth already work: only he who now letteth will let, until he be taken out of the way.

And then *shall that wicked one be revealed,* whom the Lord shall consume with the spirit of his mouth, and shall *destroy* with the brightness of his coming:

Even him (Antichrist) whose *coming is after the working of Satan* with *all power and signs and lying wonders.*

And with *all deceivableness* of unrighteousness in them that perish; because they receive not the love of the truth, that they might be saved.

And for this cause *God shall send them strong delusions,* that they should believe a lie:

That they *all might be damned* who believe not the truth, but had pleasure in unrighteousness (2 Thessalonians 2:3-12).

The premillennialists and the Jewish people share a common error relative to the future. Both foresee, for the Jews, a utopian period *before* the consummation of all things. The Jewish people are anxious for "another messiah" and the futurists are anticipating "another appearance" of *the* Messiah *after* the church is raptured. The premillennialists and the Jewish people are standing in their own light. The Jews wait in vain for "another messiah" and the futurists wait in vain for "another appearance" of Christ *after* He returns for His church.

The premillennialists teach *two appearances* of Christ in their eschatology. These two appearances are known as the "rapture" and the "revelation." The "rapture" will be secret— the church will be taken out of the world unbeknown to the rest of mankind (at least, at the moment of the rapture). After the rapture of the church, the Antichrist will appear to reign and usher in the Great Tribulation period which will last for seven years. The seven years' rule of the Antichrist will be characterized by a time of great deception and persecution. The Battle of Armageddon will follow in the wake of the Great Tribulation period, at which time

Christ will return with His saints (in their glorified bodies) and destroy the Antichrist. This second appearance of Christ is called the "revelation" — "every eye shall see Him" — hence, the term "revelation." These events will be followed by the millennial reign with Jewish predominance.

The above details on end-time events represent premillennial views in a nutshell. However, there are some differences of opinion within their own ranks. It is very obvious that the millenarians teach a *second chance* for those who are living *after* the church is raptured, especially for the Jews. This is contrary to the entire tone of Scripture relative to the Second Coming of Christ.

A good deal of premillennial "doctrine" must be held in limbo until the church is taken out of the world. The rapture of the church is just the beginning of the celebration period for the futurists. Nothing of significance has happened or is happening in the church age — the "fireworks" will not begin until the church is caught up and the first stage of the tribulation period is set in motion. C. I. Scofield contends that the "enormous majority of earth's inhabitants will be saved" *after* Jesus returns for His church (p. 977).

Walter K. Price, in his book, *The Coming Antichrist,* believes that the tribulation period will result in more converts than all the evangelical efforts of the past, from the first century to the present hour. While commenting on Revelation 7:9-13, he states:

> One hundred forty-four thousand Jews saved, plus a multitude which no man can number out of all the nations who have been washed in the blood of the Lamb! And all this within the *limits of the tribulation period.* What a revival! Neither Pentecost in the first century, nor the Reformation on the Continent, nor the evangelical revival in England, nor the Great Awakening in the Colonies, could match this spiritual awakening. Neither Luther, Wesley, Whitfield, Finney, Moody, Sunday, nor Billy Graham — individually or collectively — could muster such statistics as these. The world is yet in store for its greatest spiritual revival in which vast multitudes, beyond comprehension, will be saved.[7] (All emphasis mine.)

Mr. Price does not believe that the tribulation saints (so-called) will be regenerated *inwardly* by the Holy Spirit (p. 155), and yet he states that

---

7. Walter K. Price, *The Coming Antichrist,* Moody Press, Chicago, 1976, 158-159.

they will be "washed in the blood of the Lamb." According to Mr. Price, the work of the Holy Spirit (during the tribulation period) will be similar to that of the Old Testament dispensation — it will be an *outward* work rather than an *inward* work (pp. 148-149). For centuries, the evangelical church has maintained that the saints of God are "washed in the blood of the Lamb" by the *inward* work of the Holy Spirit in the act of regeneration (Revelation 1:5) — but Mr. Price would change all of this. As usual, he retreats to the Old Testament for his confirmation. Why shouldn't he? The premillennialists are very gifted in turning the pages of history backward — they are always backtracking — they are forever imposing ancient religious customs on us instead of the "new and living way" (Hebrews 10:20). The Scriptures teach that the "blood" and "Spirit" are in perfect agreement — they are actually one (1 John 5:6-8). In other words, it is impossible to be "washed in the blood of the Lamb" without the *inward* work of the Holy Spirit (Hebrews 9:14).

In the light of what has already been written on the millennium controversy, it would be almost anticlimactic to spend time and space refuting the *two appearances* of Christ as taught by the futurists. The distinction that has been made between the "rapture" and "revelation" by the millenarians is just another method of manipulating the Scriptures to their own advantage. The "rapture" and "revelation" are simultaneous events that occur when the Lord returns for His church.

It is axiomatic that a house begun on a faulty foundation will be followed by flaws in its superstructure. This is the whole story of premillennialism. There are "weak spots" and "cracks" to be found throughout its theological structure. Premillennial views on the Antichrist are just more defects in their doctrinal framework. Most futurists believe in the appearance of a "personal" Antichrist, but it is a matter of *when* (or the *time*) he will appear.

If we follow Paul's order of events on the reign of the Antichrist, we must conclude that the Antichrist will appear *before* the rapture of the church and the conflagration of all things. The precise details of Christ's return are set forth in the first chapter of Second Thessalonians, but there is no specific *date* or *time* given as to when Christ will return, because no one "knows the hour or the day" of His appearing (Mark 13:32). However, Paul mentions two very significant end-time events in the second chapter that should alert the church as to the nearness of His coming: (1) there must be a "falling away" of the church, and (2) there must be the "revelation of the man of sin" or the Antichrist (2

Thessalonians 2:3). The Thessalonians must not expect the particulars of chapter one until *after* the "falling away" and the "appearance of the Antichrist." The warning that Paul gives, relative to the coming of Christ, is still valid:

> Let no man deceive you by any means: for that day (return of Christ) *shall not come,* except there come a *falling away first,* and *that man of sin be revealed, the son of perdition* (2 Thessalonians 2:3).

The imminent return of Christ is not taught in the New Testament. Certain events must come to pass *before* He returns for His elect and one of those events is the appearance of the Antichrist. The unbelieving Jews, who are living at the appearance of the Antichrist, will be subject to his diabolical tactics. If they continue to *deny that Christ has come in the flesh,* and if they insist upon *another messiah* to come, they will be fertile soil for the most deceptive period in the history of mankind. The "fireworks" will begin at the appearance of Christ, but it will not be with a Jewish millennium. Paul tells us exactly what will happen after the church is raptured: "…the Lord Jesus shall be revealed from heaven with his mighty angels, *in flaming fire* taking vengeance on them that know not God, and that obey not the gospel of our Lord Jesus Christ: Who shall be punished with everlasting destruction from the presence of the Lord, and from the glory of His power" (2 Thessalonians 1:7b-9).

The role of the Antichrist will be one of imitating Christ and His church. The "falling away" of the true church will produce a vacuum for an apostate church over which the Antichrist will be the head. This, in turn, will create a climate for the "man of sin" to

> … exalt himself above all that is called God, or that is worshipped; so that *he as God sitteth in the temple of God,* showing himself that *he is God* (2 Thessalonians 2:4).

Paul is describing the most arrogant and forceful impersonation of God that will ever occur in the history of the world. The "temple" in which the Antichrist sits will be a fabrication of the temple of God and not the true temple. It would be impossible for the Antichrist to "sit in the temple of God." God does not dwell in temples made with hands (Acts 7:48). The Scriptures teach that Jesus is the "temple of God" (John 2:21) and so is His true church (2 Corinthians 6:16). The "temple" in which the Antichrist "sits" will probably be the harlot church which is antithetical to the body of Christ.

The tactics of the Antichrist will be in total agreement with man's religious, physical, and mental make-up. Man's limitations, both physical and mental, demand a *supreme being* who is able to assist him in coping with any and all adverse circumstances. However, man's religious quests are never equal to his physical and mental pursuits. Material and intellectual attainments have always taken precedence over religious endeavors. This opens the door for any religious appeal that Satan may offer, regardless of its nature. Man has always welcomed a counterfeit religion that will leave him in his sin.

Israel's history is positive proof of the above truth. The Jews were faced with many problems and needs throughout their history — both as a nation and as individuals — but generally speaking, they looked to other sources for their hope and confidence, instead of to God. A wooden or metal idol, which they could manipulate at their discretion, was more conducive to their carnal nature than obedience to God's Word. "Circumcision in the flesh," performed by the hands of men, was far less demanding in moral and ethical terms, than "circumcision of the heart." When true faith is rejected, men must settle for something less than God.

Redemptive faith places God first — material and mental needs are secondary. *Satan always reverses this order.* Jesus said: "Seek ye *first* the kingdom of God and his righteousness; and *all these things* (material things) shall be added unto you" (Matthew 6:33). Moses and the prophets taught the same thing. The first commandment insists that we "love God with all the *mind.*" Isaiah wrote: "Thou wilt keep him in perfect peace, whose *mind is stayed on thee*" (26:3). The Antichrist will fulfill man's religious, physical, and mental needs to the letter. Man will be able to satisfy his carnal desires without forsaking his sin. In other words, he can have his cake and eat it too.

It is commonly believed that the reign of the Antichrist will be almost, if not altogether, religious in nature. However, the Scriptures reveal that the rule of the Antichrist will be both religious and political. The possibility of such religious and political control can be seen from the history of the Roman Catholic Church. The Romanish church is as much political as it is religious. It has had world dominance in view for many centuries. The Roman Catholic Church *has* controlled and *will* control any country where its influence is not restrained. During the Middle Ages the papacy had many of the kings and potentates eating out of its hand. When the "man of sin" appears, he will be able to accomplish

this and more. It was the political and religious influence of the Roman
Catholic Church that caused most of the Reformers to regard it as *the*
Antichrist.

The papal system of the Roman Catholic Church is *not* the Antichrist per se. All false religious groups that have appeared over the
centuries (regardless of their nature) can be linked to the Antichrist
"spirit." The Antichrist "spirit" has many faces but it is always the "same
spirit." The religious and political power of the Roman Catholic Church
in the past centuries is only a token of the "personal" reign of the
Antichrist. The "man of sin" will be able to control both the religious and
political scene of his day. This, in turn, will dominate the economic
climate as well.

This religious and political combination can be seen in several
countries today — especially in the Middle East. Iran and Iraq are only
two examples. However, the religious and political rule of the Antichrist
will be universal in nature.

The Antichrist will be characterized by a materialistic emphasis
that will dupe his subjects. The "world and the things of the world,"
which John discourages in his first epistle, will be accentuated to their
ultimate during the time of the Antichrist. Satan will extol the very
things that the Jewish people anticipate in a messiah. The "loaves and
fishes" that Jesus provided in His day were welcomed by the Jews, but
these were only "cornhusk" of the pigsty compared to His *flesh* and
blood that men were to eat (John 6:53-58). Jesus, with His signs and
wonders, would have fulfilled the Jewish dream of an earthly kingdom
to the letter had He avoided His cross. But His death and resurrection
were to be the ultimate sign and proof of His Messiahship (Matthew
12:39-40).

There are three major agencies that Satan uses in every age to
achieve His purpose. These consist of: (1) a distortion of the Scriptures,
(2) man's depraved nature — or the flesh, and (3) the "world and the
things of the world." All of these spell doom for the Incarnation of
Christ. These were the primary instruments of the Antichrist "spirit" in
John's day and will be until the appearance of the "man of sin." The only
difference in the Antichrist "spirit" and the rule of the "person" of the
Antichrist will be a greater and more dramatic exploitation of these three
agencies.

Men must never forget that Satan is described in Scripture as the
"god (prince) of this world" (2 Corinthians 4:4; John 14:30) and the

"prince and power of the air" (Ephesians 2:2). It is a perverted view of the "world and the things of the world" that Satan uses to entice and seduce men to worship and serve him. The Antichrist "spirit" seeks to impose upon man a sense of "security" and "pride" that will blind his eyes to the true source and nature of the creation (Romans 1:18-32). All of this translates into loving and serving the creation more than the Creator. Satan emptied his quiver of arrows on Jesus when he offered Him "all the kingdoms of the world, and the glory of them" if He would worship him. Man's resistance to the "world and the things of the world" is not as great as that of our Lord.

The "world and the things of the world" are not all that man and Satan esteem them to be. According to Paul, the present creation has been subjected to "vanity" and is in the "bondage of corruption" (Romans 8:20-21). The Greek word for "vanity" *(mataiotes)* literally means: *inutility* or *depravity.* The Greek word *mataiotes* is derived from another Greek word *(mataios)* which means: *empty, profitless,* or *specifically an idol (Strong's Greek Lexicon).* By using the word "vanity," Paul says that the "world and the things of the world" are not all they appear to be and it is the work of Satan to contribute to this falsification. This "vanity" of the "world and the things of the world" comes to full fruition in the vain, false woman in the book of Revelation known as Babylon, or the *Great Whore.*

Let us say parenthetically that we cannot deal with the Antichrist "spirit" and "person" without a consideration of Babylon and its ruin. The link between the Antichrist and the "world and the things of the world" becomes full blown in the closing chapters of Revelation. Babylon represents man's religious and commercial aggrandizements in every age that excludes the true and living God. A few men fulfill their goals realistically in the symbol of Babylon — they gain great wealth and heap treasures upon themselves. But the masses realize their Babylon in an autistic manner; they only dream of Babylon. But whether real or imaginary Christ and His Word have no place in their lives.

Paul also states that the present creation is in the "bondage of corruption" (Romans 8:21). The Greek word *(phthora)* that is used to describe the corrupt state of the creation is used elsewhere to describe the corrupt condition of the human body (1 Corinthians 15:42). The creation, like the human body, is in a chaotic state due to the fall of man. The creation is in a state of flux — everything is subject to erosion, rust, and decay. The heat, rain, cold, and air take their toll on the hardest steel and the most adamant stone. According to Paul, the creation will remain in the "bondage of corruption" until the bodies of the saints are changed.

"Corruption" and "incorruption" have nothing in common — this is true regarding the creation as well as the human body (1 Corinthians 15:50). Redeemed bodies belong to a redeemed creation — the two complement each other. Saints, in their redeemed or glorified bodies, living in an unredeemed creation during the so-called millennial reign as the futurists teach, is without Scriptural grounds. The redemption of both the creation and the body is the hope of the Christian faith.

An appeal to a worldly kingdom that would appease man's carnal nature is antithetical to the whole revelation of Scripture. A "love of the world and the things of the world," which John links with the Antichrist "spirit," is discouraged in both the Old and New Testaments. As we have already shown, the entire wilderness experience under Moses was meant to wean the Israelites from depending upon the "world and the things of the world" per se. They were to learn of a power and life above and apart from this present world order. Bread alone was not sufficient for their ultimate well-being. Even in the Land of Canaan, the "world and the things of the world" were to be held with a loose hand. This mentality was to be maintained throughout the Old Testament era. An earthly kingdom that would appeal to the "lusts of the eyes and pride of life" runs counter to everything that is written by the prophets and the New Testament Apostles.

The "world and the things of the world" are oftentimes described in the Scriptures by the term "riches." We can readily discern the "vanity" and "corruption" (decay) of wealth from those who wrote the New Testament. Jesus speaks of the *deceitfulness of riches* that choke the Word of God (Matthew 13:22). Paul warns about trusting in *uncertain riches* (1 Timothy 6:17). James describes the precariousness of wealth in these words: "… your *riches are corrupted,* and your *garments are moth-eaten,* your *gold* and *silver* is *cankered;* and the *rust* of these will be a witness against you, etc." (James 5:2-3b).

From the Pentateuch to the book of Revelation, we are taught that man's mind and heart is to be occupied with a "world to come" (Hebrews 6:5), rather than the present creation. Man's attention is to be drawn toward that which is "real" and "permanent," and not to that which is subject to "decay" and "destruction." Jesus' life and words should be a constant reminder of this fact:

> Lay not up for yourselves *treasures upon the earth,* where *moth* and *rust* doth *corrupt,* and where thieves break through and steal:
> But lay up for yourselves *treasures in heaven,* where neither *moth* nor *rust* doth *corrupt,* and where thieves do not break through nor steal (Matthew 6:19-20).

Can we ignore the words of Jesus without closing our eyes to a very large block of Scripture on the same subject? Rational men are constrained to accept the intelligible language of Paul as he encourages the Colossian church to follow the same truth that Jesus taught:

> ... seek those things which are *above,* where Christ sitteth on the right hand of God.
> Set your *affection on things above, not on things of the earth* (Colossians 3:1-2).

Enough has been written to prove conclusively that the "world and the things of the world" are "vain" and "corruptible." Enlightened minds and hearts are aware of this truth and turn their thoughts and interests to "things above." The death and resurrection of Christ makes all of this possible. God's purpose in Christ was to "reconcile *all things* unto Himself." This includes both man and the creation. The *"blood* of His cross" and the *"body* of His *flesh"* are commensurate with a redeemed society and a redeemed creation (Colossians 1:20-22), and a *denial* of either is the "spirit" of Antichrist. An earthly kingdom that would gratify man's carnal nature is incongruent with everything that is taught in Scripture.

The "world and the things of the world" can also be summed up in the phrase, "love of money," which is the *root* of all evil (1 Timothy 6:10). Almost everything in this world has a monetary value in one form or another and can be considered as "money." If the "love of money is the *root of all evil,"* then it is very certain that Satan will use it as one of his chief weapons. According to the Scriptures, the "love of money" which begins with a single *root* can be divided into two major branches — (1) the secular commercial world, and (2) the false religious world. Both have their beginning and ending in the symbol of Babylon.

Man has used everything from the floors of the ocean to the constellations of the heavens to gain money. The horoscope that appears each day in almost every newspaper in this nation is not new. Astrology, which consists of studying the movements of the stars, moon, and sun, is almost as old as mankind. Men use such voodoo to "make money."

False prophets and all pseudo-religionists have their origin and perpetuity in the "love of money." We sometimes hear and read of a "scarlet thread" that is woven throughout the Bible and this scarlet thread is symbolic of the blood of Christ. There is also a "golden thread" woven throughout the Scriptures and it is symbolic of man's "love for money." The spirit of Baalim, the false prophet who "loved the *wages of unrighteousness* (or money), emerges in every age (2 Peter 2:15; Micah 3:11; Jeremiah 6:13). Fortunetelling, witchcraft, and divination continue to appear in every age of history because of man's "love for money" (Acts 16:16-19). Judas, whom Satan entered, and who is called the "son of perdition" (the same name ascribed to the Antichrist), is not the only person who has sold Christ for "thirty pieces of silver." Some of the religious "success cult" of our day have a tinge of the Antichrist "spirit."

The idea of carnal man living and reigning in a carnal kingdom is not new. It started with the tower of Babel in the book of Genesis and has its ultimate expression and termination in the symbol of Babylon that is climaxed in the book of Revelation. Babylon is not a "tinsel town" composed of hanging gardens, colorful tapestries, marble stones, rare wood, and precious metals. Babylon represents *people* of all ages who have been enticed by Satan through the "world and the things of the world." It is people who have given their allegiance and worship to him in exchange for "gold, and silver, and precious stones, and of pearls, and fine linen, and purple, and silk, and scarlet, and all thyine wood, and all manner vessels of ivory, and all manner vessels of most precious wood, and of brass, and iron, and marble" (Revelation 18:12). It is *people* who esteem the creation more highly than the Creator.

Babylon is a vain, false woman—decked with all the paraphernalia and glitter that Satan can bestow upon her. Babylon is the counterpart of the New Jerusalem, the wife of the Lamb, who is "arrayed in fine linen, clean and white: for the fine linen is the righteousness of saints" (Revelation 19:8). Babylon is the *Great Whore* seated upon the "beast" who derives his power and authority from the Great Red Dragon or Satan (Revelation 13:3-4). The Antichrist "spirit" from the beginning to the end is to attract man's attention to the "world and the things of the world" rather than to Christ and a "world to come."

The Scriptures are replete with men and nations who have "traded" their souls for the "world and the things of the world." From Esau, who sold his birthright for one morsel of meat (Hebrews 12:16), to the wealthy farmer whose barns were enlarged to contain his yield (Luke 12:16-20), men have exchanged their souls for the "world and the things of the world." According to our Lord, the "whole world" is an inferior price for the soul of man. Three of the Gospels (Matthew, Mark, and Luke) quote Jesus as saying: "For what shall it *profit* a man, if he shall *gain the whole world,* and *lose his own soul?* Or what shall a man give in *exchange* for his soul?"

Marketplace terms are oftentimes used in the Scripture to describe man's relationship to God. Such words as "purchase," "exchange," "redemption," and the phrase, "bought with a price," are used to reflect ownership and servitude. However, Peter assures us that those who are in Christ are "not redeemed with *corruptible* things, as *silver* and *gold* ... but with the *precious blood of Christ,* as a lamb without blemish and without spot" (1 Peter 1:18-19). Man's relationship to God, whether right or wrong, is reflected in *who* or *what* he serves. Jesus said: "Ye cannot serve *God* and *Mammon"* (Luke 16:13).

For men to love and serve that which is corrupt and perishable, instead of the Everlasting God, is the act of a fool (Luke 12:20). The "Land of Canaan," which the millenarians hold so dear, is a part of the "world and the things of the world." In essence, it is corrupt and perishable. If all the gold and oil of the world were concentrated in Palestine, it would have no more value than the sand dunes of the Sahara desert — and yet, this is what the futurists want to offer the Jews for an inheritance. Is it right and proper for men to anticipate that which is subject to decay, and that God (for this very reason) will one day destroy? Is it in harmony with the Scripture to desire that which God has discouraged from the beginning?

If God seeks to dispel a "love for the world and the things of the world" from mankind today, why would He offer such things to the Jews in the future? It is inconsistent with God's purpose to redeem and deliver man from the "world and the things of the world" and yet plan for a worldly kingdom as the futurists teach.

The reason that men overestimate the present world order is because they know nothing of a "world to come." The human eye has never seen or the human ear ever heard of "the things that God has prepared for them that love Him" (1 Corinthians 2:9). This is off limits to every man — only the Holy Spirit is able to reveal such things to mankind (1 Corinthians 2:10). The "sense man" has never and will never be able to attain unto such knowledge by and of himself. When the "world and the things of the world" are seen in the light of the "world to come," they fade into oblivion. When Jesus becomes the focal point of our attention, we must agree with Helen H. Lemmel, as she writes: "Turn your eyes upon Jesus, look full in His wonderful face, And *the things of earth* will *grow strangely dim* in the light of His glory and grace."

However, such a comparison may be a violation of Scripture. When writing about "spiritual" and "non-spiritual" things, Paul affirms that we are to "compare spiritual things with spiritual" (1 Corinthians 2:13). The word order for this phrase in the Greek is literally: "With spiritual things spiritual things comparing." When the English word "comparing" is fully developed in the Greek, it means that "spiritual things" are to be associated with and understood with "spiritual things" and never "non-spiritual." "Non-spiritual" things may serve as "aids" in understanding "spiritual things," but they can never be in union with each other. Jesus said that the Kingdom of Heaven is "like" a grain of mustard seed, but it can *never be a mustard seed* (Mark 4:31). These are two *distinct* and *separate* realms — they never mix or blend. The Psalmist was aware of this truth many centuries before Christ came in the flesh. David writes: "In thy (God's) *light* shall we see *light*" (Psalm 36:9b). Only *light* can shed and increase light. It is possible to substitute the word "Spirit" for "light" in this Psalm and arrive at the same conclusion: "In thy *Spirit* shall we see *Spirit.*" Spiritual things are known and enlarged by the Spirit of God and by no other means.

It is very likely that the men who drafted the Nicene Creed in 325 A.D. had the same principle in mind when they described Jesus as "… one Lord … the only Son of God, eternally begotten of the Father, God from God, *Light from Light,* true God from true God … for us and for our salvation He came down from heaven." Jesus came from "Light" — He was "Light" — and He returned to "Light." God's first and foremost objective is to bring His elect into the same substance and heavenly environment.

Those who are "spiritual-minded" are confronted with "two worlds" and they must be able to differentiate between the two. A distinction between the two realms was a constant theme of our Lord. Jesus said concerning His disciples: "They are *not of the world,* even as *I am not of the world*" (John 17:16). Jesus implies two separate realms of existence in His conversation with Nicodemus. This "master of Israel" knew nothing about "spiritual things" (John 3:10). Therefore,

Jesus said to him: "That which is born of the flesh *is flesh;* and that which is born of the Spirit *is Spirit"* (John 3:6). In order for Nicodemus to understand "spiritual things," he must first of all be "born of the Spirit." The "flesh," the "world," and the "things of the world" can never be in league with "spiritual things" and a "world to come." Those who understand this truth will appreciate the words of the French mystic, Madame Guyon, as she writes: "The rays of the sun may shine upon mire, but those rays will never be united with the mire." [8]

The person who is in the Kingdom of God is constrained to think on "spiritual things." The Holy Spirit does not have a divided loyalty — the Holy Spirit associates "spiritual things" with "spiritual," and never carnal or worldly. Therefore, the Holy Spirit *must* focus attention upon the "heavenly inheritance," and never upon the physical "Land of Canaan." Since the Holy Spirit is the ultimate source of the New Testament Scriptures, men search in vain to find the "Land of Canaan" as an inheritance for the saints of God (Jew or Gentile).

When the "Land of Canaan" and the remainder of the "creation" is viewed from God's perspective, we are constrained to see them in an entirely different light. God does not value the "things He has made" as men value them. Neither does God depend upon the "things He has made" for His good pleasure and Self-existence. When Solomon's temple became an end within itself, rather than a means to a personal relationship to God, the Lord reacted very strongly against it. The New Testament disciples recount the same protestation, and Stephen affirms that God must not be interfused with any part of His creation:

> But Solomon built him (God) a house.
> Howbeit the most High dwelleth not in temples
> made with hands; as saith the prophet,
> *Heaven* is my *throne,* and *earth* is my *footstool:*
> What house will ye build me? saith the Lord: or
> what is the *place of my rest?*
> Hath not my hand made all these things? (Acts 7:47-50).

The above passage implies that God needs a *house* or *dwelling place* for His "rest" or ultimate well-being. Is it possible to take that which God has created and build a house that will accommodate the Creator? Anything that is created suggests a greater intelligence, wisdom, and power than the thing created (Hebrews 3:3). God is much

---

8. Jeanne Guyon, *Experiencing the Depth of Jesus Christ,* Christian Books Publishing House, Auburn, Maine, 127.

greater and far superior to anything that He has made — which includes the entire cosmos. God is so majestic and great that the earth is no more than His *footstool* — *Heaven* is God's dwelling place. This metaphoric language is affirming that God's *throne*, which is heaven, is much superior to His *footstool*, which is the earth. It is difficult to believe that Christ would exchange His *throne* for a *footstool*.

Stephen deplores the idea of God finding a "rest" in the things that He has made. God's "rest" and ultimate well-being cannot be dependent upon something that men may build for Him. God's "rest" is within *Himself*. In the vernacular of our day, we would say that God is "self-contained." From a human point of view, men do not rest *in* the "things they have made," but *from* the "things they have made." God's objective is to bring men to His throne, which is *heaven*, and His eternal "rest" (which is within Himself), rather than His footstool, which is the *earth*.

The cosmetics of this present creation will one day be removed — including the "Land of Canaan." The present order of things will be seen for their true worth. This will happen with the coming of Christ when the "heavens shall pass away with a great noise, and the elements shall be burned up" (2 Peter 3:10). Only that which is permanent and everlasting will remain. Jesus died and rose again that He might deliver us from this present evil world (Galatians 1:4), and upon His return, He will fulfill the promise of "new heavens and a new earth," as told by the prophets and Apostles (2 Peter 3:13; Isaiah 65:17; 66:22).

It is impossible for God to retrograde. He is always moving forward in time and history. This progressive mood has been going on for many centuries — time and history are being brought to an ultimate conclusion. God's Kingdom is always expanding — the New Jerusalem is enlarging every day. The body of Christ is "growing into a holy temple" in the Lord (Ephesians 2:21). There is a posture of expectancy. There is a buildup of hope and anticipation in practically every verse of Scripture. The saints of all ages await the "things which God hath prepared for them that love him" (1 Corinthians 2:9b). Something glorious is on the horizon for the children of God. The New Testament assures us that God will *complete* or *finalize* that which He has undertaken. Paul is very confident that "he (God) which hath begun a good work in you will *perform it until the day of Jesus Christ*" (Philippians 1:6).

A carnal kingdom of one thousand years, as believed by the futurists, would be the most anticlimactic event in all the activities of God. It would be a retrogression for the saints who have "died in the faith" — in short, it would be a step backward. God will never recycle His elect. Canaan is not a "halfway house" to a better world. To delay the heavenly inheritance of the saints and *return* them to a worldly kingdom in which they must live for a thousand years is the Frankenstein of theology.

A backward look has no place in the Christian hope. Following Jesus means a perpetual "looking unto him as the *author* and *finisher of our faith*" (Hebrews 12:1-2). It was a *backward look* (a longing for Sodom) that resulted in Lot's wife being turned into a pillar of salt (Luke 17:32). Jesus warns men in every age with these words: "No man having put his hand to the plough, and *looking back* is fit for the kingdom of God" (Luke 9:62). The gaze of the saint is always upward and away from the "world and the things of the world."

When the phrase, "author and *finisher of our faith*" (as used above), is considered in its total context, it puts another quietus on a future earthly kingdom as taught by the premillennialists. It is very evident that the "faith" principle that is discussed in chapters 10, 11, and 12 of the epistle to the Hebrews is not *finalized* in the Land of Canaan but at the "throne of God," in "heaven" which consists of a "better and an enduring substance" (10:34), in "mount Zion ... the city of the living God," in the "heavenly Jerusalem," and amid an "innumerable company of angels," along with the "general assembly and church of the firstborn" and in the company of God and Jesus ... and in a "kingdom which cannot be moved" (Hebrews 12:22-24, 28). The "faith" of the Old Testament saints will be "finished" in the same way that the New Testament saints is "finished" — and both will result in a glorious heavenly inheritance.

It is very feasible that the reign of the Antichrist will consist of an intensified emphasis upon the "world and the things of the world." Babylon will most likely appear in all her glory just before she is brought to ruin at the return of Christ. Our generation may be on the very threshold of Babylon's most glorious era — the reign of the Antichrist. More has been accomplished in the past 50 years to create a utopia in this world than all the rest of history combined. The "world and the things of the world" are being pursued with a madness heretofore unknown. Humanism, which is a deification of man, and one of the most widespread religions of this age, is a major contributor to the Antichrist "spirit."

Today, and in centuries past, the activities of Satan are known as the "mystery of iniquity" (2 Thessalonians 2:7). As we have already shown, a "mystery" in the Scriptures is generally something that is not fully known or understood. Babylon, the harlot city of Revelation, is linked with the "mystery of iniquity" — it is called "mystery Babylon" (Revelation 17:5). Babylon represents the works of Satan upon mankind in every generation. The "mystery of iniquity" will continue until Satan appears incarnate.

Satan has never been *revealed* in his ultimate power and manifest person. At the present time, Satan is held in restraint (2 Thessalonians 2:6-7). This restraint is described as a "great chain" in Revelation 20:1-2. The two passages (2 Thessalonians 2:6-7 and Revelation 20:1-2) have very much in common. Both are describing the same restraint. When Satan appears as the "man of sin," the restraint will be removed — Satan will be revealed for *who* and *what* he really is. He will go out and "deceive the nations which are in the four quarters of the earth (Revelation 20:8) until he is destroyed at the appearance of Christ (2 Thessalonians 2:8; Revelation 20:10).

The counterpart to the "mystery of iniquity" is the "mystery of godliness" (1 Timothy 3:16). Both "mysteries" are at work in the world unbeknown to the masses of mankind. The unregenerate world is blind to both mysteries. The two mysteries will cease at the *revelation* of Satan and the *revelation* of Christ. The two superpowers of the ages will settle once and for all who is Sovereign.

God has never been revealed in all of His power and glory. God was veiled in human flesh when Christ appeared the first time. Paul describes God as the "blessed and only Potentate, the King of kings, and Lord of lords; Who only hath immortality, dwelling in the light which *no man can approach unto: Whom no man hath seen, nor can see:* to whom be honor and power everlasting" (1 Timothy 6:15b-16). At the present time, "we know in part" (1 Corinthians 13:12), but at the second coming of Christ, we "shall see him as he is" (1 John 3:2b).

The world awaits two very important and dramatic *revelations:* (1) The "man of sin" is to be *"revealed* in his time" (2 Thessalonians 2:6), whose coming is "after the working of Satan with all power and signs and lying wonders, And with all deceivableness of unrighteousness" (2 Thessalonians 2:9-10). Also, (2) the Lord Jesus shall be *"revealed* from heaven with his mighty angels" and shall destroy Satan (2 Thessalonians 1:7; 2:8).

Satan was *not destroyed* in the death and resurrection of Christ. Satan stands condemned or judged (John 16:11), but not destroyed.

Jesus conquered death and overcame Satan for Himself and for those who believe upon Him when He died and rose again. The believer reigns with Christ even now, and sits with Him in heavenly places far above all principality, and power, and might and dominion (Ephesians 2:6; Colossians 3:1). And in this sense Satan is bound; he is limited in that he cannot reach beyond his sphere. However, Christians continue to be tempted by the Evil One and are not immune to his snares. Peter says that the Devil continues to go about "as a roaring lion seeking whom he may devour" (1 Peter 5:8).

Jesus' last encounter with Satan will be in the person of the "man of sin." Satan must also become incarnate. He, too, must suffer in a body, not for the same reason that our Lord suffered, but that he might know the full import of the "place prepared for the devil and his angels" (Matthew 25:41). Since Jesus suffered in a body, it is very plausible that Satan will also suffer in a body. If Satan is to be cast into the lake of fire and brimstone, as described in Revelation 20:10, then he must have a body. Those who "receive not the love of the truth that they might be saved" will have this in common with him (2 Thessalonians 2:10b).

The bodies of men, both of the believer and non-believer, will play an important role in the resurrection. If the bodies of the saints are to be resurrected and glorified, then it is very feasible that the bodies of the wicked will suffer a contrary fate. The Scriptures declare a resurrection of both the just and the unjust at the return of Christ (Acts 24:15).

Jesus had more to say on the above topic than anyone else. When He sent His disciples on their first preaching mission, He prepared them for the opposition they would face and gave them a double warning. Fear of their fellow man was to be a secondary concern — men are limited in their destructive powers. God was to be feared more than man. The disciples were to "fear him (God) who is able to destroy both soul and *body in hell*" (Matthew 10:28). In other passages of Scripture Jesus specifies certain parts of the human body that will be affected in the punishment of the wicked. For example, He describes the plight of the unsaved with *"weeping* and *gnashing of teeth"* (Matthew 8:12). Also, a reference is made to the *eyes* and *tongue* of the rich man who suffered in hell because he ignored the needs of Lazarus while on the earth (Luke 16:19-31). In the light of such remarks by our Lord, it is very logical that Satan will also have a body in which to be punished.

Again, let it be noted that *two important events* must transpire *before* Christ returns for His church: (1) the "falling away" of the church, and (2) the appearance of the "man of sin" or the Antichrist. The two have much in common. Most likely it will be the "world and the things of the world" that will distract the church from her Lord. This is certainly happening today. At the present time, the ground work is being laid in a very dramatic way for the appearance of the Antichrist. The materialistic and humanistic mood of this age, created by the "god of this world," is "blinding the minds of them which believe not, lest the light of the glorious gospel of Christ, who is the image of God, should shine unto them" (2 Corinthians 4:4). The only means of overcoming the "spirit" of Antichrist that is already among us, or the Antichrist of the future, is to believe on Him who became *flesh* and shed His *blood* for the sins of the world.

The Holy Spirit should be the believer's primary teacher in things pertaining to Christ and the Antichrist (1 John 2:27). The humanity of Jesus, particularly His death and resurrection, are the focal points of the Spirit's revelation. The flesh and blood of Christ are the source of a redeemed humanity and a redeemed creation (Colossians 1:20), and the Holy Spirit will keep them all in their proper perspective. The Spirit of God, which John insists that we follow, rather than the "spirit" of the Antichrist, will direct the believer from the "world and the things of the world" to an "inheritance *incorruptible*, and *undefiled*, and that *fadeth not away*, reserved *in heaven* for you" (1 Peter 1:4). In the light of current events, John's words should emerge with more transparency than ever before:

> Beloved, *believe not every spirit*, but *try the spirits* whether they are of God: because many *false prophets* are gone out into the world.
> Every spirit that confesseth that Jesus Christ *is come in the flesh* is of God:
> And every spirit that *confesseth not* that Jesus Christ is *come in the flesh* is *not of God:* and this is that *spirit of Antichrist*, whereof ye have heard that it should come; and even now already is it in the world.
> Ye are of God, little children, and have *overcome them;* because greater is he that is in you, than he that is in the world.
> They are *of the world:* therefore *speak they of the world,* and the *world heareth them* (1 John 4:1-5).

From the Garden of Eden to the present hour, man's struggle has not been against flesh and blood per se. Man's struggle has been "against principalities, against powers, against the rulers of the darkness of this world, against spiritual wickedness in high places" (Ephesians 6:12). The Jews' worst enemy is not Russia and her allies (as we have seen in recent times), neither is America Russia's worst enemy. Man's real enemy is Satan who has the *power of death* (Hebrews 2:14). According to the Scriptures, both *Satan* and *death* will be destroyed and cast into the lake of fire (Revelation 20:10, 14). This will be the "second death" for those who know not Christ. The redeemed of all ages will be able to cry: *Allelujah,* for "The kingdoms of this world are become the kingdoms of our Lord, and of his Christ; *and he shall reign for ever and ever*" (Revelation 11:15).

Chapter 10

Revelation 20:1-10
vs.
The Remainder of Scripture

The Bible is perhaps the most scrutinized book that has ever been written. It has been gone over with a fine-toothed comb from the first word in Genesis to the last Amen in revelation. Every book, every chapter, every verse, every word, and even the punctuation has been brooded over, catalogued, diagramed, tabulated, and classified with the utmost diligence.

Geddes MacGregor, in his book, *The Bible in the Making*, gives a computation of the number of books, chapters, verses, and words that are found in the Bible.[1] This computation was done by the Gideons. If my addition is correct, there are 66 books, 1,189 chapters, 31,100 verses, and 777,133 words in the King James Version. In spite of all the attention given to the Scriptures, they have not readily yielded all of their content.

The millennial passage (Revelation 20:1-10) is found in only *one* of the 66 books of the Bible and comprises only a fraction of that one book. If verses 2 through 7 were removed from Revelation 20, the thousand years reign could not be found in Scripture. If these six verses were left out of the 31,100 verses, the results would be almost negligible. Yet these six verses have created more discord in the body of Christ than most well-known, doctrinal themes — all because many have majored upon the minor.

There are some outstanding themes in the Bible that should never be at cross-purposes with each other. Such themes are the sovereignty of God, the universality of sin, the righteousness of God, God's love, God's wrath, the Incarnation, the death and resurrection of Christ, repentance and faith, the return of Christ, the role of Satan, the reward of the righteous, the fate of the wicked, etc. Every student of Scripture must admit that there are a few texts that do not "fit" easily into the larger themes of Scripture — they are peripheral — and the Scriptures are not

---

1. Geddes MacGregor, *The Bible in the Making*, copyright: HarperCollins Publishers, New York, N.Y., 428-430.

strangled by such passages. Revelation 20:1-10 is one of those passages.

Premillennialism stands or falls on Revelation 20:1-10. This brief passage is the epicenter of the millennial kingdom doctrine. The futurists see the entire Bible through this tiny window. If a shade is pulled over this narrow slot of Scripture, premillennialism is left in total darkness. As William E. Cox would say, to interpret all of the Scripture in the light of this one passage, is to make the tail wag the dog. To change our analogy, the futurists have all their eggs in one basket — and a very small basket at that.

No man has all the truth. There is a certain exegetical embarrassment to most men when they are unable to speak and write with a large degree of dogmatism. Because of this, men oftentimes rush in where angels fear to tread. Three of the most difficult words for an exegete to say is, "I don't know." Exegetical pride on the part of many interpreters of the Scriptures has resulted in multiple errors. This should be avoided at all costs. It is better to stick to the major themes of Scripture than to go off on an unchartered theological tangent.

I have noted with a good deal of interest the ambiguity with which many premillennialists write. They use such words and phrases as "it seems," "it appears," "assuming," "we propose the following theory," "may," "it may be," "apparently," "perhaps," "the indications are," "it would appear," "one would suppose," "indicates," "one wonders," "suggests," "it may thus be," "may be assumed," "it would seem," "it seems clear," etc. These are not isolated words and phrases; they are reflected throughout their works. These words and phrases point to a lack of confidence in their own interpretation of Scripture.

Some of the most able scholars in the world have wrestled with Revelation 20:1-10, but there is little agreement among them. At this point in history, the evangelical church has not produced a satisfactory answer to this difficult passage of Scripture. However, we must not write it off as being incomprehensible. The Lord may initiate a future breakthrough in eschatology comparable to the discovery of "justification by faith" that resulted in the great Reformation. Until there is more agreement within the evangelical church similar to some of the major themes of Scripture, Revelation 20:1-10 should be kept on the back burner. The undue strain that has been imposed upon this passage by the millenarians cannot be justified by any stretch of the imagination. Volumes and volumes of books have been written by the futurists in conjunction with this short passage, and their opinions are as diverse as the stars in the sky. As Richard Baxter has said: "Overdoing is one way of undoing." Millennial views on Revelation 20:1-10 should be regarded as the enigma of the century.

Those who wish to study the last book of the Bible should keep in mind that it is the "revelation of Jesus Christ" (Revelation 1:1) and *not* the "revelation of national Jewry." According to *James Strong's Concordance*, there are 28 passages of Scripture in the Revelation that speak of Christ as the "Lamb." The central issue in the book of Revelation is the activity of the Lamb, seated upon a throne (in heaven), and His ultimate destruction of Satan and his cohorts. While John falls at the feet of Jesus and all heaven and earth praise, adore, and worship the Lamb upon the throne, the millenarians would draw our attention to "national" Jewry. Again, it is shown that the priorities of the futurists are out of focus. They are condemned by the very book they endeavor to interpret.

The Revelation is a book of speculation for the millenarians from the beginning to the end. A classic example of this is their attempt to remove the church from the world (rapture) before the beginning of *their* tribulation period. Some premillennialists, including C. I. Scofield, have the gall to say that Revelation 4:1, John's invitation to heaven, is synonymous with the rapture of the church (see Scofield's notes, p. 1334, note 2). There is only one conclusion that can be drawn from this interpretation. Those who accept this view take great delight in being deceived (2 Corinthians 11:20 NIV). It is a waste of energy to kick the tires on this theological vehicle; the tires were never inflated.

Another example of their speculative theology can be seen in the release of Satan at the end of the thousand years period (Revelation 20:3, 7-8). According to the millenarians, the releasing of Satan will be a *testing time* for those who will be living at the end of this unusual period. Multitudes will be deceived by Satan and accompany him in his last-ditch stand for survival. This is a monumental revelation for the futurists. It proves that an ideal government, environment, society, and economy will not change the hearts of all mankind. It will demonstrate that the human heart is rebellious and sinful even under the most favorable conditions.

One gargantuan question comes to mind relative to the above view on the releasing of Satan. *Who will benefit from this "tacked on" revelation of man's sinful nature?* God doesn't need additional information regarding man's evil heart. The Scriptures provide a storehouse of data on man's corrupt condition. Future generations will not be helped by this "extra" knowledge. The time-frame of Satan's release is but a "little season," which according to most Bible scholars, is three and one half years. Eternity will begin after the "little season" (or 3-1/2 years), and the human race in its present form will not exist. Satan doesn't need new information — he has been deceiving, testing, and trying the sons of Adam for centuries. The only people who profit from this "testing episode" are the premillennialists. It is an excellent fire escape from the *heat* they have generated for themselves. It can be classified as a self-imposed theological perk for the futurists.

There is only one passage of Scripture in the entire Revelation that can be considered favorable to the millenarians and it is laced with many difficulties. This passage is found in Revelation 7:4-8. These five verses deal with the 144,000 from the various tribes of Israel. Verses 5-8 of chapter 7, which give the number and names of the tribes, are not crucial to its interpretation. If the 144,000 in this passage are to be associated with the "great multitude that no man could number" in verse 9, as many Bible scholars belive they should be, then the 144,000 are "before the *throne,* and before the *Lamb,* clothed with *white robes,* and palms in their hands." The "throne," the "Lamb," and "white robes" suggest a "heavenly" scene for the 144,000, rather than an "earthly" one.

The same number (144,000) is used again in the fourteenth chapter of Revelation to describe a group of people (verses 1, 3), but they are not identified as either "Jew" or "Gentile." The 144,000 that are mentioned in Revelation 14:1-5 are definitely "redeemed from the *earth"* and are before the *"throne* of God" which is usually associated with "heaven."

There is a third isolated passage of Scripture that speaks of the twelve tribes of Israel in the Revelation, but it, too, is not favorable to the premillennialists. This text is found in Revelation 21:12. The twelve tribes of Israel in this passage translate into the twelve gates of the "holy Jerusalem that descends out of heaven from God" (Revelation 21:10). The "holy Jerusalem" is the "bride, the Lamb's wife" which is the church (Revelation 21:9). The walls of the "holy Jerusalem" have twelve foundations inscribed with the names of the twelve apostles (Revelation 21:14). It is very evident that the twelve tribes and the twelve apostles are associated with the holy Jerusalem that descends out of heaven from God. The twelve tribes (or gates) and the foundations of the walls of the city (12 apostles) are a unit. These are symbolic words and phrases that represent the redeemed of all ages. The saints in the Old

Testament era cannot be separated from the saints in the New Testament era as believed by some millenarians. The Apostle Paul declares that the Gentiles are *not* "foreigners" and "strangers" in the household of God but are fellowcitizens with the saints and "are built upon the *foundation* of the *Apostles* and *Prophets,* Jesus Christ Himself being the chief corner stone" (Ephesians 2:20).

We have exhausted all the direct references to the twelve tribes of Israel in the book of Revelation. It is impossible to connect Revelation 14:3-4 and Revelation 21:12 with the twelve tribes of Israel in an *earthly,* millennial kingdom. We are left with Revelation 7:3-4. As stated earlier, if the 144,000 of Revelation 7:3-4 are to be regarded as a part of the "multitude that no man could number" in verse 9, then the millenarians are left without a leg to stand on.

Most Bible scholars are unanimous in believing that the 144,000 from the various tribes of Israel is a symbolic number rather than a literal one. The 144,000 could represent the saints of the Old Testament dispensation who "needed" to be sealed *after* the death and resurrection of Christ. Redemption for the Old Testament saints was not finalized until Jesus shed His blood. This mass "sealing" could be those who "died in the faith, not having received the promise" (Hebrews 11:39). This view would certainly harmonize with what John envisioned in Revelation 14:1-3 and Revelation 21:12. The saints of all ages comprise the "holy Jerusalem that John saw descending down from God out of heaven." However, these comments are not engraved in marble. "Caution" is the key word in any interpretation of the Revelation.

In the light of what the premillennialists have imposed upon Revelation 20:1-10, it would be much easier to comment on what these brief verses *do not say* than what they do say. Nothing is said about a Jewish theocracy during the thousand years in question; nothing is said about a temple being built in Jerusalem; nothing is said about animal sacrifices being offered in the millennium; nothing is mentioned about Canaan being an inheritance for the Jews; there is no hint of mass evangelism and millions being won to Christ; nothing is said about a "rod of iron" by which Christ will rule the nations; and nothing is said about an earthly Jerusalem from which Christ will reign. Jewry is not mentioned in Revelation 20:1-10 in any shape or form. The millenarians exploit the silence of Scripture rather than enlarge upon its speech.

Revelation 20:1-10 raises many more questions than it answers.

This passage does not say that the one thousand years period occurred on the "earth." Neither does it say that it occurs in "heaven." However, the multiple "thrones" and "beheaded souls" in verse 4 lend themselves to a "heavenly" scene more readily than an "earthly" one. As for the "priest of God and of Christ" that are mentioned in verse 6, the saints of God have been "priests of God" from the beginning (Exodus 19:6; 1 Peter 2:9; Revelation 1:6). Verse 4 is perhaps the most critical passage in all of Revelation 20:1-10, but no "earthly" scene can be found in the text.

The activities of Satan seem to be associated with the "earth" in this passage, but *not* the reign of Christ. The New Testament leaves no doubt about the activities of Satan (Antichrist spirit) being abroad in the world since apostolic days (1 Peter 5:8; 2 Timothy 2:26; 1 John 4:1-3; 2 John 7). However, Christ is portrayed as being at the right hand of God seated in the heavenlies. He will remain there until He comes again to utterly destroy the Devil and cast him into the lake of fire.

Verse 3 speaks of "nations" in conjunction with the work of Satan and according to verse 8, these are "nations" of the earth. Who are these "nations" and when do they exist? The word "nations" is a blanket statement that could cover all of mankind. Are we to conclude that *all* of mankind would be free from Satanic deception for a thousand years? In verses 7 and 8 of the passage under consideration, we find that Satan will "be loosed out of his prison, and shall go out to deceive the *nations* which are in the four quarters of the *earth*." The "nations" in verse 8 cannot be any different from the "nations" in verse 3 except they are separated by a period of *time*. Will the "nations" that are free from Satanic deception in verse 3 be faced with a wholesale deception again in verse 8? Would the millenarians dare impose their "literalism" on this quandary? We are forced to resort to one of Paul's bewildering questions: "Who is sufficient for these things?"

The broad use of symbolism in Revelation 20:1-10 creates another problem for those who try to interpret this passage of Scripture. One is at a nonplus to find much "literalism" in the binding of Satan. The "key," "bottomless pit," "great chain," "dragon," and the "old serpent" are all symbolic language. If these terms are symbolic, then the "thousand years" is likely to be symbolic. There are many Bible scholars who feel that this is a *real* period of time but not necessarily a *literal* thousand years. Dr. George E. Ladd, a historical premillennialist, is one of those scholars.

In his commentary on Revelation Dr. Ladd writes: "It is difficult to understand the thousand years for which he (Satan) was bound with strict literalness in view of the obvious symbolic use of numbers in the Revelation. A thousand equals the third power of ten — an ideal time. While we need not take it literally, the thousand years does appear to represent a real period of time, however long or short it may be."[2] (Parenthesis mine.) There is no time element with God. Peter declares that "one day is with the Lord as a thousand years, and a thousand years as one day" (2 Peter 3:8).

This highly symbolical book is at the mercy of the interpreter. Symbolism is in the eyes of the beholder, and like beauty, it can be decided in a thousand and one ways. Symbolism can be compared to a "midwife" who delivers a "child" — but symbolism can never be the child. For many people, the "midwife"is more important than the "child."

Since New Testament days the church has been confronted with some of the same theological principles that are expressed in Revelation 20:1-10. The New Testament has a world of information on Satan and his relationship to Christ. According to our Lord, the only way that Satan's kingdom can be "spoiled" is by first *"binding the strong man"* or Satan (Matthew 12:29). Luke expands Jesus' analogy somewhat by saying that the strong man (Christ) takes from the weaker man (Satan) "all his armour wherein he trusted, and divideth the spoil" (11:22). Paul avers that Christ, by His cross, *"spoiled* principalities and powers, (and) made a show of them openly, triumphing over them in it" (Colossians 2:15). The hour of Christ's death was the hour when He "destroyed him that had the power of death" (Hebrews 2:14-15).

Jesus encouraged His disciples by saying that He saw "Satan as lightning fall from heaven (Luke 10:18); See also Revelation 12:9-10). A part of the Holy Spirit's ministry would be to confirm that the *"prince of this world (Satan) is judged"* (John 12:31). John comforted those to whom he wrote by declaring that Jesus was "manifested that he might *destroy the works of the Devil"* (1 John 3:8). The head of the serpent was certainly bruised when Christ died on the cross. All power has been given to Him in heaven and in earth (Matthew 28:18).

2. George E. Ladd, *A Commentary on the Revelation*, William B. Eerdman's Publishing Company, Grand Rapids, Michigan, 1985, 262

In addition to the above, the Gospels and epistles have a good deal to say about the disciples' relationship to Satan. Jesus said to the twelve: "Behold, I give you power to tread on serpents and scorpions, and *over all the power of the enemy,*" etc. (Luke 10:19). Mark's Gospel says that Jesus gave the disciples "power to cast out devils" (3:15; Matthew 10:8). Paul informed the Ephesian church that the "shield of faith" would be able to "quench *all the fiery darts of the wicked*" (6:16). A part of Paul's ministry was to open the eyes of the Gentiles and "to turn them from darkness to light, and *from the power of Satan* unto God, etc." (Acts 26:18). James affirms that an humble spirit and submission to God would result in the *flight of the Devil* (James 4:7). The disciples were told that the "gates of hell would not prevail against the church" (Matthew 16:18). John writes about a relationship to God (of such a nature) that the *"wicked one toucheth him not"* (1 John 5:18). The blood of the cross is the believer's triumph over the enemy (Revelation 12:11).

Those who are in Christ are not in a listless state of existence in their triumph over Satan. Those who believe in Christ have been delivered from the *power of darkness* and *translated* into the *kingdom of His dear Son* (Colossians 1:13). They have been *"quickened together with Christ"* and have been *raised up together* (with Christ) and *"seated together in heavenly places in Christ"* (Ephesians 2:5-6). The word "together" is used three times in this passage to confirm the believer's position *in Christ.* The term "in Christ" is used many times over in the New Testament to depict this glorious relationship and position.

There can be no question that those who are *in Christ* have been "translated," "resurrected," "quickened," "raised," and "seated" with Him in the heavenlies. Even death cannot sever this union with Christ (Romans 8:38). Paul declares that to be absent from the body is to be present with the Lord (2 Corinthians 5:6). It goes without saying that Satan's influence and power over those who are in Christ is certainly "limited" and practically nil when a right relationship to God is maintained.

There is another principle at work in the world *today* that is expressed in Revelation 20:1-10 — and that is Satanic deception. Most of the "nations of the earth" are *already* in the throes of Satan's power. Paul declares that the "god of this world (Satan) hath *blinded the minds* of them which *believe not,* lest the light of the glorious gospel of Christ … should shine unto them" (2 Corinthians 4:4). John writes: "… we know that we are of God, and the *whole world lieth in wickedness*" (1

John 5:19). John depicts the "world" as a child nestled in its mother's bosom. The "world" is nurtured in the arms of Satan. The masses of mankind are already aligned with Satan in his opposition to the Kingdom of God. Paul portrays the unbelieving world as "walking according to *this world*, according to the *prince of the power of the air* (Satan), the *spirit* that *now worketh in the children of disobedience*" (Ephesians 2:2). The greater part of mankind (the "nations of the world") are already under the influence of Satan.

The millenarians are jumping the gun. They lay stress on "tomorrow's future" rather than "today's future." Over the centuries, the "future" has been one of man's greatest enemies. While it has been favorable to many, it has been the downfall of millions of others. Man's concern for the "future" has given rise to fortunetelling, witchcraft, divination, palmistry, astrology, horoscopy, spiritualism, clairvoyance, etc. Christian theology can be turned into the same category as the aforementioned evils. Many modern day cults attest this fact. It is the height of wickedness to speculate on what God will do in the "future" without an attempt to discover His Infinite power and love *today*. What God is *today*, He will be *tomorrow*, and all of the "future" is inherent in what God is *today*.

For centuries upon centuries the Jews have tried to force God's hand and make Him into *their* own image — a reversal of God's eternal purpose (2 Corinthians 3:18; Romans 8:29; Colossians 3:10). They have schemed, connived, and manipulated the Scriptures to effect this goal. They have reduced God to a tribal, genetic, geographical, national God that will eventually come to their terms. The millenarians have joined their ranks in an effort to make this happen. At this point God has *not* blinked. After several thousand years, God has declined to bow to their expectations. But one day God will conform. He will cave in and fulfill the Jews' dream. But the millions who have wailed, begged, and even died for this *Jewish glory* will be left out in the cold. Notwithstanding this fact, God will fulfill this dream to many "unborn" Jews who have never heard of a millennial kingdom. God has "bound" Himself to these "unborn" Jews, while by-passing millions of others. Those whom God has by-passed seem to be a people born out of due season.

The above paragraph should be printed in bold, gilded letters, put in a diamond studded frame, and displayed in all of *Ripley's Believe It or Not* museums. It should attract a good deal of attention. Better still, it should be hung in every church sanctuary and Jewish synagogue across this nation and around the world — it could become a prized relic rather than an ongoing theological movement.

It is not within the scope of this work to address the entire book of Revelation. Some readers may conclude that this cliché is a "cop out" by the writer to avoid further confrontation with this polemical book. Such a conclusion would be partially correct. I make no claim of understanding all the Revelation — however, I must say in the same breath that no person or any group of persons has a monopoly on this unique book. I have found that most commentators on the Revelation write with a fair degree of uncertainty — including the premillennialists. In all likelihood the church would be better off today if there had been more "cop outs" relative to the Revelation.

The comments on the Revelation are given primarily to call attention to the limited information that it has to offer on "national" Jewry — especially Revelation 20:1-10. When Revelation 20:1-10 and the remainder of the Bible are placed side by side, the contrast is awesome. The body of knowledge in one, and the vague, meager information in the other is mind-boggling. The two ideas can be compared to the "pigsty" and the "father's house." To impose Revelation 20:1-10 upon the remainder of Scripture unduly would be in the words of Shakespear "painting the lily."

The millenarians have taken two verses from the seventh chapter of the Revelation (3-4) and developed the most complicated, sophisticated, and elaborate doctrinal system that has ever been contrived by the human mind. These *two verses* constitute the foundation and framework for all they have to say on the remainder of the Revelation and the thousand years in particular. There is an open-ended question to all of this — would any natural son or daughter of Abraham be willing to stake his or her life (and future) on such scant information?

From the writer's point of view, the jury is still out relative to Revelation 20:1-10. Until those who interpret the Scriptures are able to coordinate this passage with the major themes of Scripture, it should be kept on a leash. Man's redemption is not dependent upon his understanding this one passage of Scripture. Millions of saints have passed the scene without an understanding of this text. It is better to die without an understanding of Revelation 20:1-10 than it is to violate John's admonition in 22:18-19: "And if any man shall *take away* from the words of this prophecy, God *shall take away his part out of the book of life,* and of the holy city, and from the things which are written in this book."

Man's accountability to God will be far more than a shoebox system of keeping records. Even the slightest motive or intent of the heart are known to God (Hebrews 4:12-13). John's warning should be taken very seriously.

Most of the important themes of Scripture have been dealt with in this work and there is perfect agreement throughout. There is no way that an overblown emphasis upon the Jewish people in a carnal kingdom can be found in the outstanding themes of the New Testament. In fact, the doctrine of sin, justification by faith, the hope of heaven, etc., are like roadblocks, flashing red lights, burning flares, and screaming sirens to prevent any revival of Judaism and a carnal Jewish state. It is the mystery of mysteries that churchmen would capitalize on a chimerical, *earthly* Jewish kingdom in the future when the "unsearchable riches" of Christ's grace is available *today*.

Millenarianism can be compared to a ship carrying too much sail. The excess sail is a threat to the vessel and its cargo. Premillennialism is only added weight to the simple message of the Gospel — it is *not necessary* for man's redemption — Christ has already "weathered the storm" and proven His power over the enemy (Satan). No "extra sail" is needed to carry the cargo to the desired haven.

Chapter 11

Today's Jew vs. Yesterday's Jew

After reading a number of Jewish authors I have been greatly impressed with the admixture of pride and condemnation that seems to emerge in almost every writer. It is a strange combination. The Jewish people are proud of their Hebraic heritage but at the same time many of them resent some of the religious and cultural patterns that have characterized their forefathers.

The Jews of today are faced with a real dilemma. They are drawn between Jewish tradition and Western-Gentile culture. This tension is so strong that one Jewish writer refers to it as a split personality. This schizophrenia syndrome is resulting in mixed marriages, a disdain for Judaism, and other disruptions within the Jewish race.

Drastic measures are sometimes taken by the Jews to rid themselves of the stigma imposed upon them by their Jewish ancestors. Some have undergone cosmetic surgery to alter their facial features. Others have changed their names. Many keep a very low profile for fear of discrimination.

Over the centuries the Jewish people have created a self-destructive climate that has brought many hardships and untold sufferings into their lives. In almost every age, they have backed themselves "into a corner" as it were, by a self-made snare. Their exclusiveness has brought both the wrath of God and the Gentile world down upon them. Their kosher life style, their legal dogmas, and racial superiority (God's chosen people) have turned to be their enemy. By clinging to traditional Judaism, they have developed a stigma that has repelled many of their own kin. In many ways the Jewish people are their worst foe. Many modern day Jews would no doubt agree with Paul who said of them: "They please not God and are contrary to all men" (1 Thessalonians 2:15).

In Biblical days the Jews were not content to isolate themselves from other nations — they actually "hated" other nations and people. Their protest of the Gospel to the Gentiles was the full cup of their iniquity (1 Thessalonians 2:15-16). It is for this reason that the "wrath of God has come upon them to the uttermost (or to the end)." Bigotry is very obnoxious to God. Premillennialism, with its inappropriate emphasis upon the natural seed of Abraham, promotes this self-lauding spirit among the Jewish people. The futurists become an accessory to God's wrath upon Abraham's natural descendants.

While some Jews are trying to shake the stigma they have acquired, others are contributing to it. Jewry is not dead. Generally speaking, serious threats to a race or religion only strengthen their efforts. The holocaust against the Jews in Germany (which the writer deplores) gave the Zionist movement an acceleration heretofore unknown. It contributed to the formation of the state of Israel in 1948 and brought the Jews world-wide attention. It has bonded them together in a way that has strengthened the cause of Jewry in almost every nation. The Jews in Palestine today are able to fulfill their dream as never before. They have succeeded in isolating themselves from almost all Christian influences; a goal they have wanted to achieve for centuries. They are in a position to turn a deaf ear to the voice of God similar to their fathers of old. Premillennialism is just another handmaid to their resolve.

As stated earlier, the two dominate features that have perpetuated the Jewish people over the centures are race and religion. The natural instincts in man regarding race and religion are enough to unite and continue them indifinitely — no miracle is necessary. This has been proven over and over again in the history of mankind. Race and religion have been bedfellows for centuries. The Arab world and the Muslim religion are modern day examples. "State" religions have flourished in almost every age and generation. "State" religions, at various periods of history, have overshadowed the true church. If other races and religions can self-perpetuate apart from the grace of God, so can the Jews and Judaism.

It is not necessary to teach men to be "religious" — they are religious by nature. The first atheist is yet to be born. Atheism is not innate in man, it is acquired (Romams 1:19-20; 2:14-15). Neither is it necessary to teach men to promote their own race. Birds of feather continue to flock together — so do men. Birds and men do this without any kind of supernatural intervention. Race and religion have been one bone and one flesh for the Jewish people since the dawn of their history. When the two are rolled into one, they are almost invincible.

It is the writer's opinion that legalistic Judaism has brought more "woes" to the Jewish people than "weals." It has contributed to the "chosen people" theology more than anything else — a concept that flies in the face of sound theology. Legalism, whether in Judaism or

Christianity, has its own built-in self-destruction. Of course there are mild and extreme cases. The Jewish situation is the extreme.

Legalism produces two natures in man; pride on the one hand, in that he is keeping the law, and self-hatred on the other hand because in his conscience he knows that he is a transgressor. The Apostle Paul says that the "law worketh wrath" (Romans 4:15), i.e., it creates a conflict within one's innermost being. There is a desire to fulfill the law, but the "sin principle" in man pulls him in another direction — he is drawn betweeen two straits. The Apostle expresses this tension in his own life in the seventh chapter of Romans. It is a real struggle and is never resolved until one is liberated by the love and grace of God.

Extreme lelgalism has a very exclusive spirit. It isolates men individually and collectively — the latter being the worse. Collective legalism tends to endorse the old adage "might makes right." The larger the group the tighter the bondage, eventually becoming an accepted way of life.

In this isolated state, extreme legalism is prone to strike out at anything that threatens it. This is true whether it is found in Judaism or Christianity. Truth does not fear scrutiny or outside pressure. Truth embraces all men — even one's enemies. Any theology that does not bring men into a living, loving, and hopeful relationship to God and one's fellow man should become extinct. Religion can become a tool in the hands of Satan to deceive and damn.

The real culprit that has brought havoc to the Jewish people is not the Gentile world, race ties, or inferiority, but "legalism." Legalism produces a bondage that vexes and galls men's souls until they are beside themselves—the true self never emerges. However, God's grace liberates men intellectually, culturally, racially, geographically, and creates a love for one's self and one's fellow man.

Futuristic teachings augment the very things that have brought chaos to the Jewish people. The millenarians are only adding fuel to the fire when they make claims for the Jewish people that have spelled doom for them over the centuries. The "chosen people" mentality, with all of its ramifications, can only be a minus for the people they attempt "to help."

For this writer to bring the curtains down on the Jewish people is to beg the question. The Jewish people need not lose their physical identity with Abraham as a believer in the Gospel. Faith in Christ will enhance all relationships to Abraham of whatever kind they may be.

However, there is a loss of identity in another realm that needs to be emphasized with all the love we can muster. In God's family, race, sex, and social status count as naught — *Christ is everything.* This lack of distinction is best described in the words of Paul as he writes about the oneness of all believers who belong to the body of Christ:

> For ye are all (Jew and Gentile) the children of God by faith in Christ Jesus.
>
> For as many of you as have been baptized into Christ have put on Christ.
>
> There is *neither Jew nor Greek,* there is neither bond nor free, there is neither male nor female: for *ye are all one* in Christ Jesus.
>
> And if ye be Christ's, then are ye *Abraham's seed,* and heirs according to the promise (Galatians 3:26-29).

If any Jewish individual wishes to contest the words of Paul, let him turn to his own Scriptures where Moses wrote:

> One law shall be to him that is home born (Jew), and unto the stranger (non-Jew) that sojourneth among you (Exodus 12:49).

And that "one law" is *love* ... which is allied with *faith.*

Conclusion

This work is not written in defense of any particular view on the millennial controversy, i.e., "postmillennialism," "amillennialism," or "historical premillennialism." It is first and foremost an exposé on "dispensational premillennialism." It is hoped that enough has been written to expose the structural foundation on which premillennialism is built. If a position was held by the writer on the millennial dispute, it would be the "amillennial" position. I feel a closer kinship with this school than any of the others. This work should serve as a counteragent to both premillennialism and Judaism. Simply put, premillennialism is Judaism with a new face lift. Judaism was nailed to the cross two thousand years ago (Colossians 2:14).

Premillennialism and Judaism have a good deal in common — both are Old Testament orientated and both are built upon a false premise, namely, the carnal seed of Abraham. Premillennialists cannot deal properly with Abraham as the "father of the faithful" without destroying the foundation on which their doctrine is built. Like the Jews, they dwell upon the "fleshly" aspects of Abraham's fatherhood rather than the "faithful" aspects. At various points in their theology, when it is in their favor, they try to blend the two together, but there is no way of fusing the two; they cannot be reconciled. Because of this, they create insoluble theological problems for themselves — this is their thorn in the flesh.

The premillennialists are very adept at switching between the two seeds of Abraham without loss of reputation. Robert Louis Stephenson must have acquired some of his finesse from the futurists when he wrote *The Strange Case of Dr. Jekyll and Mr. Hyde*. This fictional writing of Mr. Stephenson could not hold a candle to the masking of the two seeds of Abraham, so well contrived by the premillennialists. Most people are unable to detect the two masks worn by the millenarians.

All kinds of errors are associated with the false premise on which premillennialism is built. It is almost impossible for the average lay Christian to "wade through" the jungle of falsehoods that have grown out of these unscriptural doctrines. Those who try to understand premillennialism are faced with many insurmountable obstacles. They must grapple with two or three second appearances of Christ — they must unscramble two or three resurrections in the future; they must struggle with two or more judgments for mankind; they must wrestle with the pre-trib, mid-trib, and post-trib theories relative to the rapture of the church; they are confronted with a mixture of glorified saints, regenerate saints in their physical bodies, and sinners living simultaneously on the earth during the millennium; there is a reversion to the old Jewish worship of temple, priest, and sacrifice that must be explained; they must differentiate between Israel as individuals today and Israel as a nation in the future; they must decide when the Antichrist will appear — before the tribulation, during the tribulation, or after the tribulation, etc. It is never appropriate in any age to play theological games as the premillennialists do.

That men would impose such a rigmarole of biblical views upon the Christian church is without excuse. Such a muddling of Scripture should be an embarrassment to the church of Christ. It is yet a greater embarrassment if the church remains indifferent toward this juggling of God's Word and allows it to continue unchallenged.

These multiple and diverse interpretations of end-time events by the premillennialists are indicative of a people who have lost their way in a wilderness of theological fadmongering. Many well meaning Christians, without a Moses or Joshua to lead them out, are wandering in this barren desert created by the futurists. These aimless meanderings lead only to more entanglements.

Premillennialism, with all of its complexities, is quite a departure from the simple pathway of faith. Isaiah writes of a "highway" that men are to travel upon and the "wayfaring men though fools, shall not err therein" (Isaiah 35:8). It is an established fact, in both the old dispensation and the new dispensation, that the farther men travel from the beaten pathway of *faith*, the more susceptible they are to deception. Premillennialism is the aftermath of a departure from "justification by faith" for the Jewish people.

The demands set forth in this book for the Jewish people in matters of redemption are the same demands made by Moses, the prophets, Jesus, Paul, and all the other biblical writers. God's anointed servants insisted upon *faith in* and *obedience to* God's Word for the Jews (and Gentiles) in every generation. This requirement is written on every page of Scripture. This truth has not changed.

If "justification by faith" was necessary in Abraham's day (Genesis 15:6), and in Ezekiel's day (Ezekiel 18:5-9), and in Habakkuk's day (Habakkuk 2:4), and in Paul's day (Galatians 3:11), and in Martin Luther's day, then it is still necessary in the twentieth century. And it will be, as long as time endures. Premillennialism, with its "unconditional promises" for the natural seed of Abraham, is a trend away from this all important doctrine—leaving the Jews in their sins. To capitalize on the carnal role of Abraham as a father (with all the implications that the premillennialists attach to it), and neglect the most significant role of Abraham as the "father of the faithful" (with all that it implies), is no less than a denial of the doctrine of "justification by faith." Those who love the Jewish people and believe in redemption *sola gratia, sole Christo,* and *sola fide** must take their stand with those who wrote the Scriptures, including the reforming fathers, and declare along with Luther: "I cannot recant! ... *Here I stand."*

The growth of premillennialism in the past few decades is no guarantee of its soundness. The papier-mache millennial kingdom that is so popular in the minds of many modern day prophets will one day be the laughing stock of succeeding generations. The title of Carl Wilson's book, *Our Dance Has Turned to Death,* would be an excellent epilogue for premillennialism. The wheels of truth turn slowly; but they, nevertheless, turn. We need to be reminded that error and falsehood have flourished in the church for centuries before being exposed and dealt with. It is not an unusual pattern for God to leave men in darkness for centuries when they refuse to walk in the light.

There is a very conspicuous silence of 400 years between the Old and New Testament dispensations when the voice of God was not heard. The doctrine of "justification by faith" lay buried for 12 or 13 hundred years beneath the pomp and ritual of the Roman Catholic Church. It was not until Martin Luther's day that it was brought to light — setting in motion the Protestant Reformation. In the past few years God has demonstrated in an unprecedented way that the gifts of the Holy Spirit did not cease with the apostolic ministries. In 1966, the gifts of the Holy Spirit, known primarily to Pentecostal groups, began to cross denominational lines in an unorthodox manner. Practically every denomination, from the "high church" status to the "low church" status, was affected by the Charismatic movement. But the same denominations, including some Pentecostal groups, refused to identify with and acknowledge what God was doing in this age. So great has been this movement that the word "charisma" has become a household word in the secular world. The question arises — when will God give such a demonstration of His gifts again?

*Solely by grace, solely by Christ, and solely by faith.

Men's rejection of God's revelation, regardless of its nature, plunges them into greater darkness. In this dark state they create new "doctrines" that only tickle men's ears — leaving the heart and soul untouched. Premillennialism, carried to its ultimate end, has no message for the Jews of today; and in reality, it has no message for them in the future. Premillennialism deserts the Jews like Absalom's mule deserted him — it leaves them dangling between the Land of Canaan and heaven with no assurance or hope of either.

The last chapter in the Middle East has not been written. God, in His providence, has permitted the formation of the state of Israel, but it is solely a political movement. Many premillennialists admit that the Zionist movement, begun by Theodor Herzl in the late 1800s, had no religious connotations whatsoever. The futurists have jumped on the political bandwagon and are doing their utmost to make it a "religious" adventure that will usher in a millennial kingdom for the Jews.

The multiple problems in the state of Israel at this hour should create a theological nightmare for the premillennialists. The dazzling six-day war of 1967, which was interpreted by the futurists as a sign of God's favor, is now eclipsed by unprecedented national setbacks. Peace has eluded this nation since its birth. Hostile Arab nations remain a constant threat to its security and endurance. Should some of the sophisticated military weaponry of the modern world fall into the hands of Israel's foes, her survival would be up for grabs.

An Arab coalition seems to be a secondary danger to the Israeli nation at this point in history. The February issue (1985) of *Reader's Digest* featured an article entitled "Israel's Hour of Danger" and opened with a quote from a former financial minister of Israel, Yigael Hurwitz. The quote does not paint a very rosy picture for Israel's economic future (p. 60). Rowland Evans and Robert Novak, co-authors of the *Reader's Digest* article list four interrelated threats to Israel's future:, (1) Internal Division, (2) Economic Problems, (3) Emigration, and (4) Political Fragmentation. Without amplifying these caution signs per se, suffice it to say that the problems are multitudinous and these writers do not stand alone in their appraisal of the Jewish situation at this hour. Financial ruin seems inevitable, unless drastic steps are taken to relieve the threat poised on this nation's doorstep.

Israel's ability to continue as a nation has been a grave concern to people on both sides of the Jewish controversy. But the outcome of the state of Israel, whether good or bad, will not change the Word of God.

The Kingdom of God does not stand or fall by the behavior of men and nations. *Faith* has been the means of entering God's Kingdom from the beginning and even God, Himself, cannot change it without betraying His character (Hebrews 11:17-18).

God's plan of redemption has not gone unchallenged. Men in every age have fabricated a lenient, legalistic religion that leaves men in their sins. This is the colossal mistake that the Jews and others have made over the centuries and premillennialism only contributes to it. The Old Testament prophets refused to alter God's Word and tell the Jews what they wanted to hear, and they were stoned and killed. Jesus declined to say what they wanted to hear, and they crucified Him. Paul followed the same example and they beat, stoned, and imprisoned him.

There are some frontrunners in the premillennial movement who are willing to play "religious games" with the political leaders in the state of Israel in order to promote millenarianism in this nation and in other parts of the world. These men luxuriate in their good fortune to rub shoulders with some of the high-ranking officials in both the state of Israel and in Washington, D. C. It is a grandiose experience to have an audience with such high-level governmental leaders — especially in the state of Israel. It is a good omen that God is preparing the stage for the millennial kingdom. Most politicians have an ear for the ring of the cash register and a hearty handshake for anyone's influence and vote. The Israeli politicians are no exception — they will kiss a "millennial baby" as well as a "Zionist baby." In other words, they will grab at straws in order to keep their "cause" alive and flourishing — the source is immaterial. The Israeli diplomats will welcome anyone or any group that will enhance their standing with the United States or any other favorable nation. The "support," "comfort," and "concern" of the futurists become a "hallelujah course" for these Jewish statesmen. This is good politics. The millenarians use the same bag of tricks.

The premillennialists are able to arouse the expectations and hopes of these Israeli politicians in exchange for a millennial boost. Any kind of dialogue with these key leaders is high drama for the futurists. However, the Gospel of Christ and His cross are kept in the background, lest its message be an offense to those they wish to impress. If the millenarians insisted upon the claims of Christ for these Israeli statesmen and all Jews, as did Paul and many other New Testament believers, the door would be slammed in their faces. An emphasis upon the "future" has become a scapegoat to avoid rejection in the "present."

Men have been playing "religious games" for centuries — a brief interview with the Old Testament prophets and the New Testament apostles will confirm this fact.

The premillennialists are saying exactly what the Jews delight in hearing. The appeal to a carnal kingdom with Jewish supremacy is music to their ears. The "chosen" people trademark is much more palatable than "sinner" or "rebel." God's "unconditional" promise without repentance and a life-changing experience should be welcomed by every carnal-minded Jew. The "foolishness of the cross" is far more acceptable to the unregenerate Jew than the "wisdom of the cross."

I must confess that I have not maintained the nonoffensive spirit that I so wanted to display throughout this work. My original intentions were to be very lenient toward those with whom I disagree. However, I find it very difficult to be calm and restrained in a theological battle of this magnitude. Such a position would compare to America's role in the Vietnam War. In this unconventional war, sane and effective battle tactics were held in check for many years, and the war could not be won. Oftentimes the American soldier was unable to distinguish between friend and foe. Over the centuries, the church has had to face similar predicaments. Exposure and reproof are a vital part of church discipline and should be welcomed in the body of Christ.

Biblical truth can be, and oftentimes is, compromised by the literary style of a writer. The cutting edge of sound doctrine can be dulled by suave words and conciliatory phrases. Christian truth must not be handled naively and tossed up for grabs. It is going to require more than a band-aid theology to convince many people of the rightness or wrongness of premillennialism. The severe criticism of premillennialism in this work is not meant to castigate those innocent individuals who have been misled and "used" by the establishment. My real controversy is with the premillennial gurus who have preyed upon the good-faith of people that are in no position to defend themselves.

Concern for the *future* has been a "weak spot" in mankind from the beginning. A good deal of the New Testament is written to combat and expose those who exploit this "weakness" in man. Premillennialism is just another means of capitalizing on this "vulnerable curiosity" which gets out of control in almost every age and generation.

The majority of Christians in this century have never been exposed to any kind of teaching that would contradict premillennialism. The Scofield Bible, with its handy notes, has become the "law and gospel" for thousands of young converts. Those coming into the Christian church have been victimized by a premillennial hierarchy and environment that intimidates them on every hand if conformity is refused. "Liberal," "modernist," "spiritual blindness," and "anti-Semitism" are some of the labels that are used to force others into their camp and keep their own disciples in line. Many believers, including hundreds of ministers, have serious problems with premillennial "doctrine" but are not knowledgeable enough in the Scriptures to break its grip upon them. Its claim to "orthodoxy" seems to cast a spell upon them from which there is no escape.

Premillennialism is little more than a status symbol for many ministers and laymen. It is not a label that has been acquired through intensive Bible study, prayer, and personal convictions, but through a bootlegged version of end-time events that leaves them stranded in a theological puzzlement. They have bits and pieces of the futuristic puzzle, but not the entire puzzle. To change our analogy, they are like a commuter who has boarded a passenger coach in the middle of a long train without knowing what is pulling the train. It can be compared to flying in the night. This status symbol must be retained at all cost because their premillennial peers are able to put the puzzle together with great facility. Many superficial adherents to premillennialism would become traumatized if they really knew and understood what the futurists believe and teach.

The futurists have been very successful in hamstringing many people with their "liberal" image. There are multitudes of Christian men and women who see the fallacies of premillennialism, but they refuse to rock the premillennial boat. They are afraid of losing favor with certain key men within a denomination or some other ecclesiastical body. They would rather have the plaudits of men than the approval of God. For this reason, they find a refuge in their silence. If the old adage "silence gives consent" is true, then these mute people are helping to swell the premillennial ranks every day.

In recent years the premillennialists have waged a psychological warfare to recruit new members and to strengthen their own fortress. The age-old "scare tactics" are used to impel the American public to "bless," "support," and "comfort" Israel. Those who read and listen to such emphasis are put on a "guilt trip" if they do not rally to the premillennial cause. The threat of God's wrath is held over the heads of men and nations if such demands for Israel are not met. In short, the premillennialists have become self-appointed curators of the Jews. But the futurists are putting the cart before the horse. Carnal Israel needs the wrath of God removed from her head (Romans 2:8-11), and the only way this is possible is through the Gospel of Jesus Christ.

The premillennialists are undertaking an impossible task. They are trying to forge "carnal Israel" into the true "Israel of God." This is a hopeless endeavor. There are *two Israels* in the Scriptures. One is "carnal Israel," born after the flesh, and the other is "faithful Israel," born of God's *Word* and *Spirit*. The paradoxical nature of the Scriptures confirms this truth over and over again. The two Israels are as different as night and day.

I am sure that many who read this work will consider me cruel and unreasonable in the position that I have taken on the Jewish controversy — and some will accuse me of being anti-Semitic. I assure the reader that such is not the case. In reading the thoughts and feelings of many Jewish writers, I have literally wept for them in their struggles for answers and for acceptance in a Gentile world that has been hostile to them for centuries. After researching several books on the Jewish situation, both past and present, I can better understand the heartbeat of the Apostle Paul when he wrote: "My heart's desire and prayer to God for Israel is that they might be saved" (Romans 10:1). I share that prayer.

Epilogue

There goes our song again!

George Grant, in his book *The Blood of the Moon,* presents a dialogue between two persons in a church parking lot who have just heard a powerful prophetic sermon by an unnamed minister (I assume a pre-millennialist). The sermon dealt with events that would most likely follow the Iraq war that was fought in the early part of 1991. One of the persons is somewhat confused over what he has just heard. Dr. Grant quotes the puzzled man as saying: "I've been hearing this stuff all my life. The same charts. The same maps, the same scenarios. Only the dates change — they keep having to push them back ... I'm not questioning the Bible. Not at all ... I just have to wonder if we're not kind of *baptizing the headlines onto the Bible instead of the other way around"* [1] (Emphasis mine).

There goes our song again!

Tremendous changes have taken place in the world arena since this manuscript was undertaken. The whole of mankind has been shocked at the turn of events in the year 1990 and the first two months of 1991. The European scene has undergone dramatic changes. Communism has run its course in most of the world and proven to be ineffective. Poland, along with many other countries of Europe, has gained her independence. The Berlin Wall has been removed and Germany now stands as a reunited nation. Panama has been liberated and Manuel Noriega at the present time is in prison. The activities of the Marxist Sandinistas in Nicaragua are no longer on the front page of our newspapers. These are some of the incredible events that have occurred within a matter of months.

The greater part of this manuscript was written before 1990. Early on, I made the statement that every time some bizarre event occurs in the Middle East, particularly in the state of Israel, the canon of Scripture is reopened by the millenarians and a new chapter is added to the Bible. In recent weeks this statement has been demonstrated to the letter. When Saddam Hussein overran Kuwait in August of 1990, the futurists began

---

1. George Grant, *The Blood of the Moon,* Wolgemuth & Hyatt, Publishers, Inc., Brentwood, Tenn., 1991, 19.

to prophesy again. As the Persian Gulf crisis began to unfold, it was back to the millennial drawing board. The premillennialists adopted their usual stance by delivering a barrage of prophetic sermons and writing many books. Armageddon loomed on the horizon — mankind was on the verge of a world holocaust — the appearance of the Antichrist was close at hand — and a new day would soon dawn in Israel. Saddam's dream of becoming Nebuchadnezzar II and the restoration of the ancient city of Babylon became real fodder for the millenarians. This new surge of events in the world was very favorable for the futurists and they rode the crest of the wave to its maximum — and a few are still riding it.

At the writing of these words, Iraq is in ruins; her military power is almost annihilated; Kuwait is liberated; Saddam's dream of a restored Babylon will probably slip back into the dust and ashes of the past; and Saddam's future is up in the air. The premillennialists scored a temporary hit with many people, but left them in a blind alley and with fewer dollars in their pockets. The futurists must *wait* for another Middle East skirmish in order to keep their "doctrine" alive. Most likely the public will be gullible for another flurry of the premillennial drama. It is indeed strange that the millenarians never see these events in Scripture until *after* they appear in the newspapers or on the television screens.

There is also a reference in the manuscript to the "Six-Day War" that Israel fought against three Arab countries in 1967. This, too, was a "high wire act" for the futurists. Such a short-lived battle was unheard of in ages past. For the futurists, it was no less than the Providence of God; God *must* be on Israel's side and fighting her battles as He did in Old Testament days. It was classified as a miracle. However, the ground war of the United States and her allies against Iraq was just as miraculous as the "Six-Day War" that Israel fought in 1967 — and perhaps more so. The most discussed and dreaded aspect of the war was the ground offensive that lasted only *four days*. One of the largest armies (fourth) in the world was devastated. The winds of Desert Storm blew out so quickly that news commentators began to speak of it in terms of hours (100) rather than days. General Norman Schwarzkopf, commander of Desert Storm Operation for the United States, stated in a newsbrief that it was no less than a miracle. The "mother of all battles" that Saddam Hussein boasted about became the "mother of all defeats."

When the magnitude of Desert Storm is taken into account, it is most likely that the United States and the coalition against Iraq suffered fewer casualties than any other battle that was ever fought in the history of the world. And it was a Gentile war from the beginning to the end — the Israelis did not fire a shot. Paul's question on the Jews and Gentiles needs to be raised again: "Is he the God of the Jews only? Is he not also of the Gentiles? *Yes*, of the Gentiles also" (Romans 3:29).

Operation Desert Storm should be an embarrassment to the premillennialists in a number of ways. This statement is made in connection with the "Yom Kippur War" of 1973 between the Israelis and two Arab countries (Egypt and Syria) in the Golan Heights region. The millenarians were not caught napping when the "Yom Kippur War" broke out. The clash between Israel and the two Arab countries was destined to become another museum piece to hang in the millennial gallery. The armored tank battle in the 1973 war was considered to be the biggest tank battle ever fought in the history of wars. The Plain of Megiddo was almost within a stone's throw of the conflict and Armageddon was sure to follow. Israel became the victor and the premillennial machinery was on a roll again but only to have its wheels come off when the battle ended *without* the war to end all wars.

There is a counterpart to the "Yom Kippur War" of 1973. When the history of Operation Desert Storm is written, we will probably learn that the surgical, high tech tank battle waged by the United States and the coalition against Iraq was a nondescript battle — it defied the imagination of those who planned it. "Phenomenal" became a stock word that was on the minds and lips of everyone. Again, the Israelis had no hand in the war — quite the contrary — Israel was encouraged to stay out of the war — which she did.

Operation Desert Storm should put a chill on another prophetic dictum coming out of the premillennial camp. For many years, the futurists have convinced themselves that certain ancient nations such as Babylon, Rome, Israel, etc., were going to be brought out of the mothballs of the past — these expired nations would live again. However, Saddam Hussein's delusion of becoming Nebuchadnezzar II and a revived Babylon should be the *mene, mene, tekel, upharsin* for the futurists. The mores of these antiquated nations should serve as "examples" or "guidelines" for the present age, but for all practical purposes they are history. The atoms of the bows and arrows, swords and shields, horses and chariots, citizens and soldiers, plows and hoes of these by-gone nations lie buried in the sands of the old world until the conflagration of all things. These remote nations are irrecoverable and should be allowed to "rest" except for the spiritual value they are able to provide.

For many decades the premillennialists have written and spoken about an enemy coming out of the "north" against Israel — the enemy from the "north" is believed to be Russia. The enemy from the "north," along with other military forces from the East, will usher in the battle of battles — the Battle of Armageddon. The Cold War era and Russia's military might convinced the futurists that they were on the right prophetic trail — history and current events were on their side. But in the past few months Russia has taken on a different image. The world has been awakened to the failure of communism and the deterioration of the Russian regime. The political scene in Russia at this hour is in chaos; the economy is practically bankrupt; civil unrest is to be seen in almost every Russian republic; at this stage a military coup is very possible *(written before the coup attempt of 1991 — editor's note.)* or there could be a civil war similar to the Bolshevik Revolution of 1917. However, there is one bright spot in all of the recent changes in Russia, but it, too, puts a damper on the premillennial scenario — Russia is now permitting religious freedom. The grizzly Russian bear of the "north" could become the "teddy bear" of the future — only time will tell.

The millenarians, if they were honest, should rework the homilies they preached during the Persian Gulf crisis (war with Iraq) and rewrite their prophetic books. By all the rules of ethics, they should apologize for their prophetic intrigues, but in all probability this will never happen. They will find some isolated passages of Scripture to shore up their prophetic demeanor and keep their eyes focused on the Middle East. The futurists have tunnel vision that will not allow them to prophesy about any other part of the globe except the Middle East. Is this the only part of the universe that God is interested in? Is God any less concerned with the daily events that occur in America, France, China, Africa, Australia, etc.? Is God oblivious to the *activities* and *future* of these nations? The obvious answer is no! He who sits in the heavens is involved in a global affair. God's love is global (John 3:16-17); the reconciliation of mankind is global (Romans 11:15; 2 Corinthians 5:19); the Gospel message is global (Matthew 24:14; 26:13); Satan's activities are global (2 Corinthians 4:4); wickedness and spiritual darkness are global (1 John 5:19); God's judgment will be global (2 Timothy 4:1). God's Kingdom and redemptive program cannot be tied to or limited to the Middle East.

The premillennialists make every effort possible to include America and Great Britain in their crystal ball, but they are hindered by the fact that these nations cannot be found in Scripture. It is worthwhile to note that the futurists have only one faint glimmer wherewithal they are able to espy Russia in their prophetic gazing, i.e., the vague, obscure country out of the "north." The futurists have a lot of theological tonnage resting on this ill-defined country out of the "north" but this is no cause for alarm — it is treated as a sure-fire prophecy. This is just another example of the shaky foundation on which millenarianism is built.

It is ironic that we also find an enemy coming out of the "north" against ancient Babylon that is depicted in the book of Jeremiah (50:3, 9, 41; 51:48). Jeremiah devotes two entire chapters (50 and 51) to the destruction of Babylon by this undefined enemy from the "north." Some of the statements used by Jeremiah to describe the destruction of ancient Babylon are used by John in the book of Revelation to describe the destruction of "spiritual" Babylon. In the Scriptures, future events are oftentimes described and foretold in the literal, historical events of the past. But these historical echos of the past reverberate into another dimension — i.e., a "spiritual" dimension. In the book of Revelation, Babylon is symbolic of the political, economic, and religious systems of the world from time immemorial. If the enemy from the "north" that came against ancient Babylon is to be understood as being both literal and spiritual, then we should apply the same principle to the enemy out of the "north" against Israel. It has already been proven that the "true Israel" is the faithful remnant or the church. The enemy from the "north" is probably a spiritual battle against the body of Christ that is both present and future. We must of necessity allow the New Testament to interpret the Old.

The Second Advent of our Lord was never meant to be a school of speculation or a throw of the dice. It was not to be a contest between "winners" and "losers" within the church. Dogmatism on trivial things of the future is out of character with the entire New Testament. The principle concern for those who are in Christ should be "readiness" and "holiness of life" when He returns. The following warning from Jesus is to be found throughout the New Testament: "Watch therefore: for ye *know not* what hour your Lord doth come ... Therefore *be ye also ready: for in such an hour as ye think not the Son of man cometh*" (Matthew 24:42, 44).

Practically all of Peter's second epistle is devoted to the Second Coming of Christ. The entire epistle can be condensed into three crucial topics. First of all, Peter warns about false prophets who "walk after their own lusts" and speak of coming events in total ignorance (3:3, 5). The "warning" on false prophets is a major theme in this letter. Secondly, Peter has a good deal to write on the destruction of the heavens and the earth that will be replaced by new heavens and a new earth. With the exception of a few verses, all of chapter three is focused in this direction. Thirdly, there is a plea for holy living: "Seeing then that all these things (heavens and earth) shall be dissolved, what manner of persons ought ye to be *in all holy conversation* (or manner of life) and *Godliness*" (verse 11). This cosmic destruction, according to Peter, should cause one to be "diligent" and to be "found in *peace, without spot,* and *blameless*" (Verse 14). These are very weighty subjects and leave no room for picayunish discussions on animal sacrifices, temple, government, Jewish dominance, etc., in a so-called millennial kingdom. Concern for government jobs in the millennial kingdom, such as a "peace officer" or a "cabinet official," is less than a bargain basement theology (ideas expressed in an article by Dr. C. S. Lovett on the subject: "What Will You do in the Millennium?")[2]

Needless to say, the Apostle Paul tells the same story as Peter. Paul describes Jesus' coming as a "thief in the night," and many people will be unprepared for the event (1 Thessalonians 5:5). But the "children of light" should not be surprised (verse 5). The Apostle admonished the Thessalonians with these words: "... let us *watch* and be *sober.* For they that sleep sleep in the night; and they that be drunken are drunken in the night. But let us, who are of the day, *be sober, putting on the breastplate of faith* and *love;* and for an *helmet,* the *hope of salvation*" (1 Thessalonians 5:6-8). "Readiness" is the key emphasis in Paul's admonition.

Those who are rooted and grounded in the Scriptures should not become unglued every time the millenarians push the Middle East panic button. An overdose on the "mark of the beast," "Armageddon," the "Antichrist," and the "Great Tribulation" is no cause for paranoia. Fear, trembling, and darkness belong to those who are "of the night" and not the "children of the day." From the very center of Paul's lengthiest discourse on the future Antichrist and the Second Coming of Christ, we find these very positive words: "Now we beseech you brethren, by the coming of our Lord Jesus Christ, and by our gathering together unto

2. *Personal Christianity,* Vol. 19, No. 3, March 1979, Baldwin Park, California.

him, That ye *be not soon shaken in mind,* or be *troubled,* neither *by spirit,*
nor *by word,* nor *by letter* as from us, as that the day of Christ is at hand.
Let no man deceive you by any means," etc. (2 Thessalonians 2:1-3a).
The watchwords for the coming of Christ are alertness, sobermindedness, comfort, stability, and holiness of life. In addition to the passages
already quoted, the reader would be rewarded by considering the
following passages also: 1 Corinthians 1:7-8; 1 Thessalonians 3:13,
5:23; 2 Thessalonians 3:5; 1 Timothy 6:14; James 5:7-8; 1 Peter 1:7-9;
and 1 John 3:2-3.

The facts presented in this epilogue are very conclusive that the
premillennialists have gotten themselves out on several prophetic limbs
in the past twenty-five years and have sawed the limbs off behind them.
This is to say nothing of their enthusiastic illusions prior to this period.
The "Six-Day War" of 1967, the "Yom Kippur War" of 1973, "Operation Desert Storm" of 1991, Saddam Hussein's dream of a revived
Babylon, and the collapse of the Russian regime are over-documented
events that have stood out like neon lights in the headlines of our
newspapers and television broadcasts. These are newly sawn limbs that
should send a message to both the church and the millenarians. Most
likely the futurists will grab another branch in their downward tumble
and continue their predictions on the Middle East.

The Apostle Paul sends a clear message to every minister of the
Gospel and every layman alike when he writes: "Study to show thyself
approved unto God, a workman that needeth not to be ashamed, rightly
dividing the word of truth" (2 Timothy 2:15). Lurid prophecies can
bring reproach upon the body of Christ. They open the door for the
Church's adversaries to scoff and mock (2 Peter 3:3-4). Immaterial and
irrelevant predictions on end-time events only strengthen the forces of
evil.

The above comments are not meant to be an oversimplification of
our Lord's Second Coming — they are not a retreat to "panmillennialism" (a term that some have coined to say that everything will "pan out"
all right in the end). However, it does mean that we should have our
antennas turned in the right direction. The Church should concern itself
with what the New Testament has to say about His Second Advent,
rather than the things that paved the way for His first coming, i.e., the
tutorage years of the Old Testament period (Galatians 4:1-5).

Those who *missed* Christ's first coming were looking in the wrong
direction. They were looking backwards rather than keeping abreast

with God's eternal plan and purpose. They were concerned primarily with the restoration of the old Davidic kingdom, Jewish racial superiority, the preservation of the Mosaic rituals and temple, signs, trivial and argumentative religious questions, the political subjugation of Rome, etc. These were *life* and *death* issues for the Jews when Christ came in the flesh. Needless to say, these ancient religious issues are still with us. The futurists have revived them and are still keeping them alive. Looking back is not very promising — men have traveled this path before and we are familiar with most of the story. Looking forward is assuring and glorious — enter, *faith, hope,* and *love.* Without these, everything else is zero (1 Corinthians 13:1-3). Compare also 1 Thessalonians 5:8).

The journey to eternal, everlasting life via the law of Moses is a long and treacherous trek—and no one has ever completed the course. There are many thorns, slippery slopes, and hidden dangers on the roadway. Those who travel this path are like John Bunyon's "pilgrim" with an unbearable load on his back. The casualties along the route are as numerous as the grains of sand upon the seashore. Just to review the results is a loathsome task. The greatest lesson that one should learn from legalism is that it is a *deadend* street — which is far more consequential than a pun.

The law of Moses is never represented as being favorable to man (Colossians 2:14-15) — not because the law is unholy but because of man's sinful nature. The initial experience at Mt. Sinai, with its physical signs and sights, along with the fear and trembling of Moses and the people, are a recapitulation of the entire Mosaic system and its adverse effect upon man. A return to the law of Moses is a return to Mt. Sinai. The premillennialists want us to *look back* to a bleak and barren desert. They would return us to Mt. Sinai that can be "touched" and that burns with fire — a mount that is surrounded with blackness and darkness — a mount that shook at the voice of God.

The futurists would revive a religious system filled with terror, death, and condemnation — all of which resulted in "children of bondage." This dismal portrayal of the law of Moses, as given in the book of Hebrews, is set in contrast to Mt. Zion, the city of the living God, the heavenly Jerusalem, the general assembly and church of the firstborn which are written in heaven ... to Jesus ... and to a kingdom that cannot be shaken (Hebrews 12:18-29).

The Mosaic system from the beginning to the end deals with sin and God's anger against it. The earth and man are under the curse of sin, and Mt. Sinai with its fire, blackness, and tempest, along with man's fear and trembling, are tokens of this truth. But Mt. Sinai has been stripped of its abject fear. Two thousand years ago, the two mountains (Mt. Sinai and Mt. Zion) met in mortal combat on another mount — Mt. Calvary. The physical signs of darkness, the quaking earth, the rent rocks, the fear and death that were displayed at Calvary are echoes of Mt. Sinai. However, God's love and grace conquered sin and death and brought to naught the dreadful consequences of Mt. Sinai. Those who are in Christ and citizens of the heavenly Jerusalem should disdain forever any remnant of Mt. Sinai. The temple, animal sacrifices, and priesthood that the premillennialists want to revive in the so-called millennial kingdom, originated at Mt. Sinai. The Gospel of Christ dispels every vestige of Mt. Sinai and the Mosaic system.

According to Paul, the law of Moses "has no glory" when compared with the glorious Gospel of Christ (2 Corinthians 3:10). The "glory" of these obsolete types and shadows (including Canaan) belongs to those who have "missed" Christ's glory in His death and resurrection. If the present Gospel age dispels the "glory" of these outmoded institutions of the Old Testament period, then what effect will Christ's *future* and *ultimate* glory have upon them? At the present time we see through a glass (mirror) darkly and we have only a partial knowledge of Christ's glory, but when He comes in *all His glory* we shall see Him "face to face" (1 Corinthians 13:12). It is inconceivable that men could be attracted to and become involved in these outdated rituals when the effulgence of Christ's glory is present.

There are several important blocks of truth in the New Testament relative to Christ's Second Coming that should demand our attention, but not trivial, vague, insignificant things. The following are some vital concepts regarding Christ's return that cannot be questioned and on which most evangelicals should be able to agree: Christ is coming again; the church will be caught up to meet Him in the air — preceded by those who are asleep in Christ; men should be ready at all times; the present heavens and earth will be dissolved; there will be new heavens and a new earth; there will be a day of judgment for all men; Satan and those who reject Christ will be cast into the lake of fire; and God's elect will reign with Him eternally.

Someone has remarked that most people are more interested in *coming events* than they are in the *coming Saviour*. For the most part, only God has the full picture of what things will be like after Jesus returns for His church. One thing can be depended upon — He has given His people enough Truth and promised them sufficient grace to prepare them for *that day* (2 Timothy 1:12). If the "grace" that God gives to His elect in this present age is a capsule of the *"exceeding riches of His grace in the ages to come"* (Ephesians 2:7), then those who are in Christ can look forward to something far more glorious than a page out of the past — a history that is already written — a religion that was nailed to the cross — untenable Jewish flesh (1 Corinthians 1:29; Philippians 3:3ff.) — and an indistinct, acataleptic, confounded earthly existence of one thousand years. It is time to put this specter of the past behind us and move on to higher and nobler realms. These ancient albatrosses have been tried and proven for what they are worth and their lessons are legion. The Latin phrase *caveat emptor* is germane to this entire discussion.

What better note can we conclude with than the lyrics of Philip P. Bliss' (1838-1876) song, "Free from the Law, O Happy Condition:"

> *Free from the law, O happy condition,*
> Jesus hath bled, and there is remission;
> *Cursed by the law* and bruised by the fall,
> *Grace hath redeemed us once for all.*

> *Now we are free — There's no condemnation,*
> Jesus provides a *perfect salvation;*
> "Come unto me," O hear His sweet call,
> Come, and He saves us once for all.

> "Children of God," O glorious calling,
> Surely His grace will *keep us from falling;*
> Passing from death to life at His call,
> Blessed salvation once for all.
> (Italics mine)

> *Soli Deo Gloria* — To God Alone Be the Glory!